CRITICAL
PERSPECTIVES
ON AGING:
The Political and Moral Economy
of Growing Old

Edited by
Meredith Minkler
and
Carroll L. Estes

with the assistance of Ida VSW Red
Editorial Consultant

POLICY, POLITICS, HEALTH AND MEDICINE Series
Vicente Navarro, Series Editor

Baywood Publishing Company, Inc.
Amityville, New York

Library of Congress Catalog Number: 90-19475
ISBN: 0-89503-075-6 (Paper)
ISBN: 0-89503-076-4 (Cloth)

Library of Congress Cataloging-in-Publication Data

Main entry under title:
Critical perspectives on aging / edited by Meredith Minkler and
    Carroll L. Estes, with the assistance of Ida Vsw Red, editorial
    consultant.
        p. cm. -- (Policy, politics, health, and medicine series)
    Includes bibliographical references and index.
    ISBN 0-89503-076-4 (cloth). -- ISBN 0-89503-075-6 (paper)
    1. Aged--United States--Social conditions. 2. Old age--Social
aspects--United States. 3. Aged--United States--Economic
conditions. 4. Old age--Economic aspects--United States.
5. Retirement--Economic aspects--United States. I. Minkler,
Meredith. II. Estes, Carroll L. III. Series.
HQ1064,U5C76 1991
305.26'0973--dc20   90-19475
                                                                    CIP

Acknowledgments

Many individuals have contributed, through their own work, to this second book of readings in critical gerontology. We are particularly indebted to our friends and colleagues for challenging debates and discussions—to Martha Holstein, Tom Cole, Ann Robertson, Diane Arnold-Driver, Patricia Morgan, Ralph Catalano and Jon Hendricks on the moral economy of aging and to Vicente Navarro for his openness to our explorations in this area; to Lisa Binney, Lenore Gerard, James Swan, and Jane Zones on the political economy of aging; to Maggie Kuhn, Jim O'Connor, John Walton, and the late Alvin Gouldner and Tish Sommers on the theory and praxis of aging, feminism, and political economy. They have taught us the meaning of the view that "nothing is impossible."

Our faculty colleagues and graduate students in the School of Public Health and the School of Social Welfare, University of California, Berkeley and the Department of Social and Behavioral Sciences and the Institute for Health and Aging, University of California, San Francisco, also provided invaluable opportunities for dialogue, and the book is enriched by their shared thoughts and perspectives. Our sincere thanks also are due Meredith's friend and former secretary, Jane Tzudiker, who was a life saver on more than one occasion and who helped tie many loose ends together and to Carroll's assistants, Barbara Griswold, whose organizational skills permitted the necessary time to complete this book and Patrick Henderson, who contributed essential and proficient bibliographic and word processing assistance.

The late Norman Cohen of Baywood Publishing Company was a strong advocate for the undertaking of this second volume, and we share Baywood's sense of loss in his death. We also extend our deep gratitude to Stewart Cohen who took over the publishing end of this book in midstream and has proven an invaluable coworker.

Finally, our deepest thanks go to our close friends, our families, and especially to our parents and husbands for moral support and love without measure.

Acknowledgment of Sources

Chapter 5, Generational Equity   This is a revised and updated version of an earlier article, "Generational Equity and the New Victim Blaming: An Emerging Public Policy Issue," which appeared in the *International Journal of Health Services*, 16(4): 539–551, 1986.

Chapter 6, Gold in Gray   An earlier version of this paper appeared in *The Gerontologist,* 29(1): 17–23, 1989. Reprinted with permission of The Gerontological Society of America.

Chapter 8, The Biomedicalization of Aging   An earlier version of this paper appeared in *The Gerontologist,* 29(5): 587–596, 1989. Reprinted with permission of the Gerontological Society of America.

Chapter 13, Older Women in the Post-Reagan Era   This is a significantly revised and expanded version of a paper appearing under the title, "Unsettled Future: Older Women—Economics and Health," in *Feminist Studies* 7(1): 3–25, 1987. Reprinted with permission of Transaction, Inc.

Chapter 14, Community Care Policies   Reprinted with permission from the *International Journal of Health Services* 17(2): 217–232, 1987.

Chapter 15, Gender, Race, Class . . .   Originally published in *The Gerontologist* 28(2): 177–180, 1988. Reprinted with permission of The Gerontological Society of America.

Chapter 17, Retirement and the Moral Economy   Reprinted from the *Journal of Aging Studies* 1(2): 125–144, 1987, with permission of JAI Press.

Chapter 18, Post-War Capitalism   Originally appeared as a chapter in Weir et al. (eds.), *The Politics of Social Policy in the U.S.*, Princeton University Press, 1988. Reprinted with permission.

INTRODUCTION

The Unique Contributions of This Volume

This volume is unique in its analysis of aging within the context of society as a whole. Rather than studying aging by focusing solely on the aged, the contributors look at the many other forces and factors that affect aging. The authors have dared to do something that is rarely attempted in the analysis of social phenomena: they have followed the Hegelian dictum that "the truth is the whole," that is, in order to understand any specific sector of society, we must first comprehend the society of which that sector is a part. Accordingly, the authors analyze aging within the social, political, and economic contexts that determine aging.

This volume, like other volumes in this series, is also unique in the way the authors perceive the totality called society. Those who look at the society of the United States as a whole frequently see it as an aggregate of interest groups competing for limited resources, and in this competition, what is equitable is determined by those with the power to define equity. The subjects of such analysis are the different interest groups and their political instruments that struggle to achieve their objectives in the political arena. Consequently, there has been a series of studies analyzing, for example, the elderly and their political instruments, such as the American Association of Retired Persons (AARP) and the National Council of Senior Citizens as major political forces behind public programs for the aged. Yet, however important such studies may be, and however valuable the information they provide, these analyses are insufficient. The AARP is one of the most powerful interest groups in the United States. Its influence on Congress is not a minor one. Yet our elderly still have fewer social benefits, including health benefits, than those in comparable Western developed societies. Why? To answer this critical question, we must look beyond the interest-group *modus operandi*.

As Baran and Sweezy have indicated, "just as the whole is always more than the sum of its parts, so the amassing of small truths about the various parts and aspects of society can never yield the big truth about the social order itself" (1). We must explain how the different interest groups are related within society as a whole. The paucity of social rights and benefits for our elderly, our workers (such as the right to organize, safe and healthy jobs, good employment and disability insurance, and comprehensive health benefits coverage), and our women (such as parental leave with pay, child care coverage, access to free health care) compared with their counterparts in other Western industrialized nations cannot be explained by looking only at our elderly, our workers, or our women. We must understand the nature of power in our society, particularly class (as well as gender and race) power and the economic structure that sustains it. Contrary to the prevalent myth, the United States is not a classless society or one in which the majority are in the middle class. Far from it. An analysis of the economic and social structures of the United States shows that there are indeed social classes. A discernment of the correlation of class forces and the dynamics of the economic system of the United States is critical to understanding the status and power of our elderly. This is the approach taken by the contributors to this volume. They do not reduce ageism to classism, but they clearly show that one cannot understand ageism without first understanding class power and the class to which most of our elderly belong. Several of the chapters show that the underdeveloped welfare state in the United States, which provides fewer rights for our elderly, workers, women, children, and minorities than are provided to their counterparts in other countries, is rooted in the weakness of the working class and the absence of political instruments—such as labor or social democratic parties—that can realize the interests of this class and translate their moral economy into concrete programs and policies.

The elderly in many European countries do not have such a powerful lobby as the AARP, but they have better benefits because labor or social democratic parties have successfully established *universal* social programs rooted in strong moral economy beliefs about the rights of elders, workers, etc. to have basic needs met. We do not have such political instruments. In the Democratic Party, labor is just one influence competing with many others, including the ubiquitous corporate interests that, through the power of money, are skewing the representative nature of our institutions. The absence of class-based behavior divides the dominated forces. These forces need to unify around their class interests and build upon their shared moral economy conceptions of fairness and social justice in opposition to corporate interests. This understanding is clearly and uniquely presented in this book. The potency of the analysis lies in its ability not only to explain the existing situation but to provide the bases for change.

The richness of the analysis provided in this volume is strengthened by the incorporation of moral economy perspectives as a complement to the book's primary political economy approach. Such topics as the evolution of pension systems and the debate over generational equity in resource allocation are examined within a broad theoretical framework that attends not only to the influence of political and economic factors, but also of ideals of fairness and reciprocity collectively held among workers and other groups in society. As several authors in this volume suggest, to ignore these moral economy considerations (e.g., underlying labor's fight for pension systems, or youth's support for old age entitlements) is to miss a critical set of factors which also influence and determine U.S. politics and policies.

The contributors to this volume provide a great variety of solutions to the problems presented based on their varied understandings of our realities, within the framework discussed in the Introduction by the co-editors, Drs. Minkler and Estes. And there is an underlying realism to the authors' proposals. The understanding that capitalist logic is at the root of our problems is not tantamount to offering the maximalist notion that unless the whole system changes nothing can be changed—this could not be further from the purposes of this book.

Great improvement can and should occur, even under current economic structures. The issue is not the validity of reforms but rather what type of reforms and through what agents? Current practice has shown that in order to improve the lives and well-being of our elderly it is not enough to strengthen the power of their lobbies. Other types of reforms are needed—universal reforms, such as a national health program—to empower the majority of our elderly, our young, our men and women, our working class, and allied classes and assure that the United States is a country of the people, for the people, and run by the people. We are far from that ideal today.

This last point merits repeating in the light of current announcements that "our system" (the American system) has triumphed over the "enemy" (the socialist system), with the Eastern European regimes given as proof of this victory. But the welcome collapse of regimes imposed by the Red Army in Eastern Europe cannot be seen as proof of the attractiveness of the U.S. model. These countries are unlikely to choose an unconstrained capitalism with a very limited welfare state, such as we have in the United States, but are more likely to choose a more humane capitalism with an extensive welfare state, such as those of Western European countries. Indeed, the majority of Americans would also prefer the latter over the former. Twenty-five percent of Americans had no health insurance for a certain period of time during one year. Our elderly live in great fear of the economic consequences of a major illness, and family members cannot afford to stop working to take care of their loved ones—this is not considered a triumph but a defeat of the U.S. system. The majority of Americans would like to live under a different system; 61 percent prefer the Canadian health care model over the U.S. model (2).

How is it, the reader may ask, that if the people want a more humane system they do not get it? How is it that basic moral economy notions underlying the people's support for more generous welfare provisions have not more heavily influenced our reality? As shown by several contributors to this volume, our political system is severely limited. *Vox populi* competes with moneyed interests. That is the drama of our democracy. The eloquent opening sentence of our Constitution: "We, the people . . ." was not referring to the extensive corporate interests that now shape the nature of our government's policy. To consider this as a sign of triumph is to have a distorted understanding of morality and history. It is this skewed nature of our political discourse that leads to reports in the media of the generational conflict as an equity issue. The young themselves deny this conflict; as noted above, most share basic moral economy assumptions which favor expansion, rather than reduction, of benefits to the elderly. So why is this issue being reproduced in the corridors of power, and why is it presented as an issue of fairness among generations?

Several contributors to this volume show that in morality—as in policy—those who have the power to pose the questions already have the answers. Why is there no debate about the morality of an economic system that does not provide security, joy, and relaxation for those citizens who have built the country through their sweat and toil? Where is the morality of a system that enables a Trump to amass millions in just a few telephone calls? Recent polls published by *The Independent* (in the United Kingdom), *La Republica* (in Italy), and *El Pais* (in Spain) showed that the overwhelming majority of Western populations support the strongly ethical position that a society should be structured so that resources are produced according to ability and distributed according to need. Most of those surveyed also felt that the unrestrained capitalism of the United States was furthest from fulfilling that ideal (3). Most of our resources are distributed according to ability to pay, which reflects the most distorted wealth and income distribution in the Western world and disregards moral economy conceptions of fairness and social justice. How can the United States proclaim that it is the society of human rights when basic rights (such as access to health care) are still denied, not because of popular mandate but because of the enormous power of unelected forces such as the insurance industry and the "medical industrial complex" (4)?

This volume provides answers to some of these critical questions, so often avoided in the official discourse. The contributions to this book are uncompromising in the sense that the authors' criticism fears neither its own results nor conflict with the powers that be. We welcome this addition to the Health Policy Series.

REFERENCES

1. Baran P., and Sweezy, P. *Monopoly Capital*, pp. 2–3. Monthly Review Press, 1968.
2. Blendon, R. J. Three systems: A comparative survey. *Health Man. Q.* 14(1): 2, 1989.
3. *El Pais*, p. 6, Febrero 19, 1990.
4. Relman, A. S. The new medical-industrial complex. *New Engl. J. Med.* 303(17): 963–970, 1980.

Vicente Navarro
Professor of Health Policy,
Johns Hopkins University
Editor, Health Policy Series,
Baywood Publishing Company

TABLE OF CONTENTS

PART I. INTRODUCTION

The introductory section of this book attempts a two-fold objective. First, it provides the reader with a detailed introduction to the book's primary theoretical framework, the political economy of aging. Second, it introduces the concept of moral economy and suggests how incorporation of the latter may enrich political economy analyses and lead to a more comprehensive understanding of the experience of aging and old age.

In Chapter 2, Estes presents the political economy of aging as a broad interdisciplinary perspective which examines how economic, political, and sociocultural factors interact to shape and determine the meaning and experience of old age. In contrast to more traditional gerontological theories which focus primarily on the micro level, the political economy approach views aging in structural rather than individual terms. By broadening the unit of analysis, and clearly linking "private troubles" with "public issues," such a perspective is seen to facilitate work in such key areas as: variations by class, gender, and aging in the "lived experience" of old age; the social construction and management of dependency by societal institutions; the role, function, and relations of the state and capital and how these affect the elderly; and the nature and consequences of our social policies for the old.

In addition to presenting a broad overview of the political economy of aging, Chapter 2 introduces three particularly promising areas of investigation and theorizing: the state, social class, and gender and aging. Each of these is seen as representing a major underdeveloped area within the political economy of aging, yet one central to a comprehensive understanding of both the experience of old age and the nature and significance of our health and social policies for the old.

While the political economy perspective has greatly enriched our understanding of the interconnections between the personal and the structural dimensions of aging, additional work is needed in surfacing and examining the often implicit norms, cultural beliefs and values that underlie societal policies and practices affecting the old.

In Chapter 3, moral economy is presented as a concept particularly useful in this regard. Defined as the shared assumptions underlying norms of reciprocity in which an economic system is grounded, moral economy is seen as helping explicate such phenomena as the evolution of retirement and social security systems, and recent debates over generational equity and the allocation of resources between age groups.

Chapter 3 describes the origins and contemporary usage of moral economy, and then demonstrates its relevance to a variety of policy and related issues within the political economy of aging.

While Chapter 3 presents a unitary notion of moral economy, an alternative perspective is presented in the final chapter in this section, which suggests that the norms implicit in moral economy vary with changes in the social context. Hendricks and Leedham thus present two ideal types of moral economy—those grounded in exchange value and in use value respectively—and argue that the latter may contribute to a conceptual framework for empowerment of the old. For unlike moral economies grounded in exchange value, which tend to discount contributions outside the labor market and hence devalue the old, moral economies based on use value are seen in Chapter 4, as attempting to structure a society that maximizes the possibilities of a decent life for all, regardless of age.

As noted in Chapter 1, scholars are just beginning to explore the relevance of moral economy for the study of aging. Alternative ways of viewing this concept are presented in this first section of the book so that readers can weigh for themselves the relative merits of different approaches in terms of their ability to enrich a broader political economy of aging framework.

Overview

Meredith Minkler

In the past decade, increasing scholarly attention has been devoted to understanding the ways in which the individual experience of aging emerges from the social, political, and economic structure of society. Research in this tradition is based on the premise that the phenomenon of aging cannot be understood in isolation from the larger sociostructural issues that shape and condition "the status, resources and health of the elderly, and even the trajectory of the aging process itself" (Estes, Chapter 2, p. 21).

The political economy of aging represents a framework for inquiry based on this perspective, and committed to viewing the experience of aging in structural rather than individual terms (Chapter 2). This conceptual approach provides the primary theoretical framework for the critical examination of aging undertaken in this volume.

The purpose of the book is threefold. First, we attempt to apply a political economy of aging framework to the analysis of such diverse problems and issues as the politics of generational equity; the "biomedicalization" of old age; and the intersections of race, gender, and class that influence how aging is experienced. In this way, the book may be seen as complementing and extending our first volume, *Readings in the Political Economy of Aging*, by applying this conceptual approach to new areas of inquiry and facilitating an in-depth analysis of such previously introduced areas as the social creation of dependency, the multibillion dollar nursing home industry, and the economics of women and aging.

The book's second goal lies in the area of theory building. As Estes notes in Chapter 2, "the central challenge of political economy is to move beyond mere critiques to develop an understanding of the character and significance of variations in the treatment of the aged and how these relate to policy, economy, and society" (p. 19). Toward this end, the book begins by looking at the state of the art of the political economy of aging as a theoretical approach, highlighting recent developments, and suggesting areas in which further refinement and expansion may be useful. Subsequent chapters build upon this base by providing new political economy analyses within the field of aging, which, we believe, are themselves contributory to the further conceptual development of the approach, as well as to its concrete application in gerontology.

The third purpose of the book is related closely to the second and involves the exploration of a particular avenue of theory development. We explore the concept and uses of moral economy as an under-utilized but fruitful perspective that can enrich the political economy of aging. Defined as the collectively shared moral assumptions underlying norms of reciprocity in which an economy is grounded (1), moral economy helps to surface and make explicit the often implicit cultural beliefs and values underlying societal policies and practices affecting the old. A moral economy perspective thus enables a deeper exploration of such issues as the evolution of pension systems, what a society perceives is "due" its older members, and current debates over the allocation of resources between generations.

Political and moral economy perspectives share some important similarities (see Chapter 3), among them the fact that both ground their analyses of topics such as aging in considerations of broader sociohistorical processes. While political economy focuses in particular on the social structural context of aging, moral economy is primarily concerned with the related context of popular consensus defining norms of reciprocity as these affect the old and resource allocation across age groups. The explicit integration of a moral economy perspective within a broad political economy of aging framework, therefore, makes possible a richer and more thorough analysis than either can achieve independently (2).

In Chapter 2 of this volume, Estes provides a comprehensive introduction to the political economy of aging, noting that the central task of this theoretical approach is "to locate society's treatment of the aged in the context of the economy national and international, the state, the conditions of the labor market, and the class, sex, race, and age divisions in society" (p. 29). In contrast to psychological and other micro-level approaches that legitimate "incremental and individualistic approaches to public policy," a political economy perspective suggests that issues such as the health and the dependency of the old are embedded within the structure of the labor market and other macro-level considerations. Estes sees special relevance in such an approach for an understanding of how the elderly have come to be "homogenized" and labelled a social problem; how the social status and treatment of the old and of subgroups within the elderly population have developed; and how resource allocation policies affecting the old have been set.

Special attention is devoted in Chapter 2 to three critical and as yet under-developed areas within the political economy of aging: the state, social class, and gender. Most scholars have tended to view the questions of aging as peripheral to state and class theorizing since the old are no longer in the "productive" or work sector of the economy. The fallacy of this oversight is demonstrated in Chapter 2, which places aging squarely within the domain of both state and class investigations. The power of the state in allocating resources and shaping and reproducing social patterns, and the continuing role of preretirement social class in shaping the experience of old age, underscore the importance of developing these key areas of study specifically with reference to aging.

Yet, as Estes suggests, "theories of the state and class that do not explicitly and adequately address the subordination of women and the 'privileging of men' fail as comprehensive frameworks for understanding social phenomenon such as aging" (p. 27). Focus is therefore given to aging and gender both in Chapter 2 and throughout this volume, with gender, class, and racial/ethnic divisions in society examined in terms of how they influence and condition the experience of aging on both the macro-level and the individual or micro-level.

The multiperspectival nature of political economy, and its consequent ability to move across narrow disciplinary boundaries, enable it to integrate related conceptual approaches. In Chapter 3, Minkler and Cole propose one such integration, introducing the concept of moral economy and suggesting its usefulness as an adjunct to political economic analyses. As noted above, Thompson's view of the moral economy as the shared assumptions underlying reciprocal relations (1) is employed in Chapter 3 and in several subsequent chapters. Following a consideration of the ambivalence surrounding moral questions that has tended to characterize the "Scientific Marxism" tradition in political economy (3), Chapter 3 makes a case for acknowledging the importance of exploring moral issues and introduces the notion of moral economy as an appropriate tool for analysis.

While Thompson (1) and others (4, 5) have argued that the concept of moral economy has relevance primarily to the study of premarket societies, Chapter 3 argues, with Kohli (Chapter 17), that this construction also holds considerable promise for enriching understanding of contemporary arenas of moral conflict, particularly in the area of aging. The creation and evolution of pensions systems, the reality versus the rhetoric of "generational equity," and the recent "senior revolt" against the Medicare Catastrophic Coverage Act in the United States are among the topics introduced in Chapter 3 as meriting further analysis within a framework combining political and moral economy. Each of these topics is explored further in the book through such a joint political and moral economy perspective.

While Minkler and Cole (Chapter 3) employ a unitary conceptualization of moral economy, an alternative perspective is offered by Hendricks and Leedham (Chapter 4). These analysts suggest that because the norms implicit in moral economy vary with changing cultural and social contexts, several forms of moral economy may exist side by side in highly fragmented societies, competing for hegemony. Two "ideal types" of moral economy are proposed in this chapter. Moral economies grounded in use values are characterized as focusing on meeting human needs and creating social arrangements that maximize life chances for all over time. In contrast, moral economies grounded in exchange value are seen as taking a utilitarian approach to the public good and ignoring both problematic issues of distributive justice and the existence of goods not easily measured in economic terms.

The policy implications of these two "ideal types" of moral economy hold particular salience for the elderly. Moral economies grounded in exchange value thus tend to devalue the old, who are excluded from most "productive" activity and whose contributions outside the labor market (e.g., as caregivers and volunteers) tend to be discounted. In contrast, moral economies based on use value, and concerned with structuring a society that maximizes the possibilities of a decent life for all, are seen to provide an important avenue to empowerment of the old.

The alternative perspectives on moral economy provided in the first section of the book are designed to acquaint the reader with some of the early thinking of scholars attempting to apply this concept within the broad field of aging. The reader is invited to critically consider the different views of moral economy provided, and to weigh for him or herself their relative usefulness in enriching an overall political economy framework for the study of aging.

CHANGING IMAGES OF THE OLD

In the United States, appeals for increasing society's commitment to meeting the needs of its members across the life course have unfortunately been counterbalanced by other efforts to pit one group against another in the fight for scarce resources. The elderly have been particularly victimized in this process and scapegoated as a cause of poverty among children and economic hardship among young workers (6, 7).

Images of older Americans as a weak, poor, impotent, and deserving subgroup have given way over the last decade to new and equally inaccurate stereotypes portraying the elderly as a wealthy, selfish, and powerful voting block. The old are said to be "busting the budget" with costly entitlement programs that unfairly syphon scarce resources away from needy children and financially strapped workers. The resulting "generational inequity" is claimed to have set a dangerous precedent and one which, left unchecked, may lead to major intergenerational conflict and possibly even "age wars" in the years ahead (8, 9).

Chapter 5 examines the assumptions underlying the concept of generational equity from a political economy perspective enriched by a consideration of the moral economy notions in which attitudes toward the old are embedded. Minkler suggests that the concept of generational equity represents a flawed basis for public policy, particularly in its tendencies to aggregate and "homogenize" the elderly and to lay out complex issues simplistically in terms of competition between generations for scarce resources. Additionally, and contrary to the rhetoric of generational inequity popular in the mass media, moral economy notions underlying entitlements for the old are seen to remain strong throughout the society, and to be reflected in the continued evidence of a widely held cross-generational "stake" in programs like Social Security and Medicare.

While the mass media and some conservative political groups have decried what they see as the growing economic and political clout of the old, to the detriment of the rest of society (7–9), the business sector has discovered that there is indeed "gold in gray." Chapter 6 examines the various factors contributing to the new business image of the old as a potent new market with considerable financial assets and a high level of discretionary spending, making this group ripe for all manner of new products and services.

Viewed in a positive light, discovery of the elderly market by business can help bring a historically devalued segment of the population into the social and cultural mainstream by providing needed visibility and conferring implicit value upon them. But as Chapter 6 suggests, the eagerness of business and industry to capitalize on the "gray market" may also reinforce age separatist policies and approaches, and create artificial needs, frequently by reinforcing gerontophobia, the cultural dread of aging so prevalent in American society (10). Finally, by contributing new images of the old as a largely affluent consumer group, business and industry may divert attention from the needs of low-income elders and undermine support for needed public services.

The emergence of a new and misleading stereotype of the elderly as a wealthy and homogeneous population group has been accompanied by new and equally simplistic images of seniors as one of the most powerful political constituencies in the United States. Citing the 31 million member American Association of Retired Persons (AARP) as a case in point, proponents of the "senior power" perspective argue that the organized elderly have surpassed both the National Rifle Association and the American Medical Association to become the largest special interest group in the nation (11).

The senior power perspective, however, assumes an aging population with collectively shared interests and values that direct their political activism (12). It assumes that the elderly consistently vote as a block and that organizations like AARP truly reflect the voice of the nation's elderly. Yet these assumptions must be carefully questioned.

In Chapter 7, the myths and the realities behind the concept of senior power are disentangled. Using as a theoretical framework Lukes' three-dimensional typology of power (13), Wallace, Williamson, Lung and Powell examine the perceived and actual *situational* power of the elderly, reflected in their ability as an electorate to influence decisions on contested public issues; their *institutional* power through senior organizations that attempt to shape political agendas and policy processes; and their *structural* power or ability to change the policy context as a consequence of the transformative influence of population aging on the social structure and the economy. The Townsend Movement of the 1930s, the impact of "Seniors for Kennedy" in 1960, and recent and effective senior organizing against the Medicare Catastrophic Coverage Act are used to illustrate the *situational power* of elders, while the passage and implementation of Social Security and Medicare are examined from the perspective of *institutional power* of the aged and their organizations. The leading senior organizations and their policy impacts also are examined, with attention to the class-based nature of these organizations, and their consequent tendency to disproportionately focus on issues of concern to middle- and upper middle-class elders, rather than their low-income counterparts. Indeed, "senior power" is a misnomer to the extent that it tends to leave out the low-income elderly, minority elders, and other groups low in political activity and whose interests and needs are not well represented by most aging organizations (14).

Elders may have a more generalized influence on *structural power*, the dimension of power relating heavily to the influence of demography. As the United States moves toward a society with more elders than children and youth, virtually every aspect of the society may be transformed, including work and retirement, the health care system, and business and industry. Such transformations, already well underway in a number of Western European nations, raise a host of ethical and practical questions, and further suggest the need for new images of the old that respect their diversity and view them as an integral, rather than a marginal, part of the larger society.

APOCALYPTIC DEMOGRAPHY AND THE BIOMEDICALIZATION OF AGING

Antithetical to an appreciation of the diversity of the old is the social construction and treatment of aging as a medical problem. Termed by Estes and Binney, the "biomedicalization of aging," this perspective encourages society to view aging as pathological and undesirable—a problem to be ameliorated through generously funded biomedical research and health policies that "reflect medicine's monopoly in the control and management of the aging" (Chapter 8, p. 124).

In Chapter 8, Estes and Binney examine in detail the biomedicalization of aging as it is reflected and played out in academia, the professions, the worlds of funding and public policy, and ultimately in the attitudes of the lay public. Although several significant sources of resistance to this model are noted, the hegemonic hold of a "gerontology of medicine" approach remains strong and diverts attention from such underdeveloped areas of inquiry as the influence of social and environmental factors on the process and experience of aging.

Just as biomedicalization narrows our vision and constricts our choices with respect to aging, so do catastrophic projections of the burdens to society posed by the aging of the population. Robertson has coined the term "apocalyptic demography" in reference to a "bankruptcy hypothesis of aging" (Chapter 9, p. 135). In this view, the unprecedented growth of the elderly population is hypothesized as depleting national budgets and robbing nations of their freshness and creativity.

In Chapter 9, Robertson challenges the apocalyptic demography approach by demonstrating how even Alzheimer's disease—one of the most dreaded and widely publicized health problems of old age—may be in part socially constructed. Within the framework of the biomedicalization of aging and of Foucault's notion of the "clinical gaze" (15, 16), Robertson presents further support for Fox's recent observation that "the discovery of Alzheimer's disease has involved a political process more than simply a biomedical discovery" (17, p. 597).

Chapter 9 builds on Fox's historical work to demonstrate how the response of the health care system to Alzheimer's disease and to the aging of the population may have contributed heavily to the cataclysmic visions of aging that permeate many advanced industrial societies.

MARKET ECONOMY HEALTH CARE

The social construction of aging as a medical problem (Chapter 8) helps explain the vast "overdevelopment" of a geriatric "medical industrial complex" (18) in countries like the United States and the related underdevelopment of social, economic, and other nonmedical approaches to helping elders meet their needs. In Chapter 10, Harrington provides a detailed analysis of the multibillion dollar nursing home industry in the United States, examining in particular the structural features of the nursing home market and industry that compromise quality of care.

Second only to the drug sector of the health care industry in terms of proprietary and chain ownership (19), the nursing home industry stands as a highly visible reminder of the problems plaguing a market economy approach to health care in the United States. As Harrington demonstrates, nursing homes have the poorest quality of care of any segment of the health care industry, despite massive infusions of public funds, and numerous exposés and investigations. Although greatly stepped up regulatory approaches are advocated, only major structural reforms are seen as holding promise for substantially improving quality of care for the nation's 1.5 million nursing home residents.

Just as long-term care in the United States has been dominated by the lucrative nursing home industry, so has care of the elderly with mental illnesses been disproportionately institutional in nature. Despite the deinstitutionalization movement of the late 1960s and early 1970s, the "the cornerstone of mental health policy" for the elderly continues to be institutionalization, with a shifting venue from the back wards of public hospitals to nursing homes (20).

In Chapter 11, Binney and Swan examine mental health care for the elderly within a political economy framework. Mental illness in the elderly is seen as an inherently political issue, with illness rates, definitions, treatment, and management approaches heavily influenced by race, gender, and class, and by the nature of social and economic relations under capitalism.

Building on themes introduced in Chapters 8 and 9, Binney and Swan also explore the biomedicalization of mental health problems, and in particular the role of a growing "Alzheimer's Disease Enterprise" in heavily skewing policy and funding priorities. The class basis of mental health and aging policies is underscored, and a case made for developing Marxist models that can further our understanding of this critical and neglected problem area.

The high costs of long-term care—whether for severe mental or physical health problems—have made this area, in poll after poll, older Americans' top priority issue for Congressional action (21).

Despite the primacy of this concern, however, recent efforts to significantly expand Medicare all but ignored long-term care, focusing instead on the provision of coverage for catastrophic acute care needs (22). Although the rise and fall of the Medicare Catastrophic Coverage Act appears at first a simple case of interest group politics in action, such limited analysis fails to explicate some of the more fundamental issues beneath the U.S. experience with Catastrophic Coverage. In Chapter 12, Holstein and Minkler use a combined political and moral economy framework to examine the passage and repeal of this legislation. As they demonstrate, the peculiar form of the legislation—omitting coverage for long-term care and including a self-financing mechanism—must be understood within the context of both long-term and immediate political and economic developments. A political economy framework is useful in understanding how and in what form the legislation came into being, and moral economy concerns with just and unjust taxation help explain the strength of the "senior backlash" and the consequent repeal of the Act.

RACE, CLASS, GENDER, AND AGING

As noted above, a major contribution of the political economy perspective is its ability to highlight the intersections of race, class, gender, and aging as they shape and determine the experience of growing old. Since race, class, and gender are, like age, major stratifiers in society, attempts to study and understand aging without reference to these critical factors and their interactions are doomed to failure.

In Chapter 13, Arendell and Estes examine the health and economic issues confronted by older women in the United States, pointing out that the often adverse circumstances faced by women in late life are not a result of old age *per se*, but of "lifelong patterns of socio-economic and gender stratification" in society (p. 209).

The disproportionate representation of women in the peripheral or secondary sector of the labor market, wage discrimination, the sexual division of labor, and the devaluation of caregiving are among structural inequalities that help explain the economic dependence of women on men and the continued economic vulnerability of many older women. In the face of these problems, moreover, there is another persistent pattern: federal budget cutbacks continue to fall dispropor-tionately on programs and services (e.g., public housing, Medicaid, and legal assistance) used most heavily by poor women, and particularly by women of color and advanced age (23).

Consequently, as Chapter 13 suggests, although the 1980s witnessed some public policy gains for older women in areas such as Social Security and health coverage, the decade may, on balance, be characterized as one of policy losses that further eroded the already vulnerable position of many older women.

Some cost containment policies of the eighties, moreover, such as the DRG hospital reimbursement system under Medicare, have had the effect of doubly burdening older women: not only are they themselves being sent home from hospitals "quicker and sicker" (24, 25), but as primary caregivers to their spouses and elderly parents and in-laws, they are assuming responsibility for increasingly demanding levels and amounts of care. Estes and her colleagues have documented that families and communities have by necessity absorbed 21 million extra days of caregiving each year since DRGs went into effect (26). This caregiver burden falls principally on middle-aged and older women.

In the area of caregiving for the impaired elderly, the intersections of race, class, gender, and age are classically played out. Women represent over 90 percent of the paid attendants for the elderly both in the home and in nursing homes (27). Attendants are disproportionately women of color and of low socio-economic background. Low status, coupled with low pay, and the dead-end nature of the work, reinforces the devalued position in society of women who work as paid attendants.

Women also provide most of the unpaid caregiving to the elderly, with "family care" being a euphemism for care by women, typically older wives and adult daughters and daughters-in-law (28). The health, social, and economic costs to women caregivers are only beginning to be realized, as are the differences in the caregiving burden of women by race and class. Research attention is merited, for example, on the greater direct parent care role shouldered by working-class women (29) and on the special problems faced by low-income black women serving as primary caretakers for grandchildren as a result of the crack cocaine epidemic (30).

Chapter 14 examines how the provision of community care to the elderly interacts with the feminized structure of family caregiving to create and maintain inequities for women, who provide the bulk of this unpaid care. Constricted choices for women in the workplace are shown to be further reinforced by a conservative political climate in which the marketplace is considered "an efficient and sufficient mechanism for distributing services to families" (p. 230). A direc-tion for future policy development is suggested to assure "gender justice" by providing alternatives that enable individuals to freely choose whether and to what extent to perform the caregiving role.

As noted above, the gender inequalities faced by many older women are compounded for those who are also people of color and members of low socioeconomic groups. As Dressel suggests in Chapter 15, however, to view oppression in an additive way—looking, for example, at gender inequities and then simply adding on the effects of inequities based on race or class—misses the fact that to be an old, black woman is *qualitatively* and not just *quantitatively* different from being an old white woman.

Further, an "add and stir" approach to oppression (31) tends to operate as if one filter (e.g., sexism) were the most important through which to view social problems, rather than acknowledging that racism, sexism, and classism all are potent forces for social inequity.

In Chapter 15, Dressel demonstrates the limitations and distortions of the add and stir approach, using as a case study the feminization of poverty in late life. As she points out, although the feminization of poverty thesis has been useful politically in consciousness-raising and related activities, it ignores critical data (e.g., the very high poverty rate among older black men) that a more interactive focus on race, class, gender, and aging would illuminate.

Such an interactive focus is demonstrated again in Chapter 16. The health care of elderly blacks is used as a case study for examining how theories based on culture, race, and class factors each alternatively would account for the inequities in health status and medical services that continue to persist between older blacks and whites in the United States. Wallace demonstrates in Chapter 16 that the continued inferiority in the quality of care received by elderly blacks cannot be adequately explained by culture theories that fail to explore such structural forces as institutional racism and the profit motive in health care, both of which heavily influence access to care and quality of care. Moreover, neither class theory nor race theory is sufficient alone to explain health care differences between aged blacks and whites because some differences (e.g., discrimination against blacks in nursing home admissions) primarily reflect racial forces, but others (e.g., disparities in income and health insurance coverage) appear most closely related to social class variables. Policies, such as national health insurance, that address income but not racial barriers to care thus are seen as necessary but insufficient avenues for change. Similarly, efforts to end institutional racism in the medical care sector are necessary, but not enough, to provide true parity in quality of health care for older blacks.

RETIREMENT, SOCIAL SECURITY, AND ECONOMIC DEPENDENCY

The social creation of old age is nowhere better illustrated than in the spheres of retirement and social security. As Myles has argued, the very right to retire and "become old" is established through legislation so that "politics, not demography" has become the main determinant of the size and economic circumstances of the elderly population (32). Critiques of the modern welfare state in general and of social security schemes in particular correctly argue that such systems often reproduce market-based inequalities, in part because they are grounded in and shaped by the needs of capital.

Yet political economic analyses which attempt to understand the development of public pensions and other welfare schemes solely in market terms miss other and equally compelling aspects of these social developments. As Myles (Chapter 18) points out, for example, labor rather than capital provided political support after World War II for the expansion of pensions into a retirement wage in the United States and other advanced capitalist countries. Moreover, the embedding of retirement in the moral economy of modern societies is critical to its viability and must therefore be understood in moral, as well as economic and political, terms.

In Chapter 17, Kohli uses the concept of moral economy to explicate the development of the world's first pension system and its grounding in notions of reciprocity based on shared moral assumptions of solidarity between the generations. The German public insurance system, with pensions as its largest component, is seen to have had as its aim the construction of a reliable life course which would provide coverage for disability, old age and sickness—the risks connected to the new organization of work. The pension scheme which Germany developed thus helped address some of the structural problems that occurred with the transition from a household economy to a modern work society. Key among these, it gave workers an increased stake in the social order, thereby increasing both their integration and their social control.

Chapter 17 argues that the welfare state and retirement successfully met their goals in that they "embedded the emerging capitalist market economy within the new moral economy of the work society, and thus made it socially viable" (p. 277). Moreover, this embeddedness has been so firm that frightened conservative governments have been moving away from attempting to radically cut social insurance schemes as a cost saving mechanism.

While moral economy helps explain such phenomena as the significant role of labor and of popular consensus in protecting pension coverage, a careful look at the needs of capital in shaping the history of pension systems also is in order. In the United States, for example, a political economy perspective helps illuminate how retirement initially served the needs of business and industry by enabling these sectors to remove their older, most expensive workers and reducing dangerously high unemployment rates. By the mid-1970s, however, the modernization of the Social Security system, which greatly expanded "social wages," led business to mount a strong, albeit largely unsuccessful, attack on this hallowed institution.

In Chapter 18, Myles examines the expansion of Social Security into a true "retirement wage," and the corresponding changes in business' attitudes, leading to the latter's attempts to create a perceived "Social Security crisis" which might in turn generate political support for cutbacks. While the subsequent strong public reaction against tampering with Social Security underscored the extent of popular support for this program, the fact that incremental cuts *were* successfully made suggests, according to Myles, the need to safeguard against an incremental dismantling of this centerpiece of the welfare state in the years ahead.

Analyses of economic dependency and social security for the elderly typically focus on the conditions of the old in Western industrial and postindustrial societies. Such a focus, however, necessarily ignores the situation of the 60 percent of the world's elderly who live in Third World nations (33).

Political economy perspectives can enhance an understanding of aging in the Third World by enabling a systematic examination of the social conditions of the old as they reflect location in the social structure, the nature of social policies, and related factors. In a similar manner, moral economy approaches can enrich an understanding of aging in the Third World by illuminating collectively held assumptions underlying norms and beliefs about what a society owes its elderly, the just allocation of scarce resources across age groups, and filial responsibility norms and customs.

In Chapter 19, Neysmith uses a political economy framework, enhanced by moral economy considerations, to examine the social creation and reinforcement of dependency among the elderly in the Third World. The intersections of gender, class, race, and age discrimination, coupled with deteriorating social and economic conditions in much of the Third World in the 1980s, are shown to have aggravated the already economically vulnerable situation of many of the old in these countries.

Traditional approaches to development that disproportionately favor middle- and upper-income groups are seen to reinforce the disadvantaged position of the old and other vulnerable populations. Further, while some recent approaches (e.g., the new focus on micro- and not merely macro-scale development) have given new visibility to such "invisible" sectors as unpaid female labor in caregiving, strong patriarchal attitudes and moral economy notions stressing family responsibility for care of the old suggest that such visibility alone is insufficient to bring about change. A "renegotiated social contract" between the developed and developing worlds is necessary in setting a stage for improved social conditions for elders and other high-risk groups in the Third World of the nineties. Recommended micro-development approaches shift the focus from national elites to the needs of the most oppressed social groups and incorporate a level of social analysis that enables a reconsideration of the position of the old, and of women as the chief unpaid caregivers for the old.

FUTURE POLICY DIRECTIONS

The tremendous diversity of the elderly both within the United States and in other countries constitutes a central theme threaded through this volume. A second and contradictory theme, however, is also apparent and relates to the growing tendency, particularly in the United States, to stereotype the old as a wealthy and politically powerful population block siphoning resources from the young (6, 7). Such juxtapositions have led to reevaluations of the once unquestioned "deservingness" status of the old (34), which, coupled with cost containment considerations and other factors, may weaken public support for old age entitlements in the 1990s.

In Chapter 20, Shindul-Rothschild and Williamson examine the future prospects for U.S. aging policy reform against the backdrop of these changing images of the old and other recent political, social, and economic developments. Although not envisioning major cutbacks in programs for the elderly in the near future, these investigators suggest that the above-mentioned factors, combined with such recent developments as negative fallout from the senior revolt against the Medicare Catastrophic Coverage Act, may mitigate against significant policy gains in the years ahead. Viewed retrospectively, they argue, advocates for the elderly "have done well emphasizing programs and policies that are *particularistic* in providing benefits targeted for the elderly to the exclusion of other age groups, but *universalistic* in the sense of providing benefits to as many of the aged as possible" (p. 338, emphasis added).

In the future, however, an alternative policy strategy is needed—one stressing benefits that are particularistic in being aimed at elders in need, but universalistic in providing benefits for the non-aged as well as the middle-aged and low-income groups. While some exceptions are noted (e.g., meeting the long-term care needs of the frail elderly regardless of economic status), the overall strategies proposed constitute an ethically and politically sound means of combining concerns for fairness and equity with those of cost effectiveness. In Estes' words, such a shift would involve a move away from the "selfish separatism" of an aging lobby advocating only for the elderly, and toward activism on behalf of policies supportive of young and old alike (35).

Several of the concerns expressed by Shindul-Rothschild and Williamson in the book's final chapter echo themes that are woven through this entire volume. Key concepts are the primacy of politics and the needs of the economy in the shaping of policies for the old; the role of such policies in reinforcing existing structural inequities; and the increasing necessity for policies and programs that address human needs across generations, in the process strengthening moral economy concerns for reciprocity and fairness.

It is our hope that through its treatment of these and related themes, the book will contribute to the theoretical development of the political economy of aging, and to its use in explicating the status and treatment of the old in a broad sociostructural context. In addition, if the book succeeds in acquainting readers with a new conceptual area, the moral economy of aging, and demonstrating its potential for enriching political economy analyses, it will have achieved another major objective. Finally, although the book is geared to understanding the way in which the experience of aging is shaped and conditioned by its embeddedness in larger contextual arenas, such understanding is of little consequences unless it, in turn, is translated into action based on critical reflection. It is our hope that the critical perspectives on aging offered in this volume will ultimately be reflected in *praxis* geared toward overcoming the devalued and dependent position of the elderly and fostering empowerment across the lifespan.

REFERENCES

1. Thompson, E. P. *The Making of the English Working Class*. Vintage Books, New York, 1966.
2. Brocheux, P. Moral economy or political economy? The peasants are always rational. *J. Asian Studies* 42(4): 791–803, 1983.
3. Lukes, S. *Marxism and Morality*. Oxford University Press, Oxford, United Kingdom, 1985.
4. Claeys, G. *Machinery, Money and the Millennium: From Moral Economy to Socialism, 1815–1860*. Polity Press, Cambridge, United Kingdom, 1987.
5. Scott, J. C. *The Moral Economy of the Peasant Rebellion and Subsistence in South East Asia*. Yale University Press, New Haven and London, 1976.
6. Preston, S. Children and the elderly in the U.S. *Scient. Am.* 251: 44–49, 1984.
7. Chakravarty, S. N., and Weisman, K. Consuming our children. *Forbes Magazine* November: 222–232, 1988.
8. Hewitt, P. Case Statement. Americans for Generational Equity, Washington, D.C., 1986.
9. Longman, P. Age wars: The coming battle between young and old. *The Futurist* 20(1): 8–11, 1986.
10. Fischer, D. H. *Growing Old in America*. Oxford University Press, New York, 1978.
11. Dychtwald, K., and Flower, J. *Age Wave: The Challenges and Opportunities of an Aging America*. Jeremy P. Tarcher, Inc., Los Angeles, 1989.
12. Rosenbaum, W. A., and Button, J. W. Is there a gray peril? Retirement politics in Florida. *The Gerontologist* 29: 300–306, 1989.
13. Lukes, S. *Power: A Radical View*. Macmillan, New York, 1974.
14. Schick, F. L. (ed.), *Statistical Handbook on Aging Americans*. Oryx Press, Phoenix, 1986.
15. Foucault, M. *The Birth of the Clinic*. Vintage Books, New York, 1975.
16. Foucault, M. *Discipline and Punish: The Birth of the Prison*. Vintage Books, New York, 1979.
17. Fox, P. From senility to Alzheimer's disease: The rise of the Alzheimer's disease movement. *Milbank Mem. Fund Q.* 67(1): 58–102, 1989.
18. Relman, A. The new medical industrial complex. *New Engl. J. Med* 303(17): 963–970, 1980.
19. Strahan, G. Characteristics of registered nurses in nursing homes: Preliminary data from the 1985 National Nursing Home Survey. *Advance Data from Vital and Health Statistics*, No. 131, DHHS Publ. No. (PHS) 87-1250. National Center for Health Statistics, U.S. Public Health Service, Hyattsville, Maryland, 1988.

20. Gatz, M., Smyer, M. A., and Lawton, M. P. The mental health system and the older adult. In *Aging in the 1980's: Selected Contemporary Issues in the Psychology of Aging*, edited by L. W. Poon. American Psychological Association, Washington, D.C., 1980.

21. Personal communication from Jeff Kirsch, Field Director, Families U.S.A. Foundation, May 15, 1990.

22. Torres-Gil, F. The politics of catastrophic and long term care coverage. *J. Aging and Soc. Pol.* 1: 61–86, 1989.

23. Minkler, M., and Stone, R. The feminization of poverty and older women. *Gerontologist* 25(4): 351–357, 1985.

24. Bergthold, L. The impact of public policy on home health services for the elderly. *The Pride Institute J. of Long Term Home Health Care* 6(1): 12–21, 1987.

25. Shaughnessy, P. W., and Kramer, A. M. The increased needs of patients in nursing homes and patients receiving home health care. *New Engl. J. Med.* 332(1), January 4, 1990.

26. Estes, C. L. Cost containment and the elderly: Conflict or challenge? *J. Am. Geriat. Soc.* 36: 68–72, 1988.

27. Employed persons by detailed occupation, sex and race. *Annual Averages Employment and Earnings*, vv25–35, January 1977–88. Cited in Quinlan, A. *Chronic Care Workers: Crisis Among Paid Caregivers of the Elderly*. Older Women's League, Washington, D.C., 1988.

28. Brody, E. M. 'Women in the middle' and family help to older people. *Gerontologist* 21(5): 471–480, 1981.

29. Archbold, P. G. Impact of parent-caring on women. *Fam. Rel.* 32(1): 39–45, 1983.

30. California Assembly Human Services Committee. Hearing on drug exposed infants: The role of grandmothers as caretakers. San Francisco, California, October 30, 1989.

31. Anderson, M. L. *Thinking About Women: Sociological and Feminist Perspectives*. Macmillan, New York, 1983.

32. Myles, J. F. Conflict, crisis, and the future of old age security. In *Readings in the Political Economy of Aging*, edited by M. Minkler and C. L. Estes, pp. 168–176. Baywood Publishing, Amityville, New York, 1984.

33. United Nations Department of International Economic and Social Affairs. *Economic and Social Implications of Population Aging*. United Nations, New York, 1988.

34. Katz, M. B. *The Undeserving Poor: From the War on Poverty to the War on Welfare*. Pantheon Books, New York, 1989.

35. Estes, C. L. The aging enterprise: In whose interests? *Int. J. Health Serv.* 16(2): 243–251, 1986.

CHAPTER 2

The New Political Economy of Aging: Introduction and Critique

Carroll L. Estes

A political economy perspective on aging and old age emphasizes the broad implications of economic life for the aged and for society's treatment of the elderly. It is a systemic view predicated on the assumption that old age can only be understood in the context of problems and issues of the larger social order. Significantly, the aged are not treated as a homogeneous group or category. Rather, a key element is the analysis of the implications of class, gender, and race for all aspects of the definition and management of the elderly.

The central challenge of the political economy of aging is to understand the character and significance of variations in the treatment of the aged and to relate them to broader societal trends. A major task is to understand how the aging process itself is influenced by the treatment and location of elders in society. The political economy perspective requires an interdisciplinary and sociohistorical approach that draws upon sociology, economics, political science, epidemiology, history, and health services and health policy research. In building toward a comprehensive gerontological framework, the political economy of aging offers a theoretical and empirical perspective on the socioeconomic determinants of the experience of aging and old age and on the policy interventions that emerge in the context of capitalist society. The lived experience of aging is to be understood in relation to the lives of other generations and segments of society, and these in relation to the broader material and symbolic order. The political economy perspective proposed here examines (1, p. 19):

> interrelationships between the polity, economy, and society, or more specific- ally, the reciprocal influences among government . . . the economy, social classes, strata, and status groups . . . [and] the manner in which the economy and polity interact in a relationship of reciprocal causation, affecting the distribution of social goods.

19

Work on the political economy of aging has begun to specify how the meaning and experience of old age and the distribution of resources to the aging are directed by economic, political, and sociocultural factors (2–22). A major contribution of this work is its illumination of how social policy for the aged mirrors the structural arrangements of U.S. society and the distribution of material, political, and ideological resources within it. Public policy reflects and reinforces the "life chances" associated with each person's social location within the class, status, and political structures that comprise society (23). The lives of each succeeding generation are similarly shaped by the extent to which social policy maintains or redistributes those life chances.

The sociohistorical, political, and economic context in which persons age and become a "problem group" is relevant to understanding the relative influence of the state and class relations as they impinge upon the resources allocated to different subgroups of elders. Class is broadly conceived to include the impact of gender and racial/ethnic relations on the relations of production.

Questions concern the social-structural features that manifest change and elevate concepts of "private troubles" to the level of public issues at particular historical moments (24); how the definition of public issues reflect the dominance and structural location of specific interests, institutions, and classes; and how the health and subjective experiences of individuals in old age are shaped by these social forces. The structure and operation of the major societal institutions (for example, family, workplace, and medical and welfare institutions) are of particular interest as they shape both the subjective experience and objective condition of individual older persons.

Particularly fruitful areas of work on aging include studies of:

- The socially and structurally produced nature of aging and the lived experience of old age as they vary by class, gender, and race;
- Ideology as a central element in the social and political processing of the old and old age in society;
- The social construction and management of dependency by societal institutions;
- The types of social interventions that are legitimated by the dominant social construction(s) of aging;
- The role, function, and relations of the state, capital, and labor and how these affect the aging; and
- The nature and consequences of social policy for the elderly, with particular attention to the effects of societal divisions of class, gender, and racial/ethnic status.

The focus is on aging status and class and the intersections between them as they are structurally embedded and conditioned by economics, politics, and society. This approach is distinguished from other gerontological perspectives by viewing the situation of aging as the product of social structural forces rather than natural or inevitable individual biological and psychological processes. The latter perspectives, by definition, 1) take for granted existing structural arrangements and the overriding importance of the market in distributing rewards in society (2); and 2) explain the dependency status of the elderly according to individual lifecourse "choices" in work and behavior (25–27).

In contrast, the structural view of aging commences with the proposition that the status, resources, and health of the elderly, and even the trajectory of the aging process itself, are conditioned by one's location in the social structure and the relations generated by the economic mode of production and the gendered division of labor. These relations are sociohistorically framed through the interaction of economic, political, and ideological forces and the social struggles they create. The dependency of the elderly is understood as a social product of the market and the social relations it produces. Policy interventions consistent with this perspective would address institutionalized structures of society such as the labor market and patriarchy (28), in contrast to interventions that would address problems on an individual level (e.g., with counseling or individual services). Three particularly promising areas of investigation and theorizing are: 1) the state, 2) social class, and 3) gender and aging.

THE STATE

The political economy perspective proposed here necessarily draws heavily on state theory and all varieties of neo-Weberian and neo-Marxist theoretical developments therein. What is new is that questions of aging are seen as central, not peripheral, to the investigation of society and the state. A central dynamic is the examination of the contradictions between the organization of work (capitalist modes of production) and social needs, and how these contradictions affect the lifecourse.

Older persons are more dependent on state policy than younger persons. Further, older women are more dependent on the state than older men because of women's increased dependency on the state earlier in their lifecourse (29). Over the past several decades, women's dependence has shifted from private relations with men to public dependence on the state. Women are linked to the state in three types of status: as citizens with political rights, as clients and consumers of welfare services, and as employees in the state sector (29–31).

Issues of the role and power of the state, constraints on state intervention, and state legitimation functions in the distribution of benefits have, with few exceptions (13, 28), not been examined in direct relation to the aged, although Ginsberg (32), O'Connor (33), Gough (34), and others have indirectly addressed these issues. In the health field, however, major contributions to a political economy framework have been made (35–41).

The study of the state is central to the understanding of old age and the life chances of elders since it has the power to: 1) allocate and distribute scarce resources to ensure the survival and growth of the economy, 2) mediate between the different segments and classes of society, and 3) ameliorate social conditions that could threaten the existing order. The power of the state, moreover, extends beyond the distribution of resources to the formation and reformation of social patterns (42). For example, the state does more than regulate institutions and relations like marriage and motherhood as it manages them (42). The state actually constitutes "the social categories of the gender order," as "patriarchy is both constructed and contested through the state" (42). Similarly, relations associated with age, racial/ethnic status, and class are constructed and contested in the state.

The state is comprised of major social, political, and economic institutions including the legislative, executive, and judicial branches of government; the military and criminal justice systems; and public educational, health, and welfare institutions (43). Although there are many theories of the state (33, 44–47), most theorists agree with Max Weber's contention that the first role of the state is to assure the survival of the economic system (48).

Within the political economy perspective, state theory (49, 50) assumes the conflict paradigm, which conceives of the social order as held together by the dominance of certain groups over others. The outcomes of conflict and power struggles are posited as explanations for how society is organized and functions, and society is seen as held together by constraint, rather than consensus (51). Societal institutions such as work organizations and medicine are organized and operate the ways they do because some manage to successfully impose their ideas, material interests, and actions on others.

The state not only actively participates in these struggles, but also reflects various forms of the interests to the most powerful. A variety of neo-Marxist and neo-Weberian theories of the state fall within this perspective. A contrasting view of the state emerges from the social order paradigm, built on consensus theories which posit that society is held together by shared values and agreement about the way it functions (52). The liberal political and pluralist theories within the social order paradigm portray the state as a neutral entity, operating in the universal interest of all members of society. The social order paradigm has been faulted for idealizing democracy and "public choice" while overlooking the power of large-scale vested interests and the "mobilization of bias" built into interest group politics (53).

Offe and Ronge identify four characteristics of the state in capitalist societies (44): 1) property is private, and privately owned capital is the basis of the economy; 2) resources generated through private profit and the growth of private wealth indirectly finance the state (e.g., through taxation); 3) the state is thereby "dependent on a source of income which it does not itself organize . . . thus [it] has a general 'interest' in facilitating" the growth of private property in order to perpetuate itself (54, p. 192; and 4) in democracies such as the United States, political elections disguise the basic fact that the resources available for distribution by the state are dependent on the success of private profit and capital reinvestment, rather than on the will of the electorate. A fifth attribute of the state is its accountability for the success of the economy; the state bears the brunt of public dissatisfaction for economic difficulties.

Elite/managerial and class theories of the state gained prominence in the 1980s. The former, sometimes called independent state theory (4), argues that state managers act, not as direct agents of the ruling class, but in the interest of preserving their own bureaucratic power (55), and that in doing so they contribute to the maintenance of the political and economic order. The state is seen as neither completely autonomous nor a tool of the capitalist class, but instead as a mediating body between power blocks (49, 56, 57). In Offe's view, "the state is an 'independent' mediator of the class struggle inherent in the capital accumulation struggle, independence hinging on the inability of both capitalist and working class to organize themselves as classes" (49, p. 251).

Important developments in class theorizing on the state include structural and capital logic (58, 59), instrumental, and class struggle theories (33, 46). Structural theories emphasize the economic role of the state as "a self-contained institutional system guided by the interests of political officials and organizations" in the context of deep structural forces at work (60, p. 907, 61); structuralists theorize that no intervention is needed by capital to ensure that the state will act to maintain the system. Instrumentalist theories emphasize the state as a neutral arena for reconciling upper-class interests (62). Class struggle theories are the most fertile of recent developments in state theory, with at least three theoretical strands: mass turmoil thesis, elite dominance thesis, and power resource theory (49, 56). Each of these theories shares a vision of the state as the "material condensation of class forces," in Poulantzas' words (59). State structure incorporates the results of previous struggles and policy subject to class forces. Much of this literature suggests that the state, rather than the mode of production, is the principal site of class struggle, hence the principal focus of analysis. This theory represents a revision in recent Marxist thought, with politics assuming a new primacy (49). Recent efforts to revise and improve class struggle theory include the work of Jenkins and Brents (60) on political struggle theory and that of Quadagno (56) on race, class, and gender. Jenkins and Brents underscore "the distinctive logic of the political struggles defined by liberal democratic capitalism" (60, p. 907), emphasizing the role of social protest and intercapitalist political competition in state theory. Quadagno faults class theory for its inattention to the role of state policy in mediating race relations and for its blindness to " a defining feature of social provision: its organization around gender" (56, p. 14).

Pascall notes that the state sustains the subordination of women through social policy based on a particular family form, the nuclear family with a male breadwinner and a dependent wife (63). Dependent relations are sustained by Social Security and other agencies of the welfare state that lock women into a spousal wage relationship. The state also supports this relationship through the labor market and the refusal to pay for the caring work of women (64, see also Chapter 13). As a result of no pay or low pay to predominantly women caregivers, "the price of such caring work is economic dependence . . . [which] amounts to the exploitation of one kind of dependency to deal with another" (63, p. 29). Any comprehensive theory must articulate not only the relations between state and economy, but also those with the household (65). The role of the state in social reproduction must be examined from the position of women (63).

Regrettably, gerontological work on aging and the state is extremely limited and remains largely the province of state theorists who treat it almost incidentally; serious treatment of older women and the state is even more scarce. Theorists of aging and the state include John Myles in Canada (11); Anne Marie Guillemard in France (19, 20); and Jill Quadagno (56, 62, 66) and Carroll Estes and her colleagues (9, 28, 67, 68) in the United States, as well as several British scholars including Alan Walker (69) and Chris Phillipson (70).

The state and state policy on aging need to be examined more closely in terms of how they promote and reproduce the dominant institutions. One example is the consideration of how state policies that treat aging issues as individual and medical problems (e.g., requiring medical services sold for a profit) are ideologically and practically consistent with state roles in the process of capital accumulation and in legitimation of capitalist social relations through processes of social control (e.g., welfare) and social integration (e.g., democratic processes). The political economy perspective renders the aged and state policy an intrinsic part of the broader phenomenon of crisis construction and management in advanced capitalism and considers how the aged and old age policy are used in these processes (68). The task is to specify how the aged and state policy are implicated in crisis formation and trajectory and the role of ideology therein.

CLASS

According to Giddens, there is widespread confusion and ambiguity in use of the term, "class" (71). This seems particularly so for those who have attempted an analysis of aging and class (21, 72, 73, 74). Gerontology from a political economy perspective demands attention to class; nevertheless, work on the topic is surprisingly underdeveloped. James Dowd is one of the few who have examined exchange, power, and class issues in the negotiation of exchange rates between the aged and others in society. Dowd notes that (21, pp. 21–22):

> the individual experience of growing old and the nature of age relations vary so significantly by social class that there is a need for unified analysis in which both age *and* class are considered.

One difficulty in applying class theory to the aged is that the elderly are no longer in the socially defined "productive" sector of the economy (21). yet, this is precisely the point of examination critical to the political economy approach (3, 4, 17, 18). In capitalist society, the relation of class and age is profoundly influenced by the fact that being old is characterized by disattachment from the productive process. Although retirement alters class dynamics by removing the aged from the immediate relations of the workplace, these relations continue to "live" as part of the individual retiree's everyday life and in the relationships among retirees with common work histories. They are extremely important in old age (17), even affecting postretirement life expectancy. Nevertheless, this disattachment from the productive process, as defined in the traditional Marxist sense, means that the relations of the workplace do not constitute the primary dynamic of class relations for the aged.

One particularly useful concept of class is the Ehrenreich and Ehrenreich definition of class in terms of a "common relation to the economic foundations of society" (75). Class is (75, p. 11):

> characterized by a coherent social and cultural existence; members of a class share a common life style, educational background, kinship networks, consumption patterns, work habits, and beliefs.

This conceptualization of class may be of special importance to the study of age and class because it is concerned with dynamics that continue operating for elders when they are no longer in the workplace. In particular, it is a concept that embraces the relationship between the aged who receive state benefits and the agents of public and private social welfare bureaucracies. Although the Ehrenreichs note that there is no easy way to define class for some categories of professional workers as a group, certain professional-client relationships can be seen as inherently class relationships. In this sense, the professionals, bureaucrats, and service providers who constitute the "aging enterprise" (9) contribute to the dependency of the aged as they exert social control over them. The resulting systems of services reinforce preexisting class relationships (76). Similar observations can be made for the design and delivery of services and the resulting gender and racial/ethnic hierarchies imposed through social welfare services where "the professionalization and bureaucratization of care has made room for men at the top" (63, p. 31). By extension, the policies of the "aging enterprise" are not only class-based (9, 10, 77), but also constitute an important part of class relations and of the reproduction of class relations among the elderly.

The dependent status of many older persons subjects them to a greater degree than younger persons to the social relations of subordination to public and private service agencies that act to reproduce capitalist culture and class relations. Analyses of class and age must be concerned with understanding how individual elders, given their unique biographies and historical moment, are made differentially dependent according to their preretirement class, gender, and racial/ethnic status. A "differential process of devaluation" occurs based on class and gender (77). Working-class elders are more rapidly devalued in the labor market and in the society as a whole than are the aged of other classes. Similarly, women, whose labor is not generally considered productive, are more devalued than men in old age (78).

Property ownership and income sources continue to serve as the basis of class divisions in old age, and these divisions are reinforced by social welfare policy. However, according to Wright's definition of class, the ownership of wealth without effective control over investment and physical means of production leaves even the wealthy elderly on the periphery of the class dynamics of the larger society (79). Several important issues are raised. For example, how is the class of elderly men to be assessed when retirement severs connection to the means of production and their economic status deteriorates with fixed incomes and advancing age? Questions of age and class are further compounded when we explicitly take gender into account. Are older women in their own, or their husband's class; and is this the class of preretirement origin or the class of destination based on retirement income? For older women who experience changes in marital status, is class derived from (i.e., mediated by) the class of their former husbands, or from their own (likely, downwardly mobile) direct relation to productive resources? When an older male spouse dies, the economic status of the surviving female spouse often changes dramatically, usually negatively. The issue of direct and mediated class location is profoundly important (80) and has implications, not only for class identification, but also for the "treatment" of the condition of older women through state policy.

Consideration needs to be given both to the differential implications of retirement and old age *by* class, and the implications of retirement and old age *for* class relationships—and both according to gender and racial/ethnic status. The fact that most of the aged must face life on a fixed income is itself both a reflection of class relations and a factor in the analysis of class and aging. While the class analysis of aging may present different problems than does a more general analysis of the class dynamics of society, the consideration of class theory needed to "account for" the aged is likely to shed light on class analysis in general, especially as it deals with other "nonproductive" groups.

Promising areas of inquiry concern uses of the elderly and social policy in the intensified conflict between the contradictory demands on the state arising from the state's need to: 1) promote conditions favorable to business, and 2) provide sufficient benefits to those left behind by the market to ensure loyalty to the existing system. It is important to differentiate conditions under which class-based coalitions emerge and override age interests, and those under which status issues such as age account for state policy outcomes. This work will show the utility of examining the interconnections between class and status in political movements and their consequences for societal treatment of the aged.

GENDER

A major undeveloped area of great significance in the political economy of aging concerns the differential gendered consequences of aging from a lifecourse perspective. Substantial developments have occurred in the past decade in feminist theoretical and empirical work relevant to social policy (30, 63, 65, 81–83). Although this literature does not directly address the issue of aging, it lays the groundwork for an important research agenda that acknowledges the import of reproductive as well as productive relations.

Joan Acker maintains correctly that theories of the state and class that do not explicitly and adequately address the subordination of women and the "privileging of men" fail as comprehensive frameworks for understanding social phenomena (82). She observes: 1) that "understanding class and gender discrimination and exploitation is integral to understanding the place (and oppression) of women [and, we would add, older women] in industrial capitalist societies;" and 2) that the relations that produce class are gendered processes, structured through relations of *distribution* as well as relations of production. Personal relations (particularly marriage), the wage, and the state are all locations of gendered distribution. Distribution is vitally affected by: 1) the dominance of market relations as the basis of distribution; and 2) the indifference of the economic system to the reproduction of the working class and the demands of working-class daily life (82, p. 479).

The focus on reproductive relations has at least two major redeeming features for the political economy of aging: First, it places the gendered division of labor and the unpaid (informal) work of women throughout the lifecourse squarely at the center of analysis, explaining much about the condition and situation of older women in the United States (78). Second, attention to the concept of social reproduction offers the potential of casting a new and more accurate light on the role of both women and the elderly (men and women) in the daily activity of the productive sphere since it moves beyond the traditional labor market concept of production with its inherent age and gender bias (84). With the concept of social reproduction, the elderly may be seen as contributing to the creation and use of new medical technologies (a form of created consumption) that are instrumental in the development and expansion of a large and profitable medical industrial complex. The commodification of the needs of the elderly (9) and the state role in underwriting this complex (e.g., state-financed third-party reimbursement) illustrate how the elderly support the economy (i.e., in reproducing the capitalist system). Caregiving and the ideology of community care legitimate minimal state activity in long-term care by defining care as the private sphere of home and family (63, 69). Thus, even more caring work may be transferred from the formal to the informal sector (as in the case of hospital cost containment under Medicare prospective payment) when the state is pressured to redirect its resources from meeting human needs to underwriting various aspects of capital accumulation (85).

THE MICRO IN THE MACRO

While elaborating the macrosociological perspective associated with a political economy approach, the microsociological level requires consideration. The power of language, concepts, and labeling are repeatedly demonstrated (86, 87). Symbolic interactionist, labeling, and deviance theories delineate the significance of social perceptions in the processing and treatment of individuals as members of collective groups in society (87–89). One argument, for example, is that the experience of growing old is "produced" socially in that it is neither immutable nor given by the character of external reality (9, 90).

How old age is regarded by members of the society is socially constructed by the attributions and imputations of others, and it is differentially influenced by those with sufficient power to impose their constructions of reality (9), thereby controlling the dominant reality. These attributions, in turn, shape how old age is processed and treated by society. Thus the conceptualization of old age and of the aged as inherently sick is socially created in the sense that it is not determined solely by objective facts. Two processes create these constructions: 1) the interpretation and ordering of perceptions of "facts" into ways of thinking, and 2) the relative power and influence of those who interpret and disseminate facts (91). In this sense, the problems of the elderly are only those that experts, policymakers, and the public media define as true for them (9). Such attributions are framed by available theories, methodologies, and research data that channel the conceptualization, conduct, analysis, and interpretation of data, as well as by the dominant social, economic, and political forces and intellectual fashions of the period (91).

An important aspect of the link between the micro and the macro is found in the different ways in which the aged are defined and treated and their relation both to one's interpersonal relations and self-concept (92–95) and to the structural arrangements and resource disparities in the society. Problem definitions and prescriptions of treatment must be seen in terms of power relations (96). Much labeling of the aged involves a focus on physical debility and physiological decline (9). Elders are expected to adopt a social role with the characteristics of a sick role even when there is no medically diagnosed pathology (97). Sick role expectations (52) applied to old people include withdrawal from the social world, reduction of normal social and occupational responsibilities, and dependency on others in an imbalanced power relationship (97).

Those who control definitions of aging in effect control access to old age benefits such as medical care, as well as the personal and public costs of care and the structure of health care delivery (98). Currently, public money and professional effort are disproportionately expended on institutional (hospital and nursing home) medical services for the elderly. Both reflect a definition of health and health care that is a product of the professional dominance of medicine and a guarantee of a profitable medical care industry.

Further, the myth of pervasive debility in old age persists and may become self-fulfilling in the loss of effectiveness and personal control (94). Insinuations of loss of competence or mental illness are two major vehicles that usher the elderly into productive custody and long-term care institutions where they are particularly susceptible to external management. Attributions of physical decline and personal incompetence to the aging process effectively depoliticize (99) issues related to institutionalization or legal responsibility, and focus attention on the individual and individual treatment rather than the social situation creating the need for treatment.

Nevertheless, human beings do not relinquish power over their lives without strong objection. Protestations by the elderly about their social situation and treatment are generally considered unseemly, leading to the application of age-stereotyped epithets such as "cantankerous," "crotchety," and "dyspeptic." Conrad and Schneider hypothesize that such "misbehavior," and the deviant labels attached to it, are more likely to fall under the purview of medicine when the problem becomes a middle-class one rather than solely a lower-class one (89). They also posit the probability of the medicalization of a social problem increases when there is a potential for economic profitability and previous systems of social control have failed.

Although some elders experience chronic and acute illnesses, statistics belie the notion that all, or even most, elders are sick. More older people in our society are living to advanced ages and prolonging their "productive" (that is, disease-free) life spans than ever before. If, however, elders were permitted to enter times of illness without shame and guilt about dependency for personal care and financial support, and if health and aging policy accommodated the social and economic needs of elders, old age would not be the burden it has become.

Social gerontologists in the United States have legitimized incremental and individualistic approaches to public policy by focusing their analyses largely on the individual and social-psychological levels, in which their questions and concepts render the economic and political structure residual in explaining old age. Not surprisingly, such research has been more concerned with psychological models of aging than with societal effects.

CONCLUSION

The significance of the political economy literature is in the attention it directs to the relationship of the treatment of older people in society and the experience of old age itself to a capitalist economy with boundaries no longer limited to the United States alone but including worldwide economic and political conditions (100–102). The task of the political economy of aging is to locate society's treatment of the aged in the context of the economy (national and international), the state, the conditions of the labor market, and the class, sex, race, and age divisions in society. Serious consideration of the relationship of capitalism to aging is required (70, 103). Issues to be examined include the dilemmas and contradictions in maintaining both a market economy and democracy—that is, jointly advancing public interest in a democracy and private profit through capitalism.

Social policy on aging is a product of the tensions between the state, capital, and labor in working through the contradictions of capital and the crisis tendencies they create (68). Aging policy is a major battleground on which the social struggles presently engulfing the state are being fought as the state attempts to address the tensions between capitalism and democracy. Important considerations are the ways in which state policies are ideologically and practically consistent with the state role in the process of capital accumulation and its legitimation through processes of social control and social integration. It is equally important to consider how the aged and aging policy contribute to problems of the state, capital, and/or labor, and in what respects. Aging policy needs to be examined more closely in terms of how it promotes and reproduces the dominant institutions and the role of ideology in these processes. The moral economy approach proposed in this volume (see Chapter 3) will contribute to understanding the role of cultural beliefs, values, and norms undergirding societal institutions and practices vitally affecting the old.

The construction of population aging as a crisis reflects aspects of two ideological dimensions. First, the concept of the "demographic imperative" created a rallying point for those who argue that the elderly are living too long, consuming too many societal resources, and robbing the young, an argument used to justify roll-backs of state benefits for the aged (104–106). Additional antistatist sentiments have been expressed in the unfounded contention that state policy to provide formal care will encourage abdication of family responsibility for the aging, which, in turn, will bankrupt the state. This line of reasoning is consistent with continuing state refusal to provide for long-term care, reinforcing the nation's long-term care policy that such care is (and should remain) the responsibility of the informal sector and the unpaid labor of women.

Second, the projected chronic illness burden of pandemic proportions (another version of the crisis) was useful in the Reagan Administration's ideological warfare on health care as a right and contributed to the social production of intergenerational tensions. One result of this construct is that the elderly have been accused of crippling the state and capital with unsupportable demands. Daniel Callahan's argument that society must "set limits" on the aged (107) is a case in point, for it indicts those who advocate for elderly rights as encouraging "unreasonable," "unfair," and "selfish" expectations in the old concerning life expectancy, quality of life, and societal allocations. One aspect of this intergenerational struggle is the battle for the intellectual high ground in constructing resource and equity issues for the elderly (106). The seriousness and import of this struggle is reflected in the crucial role played by intellectuals both in maintenance of the status quo and in meaningful sociohistorical change (108).

The political economy approach to aging is based on the following premises:

- The social structure shapes how older individuals are perceived and how they perceive themselves, affecting their sense of worth and power.
- Attributional labels applied to the elderly not only shape the experience of old age, but also societal decisions concerning public policy for the elderly.
- Social policy and the politics of aging mirror the inequalities in social structure and the outcomes of power struggles around those structured arrangements. As such, policy is neither neutral nor quixotic; it reflects the advantage and disadvantage of capital and labor, whites and nonwhites, and men and women in society.
- Social policy reflects the dominant ideologies and belief systems that enforce, bolster, and extend the structure of advantage and disadvantage in the larger economic, political, and social order.

In summary, the political economy of aging is attendant to the sociostructural conditions and dynamics of aging and aging policy. It is essentially concerned with class, gender, and racial/ethnic divisions in society as they explain resource distributions in old age as a function of the relations of capital and the state. In my view, a proper political economy will, by definition, be sensitive to the integral connections between macrostructural conditions and the private and intimate experience of old age.

Acknowledgment — Parts of this chapter are adapted from the following sources: C. L. Estes, Austerity and aging in the U.S., *International Journal of Health Services,* 12:4, pp. 573–584, 1982; C. L. Estes, J. H. Swan, and L. Gerard, Dominant and Competing Paradigms in Gerontology: Toward a Political Economy of Ageing, *Ageing and Society,* 2:2, pp. 151–164, July 1982; C. L. Estes, L. Gerard, J. S. Zones, and J. H. Swan, *Political Economy, Health and Aging,* Little-Brown, Boston, 1984. I am indebted to my coauthors for contributions to this earlier work.

REFERENCES

1. Walton, J. Urban political economy. *Comp. Urban Res.* 7(1): 5–17, 1979.
2. Walker, A. The social creation of poverty and dependency in old age. *J. Soc. Pol.* 9: 49–75, 1980.
3. Walker, A. Towards a political economy of old age. *Ageing and Soc.* 1(1): 73–94, 1981.
4. Townsend, P. The structured dependency of the elderly: A creation of social policy in the twentieth century. *Ageing and Soc.* 1: 6, 1981.
5. Townsend, P. *The Last Refuge.* Routledge and Kegan Paul, London, 1962.

6. Townsend, P. *Poverty in the United Kingdom*. Penguin Books, Harmondsworth, Middlesex, 1979.

7. Townsend, P., and Wedderbum, D. *The Aged in the Welfare State*. Bell, London, 1965.

8. Estes, C. L., Swan, J., and Gerard, L. Dominant and competing paradigms in gerontology: Toward a political economy of ageing. *Ageing and Soc.* 2(2): 151–164, 1982.

9. Estes, C. L. *The Aging Enterprise*. Jossey-Bass, San Francisco, 1979.

10. Olson, L. *Political Economy of Aging*. Columbia University, New York, 1982.

11. Myles, J. F. The aged, the state, and the structure of inequality. In *Structural Inequality in Canada*, edited by J. Harp and J. Hofley, pp. 317–342, Prentice-Hall, Toronto, 1980.

12. Myles, J. F. Income inequality and status maintenance. *Res. on Aging* 3: 123–141, 1981.

13. Myles, J. F. The aged and the welfare state: An essay in political demography. Paper presented at the International Sociological Association, Research Committee on Aging, Paris, July 8–9, 1981.

14. Myles, J. F. *The Political Economy of Public Pensions*. Little, Brown, Boston, 1984.

15. Nelson, G. Social class and public policy for the elderly. *Soc. Serv. Rev.* 6(1): 85–107, 1982.

16. Tussing, A. The dual welfare system. In *Social Realities*, edited by L. Horowitz and C. Levy. Harper and Row, New York, 1971.

17. Guillemard, A. M. Retirement as a social process, its differential effects upon behavior. Communication presented to the 8th World Congress of Sociology, Toronto, Canada, August 21, 1974.

18. Guillemard, A. M. A Critical analysis of governmental policies on aging from a Marxist sociological perspective: The case of France. Center for the Study of Social Movements, Paris, France, October 1977.

19. Guillemard, A. M. The making of old age policy in France. In *Old Age and the Welfare State*, edited by A. M. Guillemard. International Sociological Association, Sage, New York, 1983.

20. Guillemard, A. M. *Le Decline du social, formation et crise des politiques de la vieillesse*. Presses Universitaires de France, Paris, 1986.

21. Dowd, J. *Stratification Among the Aged*. Brooks/Cole, Monterey, California, 1980.

22. Evans, L., and Williamson, J. Social security and social control. *Generations* 6(2): 18–20, 1981.

23. Weber, M. Class, status and party. In *From Max Weber: Essays in Sociology*, edited and translated by H. H. Gerth and C. W. Mills. Oxford University Press, New York, 1946.

24. Mills, C. W. *The Power Elite*. Oxford University Press, New York, 1956.

25. Henretta, J., and Campbell, R. Status attainment and status maintenance: A case study of stratification in old age. *Am. Soc. Rev.* 41: 981–992, 1976.

26. Samuelson, R. J. Benefit programs for the elderly: Off limits to federal budget. *Nat. J.* 13(40), 1981.

27. Baum, M., and Baum, R. C. *Growing Old*. Prentice-Hall, New York, 1980.

28. Estes, C. L., Gerard, L., Zones, J. S., and Swan, J. *Political Economy, Health and Aging*. Little Brown, Boston, 1984.

29. Hernes, H. *Welfare State and Woman Power*. Norwegian University Press, Oslo, 1987.
30. Sassoon, A. *Women and State*. Hutchinson, London, 1987.
31. Estes, C. L., Gerard, L., and Clark, A. Women and the economics of aging. *Int. J. Health Serv.* 14(1): 55–68, 1984.
32. Ginsberg, N. *Class, Capital and Social Policy*. Macmillan, London, 1979.
33. O'Connor, J. *The Fiscal Crisis of the State*. St. Martin's, New York, 1973.
34. Gough, I. *The Political Economy of the Welfare State*. Macmillan, London, 1979.
35. Kelman, S., ed. Special section on political economy of health. *Int. J. Health Serv.* 5(4): 535–642, 1975.
36. Renaud, M. On the structural constraints to state intervention in health. *Int. J. Health Serv.* 5: 559–571, 1975.
37. Renaud, M. Special issue on the political economy of health. *Rev. Rad. Polit. Econ.* 9, Spring 1977.
38. Alford, R. The political economy of health care: Dynamics without change. *Pol. and Soc.* 2: 127–164, 1972.
39. Lichtman, R. The political economy of medical care. In *The Social Organization of Health*, edited by H. Dreitzel, pp. 265–290. Macmillan, New York, 1971.
40. Navarro, V. *Medicine Under Capitalism*. Prodist, New York, 1976.
41. Navarro, V. (ed.). *Health and Medical Care in the U.S.: A Critical Analysis*. Baywood Publishing, Amityville, New York, 1973.
42. Connell, R. W. *Gender and Power*. Stanford University Press, Stanford, California, 1987.
43. Waitzkin, H. *The Second Sickness: Contradictions of Capitalist Health Care*. Free Press, New York, 1986.
44. Offe, C., and Ronge, V. Thesis on the theory of the state. In *Classes, Power and Conflict*, edited by A. Giddens and D. Held, pp. 249–256. University of California Press, Berkeley, 1982.
45. Frankel, B. On the state of the state: Marxist theories of the state after Leninism. In *Classes, Power and Conflict*, edited by A. Giddens and D. Held. University of California Press, Berkeley, 1982.
46. O'Connor, J. *Accumulation Crisis*. Basil Blackwell, New York, 1984.
47. Gough, I. *The Political Economy of the Welfare State*. Macmillan, London, 1979.
48. Navarro, V. The political economy of medical care. *Int. J. Health Serv.* 5(1): 65–94, 1975.
49. Carnoy, M. *The State and Political Theory*. Princeton University Press, Princeton, New Jersey, 1984.
50. Vincent, A. The nature of the state. In *Theories of the State*. Basil Blackwell, New York, 1987.
51. Collins, R. Comparative approach to political sociology. In *State and Society*, edited by R. Bendix, et al. Little Brown, Boston, 1968.
52. Parsons, T. *The Social System*. Free Press, New York, 1951.
53. Schattschneider, E. E. *The Semi-Sovereign People*. Holt, New York, 1960.
54. Giddens, A., and Held, D. (eds.). *Classes, Power and Conflict: Classical and Contemporary Debates*. University of California Press, Berkeley, 1982.

55. Skocpol, T. *States and Social Revolutions: A Comparative Analysis of France, Russia, and China.* Cambridge University Press, Cambridge, 1979.
56. Quadagno, J. Race, class, and gender in the U.S. welfare state: Nixon's failed family assistance plan. *Am. Sociol. Rev.* 55: 11–28, 1990.
57. Block, F. The ruling class does not rule: Notes on the Marxist theory of the state. *Socialist Revol.* 33: 6–28, 1977.
58. Althusser, L. *Lenin and Philosophy and Other Essays.* Monthly Review, New York, 1972.
59. Poulantzas, N. *State, Power, Socialism.* Verso and New Left Books, London, 1980.
60. Jenkins, J., and Brents, J. Social protest, hegemonic competition, and social reform: A political struggle interpretation of the origins of the American welfare state. *Am. Sociol. Rev.* 54: 891–909, 1989.
61. Gold, G., Lo, C., and Wright, E. O. Recent developments in Marxist theories of the state. *Monthly Rev.* 5(6): 29–43, 1975.
62. Quadagno, J. Welfare capitalism and the Social Security Act of 1935. *Am. Sociol. Rev.* 49: 632–647, 1984.
63. Pascall, G. The family and women's work. In *Social Policy: A Feminist Analysis.* Tavistock, New York, 1986.
64. Finch, J., and Groves, D. *A Labour of Love: Women, Work and Caring.* Routledge and Kegan Paul, London, 1983.
65. Dickinson, J., and Russell, B. (eds.). *Family, Economy and State.* Garamond Press, Toronto, 1986.
66. Quadagno, J. *The Transformation of Old Age Security: Class and Politics in the American Welfare State.* University of Chicago Press, Chicago, 1988.
67. Estes, C. L. The politics of ageing in America. *Ageing and Soc.* 6(2): 121–134, 1986.
68. Estes, C. L. The Reagan legacy: Privatization, the welfare state and aging. In *Old Age and the Welfare State*, edited by J. Quadagno and J. Myles. Temple University Press, Philadelphia, 1990.
69. Walker, A. Community care and the elderly in Great Britain: Theory and practice. In *Readings in the Political Economy of Aging*, edited by M. Minkler and C. L. Estes. Baywood Publishing, Amityville, New York, 1984.
70. Phillipson, C. *Capitalism and the Construction of Old Age.* Macmillan, London, 1982.
71. Giddens, A. *The Class Structure of the Advanced Societies.* Harper and Row, New York, 1975.
72. Atchley, R. C. Social class and aging. *Generations* 6(2): 16–17, 1981.
73. Streib, G. Social stratification and aging. In *Handbook of Aging and the Social Sciences*, edited by R. Binstock and E. Shanas, pp. 339–368. Van Nostrand Reinhold, 1985.
74. Riley, M. W. Social gerontology and the age stratification of society. *The Gerontologist* 11(1, pt. 1): 79–87, 1971.
75. Ehrenreich, B., and Ehrenreich, J. The professional managerial class. In *Between Labor and Capital*, edited by P. Walker, p. 5. South End, Boston, 1979.
76. Sjoberg, G., Brymer, R. A., and Farris, B. Bureaucracy and the lower class. *Sociol. and Soc. Res.* 50: 325–334, 1966.

77. Nelson, G. Social class and public policy for the elderly. *Soc. Serv. Rev.* 56(1): 85–107, 1982.
78. Estes, C. L., and Binney, E. A. Older women and the state. Unpublished manuscript, Institute for Health and Aging, University of California, San Francisco, 1990.
79. Wright, E. O. *Class, Crisis and the State*. Verso, London, 1978.
80. Wright, E. O. Women in the class structure. *Polit. and Soc.* 17(1): 35–66, 1989.
81. Abramovitz, M. *Regulating the Lives of Women*. South End Press, Boston, 1988.
82. Acker, J. Class, gender, and the relations of distribution. *Signs* 13(3): 473–493, 1988.
83. Redclift, N. The contested domain: Gender, accumulation, and the labour process. In *Beyond Employment*, edited by N. Redclift and E. Mingione. Basil Blackwell, New York, 1985.
84. Binney, E. A. Personal communication, 1990.
85. Binney, E. A., Estes, C. L., and Humphers, S. Informalization. Unpublished manuscript, Institute for Health and Aging, University of California, San Francisco, 1990.
86. Estes, C. L. Construction of reality: Problems of aging. *J. Soc. Issues* 36(2): 117–132, 1980.
87. Becker, H. S. *Outsiders*. Free Press of Glencoe, New York, 1963.
88. Matza, D. *Becoming Deviant*. Prentice Hall, Engelwood Cliffs, New Jersey, 1969.
89. Conrad, P., and Schneider, J. W. *Deviance and Medicalization: From Badness to Sickness*. Mosby, St. Louis, 1980.
90. Gusfield, J. Literary rhetoric of science. *Am. Sociol. Rev.* 41: 1–33, 1976.
91. Gouldner, A. *The Coming Crisis of Western Sociology*. Basic, New York, 1970.
92. Thomas, W. I. *The Unadjusted Girl*. Gannor, Santa Fe, New Mexico, 1970.
93. Scott, R. *The Making of Blind Men*. Russell Sage Foundation, New York, 1970.
94. Rodin, J., and Langer, E. Aging labels: The decline of control and the fall of self-esteem. *J. Soc. Issues* 36(2): 12–29, 1980.
95. Rodin, J. Sense of control: Potentials for intervention. *The Annals*, 503: 29–42, 1989.
96. Friedson, E. *Profession of Medicine*. Dodd, Mead, New York, 1970.
97. Arluke, A., and Peterson, J. Accidental medicalization of old age and its social control implications. In *Dimensions: Aging, Culture, and Health*, edited by C. L. Frye. J. F. Bergen, Brooklyn, New York, 1981.
98. Estes, C. L., and Binney, E. A. The biomedicalization of aging: Dangers and dilemmas. *The Gerontologist* 29(5): 587–596, 1989.
99. Zola, I. K. *Disabling Professions*. Marion Boyers, Boston, 1977.
100. Amin, S., et al. (eds.). *Dynamics of Global Crisis*. Monthly Review, New York, 1982.
101. Mandel, E. *The Second Slump: A Marxist Analysis of Recession in the Seventies*. NLB, London, 1978.
102. Castells, M. *The Economic Crisis and American Society*. Princeton University Press, Princeton, New Jersey, 1980.
103. Myles, J. F. Conflict, crisis and the future of old age security. *Milbank Mem. Fund Q.* 61: 4, 1983.

104. Minkler, M. Blaming the aged victim: The politics of retrenchment in times of fiscal conservatism. *Readings in the Political Economy of Aging*, edited by M. Minkler and C. L. Estes. Baywood Publishing, Amityville, New York, 1984.
105. Binney, E. A., and Estes, C. L. The retreat of the state and its transfer of responsibility: The intergenerational war. *Int. J. Health Serv.* 18(1): 83–96, 1988.
106. Binney, E. A., and Estes, C. L. Setting the wrong limits: Class biases and the biographical standard. In *A Good Old Age? The Paradox of Setting Limits*, edited by P. Homer and M. Holstein. Simon and Schuster, New York, 1990.
107. Callahan, D. *Setting Limits*. Simon and Schuster, New York, 1987.
108. Gramsci, A. *Prison Letters*. Pluto Press/Unwin Hyman, United Kingdom, 1988.

cultural justifications for social patterns

Political and Moral Economy:
Not Such Strange Bedfellows

Meredith Minkler and Thomas R. Cole

As we have seen in the preceding chapter, political economy provides a valuable framework for understanding how polity, economy, and society shape the conditions, experiences, treatment, and health of older people. "The central problem of the political economy perspective," writes Walton, "is the manner in which the economy and polity interact in a relationship of reciprocal causation, affecting the distribution of social goods" (1, p. 9). The trajectory of growing old, from this perspective, is intimately tied to one's class position or location in the larger social order.

Political economy has contributed a great deal to the development of social gerontology, whose early social and psychological theories were insufficiently attuned to issues of social structure, power, ideology, and history (2). In particular, political economy has helped explain variations in the treatment of the old and has explicated the influence of race, class, gender and labor market conditions on aging (3–5). By acknowledging the importance of historical context and social/political processes, it enables social gerontology to "tap into the dynamic interrelationships of individual and structure" (Chapter 4, p. 53).

Because political economy is multiperspectival and moves across narrow disciplinary boundaries, it retains the ability to integrate related conceptual frameworks. Many political economists have taken advantage of this flexibility by including in their work careful considerations of the sociocultural dimensions of phenomena under study (cf. 6–11). At the same time, however, certain mechanistic versions of political economy have tended to treat culture as a mere reflection of social structure, ignoring the elusive and contingent aspects of the historical process.

We believe that cultural questions such as individuality, subjectivity, spirituality, or morality are not simply "dependent variables" to be explained by

37

material factors (12, 13). To avoid the dangers of reductionism, political economy must make increasing conceptual room to understand moral and existential issues not as mere epiphenomena, but as necessary and irreducible elements of social processes. Especially in the study of aging, where humanistic interest in these questions is growing (14–16), it has become increasingly important to tear down invisible Berlin-like walls and encourage rapprochement, if not reunification. By exploring the concept and uses of moral economy, this chapter suggests one line of thought that can enrich the political economy of aging.

The chapter will begin by examining the uneasiness around moral questions which has tended to characterize Marxist political economy in the tradition of "Scientific Marxism" (17). It will suggest that concerns with justice, fairness, rights, and obligations—which Marx rejected in his later writings as illegitimate and ideological (18)—serve some positive functions (e.g., in protecting against certain forms of oppression), which should not be overlooked.

The chapter then will introduce the concept of moral economy, or collectively shared assumptions defining norms of reciprocity (19), as a useful complement to political economy making possible a richer and more thorough analysis than either can achieve independently. The origins of the concept of moral economy and its applications will be highlighted.

The chapter will end with a discussion of the usefulness of this concept in enriching our understanding of aging. A case will be made for integrating moral economy into a broader political economy perspective, and for applying Marx's ideas about "emancipated morality" to the political economy of aging.

MARXISM AND MORAL QUESTIONS:
A CASE STUDY IN AMBIVALENCE

In the Marxist tradition of political economy, moral questions in general have been treated with ambivalence, if not repression (18, 20). This treatment derives from a paradox embedded in Marx's own ideas about morality (20, 21), particularly in his later years when, as Gouldner suggests, Scientific Marxism "counterposed determinism to voluntarism" and held philosophy in general as "suspect and demodé" (17). On the one hand, Marx believed "that morality is a form of ideology, and thus social in origin, illusory in content, and serving class interests; that any given morality arises out of a particular stage in the development of the productive forces and relations and is relative to a particular mode of production and particular class interests" (18, p. 3). The later Marx saw his critique of capitalism as scientific rather than moral; and it is said that whenever "anyone started to talk to [him] about morality, he would roar with laughter" (20, p. 22).

On the other hand, both Marx's early work and his later writings are filled with compelling moral judgments and fueled by powerful commitment to a more just society. Marxian political economy bristles with outrage at the evils of capitalism: exploitation, alienation, and the moral degradation of an economy ruthlessly driven by the search for marketplace advantage and the extraction of surplus-value. How would Marx reject morality yet still make moral judgments?

Lukes (18) answers this question by helping us see that Marx distinguished between what he considered the ideological morality of *Recht*—a form of false consciousness—and the true morality of *emancipation*. The German word *Recht* has no direct English translation. It refers to aspects of law and morality such as justice, fairness, rights, and obligation (18). Hegel used the word broadly to refer to civil law, morality, ethical life, and world history (22). In particular, Hegel saw private property rights and principles of contractual justice as a means of restraining competitive, egoistic relations in an emerging bourgeois society (22).

Marx, however, argued that the morality of *Recht* was neither an objective nor a fair means of ordering social relations (23). He argued instead that the principles of *Recht* simply governed and stabilized capitalist social relations while claiming to protect the rights of man in general. He appealed to a morality of *emancipation*, based on an imagined harmony of social unity and individual self-development. For Marx, human emancipation required emancipation from the morality of *Recht*, and from the conditions of exploitation and wage-slavery that called it into being (18, 23).

It is beyond the scope of this chapter to discuss the complex philosophical issues involved in Marx's ideas about morality. Nor can we discuss the implications of the recent integration of socialist criticism into liberal political theory, which Scientific Marxists traditionally dismiss for its alliance with the morality of *Recht* (18). We welcome, however, the revival of moral questions in the Marxist tradition of political thought and practice (8–11). And we suggest that moral economy, understood as part of an expanded conception of *Recht*, can help guide future work in the political economy of aging.

MORAL ECONOMY: HISTORY AND CURRENT USAGE

A more detailed look at moral economy in historical context is provided elsewhere (24, 25). Since an understanding of the evolution of moral economy is necessary for appreciating its contemporary relevance to the study of aging, however, we begin this section with a brief historical note.

In his seminal work, *The Making of the English Working Class*, Thompson (24) builds upon the social anthropological foundation of Durkheim (26) and others to develop the concept of moral economy, or popular consensus concerning the legitimacy of certain practices, on the basis of shared views of social norms or obligations (See Chapter 17). In particular, Thompson uncovered the collectively shared moral assumptions which empowered artisans, peasants and laborers who rioted in response to scarcity and soaring food prices in the late eighteenth and early nineteenth centuries. Workers of this period held that, especially in times of shortage, the price of bread should not be based solely on impersonal market forces, but also on considerations of fairness and custom. The riots "were popularly regarded as acts of justice" (24, p. 65) legitimated by an old moral economy which an emerging working class carried into a new capitalist economy.

Historical investigation of *Recht*, in this sense of moral economy, has only begun and holds great promise for expanding the knowledge and vision of political economy. Claeys, for example, has sketched the evolution of conceptions of just price, fair exchange, the duty to give charity, and the question of community of property from the ancient world until 1800 (25). He suggests that while the Christine doctrine of just price achieved prominence in the twelfth century, its roots may be traced to a period 500 years earlier, when Augustine popularized the notion that human need should be a major consideration in the determination of just price.

Belief in the God-given and hence communal nature of land was fundamental to the notion of moral economy, and was reasserted by Christian moral philosophers throughout the Renaissance period as an important rationale redressing social inequalities (25). By the end of the eighteenth century, however, increasingly secular justifications of private property, declines in government regulations, the popularity of laissez-faire, and changing attitudes toward labor combined with rising poverty rates, the food riots, and other factors to greatly increase hostility toward the poor.

In this climate, the old moral economy in many parts of Western Europe quickly unraveled and "a fundamental watershed in our thinking about poverty" occurred (25, p. 19). Malthusian population doctrine, and the hated Poor Law Amendment Act of 1834 which it helped spawn, thus denied that the poor had any claim on society for subsistence, beyond what their labor could buy. The functioning of natural economic laws became, in Claeys' words, "the supreme arbiter of all questions of social welfare" (25, p. 21) and, together with Malthusian population principles, took priority over notions of Christian charity and the rights of the poor to a living. Moral economy, in this sense, was seen by Thompson (24), Claeys (25) and others as having collapsed under the weight of these changes, to be followed and replaced by the market economy.

Current usage of the concept of moral economy has tended to reflect this historical interpretation. Most contemporary applications thus involve anthropological and sociological studies of premarket societies in Asia, Africa, and elsewhere (27–30).

On the one hand, such applications have considerable relevance for our understanding of aging in many parts of the Third World. Scott, for example, has demonstrated that the moral economy of the subsistence ethic in precapitalist peasant societies dictated that all members of a community had a right to a living, including sufficient provision to carry out such culturally and economically dictated roles as caring for elderly parents (27).

On the other hand, however, to limit the usage of the concept of moral economy solely to analyses of aging and other phenomena in premarket economies is to ignore its larger relevance. Indeed as Kohli (Chapter 17) has argued, the dichotomy between moral and market economy which these scholars erect is in fact a false dichotomy and one that robs the concept of moral economy of some of its contemporary usefulness in understanding advanced Western societies. In his view, the market economy should be viewed instead as (Chapter 17, p. 277):

> . . . a new form of economic organization giving rise to its own moral economy, on which it depends for functioning . . . What occurs is not a collapse of the moral economy but a shift of the main arena of moral conflict from the consumption market to the labor market: it concerns no longer the price of goods, but the 'just reward' for work.

It is a premise of this book that the concept of moral economy is indeed a useful one today for examining the place of consensual assumptions regarding reciprocal obligations not only in attitudes toward and treatment of elders in peasant societies in the Third World, but also within the market economy in the United States and other advanced industrialized nations. Moreover, as Kohli suggests, by looking to new "arenas of moral conflict," e.g., the labor market, social security, and resource allocation among different age groups, the particular usefulness of a moral economy approach employed in conjunction with a political economy framework becomes apparent.

While the final sections of this chapter will focus exclusively on the moral economy of aging, it should be noted that recent applications of this concept in the United States have tended to focus not on aging *per se*, but on the history of labor organizing around the age-related issue of seniority (31–33). Unions indeed have been characterized in the United States as "instruments for implementing a moral economy of the working class" (31) which challenged a "possessive market economy," that had been unbridled by custom or status and had in turn created for all "equal insecurity and equal subordination to the market" (32, p. 272).

Using the U.S. automobile industry as a case in point, Gersuny and Kaufman demonstrate how seniority became the cornerstone of the workers' moral economy and a key demand in auto industry-United Automobile Worker (UAW) disputes (31).

Without underemphasizing the significant social control functions of seniority systems (e.g., in reinforcing dependency and increasing the pool of older, more disciplined workers), such analyses illuminate other, often overlooked aspects of the evolution of labor practices in the United States. Further research is needed, however, to better answer such questions as why seniority, rather than pensions, constituted the centerpiece of the workers' moral economy in the United States (34).

MORAL ECONOMY AND THE STUDY OF AGING

In Chapter 17 of this volume, Kohli's historical analysis of the German experience with retirement is presented as an illustration of the usefulness of the concept of moral economy for explicating another phenomenon—the creation and evolution of pension systems—which cannot be understood solely in terms of social control or class relations. While the centrality of these more traditional political economy concerns must not be underemphasized, the usefulness of moral economy as a complementary explanatory tool is apparent in his analysis.

Briefly, Kohli suggests that the "moral impact" of pensions and other forms of welfare relate to their creation of "lifetime continuity and reciprocity." Retirement thus meant "the emergence of old age as a distinct life phase, structurally set apart from active life and with a clear chronological boundary" (p. 277). With its emergence, the "moral universe" moved beyond the family or local community to the formal work sector of the market economy—with profound political implications.

Kohli's work represents perhaps the first explicit attempt to apply moral economy as an analytical approach to the study of a central theme within aging in modern societies. Yet several other analysts have examined pension systems (34–36), resource allocation questions (37–39), and other aging and social policy considerations within a life course context in which norms regarding reciprocity are implicitly embedded.

We thus find Myles' comparative examination of pension systems and particularly his notion of a "living wage" based on substitutive benefits consonant with a moral, as well as a political economy perspective (35). As Myles (Chapter 18) has suggested, the belief that pension benefits should be at "a level sufficient to allow continuity in living standards" is one of the hallmarks of the modern welfare state. And embedded in this notion of substitutive benefits are strong moral economy notions concerning what is due the "deserving elderly"—those who have contributed to the economy through their "productive" lives and therefore are believed to merit a decent, living wage in their later years.

That the notion of deservingness is not extended to those who fall outside the primary sector of the economy—the underemployed or unemployed, etc.—suggests a limitation of the moral economy in the United States and one that helps explain the differences between the welfare state in this country and that of Canada, the United Kingdom, and other Western societies (34, 35, 40). The notion of moral economy indeed may be a useful one for analysts exploring further the historical roots of our preoccupation with distinguishing between the "deserving" and the "undeserving" elderly, poor, etc., as this in turn continues to shape our public policy (40). (See Hendricks and Leedham's [Chapter 4] differentiation between moral economies grounded in exchange value and those based on use value for an interesting analytical approach that may be helpful in this regard.)

The evolution of pension systems in North America and Western Europe well illustrates the fit between moral and political economy approaches, and the ways in which their joint application may enrich our understanding of this and other phenomena within the broad field of aging.

A key tenet of moral economy, for example, is that the shared moral assumptions underlying norms of reciprocity serve and reflect not only the values of the subordinate, but also of the dominant groups. In this way, the demands of the subjugated group—whether of English peasants for a just price for bread or of older workers and the elderly for a pension system—also have important social control functions that serve the interests of the dominant class. In the latter case, retirement in advance of physiological necessity enabled employers to rid themselves of their most expensive workers and further served a social control function by creating and reinforcing dependence and reducing dangerously high levels of unemployment in young men (36). Thus, while achieving a pension system was a primary goal of the older workers' and elders' moral economy, its institutionalization had a flip side which worked to the benefit of employers, and of larger capitalist interests (36).

Political economy has traditionally helped examine and explain such factors as the social control functions of social security systems. Yet as the above example suggests, it is moral economy as an analytic approach which best explicates the shared assumptions regarding norms of reciprocity that undergird pensions as a demand of older workers and elders, highly consonant with their moral economy. As this example illustrates, it is the use of moral and political economy perspectives together that enables a more thorough analysis of the significance of such developments than either can achieve independently.

The perspective offered by moral economy also is helpful in explicating recent debates in the United States over generational equity. As suggested later in this book (Chapter 5), while the concept of generational equity or justice between generations is a flawed basis for public policy, proponents of this perspective do a service in pointing up the need for far greater attention to meeting the needs of impoverished children, low-income workers and other nonelderly segments of society.

On the one hand, the moral economy of the life course may be seen as forming an unspoken historical foundation of the views of some scholars [e.g., Callahan (37) and Daniels (39)] concerning justice among young and old in an aging society. Such analysts are aware of the need to rethink moral obligations among age groups and to reformulate the moral economy of the life span in a new demographic context (41). On the other hand, however, such characterizations tend to overlook how much has been lost by the secularization and modernization of the life course. If indeed it was once the case that "To every thing there is a season, and a time to every purpose under the sun," one must question whether this holds true for the season of old age in late twentieth-century America. That demeaning of old age and the marginalization of the elderly that is now embedded in the bureaucratized life course of the welfare state (41) must be considered in any attempt to understand alienation within, and potentially between, generations.

In spite of the trivialization of old age, however, and despite the media rhetoric of conflict between generations over the high cost of Social Security and Medicare, there is in fact relatively *little* support among young people in the United States for cutting back entitlements for the old. Instead, opinion polls and other data suggest strong continued societal and cross-generational support for programs directed at the elderly, even among those "Baby Boomers" who are under the erroneous notion that Social Security will be bankrupt before they are old enough to reap its benefits (Chapter 5).

The cross-generational stake in old age entitlements is discussed in detail in Chapter 5. Of particular relevance here, however, is the persistence of strong moral economy notions of reciprocity and of what is "due" the old as reflected in young people's continued support for these programs. As Hendricks and Leedham suggest in Chapter 4, such support is consistent with a moral economy grounded in use value, in which human needs are envisioned as being met across time and over the life course, rather than through isolated exchanges.

In a related way, a moral economy approach also is helpful in examining recent calls for "setting limits" on medical care for the old, and for understanding as well the strong societal reactions against such proposals. In a recent book by that title, ethicist Daniel Callahan argued in part for setting limits on government funded life extending treatment for the very old, suggesting instead that scarce resources be diverted to improving quality of life for the elderly and a world "worthy of bequest" for the young (37).

While stating that such limit setting is necessary to add meaning to old age, Callahan also invoked the concept of a "moral community," to suggest that elders should see their primary role as one of stewardship on behalf of future generations and service to the young.

Callahan's attempt, in short, was to suggest a reordering of the moral economy and a reassessment of society's unquestioned allegiance to such principles as unlimited high technology treatment, regardless of the age of the recipient. Ironically however, the strong opposition he and others (42) have encountered for advancing such notions has itself been firmly rooted in moral economic arguments. In particular, Callahan's call for setting limits on life extending treatment for the very old has been criticized for ignoring basic principles of equity, equality, and social justice which dictate that no one shall be denied the right to live on the basis of age.

Moral economy considerations around distributive or economic justice in later life also are implied in the recent work of Tindale and Neysmith (38) and others. Neysmith thus examines the "shoulds" or moral bases of alternative principles guiding social distributional policies for the elderly in Canada (43). In demonstrating the inherently contradictory nature of these principles (which in turn rely on contradictory notions of equity), she offers an analysis which bridges political and moral economy considerations in the complex area of resource allocation in an aging society.

The above examples have focused on the utility of a combined political and moral economy perspective for examining and understanding broad questions concerning such issues as the evolution of pension schemes and societal attitudes toward and policies for the old.

On another level, however, notions of reciprocity and fairness, and collective moral assumptions regarding what is "due" the old, also are helpful in explaining such developments as the dramatic "senior revolt" against the Medicare Catastrophic Coverage Act passed in the United States in 1988 and quickly repealed the following year. As noted in Chapter 12, the primary reason for the elderly backlash against this legislation was a combination of misinformation and grave concerns over fairness. In particular, the "seniors only" nature of the Medicare surtax was deemed a radical and unfair departure from the notion that taxes should be spread throughout the society, and not simply imposed on special subgroups. It was, in short, the Act's perceived disregard for popular consensus concerning what constituted legitimate and illegitimate taxation that in large part led to the downfall of this landmark decision.

Still another area within the political economy of aging that may lend itself to investigation partially through moral economy lenses is that of gender justice and care of the elderly. As Campbell and Brody have demonstrated, while women in the United States and Japan have increasingly expressed egalitarian attitudes toward parent care, comparable shifts have not occurred in practice (44). Consequently, women in both countries, and indeed in most of the world (Chapter 19), have retained primary responsibility for care of elderly parents.

The importance of viewing care of the elderly and gender justice within a political economy perspective has of course been well demonstrated (See Chapters 13 and 14). At the same time, however, and to the extent that there is indeed popular consensus concerning norms of reciprocity *vis a vis* the unpaid care of the old by women, moral economy considerations, and possible shifts in such underlying norms, are deserving of study. Moreover, as Neysmith suggests (Chapter 19), such analyses are needed not only in advanced industrial societies, but in Third World countries as well. In the latter nations, she notes, policy and programmatic reforms focused on the needs of the old "will be isolated unless micro-macro connections become central rather than peripheral to our analyses" (p. 320). The latter would include explication of not only the political economic forces underlying gender inequality in caregiving, but equally important, the assumptions and underlying norms of reciprocity in care for the old that assign responsibility to a society's adult daughters, but not its sons.

The limitations and inequities underlying moral economy notions in this and other areas indeed represent an important area for further research.

In sum, as the above examples illustrate, whether we are examining the experience of aging in Third World countries, in advanced industrialized socialist economies, or in capitalist nations, shared moral assumptions about reciprocity and fairness, and collective visions of what is due the old, should form an integral part of the data base we are exploring. A more thoughtful integration of moral economy with political economy perspectives on aging will require uncovering, critically analyzing and historically interpreting such assumptions.

While we have examined in this chapter the role that moral economy perspectives can play in enriching political economy of aging analyses, a fundamental similarity between these approaches also must be underscored. Both moral economy and political economy thus examine topics such as aging in terms of their embeddedness in a larger whole. Both ground their analyses in a sociohistorical context, with political economy focusing in particular on the social structural context of aging and moral economy on the related context of popular consensus defining norms of reciprocity as these affect the old and resource allocation across age groups.

Further, both political and moral economy provide important alternatives to the increasingly technical and instrumental orientation of academic gerontology (45). In this regard, and building on Habermas' notion of the colonization of the life world of old age (7), Moody argues that "The problems of later life are treated with scientific and managerial efficiency but with no grasp of their larger political or existential significance. The life world of the last stage of life is progressively drained of meaning" (45, p. 82). By examining the last stage of life with attention to these larger issues of significance and meaning, political and moral economy approaches to aging greatly enrich academic gerontology.

CONCLUSION: TOWARD A MORALITY OF EMANCIPATION IN LATER LIFE

We began this chapter by criticizing Marx's tendency, particularly in his later writings, to dismiss questions of justice, fairness, rights, and obligations—the morality of *Recht*—and argued that popular norms regarding reciprocity and fairness in fact played an important role in the evolution of a self-conscious working class. We also argued that moral economies of the life course in Western welfare states provide strong cultural justification for public pensions and other policies affecting the old. Finally, we noted that in contrast to the later Marx's narrow and harsh view of the "rights of man," his vision of a morality of emancipation was both broad and inspiring. We believe that it holds particular promise with reference to individual and societal aging.

As we have seen, Marx's notion of the morality of emancipation was based on an ideal of individual self-development achieved through mutual identification and community with others. Marx saw life under capitalism as alienating in part because it encouraged conflict and mutual indifference, which in turn stunted the possibility of human development for all members of society. He looked forward to the time when human social relations and economic productivity would create a society in which human development could take place unhindered by alienation and the struggle to eke out a living.

Marx's view of freedom and alienation has special relevance for our aging society, where mass longevity has created a new abundance of later life that is plagued by the absence of vital cultural meaning. As Moody puts it, the "collapse of meaning and the erosion of quality of life in old age reflect a deeper failure unacknowledged by the optimistic prophets of postmaterialist abundance: namely a failure of communication and legitimation in the social order as a whole" (45, p. 81). Confronting this crisis will mean building a new moral economy of the life course and the institutions that support it. The need to create a just distribution of goods and services remains central: "as long as the political economy is organized in ways that prevent abundance from actually becoming available to all" (45, p. 81), the emancipatory possibilities of our new abundance of life cannot be realized.

We believe that the challenge to aging societies lies not only in creating a just distribution of resources between and within age groups but also in forcing us to move beyond the alienated form of old age common in advanced industrial society, where old people are pressured into retirement and encouraged to opt for trivialized leisure or the consumption of professional services. Marx's morality of emancipation was predicated on the idea that free time would be spent for genuine humane development. A new moral economy of later life will require attention to quality of life issues in education, work, productivity, and health care at each stage of the life course. It will require social support for higher forms of activity: education, new forms of paid and unpaid work, and new arenas that bring old and young together. It will require too a vision of the whole life course which reaffirms the intimate interdependence of generations.

REFERENCES

1. Walton, J. Urban political economy. *Com. Urban Res.* 7: 1, 9, 1979.
2. Estes, C. L., Swan, J. H., and Gerard, L. E. Dominant and competing paradigms in gerontology: Toward a political economy of aging. In *Readings in the Political Economy of Aging*, edited by M. Minkler and C. L. Estes. Baywood Publishing., Amityville, New York, 1984.
3. Walker, A. Toward a political economy of old age. *Ageing and Soc.* 1: 73–94, 1981.
4. Olson, L. K. *The Political Economy of Aging.* Columbia University Press, New York, 1982.
5. Guillemard, A. M. Old age, retirement and the social class structure: Toward an analysis of the structural dynamics of the latter stages of life. In *Aging and Life Course Transitions: An Interdisciplinary Perspective*, edited by T. K. Hareven and K. J. Adams. Guildford, New York, 1982.
6. Gramsci, A. *Selections from The Prison Notebooks*, edited and translated by Q. Hoare and G. Nowell Smith. Lawrence and Wishart, London, 1971.
7. Habermas, J. Introduction. In *Observations on 'The Spiritual Situation of the Age'*, edited by J. Habermas, translated by Andrew Buchwalter, pp. 19–20. MIT Press, Cambridge, Massachusetts, 1984.
8. Frazer, N. *Unruly Practices: Power, Discourse and Gender in Contemporary Social Theory.* University of Minnesota Press, Minneapolis, 1989.
9. Walzer, M. *Spheres of Justice.* Basic Books, New York, 1983.

10. Mouffe, C. Hegemony and new political subjects: Toward a new concept of democracy. In *Marxism and the Interpretation of Culture*, edited by C. Nelson and L. Grossberg, pp. 89–104. University of Illinois Press, Urbana, 1988.
11. Sandel, M. J. *Liberalism and the Limits of Justice*. Cambridge University Press, New York, 1982.
12. Bolough, R. W. *Dialectical Phenomenology: Marx's Method*. Routledge and Kegan Paul, Boston, 1979.
13. Schmidt, A. *History and Structure*, translated by Jeffrey Herf. Massachusetts Institute of Technology Press, Waltham, Massachusetts, 1983.
14. Spicker, S., Woodward, K., and Van Tassel, D. D. (eds.). *Aging and the Elderly: Humanistic Perspectives in Gerontology*. Academic Press, New York, 1978.
15. Cole, T. R., and Gadow, S. A. *What Does It Mean to Grow Old? Reflections from the Humanities*. Duke University Press, Durham, North Carolina, 1986.
16. Cole, T. R., Van Tassel, D. D., and Kastenbaum, R. (eds.). *Handbook of Aging and the Humanities*. Springer, New York, 1991 (in press).
17. Gouldner, A. *The Two Marxisms: Contradictions and Anomalies in the Development of Theory*. Seabury Press, New York, 1980.
18. Lukes, S. *Marxism and Morality*. Oxford University Press, Oxford, 1985.
19. Thompson, E. P. *The Poverty of Theory and Other Essays*, pp. 363–364. Merline Press, London, 1978.
20. Vorlander, K. *Marx und Kant*. Vortrag genhalten in Wien am 8 April 1904. Verlag der "Deutschen Worte." Vienna.
21. Marx, K. and Engels, F. *Manifesto of the Communist Party*. MECW 6, 1848.
22. Hart, H. L. A. Are there any natural rights. *Phil. Rev.* 64: 177–178, 1955.
23. Marx, K. and Engles, F. *The German Ideology*. MECW 5, 1845–1846.
24. Thompson, E. P. *The Making of the English Working Class*. Vintage Books, New York, 1966.
25. Claeys, G. *Machinery, Money and the Millennium: From Moral Economy to Socialism, 1815–1860*. Polity Press, Cambridge, United Kingdom, 1987.
26. Durkheim, E. *The Division of Labor*. Macmillan, New York, 1933 (1893).
27. Scott, J. C. *The Moral Economy of the Peasant Rebellion and Subsistence in South East Asia*. Yale University Press, New Haven and London, 1976.
28. Evans, G. From moral economy to remembered village. Working Paper #40. Center for South East Asian Studies, Monash University, Australia, 1986.
29. Ravallion, M., and Dearden, L. Social security in a moral economy: An empirical analysis for Java. *Rev. Econ. and Stat.* 70: 36–44, 1988.
30. Brocheux, P. Moral economy or political economy? The peasants are always rational. *J. Asian Stud.* 42: 791–803, 1983.
31. Gersuny, C., and Kaufman, G. Seniority and the moral economy of U.S. automobile workers, 1934–1946. *J. Soc. Hist.* pp. 463–475, Spring 1985.
32. McPherson, C. B. *The Political Theory of Possessive Individualism*. Clarendon Press, Oxford, United Kingdom, 1962.
33. Perlman, S. *A Theory of the Labor Movement (1928)*. McMillan, New York, 1949.
34. Quadargo, J. "Organized Labor, State Structures and Social Policy: A Case Study of Old Age Assistance in Ohio, 1916–1940" *Soc. Prob.* 36(2): 181–196, 1989.

35. Myles, J. *Old Age in the Welfare State: The Political Economy of Public Pensions*. University Press of Kansas, Lawrence, Kansas, 1989.

36. Graebner, W. *The History of Retirement*. Yale University Press, New Haven, Connecticut, 1980.

37. Callahan, D. *Setting Limits: Medical Goals in an Aging Society*. Simon and Schuster, New York, 1987.

38. Tindale, J. A. and Neysmith, S. M. Economic Justice in Later Life: A Canadian Perspective. *Soc. Just. Res.* 1: 461–476, 1987.

39. Daniels, N. *Am I My Parents Keeper?* Oxford University Press, Oxford, 1988.

40. Katz, M. B. *The Undeserving Poor: From the War on Poverty to the War on Welfare*. Pantheon Books, New York, 1989.

41. Cole, T. The spectre of old age: History, politics and culture in America. *Tikkun* 3: 14–18, 93–95, 1988.

42. Lamm, R. Long time dying, *The New Republic*, pp. 20–23. August 27, 1984.

43. Neysmith, S. M. Social policy implications of an aging society. In *Aging in Canada* (2nd edition), edited by V. Marshall. Fitzhenry and Whiteside, Toronto, 1987.

44. Campbell, R. and Brody, E. M. "Women's Changing Roles and Help to the Elderly: Attitudes of Women in the United States and Japan." *The Gerontologist* 25(6): 584–592, 1985.

45. Moody, H. R. *Abundance of Life: Human Development Policies for an Aging Society*. Columbia University Press, New York, 1988.

CHAPTER 4

Dependency or Empowerment?
Toward a Moral and Political Economy
of Aging

Jon Hendricks and Cynthia A. Leedham

All too frequently, being old has been equated with dependency and helpless-ness. Yet gerontologists are increasingly recognizing that dependency is in part socially created, and that empowerment of the old is both possible and beneficial (1). This chapter explores the roots of dependency and empowerment of the elderly, in the process developing a dynamic framework for setting patterns of aging in broader context.

Over the past decade, concern with making apparent the links between social structures, policies, and individual lifeworlds have given rise to political economy, which examines the implications of structure, and social psychology, which focuses on individual responses to structural constraints (2–8). Within these traditions, social analysts have explored the creation of dependency in the elderly, the varied options to them within structural constraints, and the ways in which structure is shaped by individual and group interests. Still lacking, however, is a coherent conceptual paradigm for empowerment of the elderly. We argue that a key to understanding both the empowerment and the dependency of old people lies in Gramsci's concept of hegemony as moral and philosophical leadership with the active consent of members of society, grounded in taken-for-granted assump-tions about proper modes of social organization (9, 10). Few would question the centrality of economic factors to forms of social organization conducive to either dependency or empowerment. Assumptions about norms of reciprocity—or moral economy—therefore lie at the heart of hegemony.

Thompson (11) and Claeys (12) argue that eighteenth-century moral economy, protecting the right of the poor to buy bread through the idea of a just price, has been replaced by the new ideology of political economy in which rulers and capital unite in the interests of profit. The bread riots of the eighteenth century and their repression centered around the growing tendency of merchants to sell grain at the highest price it would fetch (11). Kohli suggests that rather than moral economy being totally supplanted, previous forms of moral economy have been replaced by forms reflecting advanced industrial society and its political economy. We contend that moral economy as described by Thompson (11)—linked to Marx's concept of production for use value by its focus on human welfare—has been replaced by a moral economy grounded in exchange value—focusing on production for the market (13–15). The path toward empowerment of the elderly and, indeed, of all generations, lies in adoption of a moral economy grounded in use value appropriate to advanced industrial societies.

After discussing the advent of the individual-structure dialectic into the limelight of political economy and social psychological theories, we explore the concept of hegemony and its relevance for dependency and empowerment in the elderly. This leads to a discussion of the various forms of moral economy and their social policy implications. In conclusion, we propose a moral and political economy grounded in use value as a key to discovering avenues for empowerment across the lifecourse.

TOWARD A DIALECTICAL FRAMEWORK IN GERONTOLOGICAL THEORY

The dialectic between individual and society has developed from a largely unacknowledged *leitmotif* to a major concern of gerontological theory. Understandings of this dialectic are clearly vital to issues of dependency and empowerment. Inattention to societal forces may lead to overestimating individual dispositional causes of dependency residing in actors (16, 17). Overemphasis on social structure, by contrast, closes off awareness of capacity for intentional action and variable responses to given circumstances (18–20). We need a reciprocal perspective that can capture how societal factors inhibit or enhance empowerment and how individuals affect social structure by challenging or submitting to situational constraints.

The Individual-Structural Dialectic in Past and Present Theories

The approach of gerontological theory to the individual-structure dialectic may usefully be cast in terms of thesis, antithesis, and synthesis. While clearly not doing justice to the subtleties and contributions of individual theories, this ideal-typical history sets broad approaches in bold relief, thus contributing to our understanding of the issues. First generation theories like disengagement and activity theory—the thesis—focus on individual adaptation to the circumstances of aging, taking structure as an unexamined given. Second generation theories, such as modernization and age stratification theory—the antithesis—focus on social structure without reference to intentionality. Third generation theories—the synthesis—seek to bridge the gap between social structure and individual lifeworlds. The point of departure for political economy is in social structure whereas social psychology begins in individual intentionality.

The Political Economy of Aging — Political economic theories attempt to tie individual experiences to macro-level structural factors by investigating the nature and constitution of structure itself (3–5). They are centered around the insight that the situation of the elderly develops from their ongoing relationship with society. Old people age differently in part because of the way material and social resources are allocated. Different futures could be invented by altering patterns of allocation (21). There are two major facets to the political economy of aging: investigation of how social location affects patterns of aging, and analysis of the dynamic, ever-changing relationship between distribution of power and forms of economic organization as various groups strive to attain and maintain a measure of control. The "structured dependence of the elderly" (4) comes about because of changing perceptions of their utility as producers and consumers due to shifts in the economy and relations of production. The old are deprecated not merely because they are elderly, but because they are believed to embody traditional, particular-istic values potentially inimical to the impersonal efficiency demanded by a modern market economy.

Because they arise from a broad analytic framework rather than a substantive picture of the way society ought to be, political economic theories present a rich diversity of models. They tap many levels, from consequences of involvement in the world of work to international relations. Their basic contention is that aging does not come about ex nihilo. Material conditions, political priorities, values, and public policy influence an individual's economic and psychosocial resources. Within the economic realm, labor markets provide differential opportunities for saving or accru-ing pension rights, which affect patterns of individual adjustment. Location in the labor market, and the perquisites that go with it, are influenced by an array of other social attributes. Notable among these are gender, race, and class. The impact of government policies varies among different categories with profound effects.

As discussed in Chapter 2 of this book, the impetus for political economic perspec-tives came in the late 1970s and early 1980s. Among early efforts, Estes undertook a critical examination of the role of policies and services in segregating old people from the mainstream (2). At nearly the same juncture, Walker offered an outline of the impact of age-based policies on the creation of their social ills and dependency (22). Olson's contribution was to focus on how the negative effects of market, class, gender, and race relations across the lifecourse engender even more adverse condi-tions during old age (5). From these beginnings, more systematic statements of a political economy of aging were developed by Estes and Walker (3, 6, 23).

Estes points out that the central challenge of political economy is to move beyond mere critique to an understanding of the character and significance of variations in the treatment of the aged and how these relate to polity, economy, and society (3). The experience of the elderly must be considered in the context of world and national economies, the state, labor market conditions, class, race, gender, and age divisions. The status and resources of different groups of elderly and trajectories of aging are always conditioned by social location. Of particular importance are position in the labor market and resulting social relations (4, 6). Like so many other components of our lives, aging inevitably reflects modes of economic organization. Fiscal austerity, cost-cutting, reemerging federalist rejection of national responsibility for basic human needs, deregulation, market-competition, and the rise of the "medical-industrial complex" (24) with its market model of health care affect the way we age.

In recent years, the political economic perspective on aging in America has gained in popularity. Hardy's focus on retirement policies, how these create dependency by limiting economic access, and the impact of class and labor-market differences on control over the nature and timing of retirement is but one example (25). Baron and Bielby (26) and Minkler and Stone (27) also point to ways labor market segmentation and other factors exacerbate economic risks for women across the lifecourse thereby resulting in feminization of poverty during old age. In fact, political economic perspectives have greatly enhanced our insight into the impact of gender on basic age-related issues. Hess uses it to analyze gender biases in retirement and health policy (28). Zones, Estes and Binney, among others, consider how the situation of the oldest old, who are primarily women, results from the impact of historical factors throughout life (29). Dressel (Chapter 15) calls attention to the need to broaden gender-based perspectives to examine the complex interplay of race and class with gender in creating patterns of poverty in old age.

Social Psychological Theories — Passuth and Bengtson criticize political economy for focusing too exclusively on social structure at the expense of inter-pretation and meaning (18). Social psychological perspectives, by contrast, specif-ically look at self-creating aspects of aging within biological and structural con-straints (19). Dannefer, among others, draws attention to the role of intentional, albeit socially constrained, action in producing patterns of aging (20). He notes "a theory of aging must systematically consider the implications for aging of differ-ent modes of action, consciousness, and selfhood and their relationship to differ-ent social forms" (20). He compares exclusively structural descriptions of aging and normative lifecourse development models to Barthes' concept of "white writing" (30). White writing masquerades as objectivity, obscuring the subjec-tivity of the writer. Similarly, theories may normalize socially constructed patterns of aging, such as age sixty-five automatically bringing retirement, or passivity among institutionalized elderly, as if they were immutable. Dannefer calls for longitudinal studies highlighting individual intentionality and the plasticity of social structures. In a somewhat similar vein, Rowe and Kahn point up the plasticity of biological aging, stressing the importance of autonomy and control (31). They identify two modes of normal aging. In *usual aging*, extrinsic environmental factors heighten potentially negative effects of aging. In *successful aging*, the social and physical environment play a neutral or positive role. They call for research into lifestyle, psychosocial, and policy factors to elucidate how a transition of usual to successful aging can be facilitated.

Marshall sees social structure as limiting possibilities for action, yet created and shaped by individuals. His purpose is to capture the impact of social arrangements in interpretive terms, taking account of individual intentions (7, 8). He identifies a constant tension between stability flowing from structural constraints and social consensus and instability flowing from human intentionality. The emphasis is on the importance of understanding connections between personal, individual, and structural levels to identify how "personal troubles" of the elderly stem from "public issues" limiting access to opportunities (7, 8, 32).

Notwithstanding Passuth and Bengtson's charge that political economy short-changes individual interpretation (18), many writing within the political economy tradition share Marshall's concern with the links between structure and individual lifeworlds. They seek to show that the "personal is political" and its parameters are subject to change. Their purpose in uncovering the sociohistorical under-pinnings of policies affecting the elderly is to make apparent the possibility of alternative constructions (27, 33). Yet a conceptual framework for articulating the dynamics of the interplay between individual and structure so as to open avenues for empowerment is not specified within either tradition. Such a framework may be found within Gramsci's concept of hegemony and the economic assumptions implicit in particular forms of hegemony.

Hegemony and Moral Economy: The Missing Links

Hegemony is constituted out of taken-for-granted assumptions underlying active consent to existing forms of leadership and social organization. It may be a worldview permeating economic activity, politics, and civil society with the effect of normalizing dominance of one group over another into a kind of cultural permanence. In this case, active consent is based on a misapprehension of the situation and thus is similar to the Marxian idea of false consciousness. People accept as legitimate the conditions that lead to their own exploitation. Women, for instance, might accept lower wages and benefits throughout the lifecourse and resultant impoverishment in old age as the norm. While concerned with ways in which hegemony might reinforce dominance, Gramsci also aspired to a new moral and philosophical leadership—a state of hegemony to which people could give full and informed consent because the policies to which it gives rise are in their own best long-term interests. Such a state would be grounded in a fundamental, common, freely shared set of ideals and values constituting a basic notion of what is appropriate. Failure of hegemony opens the way for competition between a variety of groups to advance their own narrow economic corporatist interests, which may not be in the best interest of the bulk of the population. Alternatively, absence of hegemony may lead to domination—the maintenance of order through sheer force—always difficult to sustain in the long run (34).

Hegemony in the first sense may create dependency among the elderly, for instance, normalizing their exclusion from the economic mainstream. An understanding of the dynamics of hegemony as false consciousness may, however, serve as a first step toward empowerment of the elderly by affording insight into the mechanics of their disempowerment. Gramsci's idea of a new hegemony calling forth free assent serves as a stimulus to conceptualizing principles of social organization to which people could consent as maximizing their chances for a decent life at all ages. As political economy has amply demonstrated, the effects of economic factors on individual lifechances are a central concern. Fundamental to emancipatory hegemony is the form of moral economy in which it is grounded.

By moral economy we mean shared assumptions about norms of reciprocity (cf., Kohli in Chapter 17 and Minkler and Cole in Chapter 3). Two ideal types of moral economy may be distinguished: moral economy grounded in use value and moral economy grounded in exchange value. Since they are ideal types, neither is likely to be found in pure form, and there will always be a dialectical tension between the two in any given society. The recent history of Western society has, however, witnessed a shift away from moral economy grounded in use value toward moral economy grounded in exchange value. Moral economies grounded in exchange value lend themselves to hegemony as false consciousness. By concentrating on the monetary aspects of exchanges, they may obscure underlying exploitation. Moral economies grounded in use value, by their focus on meeting human need, are consonant with the new hegemony toward which Gramsci aspired. Empowerment of the elderly—and of all generations—could be served by development of a moral economy grounded in use value appropriate to advanced industrial society.

MORAL ECONOMIES OF AGING

The overriding social goal of moral economies grounded in exchange value is advantage or profit in individual transactions. Commodities are seen as being produced primarily for the market. Individuals are evaluated in terms of market potential—their capacity for economically productive labor. In considering the situation of workers, the focus is on what is considered a fair monetary return for hours worked rather than on life chances. The underlying purpose of moral economies grounded in use value, in contrast, is meeting human needs (cf. 13–15). The key question is how to create social arrangements that maximize lifechances for all members of society over time, given resource constraints. The differences between these forms of moral economy are associated with a number of dichotomies in Western culture including the dichotomy between structure and individual, between production and consumption, and between generations and stages of the lifecourse. After outlining the relationship of the two forms of moral economy to these dichotomies, we explore them in greater depth.

A variety of conceptual approaches to social structure is possible. Moral economies grounded in exchange value tend to be associated with structuralist and individualist models that disenfranchise people by fracturing the organic link between individual and society, thus discounting possibilities for conscious social change. Structuralist approaches pose social structure and its imperatives as unanalyzed givens against which individuals are powerless. In some cases, they may be a matter of scientific mystique without immediately apparent political implications. In other cases, they may be a matter of overt or unconscious ideology with what actually turns out to be the interests of those in power being presented as structural imperatives. Calls to workers to sacrifice wage increases and benefits in order not to vitiate the economy by decreasing profit margins could be an example of the latter. Past appeals to the invisible hand of the market lent themselves both to scientific mystique and to ideology. An emphasis on exchange value may also lean toward methodological individualism by focusing on isolated exchanges taken out of social and temporal context. In contrast, moral economies grounded in use value are associated with a dialectical approach that views structure as socially created, yet with an intrinsic logic, and individuals as both shaped by and shaping social structure. This perspective raises the challenge of teasing out hidden interests from unforeseen structural consequences— the impact of individual and group actions for structure and of structure for individuals.

Focusing on individual transactions without regard for social and temporal context means that moral economies grounded in exchange value shy away from larger social issues addressed by use value. By evaluating production exclusively in terms of economic profitability, exchange value fractures production from consumption and economic activity from the meeting of human needs. Decisions are based on whether a particular product will sell and make a profit, not its utility to the consumer or society at large. The idea of use value poses its own challenge of how to link the productive activities of society with human needs. Production decisions take account of both utility of the product and its potential negative effects for society and the environment. Exchange value also tends to focus on the isolated moment, segmenting the lifecourse, and generations, from each other, thus opening the way for framing policy debates in terms of intergenerational inequity. Use value focuses attention on how to create decent living conditions across the lifecourse. Exchange value is dehumanizing in its unrelenting imposition of economic rationality. Human development is, by contrast, central to use value.

Moral Economies Grounded in Exchange Value

In its structuralist manifestation, moral economy grounded in exchange value is associated with what House terms the utilitarian approach to the public good (35). This view sees the general good as maximizing satisfactions or their proxies in society at large regardless of social distribution. Generally, these satisfactions are measured in terms of some global quantitative economic indicator such as the

Gross National Product. This approach is problematic in its failure both to take account of problems of distributive justice and to acknowledge the existence of goods or satisfactions not readily measurable in economic terms. It tends, therefore, to devalue the elderly since the structure of the labor force excludes most elderly from productive economic activity. It also draws attention away from social contributions of the elderly outside the labor market in terms of volunteer work, caring for family members, or other nonmarket activities, and from the plight of the elderly poor. Its presentation of economic indicators as sole measures of the public good may be characterized as ideological in the Marxian sense of mistaken beliefs that create false consciousness leading people to accept oppression. Increased productivity in terms of profits may be bought at the expense of the economically marginal sectors of the population.

In their individualist version, moral economies grounded in exchange value view society as constituted or self-interested individuals pursuing their interests through market exchanges. This perspective is commensurate with House's "liberal approach," which sees the public interest as the right of individuals or groups to maximize their own subjectively defined satisfactions (35). This view, too, poses problems because it presents the opportunity for some to exploit others. For individuals and groups to adopt outlooks based exclusively on their own fairly immediate economic interest—termed economic corporatist views by Bocock (10)—may run contrary to the long-term interests of society as a whole, for instance giving rise to environmental pollution that creates long-term social problems (10, 35). Such views are invidious for the aging because they prevent the young and middle-aged from realizing their own interest in creating a viable system of income security that will persist into their own old age. When adopted by the elderly, economic corporatist views lend fuel to the intergenerational inequity debate. The individual economistic approach may be characterized as a failure of hegemony in that it does not develop a viable concept of communal social interest or link individuals with their societal context. It is ideological in the Mannheimian sense of a worldview or frame of reference that tends to pervade and circumscribe our thought (36).

Moral Economy Grounded in Use Value

As indicated above, the overriding goal of moral economies grounded in use value is individual and social utility. The central issue is how to structure society so as to maximize possibilities of a decent life for all. Such moral economies could form a foundation for a new hegemony in Gramsci's sense of a basis for policy to which the major groups in society can give informed consent (9). They are consonant with House's third conception of the public good: the public interest as a negotiated rule structure to which people adhere even though it may run counter to their own immediately desired satisfactions since it improves overall opportunities of obtaining satisfaction (35). Citizens are seen not as passive recipients or consumers of public policy but as active moral agents (37).

Moral economy grounded in use value can chart the narrow course between the Scylla of a needs-based view of equity calling for the satisfaction of needs regardless of resource constraints, and the Charybdis of basing access on ability to pay without questioning resource distribution or the structure of the labor market. Use value challenges policymakers to work toward a decent minimum concept of equity whereby available resources and productive capacity are directed toward the meeting of human needs (38). Yet resource availability itself is not seen as immutable. Although partly resulting from extrinsic limiting factors, it is also socially constructed and a result of allocation, which should be critically evaluated with an eye to the need for change. Use value takes account of resources for meeting needs outside the economic market, including contributions of the elderly and women not in the labor force. Human needs are not met through isolated exchanges, but across time and throughout life. Resource allocation is therefore conceptualized not so much in terms of competition between generations as of the resource allocation we would judge appropriate for ourselves at various times in the lifecourse (39).

Moral economy grounded in use value supports Clark's four-fold scheme of empowerment in old age—and indeed across the lifecourse (1), which builds on Rawls (40). The first of Clark's four dimensions is social goods and political activism. It "does little good to speak of personal empowerment without at least some initial consideration of the need to provide sufficient social resources to enable individuals to exercise choice in their lives" (1). Acknowledging both the role of social policy in patterning life choices, and the need to involve older people in the policy process is a first step. Secondly, empowerment is effective deliberation: the ability to think consciously about complex actions. This means treating people as autonomous, giving them access to adequate information about key decisions and policies, and, where necessary, education in decision making. By raising the question of their real long-term interests as members of a social community, moral economy can provide a framework for effective deliberation. Thirdly, Clark reminds us that empowerment is a long-term process. The conditions of dependency and its grounding in social policy stretch across life rather than beginning fresh in old age. Finally, Clark sees empowerment as balance and interdependence, an ability to come to terms with the realities of one's personal history, present situation, and needs for support and assistance while maintaining a measure of freedom and independence. It calls for a balancing of needs and visions of one's own generation and those of others within existing resource constraints. This is precisely the challenge posed by moral economy grounded in use values.

SOCIAL POLICY IMPLICATIONS

The prime policy concern of moral economies grounded in exchange theory is economic productivity. Profitability and capital accumulation are regarded as ends in themselves, leading to judgment of policies almost exclusively on the basis of cost. In moral economies grounded in use value, productivity is contingent on human need, and policies are judged in terms of the quality of life made possible for all members of society. The Gramscian ideal of hegemony also implies structuring organizations so that the elderly and other interested parties may participate in formulating policies and decisions affecting their lives. In Ladd's terms, they are to become active moral agents in the social policy process (37). A state of true hegemony calls on groups to transcend narrow corporatist perspectives based on maximizing their own immediate interests at all costs in order to negotiate policy frameworks that afford long-term benefits for all.

Adopting a moral economy grounded in use value would mean that competition between generations for resources would be replaced by the question of how to allocate resources so as to provide an acceptable standard of living throughout life. This implies balancing a modicum of income security for both present and future generations of elderly, the exigencies of midlife, and the need to educate a viable workforce for the future. On one plane, Callahan may be seen as attempting to balance the needs of young against old (41). Strands within his perspective, however, risk subordinating the needs of the old to those of the young, as when he proposes withholding life-saving treatments after "the normal lifespan." This proposal runs counter to a hegemonic moral economy grounded in use value, attentive to the needs of all members of a community. Indeed, it borders on hegemony as creating false consciousness in the elderly. Some, like Quadagno (42, 43), have even suggested that the intergenerational equity debate serves to obscure basic class conflicts over benefits between labor and corporate interests. In considering allocation of health resources, it is important to examine the effectiveness of health care in improving quality of life at any age, the long-term effects of uneven access to basic necessities within generations, and possibilities for changing resource use within society as a whole. At the budgetary level, the question is not how to allocate fixed health and welfare dollars, but how the allocation of resources within the total budget contributes to the meeting of human needs. How to capitalize on the productivity of all generations, including the elderly, is a crucial issue. The concept of use value draws attention to the issue of distributive justice, the plight of the elderly poor, and its roots earlier in life. Social justice is evaluated in terms of adequacy of results and what it takes to make possible a decent minimum standard of living rather than quantitatively equal benefits for all.

Health care systems are judged in terms of cost effectiveness—outcomes obtained with available resources—rather than cost efficiency—keeping dollar expenditures down. As Mechanic notes (44):

(t)he quality of a health care system is truly measured not by what it spends or the number of sophisticated procedures it performs, but how it enhances the potential of the population to fulfill its personal and social choices and the extent to which it limits suffering.

Health is defined as a use value in terms of the type of life it makes possible for clients rather than exclusively in terms of productivity and economic returns. Emphasis on ability to function even in the face of incurable chronic disease is as important as cure. Increasingly, geriatricians are emphasizing functional independence in the old, rather than focusing exclusively on issues of morbidity. Peterson and Coberly similarly note that many elderly are able to compensate for chronic conditions by adaptations facilitating work and relatively normal lives. It is nonetheless vital to seek sources of chronic illness in lifestyle and policy factors earlier in life in an effort toward prevention (45).

An income maintenance policy based on use value would seek to reconcile provision of a decent minimum income for all with sustaining a viable economy, productive enough to meet societal needs. In addition to developing equitable benefit structures, this policy implies facilitating productivity and finding cost-effective ways of providing for basic needs. Drawing on the capacities of growing numbers of healthy elderly—both able and willing to work—has been proposed as a solution to impending threats of fiscal crisis resulting from a shrinking labor force. Some have even suggested that seventy-five may be a more appropriate retirement age than sixty-five, given the physiological and intellectual vigor of many of today's elderly (46). Yet trends toward early retirement and decreased labor-force participation over age fifty-five have continued in spite of restructuring of social security benefits to encourage later retirement. Reducing early benefits to force the elderly to remain in the labor force without creating opportunities for meaningful employment can only lead to conditions of hardship. At a deeper level, a viable income maintenance policy requires attention to the overall structure of the labor market, ageism and other forms of discrimination in employment, and opportunities for education and job retraining throughout life. The Swedish public pension system, which uses worker's contributions to purchase bonds for collective industrial development, is an interesting example of how to combine economic growth with the welfare of present and future retirees (47–49).

All of this implies a cradle-to-grave approach to health and income policies. This means ensuring a safety net for all within limits of resource availability. Such an approach would both improve quality of life for marginal young and middle-aged persons and, through its preventive impact, decrease the prospect of dependency as they age. Within this framework, policies for elderly persons would be designed to maximize functioning and tap the skills and resources they have to offer. Income support, adequate housing, health care, and a range of community-based services should be there to enable the elderly needing them to cope creatively with limitations without infantilization due to overly protective services. If failing capacities mandate an institutional environment, every effort should be made to foster a sense of control and a variety of options (50).

CONCLUSION: TOWARD A MORAL AND POLITICAL ECONOMY OF OLD AGE

The notions of hegemony and moral economy grounded in use value can complement political and social psychological perspectives to create a dialectical view of aging. Political economy draws our attention to the influence of social location on patterns of aging, issues of resource allocation, and political power. It affirms the need to set aging issues in national and international political and economic contexts. Social psychological—and more recent humanistic— approaches point up the creativity of aging individuals in dealing with structural constraints. Hegemony and moral economy can provide ways of understanding the links between personal troubles and public issues. The contrast between hegemony as legitimating domination and Gramsci's true hegemonic leadership challenges us to a critique of ideology designed to understand the ways in which the organization of work, gender roles, age stereotypes, and political order delimit possibilities throughout life; the unanalyzed assumptions in which these are grounded; and social conditions conducive to human emancipation (cf. 1, 51, 52). The idea of a moral economy grounded in use value answers Estes' call and moves beyond mere critique (3) by proposing a grounding for models of social organization allowing for the emancipation of older and younger citizens alike.

REFERENCES

1. Clark, P. G. The philosophical foundation of empowerment. *J. Aging and Health* 1(3): 267–285, 1989.
2. Estes, C. L. The Aging Enterprise, Jossey-Bass Publishers, San Francisco, California, 1979.
3. Estes, C. L. The politics of ageing in America, *Ageing and Soc.* 6(2): 121–134, 1986.
4. Townsend, P. The structured dependency of the elderly. *Ageing and Soc.* 1(1): 5–28, 1981.
5. Olson, L. K. *The Political Economy of Aging: The State, Private Power, and Social Welfare.* Columbia University Press, New York, 1982.
6. Estes, C. L., Swan, J., and Gerard, L. Dominant and Competing Paradigms in Gerontology: Toward a Political Economy of Ageing. Ageing and Society 2(2): 151–164, 1982.
7. Marshall, V. Societal toleration of aging: Sociological theory and social response to population. In *Adaptability and Health*, I: 85–104. International Center of Social Gerontology, Paris, 1981.
8. Marshall, V. Dominant and emerging perspectives in the social psychology of aging. In *Later Life: The Social Psychology of Aging*, edited by V. Marshall, pp. 9–31. Sage, Beverly Hills, 1986.
9. Gramsci, A. *Selections from the Prison Notebooks*, edited and translated by Q. Hoare and G. Nowell Smith. Lawrence and Wishart, London, 1971.
10. Bocock, R. *Hegemony*. Tavistock Publications, London, 1988.
11. Thompson, E. P. The moral economy of the English crowd in the eighteenth century. *Past and Present* 50: 76–136, 1971.

12. Claeys, G. *Machinery, Money and the Millennium: From Moral Economy to Socialism, 1815–1860*. Polity Press, Cambridge, United Kingdom, 1987.
13. Marx, K. *Capital, Vol. I*, edited by F. Engels. International Publishers, New York, 1967.
14. Marx, K. *The Economic and Philosophic Manuscripts of 1988*, edited by D. J. Struik, pp. 110–112. International Publishers, New York, 1964.
15. Marx, K. *The German Ideology*, edited by C. J. Arthur, pp. 54–56, 68–77. International Publishers, New York, 1970.
16. Ross, L., Amabile, T., and Steinmetz, J. Social roles, social control, and bias in social perception processes. *J. Pers. and Soc. Psy.* 35: 485–494, 1977.
17. Hendricks, J. and Leedham, C. A. Creating psychological and societal dependency in old age. In *Psychological Perspectives of Helplessness and Control in the Elderly*, edited by P. S. Fry, pp. 369–394. Elsevier Science Publisher B. V. (North Holland), Amsterdam, 1989.
18. Passuth, P. M. and Bengtson, V. L. Sociological theories of aging: Current perspectives and future directions. In *Emergent Theories of Aging*, edited by J. E. Birren and V. L. Bengtson, pp. 333–355. Springer Publishing Company, New York, 1988.
19. Kenyon, G. M. Basic assumptions in theories of human aging. In *Emergent Theories of Aging*, edited by J. E. Birren and V. L. Bengtson, pp. 3–18. Springer Publishing Company, New York, 1988.
20. Dannefer, D. Human action and its place in theories of aging. *J. Aging Stud.* 3(1): 1–20, 1989.
21. Maddox, G. L. Aging differently. *The Gerontologist* 27(4): 557–564, 1987.
22. Walker, A. The social creation of poverty and dependency in old age. *J. Soc. Pol.* 9(1): 49–75, 1980.
23. Walker, A. Towards a political economy of age. *Ageing and Soc.* 1(1): 73–94, 1981.
24. Relman, A. S. The medical-industrial complex. *New Engl. J. Med.* 303(17): 963–970, 1980.
25. Hardy, M. Vulnerability in old age: The issue of dependency in American society. *J. Aging Stud.* 2(4): 311–320, 1988.
26. Baron, J. N. and Bielby, W. T. Organizational barriers to gender equality: Sex segregation of jobs and opportunities. In *Gender and the Lifecourse*, edited by A. S. Rossi, pp. 233–251. Aldine, New York, 1985.
27. Minkler, M. and Stone, R. The feminization of poverty and older women. *The Gerontologist* 25(4): 351–357, 1985.
28. Hess, B. B. Aging policies and old women: The hidden agenda. *Gender and the Lifecourse*, edited by A. S. Rossi, pp. 319–331. Aldine, New York, 1985.
29. Zones, J. S., Estes, C. L., and Binney, E. A. Gender, public policy and the oldest old. *Ageing and Soc.* 7(3): 275–302, 1987.
30. Barthes, R. *Writing Degree Zero*, translated by A. Levers and C. Smith. Hill and Wang, New York, 1987.
31. Rowe, J. W. and Kahn, T. L. Human aging: Usual and successful. *Science* 237: 143–149, 1987.
32. Mills, C. W. *The Sociological Imagination*. Oxford University Press, New York, 1959.
33. Harrison, J. Women and ageing: Experience and implications. *Ageing and Soc.* 3(2): 209–233, 1983.

34. Hamilton, P. Editor's foreword. In *Hegemony*, R. Bocock, pp. 7–8. Tavistock, London, 1988.
35. House, E. R. *Evaluating with Validity*. Sage, Beverly Hills, California, 1980.
36. Tesh, S. N. *Hidden Arguments: Political Ideology and Disease Prevention Policy*. Rutgers University Press, New Brunswick, 1988.
37. Ladd, J. Policy studies and ethics. *Pol. Stud. J.* 2(1): 38–43, 1973.
38. U.S. Congress, Office of Technical Assessment. *Medicare's Prospective Payment System. Strategies for Evaluating Cost, Quality and Medical Technology*, U.S. Government Printing Office, Washington, D.C., 1985.
39. Clark, P. G. The social allocation of health care resources: Ethical dilemmas in age-group competition. *The Gerontologist*, 25(2): 119–125, 1985.
40. Rawls, J. *A Theory of Justice*. Belknap Press, Cambridge, Massachusetts, 1971.
41. Callahan, D. *Setting Limits. Medical Goals in an Aging Society*. Simon and Schuster, New York, 1987.
42. Quadagno, J. Generational equity and the politics of the welfare state. *Pol. and Soc.* 17(3): 353–376, 1989.
43. Quadagno, J. Interest group politics and the future of U.S. social security. In *Old Age in Transition: International Perspectives on Labor Markets and Social Delivery*, edited by J. Myles and J. Quadagno. Temple University Press, in press.
44. Mechanic, D. Health issues in an aging society: The research agenda. In *Proceedings of the 1987 Public Health Conference on Records and Statistics*, pp. 17–20. U.S. Department of Health and Human Services, U.S. Government Printing Office, Washington, D.C., 1987.
45. Peterson, D. A. and Coberly, S. The older worker: Myths and realities. In *Retirement Reconsidered: Economic and Social roles for Old People*, edited by R. Morris and S. A. Bass, pp. 116–128. Springer Publishing Company, New York, 1988.
46. Morris, R. and Bass, S. A. Toward a new paradigm about age and work. In *Retirement Reconsidered: Economic and Social Roles for Older People*, edited by R. Morris and S. A. Bass, pp. 3–14. Springer Publishing Company, New York, 1988.
47. Kuttner, R. *The Economic Illusion: False Choices Between Prosperity and Justice*. Houghton Mifflin, Boston, 1984.
48. Moody, H. R. The contradictions of an aging society: From zero sum to productive society. In *Retirement Reconsidered: Economic and Social roles for Older People*, edited by R. Morris and S. A. Bass, pp. 15–34. Springer Publishing Company, New York, 1988.
49. Hudson, R. B. Politics and the new old. In *Retirement Reconsidered: Economic and Social Roles for Older People*, edited by R. Morris and S. A. Bass, pp. 59–70. Springer Publishing Company, New York, 1988.
50. Labouvie-Vief, G. Intelligence and cognition. In *Handbook of the Psychology of Aging, 2nd. edn.*, edited by J. E. Birren and K. Warner Schaie, pp. 500–530. Van Nostrand Reinhold, New York, 1985.
51. Moody, H. R. Toward a critical gerontology: The contribution of the humanities to theories of aging. In *Emergent Theories of Aging*, edited by J. E. Birren and V. L. Bengtson, pp. 19–40. Springer Publishing Company, New York, 1988.
52. Habermas, J. *Knowledge and Human Interests*, translated by J. J. Shapiro. Beacon Press, Boston, 1971.

PART II. NEW IMAGES OF THE OLD AND THE DEBATE OVER RESOURCE ALLOCATION

The past two decades have seen a dramatic change in American stereotypes of the elderly. Once perceived as a "deserving subgroup" of poor, frail, and politically powerless individuals, the elderly increasingly are portrayed by the mass media, policy makers, and others as "greedy geezers"—wealthy, political powerful, and prospering at the direct expense of younger and future generations.

In this section of the book, three different perspectives on our new images of the old are presented. We begin in Chapter 5 by examining new stereotypes concerning the economic well-being of older Americans, looking in particular at the flawed assumptions underlying new and homogenous images of the "affluent elderly." By disaggregating the old and examining more closely how poverty is measured in the United States, the chapter presents a more heterogeneous and realistic picture of the true financial status of America's elders.

Chapter 5 also lays out and critiques the arguments behind a "generational equity" approach to public policy, which tends to blame poverty in children and other complex economic problems on costly entitlement programs for the nation's elderly. Such a framework is consistent with recent government attempts to delegitimize the claims of the elderly. But it is inconsistent with American attitudes and values, which suggest the continued strength of moral economy notions of reciprocity and of cross-generational interdependence rather than conflict.

While proponents of a generational equity policy framework frequently view America's elderly as a "gray peril," a far more optimistic view of the aging of the population is being put forward by growing segments of the business community. In Chapter 6, Minkler examines business and industry's discovery of the elderly market, and their realization that there may indeed be "gold in gray." While business' belated attention to older consumers is seen as having some positive consequences (e.g., in conferring visibility and status on a previously often invisible population group), its potential and actual negative consequences are seen as troubling. Current efforts to develop and capture the aging market thus sometimes reinforce age-separatist policies and approaches and divert attention from the needs of low income elders who don't fit the new affluent consumer stereotype. Concepts such as privatization, consumerism and the rise of a geriatric "medical industrial complex" are used in Chapter 6 to understand these developments and their implications.

Still another way to view the changing images of the old has to do with the perceived political power of this group. In Chapter 7, the myths and realities behind "senior power" are explored, with attention to the electoral, organizational, and structural power of the old. Although a number of examples are presented of issues where seniors have had considerable influence over specific public policies, no enduring pattern of power is observed comparable to that of business, the new right, or other groups with more focused policy agendas. In addition, and despite media portrayals of the power of the elderly as benefiting all elders equally, senior power in reality tends to represent the interests and the political clout of middle and upper income elders. As a consequence, it tends not to be as visible around issues such as Supplemental Security Income (SSI) of greatest concern to the low income elderly. Finally, since the interests of the aged as a group will continue to be subordinated to class interests, "senior power" is not likely to have the primary role in shaping public policy that popular media portrayals would have us believe.

"GENERATIONAL EQUITY" AND THE
NEW VICTIM BLAMING

Meredith Minkler

> This policy and reverence of age makes the world bitter to the best of our
> times; keeps our fortunes from us till our oldness cannot relish them. I begin
> to find an idle and fond bondage in the oppression of aged tyranny, who
> sways, not as it hath power, but as it is suffer'd.
>
> King Lear, I, ii, 47

Stereotypic views of the elderly in the United States as a wealthy and powerful
voting block have replaced earlier stereotypes of this age group as a poor, impotent, and deserving minority (1). Capitalizing on and contributing to these changing perceptions, the mass media and a new national organization, Americans for
Generational Equity (AGE), prophesize a coming "age war" in the United States,
with Social Security and Medicare as the battleground (2). Like Gloucester's
young son in *King Lear*, they argue that entitlement programs for today's affluent
elderly "mortgage our children's future" and contribute to high poverty rates
among the nation's youth.

The framing of complex public policy issues in terms of conflict between
generations, however, tends to obscure other, far more potent bases of inequities
in our society. Indeed, in Binstock's words (1, pp. 437–438):

> To describe the axis upon which equity is to be judged is to circumscribe
> the major options available in rendering justice. The contemporary preoc-
> cupation with . . . intergenerational equity blinds us to inequities within age
> groups and throughout society.

This chapter will examine the assumptions underlying the concept of generational equity, with particular attention to notions of fairness and differential stake
in the common good. Tendencies by policy makers, scholars, and the mass media
to statistically homogenize the elderly and to utilize inadequate and flawed

measures of poverty further will be examined and seen to contribute to the myth of a monolithic and financially secure elderly population. Finally, the false dichotomy created between the interests of young and old will be found to illustrate a new form of victim blaming, whose employment is inimical not only to the elderly but to the whole of society.

THE MAKING OF A SOCIAL PROBLEM

In his trenchant look at the cyclical nature of social problems, O'Conner noted that when the economy is perceived in terms of scarcity, social problems are redefined in ways that permit contracted, less costly approaches to their solution (3). Thus, while the economic prosperity of the 1960s permitted us to discover and even declare war on poverty, the recession of 1973 and its aftermath resulted in a redefinition of poverty and the subsequent generation of less costly "solutions."

The discovery of high rates of poverty and poor access to medical care among America's elderly in the economically robust 1960s and early 70s helped generate a plethora of ameliorative programs and policies including Medicare and Social Security cost of living increases (COLAs). By the mid-1970s however, amid high inflation and unemployment, Social Security and Medicare were themselves being defined as part of the problem. By implication, the elderly beneficiaries of these programs frequently were characterized by the mass media as targets of special resentment. The "compassionate ageism" which had enabled the stereotyping of the elderly as weak, poor and dependent, from the 1930s through the early 1970s (1) gave way to new images of costly and wealthy populations whose favored programs were "busting the federal budget."

In the mid-1980s, a new dimension was added to this socially constructed problem when the rapidly increasing size of the elderly population and the costliness of programs like Social Security and Medicare were directly linked to the financial hardships suffered by younger cohorts in general and the nation's children in particular. Indeed, in a widely publicized article in *Scientific American*, Samuel Preston, then President of the Population Association of America, argued that the elderly now fare far better than children in our society (4): In the twelve years from 1970 to 1983, he pointed out, the proportion of children and elders living in poverty was reversed, with the proportion of children under fourteen living in poverty growing from 16 percent to 23 percent and the percent of elderly poor dropping from 24 percent to only 15 percent. While public outlays for the two groups had remained relatively constant through 1979, moreover, many public programs for children were cut back in the 1980s, at the same time that programs for the politically powerful elderly were expanded. Preston's widely quoted paper went on to compare the elderly and children on a variety of parameters including suicide rates and concluded with a plea for redressing the balance of our attentions and resource allocations in favor of youth.

Following closely on the heels of Preston's analysis, the President's Council of Economic Advisors reported in February of 1985 that the elderly were "no longer a disadvantaged group," and indeed were better off financially than the population as a whole (5).

These two publications helped generate a new wave of media attention to the "costly and wealthy elderly." They further provided much of the impetus for a new, would-be national organization devoted to promoting the interests of younger and future generations in the national political process. With the backing of two prominent congressmen and an impressive array of corporate sponsors, Americans for Generational Equity (AGE) attacked head on government policies which, under pressure from a powerful gray lobby, were seen as creating a situation in which "today's affluent seniors are unfairly competing for the resources of the future elderly" (6).

The mass media, AGE, and other proponents of an intergenerational conflict framework for examining current U.S. economic problems have successfully capitalized on growing societal concern over certain facts of life which have coincided with the graying of America. These include:

- a massive federal deficit;
- alarming increases in poverty rates among children, with one in five American children now living in poverty (7); and
- a 76 million strong "Baby Boom" generation whose real incomes have declined 19 percent over the last fifteen years.

These statistics have been coupled with another set of facts and figures used to suggest that the growing elderly population is itself part of the problem:

- The elderly, while representing only 12 percent of the population, consume 29 percent of the national budget and fully 51 percent of all government expenditures for social services (8);
- Since 1970, Social Security benefits have increased 46 percent in real terms, while inflation-adjusted wages for the rest of the population have declined by 7 percent (9).

The picture presented is one of a host of societal economic difficulties "caused," in part, by a system of rewards that disproportionately benefits the elderly regardless of their financial status.

The logic behind the concept of generational equity is flawed on several counts, each of which will be discussed separately. In addition to these specific inaccuracies, however, a broader problem will be seen to lie in an approach to policy which lays out the issues in terms of competition among generations for scarce resources. Each of these problems will now be discussed.

THE MYTH OF THE HOMOGENEOUS ELDERLY

Basic to the concept of generational equity is the notion that elderly Americans are, as a group, financially secure. Borrowing statistics from the President's Council of Economic Advisers, proponents of this viewpoint argue that the 1984 poverty rate for elderly Americans was only 12.4 percent (compared to 14.4 percent for younger Americans), and dropped to just 4 percent if the value of Medicare and other in-kind benefits was taken into account (5).

While the economic condition of the elderly as a whole has improved significantly in recent years, these optimistic figures obscure several important realities. First, there is tremendous income variation within the elderly cohort, and deep pockets of poverty continue to exist. Close to a third of black elders are poor, for example (32%), as are 24 percent of older Hispanics and 20 percent of all women aged eight-five and above (10).

Minority elders and the "oldest old," aged eighty-five and above, not only have extremely high rates of poverty, but also comprise the fastest growing segments of the elderly population. Thus, while only about 8 percent of blacks are aged sixty-five and over, compared to over 13 percent of whites, the black elderly population has been growing at a rate double that of the white aged group. The number of black elders further is increasing at twice the rate of the younger black population (11). In a similar fashion, the "oldest old" in America—those aged eighty-five and above—are expected to double in number by the turn of the century, from 2.5 million in 1985 to some 5 million by the year 2000 (12). The very high rates of poverty in the current generation of "old old" may reflect in part a Depression-era cohort effect. At the same time, however, the heavy concentration of women in the eighty-five and over age group, coupled with continued high divorce rates and pay and pension inequities, suggest a significant continuing poverty pocket as the population continues to age (13).

The myth of a homogenized and financially secure elderly population, in short, breaks down when the figures are disaggregated and the diversity of the elderly is taken into account.

PROBLEMS IN THE MEASUREMENT OF POVERTY

Analyses which stress the low poverty rates of the aged also are misleading on several counts. First as Pollack has noted, comparisons which stress the favorable economic status of the aged *vis-à-vis* younger cohorts fail to acknowledge the use of two separate poverty lines in the United States—one for those sixty-five and above and the other for all other age groups (14). The 1987 poverty line for single persons under sixty-five thus was $5905—fully 8 percent higher than the $5447 poverty line used for elderly persons living alone (15). If the same poverty cutoff had been used for both groups, 15.4 percent of the elderly would have fallen below the line, giving the aged a higher poverty rate than any other age group except children.

The inadequacy of even the higher poverty index also merits attention. It is telling, for example, that Molly Orfshanksy, the original developer of the poverty index, dismissed it some years ago as failing to accurately account for inflation. By her revised estimates, the number of elderly persons living in or near poverty almost doubles (16).

Discussions of the role of Social Security and other in-kind transfers in lifting the elderly out of poverty also are problematic. Blaustein thus has argued that while Social Security and other governmental transfers helped lift millions of elders out of poverty, they for the most part succeeded in "lifting" them from a few hundred dollars below the poverty line to a few hundred dollars above it (17). Indeed, some 11.3 million elders, or 42.6 percent of the elderly, live below 200 percent of the poverty line, which for a person living alone is about $10,000 per year (15).

Recent governmental attempts to reduce poverty by redefining it also bear careful scrutiny in an effort to uncover the true financial status of the elderly and other groups. The argument that poverty in the aged drops to 4 percent when Medicaid and other in-kind transfers are taken into account thus is extremely misleading. By such logic, an elderly women earning less than $5000 per year may be counted as being above the poverty line if she is hit by a truck and has $3000 in hospitalization costs paid for by Medicaid. The fact that she sees none of this $3000 and probably incurs additional out of pocket health care costs in the form of prescription drugs and other deductibles is ignored in such spurious calculations (14).

The continuing high health care costs of the elderly are themselves cause for concern in any attempt to accurately assess the income adequacy of the elderly. The elderly's out of pocket health care costs today are about $2400 per year— three and one-half times than that of other age groups, and higher proportionately than the amount they spent prior to the enactment of Medicare and Medicaid more than two decades ago (18). Contrary to popular myth, Medicare pays only about 45 percent of the elderly's medical care bills and recipients have experienced huge increases in cost sharing (e.g., a 141 percent increase in the Part A deductible) under the Reagan administration (14). Inflation in health care at a rate roughly double that of the consumer price index further suggests that the *de facto* income adequacy for many elderly may be significantly less than the crude figures imply.

MORAL ECONOMY AND THE CROSS-GENERATIONAL STAKE IN ELDERLY ENTITLEMENTS

Another criticism of the logic behind intergenerational equity lies in its assumption that the elderly alone have a stake in Social Security, Medicare, and other governmental programs which are framed as serving only the aged. Arguing that the nation's future "has been sold to the highest bidder among pressure groups and special interests" (6), Americans for Generational Equity and the mass media thus cast Social Security and other income transfers to the aged in a narrow and simplistic light. For even if one disregards the direct benefits of Social Security to nonelderly segments of the society (e.g., through survivors benefits to millions of persons under age sixty-five), the indirect cross-generational benefits of the program are significant. By providing for the financial needs of the elderly, Social Security thus frees adult children from the need to provide such support directly. As such, according to Kingson et al., it may reduce interfamilial tensions while increasing the dignity of elderly family members who receive benefits (19). Research by Bengston et al., has suggested that the family is not perceived by any of the major ethnic groups in America as having major responsibility for meeting the basic material needs of the elderly (20). Rather, families are able to provide the support they do in part because of the availability of government programs like Social Security. When these programs are cut back, the family's ability to respond may be overtaxed, to the detriment of young and old alike (21).

Programs like Social Security are not without serious flaws (see Chapter 18). Yet despite these problems, and contrary to recent media claims, there has been little outcry from younger taxpayers to date about the high costs of Social Security and Medicare. Indeed, in an analysis of some twenty national surveys conducted by Louis Harris and Associates over a recent two-year period, Taylor found no support for the intergenerational conflict hypothesis (22). While the elderly appeared somewhat more supportive of programs targeted at them than did younger age groups, and vice versa, the balance of attitudes in all generations was solidly on the same side. The majority of both elderly people, and young people under thirty, thus opposed increasing monthly premiums for Medicare coverage, opposed increasing the deductible for Medicare coverage of doctors' bills, and opposed freezing Social Security cost of living increases. Similarly, both young and old Americans opposed cutting Federal spending on education and student loans, and overwhelmingly opposed cutting Federal health programs for women and children (22). In short, while young and old differ significantly on questions relating to values and lifestyle, issues of government spending and legislation affecting persons at different stages of the life course appeared to evoke intergenerational *consensus* rather than *conflict*.

The strong support of younger Americans for Social Security and Medicare is particularly enlightening in the wake of recent and widely publicized charges that these programs may be bankrupt before the current generation of young people can reap their benefits. Such charges, while poorly substantiated, have made an impact: poll data suggest that today's younger workers are pessimistic about the chances of Social Security and Medicare being there for them when they retire. In light of this pessimism, how might their continued high level of support for elderly entitlements be explained?

As noted earlier this phenomenon reflects in part the fact that younger people in the workforce prefer to have their parents indirectly supported than to shoulder this burden themselves in a more direct way.

Yet on a more fundamental level, the continued support of younger generations for old age entitlements they believe will go bankrupt before their time reflects what Hendricks and Leedham described in Chapter IV as a moral economy grounded in use value—one whose central goal is "to structure a society so as to maximize possibilities of a decent life for all." As these analysts go on to note, moral economies grounded in use value envision the public interest as "a negotiated rule structure, to which people adhere *even though it may run counter to their own immediately desired satisfactions* since it improves overall opportunities of obtaining satisfaction" (emphasis added). Further, a moral economy based on use value or individual and social utility views citizens "not as passive recipients or consumers of public policy, but as active moral agents." Within such a vision of moral economy, resource allocation would be viewed not in terms of competition between generations, but in Rawls' sense, as allocations appropriate to ourselves at various points over the life course (23) (Chapter IV).

Generational equity proponent Daniel Callahan has argued that such life course perspectives are flawed in their failure to adequately address the fact that the huge demands made by unprecedented numbers of elders in recent years "threaten to unbalance any smooth flow of an equitable share of resources from one generation to the next (24, p. 207). Yet he and other proponents of generational equity similarly evoke a notion of moral economy in support of their arguments that the purpose of old age in society should be reformulated as involving primarily service to the young and to the future—in part through an acceptance of the need for "setting limits" on government support for life-saving medical treatment for those over a given age.

Callahan indeed proposes a shifting of the existing moral economy and a questioning of some of its basic assumptions. In particular, a fundamental tenet of the existing moral economy—that health care not be rationed on the basis of age—should, he argues, be reconsidered in light of current and growing inequities in the distribution of scarce public resources for health care between young and old (24).

The strong public outcry against age based rationing, coupled with the considerable evidence of the continued popularity of Social Security and Medicare among young and old alike, suggests, however, that the older moral economy notions of what is just and "due" the old have continued to hold sway. For both young and old, it appears, elderly entitlement programs like Social Security are not simply the way things are, but the way they should be. The reality, in short, stands in sharp contrast to the rhetoric which claims that Social Security is "nothing less than a massive transfer of wealth from the young, many of them struggling, to the elderly, many living comfortably" (25). Instead, the program, firmly grounded in American moral economy, is one which all generations appear to support, and from which all see themselves as receiving some direct or indirect benefit.

AGE/RACE STRATIFICATION AND INTER-ETHNIC EQUITY

Arguments that young and old alike have a stake in programs like Social Security and Medicare may break down, according to some analysts, when the element of ethnicity is introduced.

Indeed, Hayes-Bautista et al. suggest that there may be strong resentment of entitlement programs for the elderly thirty to fifty years from now in age/race stratified states like California (26). Within such states, the burden of support for the large, predominantly white elderly population is expected to fall heavily on the shoulders of a young work force composed primarily of Latinos and other minorities.

Utilizing California demographic projections as a case in point, Hayes-Bautista et al., note that unless major shifts take place in fertility and immigration patterns, and/or in educational and job policy achievements, the working age population of the future will not only be heavily minority, but also comprised of individuals whose lower total wage base will require that larger proportions of their income go simply to maintaining current Social Security benefit levels for the white elderly Baby Boom generation. Under such conditions, they argue, the nation may be ripe for an "age-race collision."

While these investigators go on to suggest policy measures that might avert such a catastrophe, the "worst case scenarios" which they and other analysts (27, 28) describe have unfortunately received far more media attention than their recommended policy solutions. It is precisely because of the popularity of these "age wars" predictions, moreover, that a deeper look at the current reality is in order.

While it is of course impossible to project attitudinal shifts in the population in the way that demographic changes can be forecasted, current national opinion poll data on the attitudes of Latinos and other minorities toward entitlement programs for the elderly are instructive.

If the hypothesis is correct that there may be substantial resentment of Social Security and Medicare in the future on the part of a large minority working class population left to shoulder this burden, one might expect hints of such resentment now. Contrary to expectation, however, opinion poll data show Hispanics, blacks and other minorities to be strongly supportive of Social Security and Medicare and indeed often more opposed than whites to proposed budget cuts in these programs (22).

The hypothesis of growing minority resentment of elderly entitlement programs also may be questioned on demographic grounds. Thus, while minorities make up only about 10 percent of the aged population today, that figure is expected to increase by 75 percent by the year 2025. [The Comparable increase among white elders will be only about 62 percent (29).]) Elderly Hispanics, already the fastest growing subgroup within the older population, will see their numbers grow even more rapidly, quadrupling by the year 2020 (30). From 2025 to 2050, the period corresponding to the graying of the huge Baby Boom generation, the proportion of elderly within the nonwhite population is projected to increase another 29 percent, compared to only 10 percent for the white population (29). While the minority aged population will remain small numerically compared to the elderly cohort, the fact that greater proportions of working aged Latinos, blacks and other minorities will have parents and grandparents reaching old age suggests again an important phenomenon which may work against the reification of an age/race wars scenario.

A final factor which may mitigate against the likelihood of increasing minority resentment of elderly entitlement programs concerns the differential importance of programs like Social Security to the economic well-being of whites, blacks, and Hispanics. The disadvantaged economic position of elderly blacks and Hispanics relative to whites, for example, means that higher proportions rely on Social Security as their only source of income, and that far fewer have private insurance and other nongovernment resources to cover the costs of medical care. Under such conditions, more rather than less support for elderly entitlement programs might be expected among these economically disadvantaged minority groups, and that is indeed what the survey data appear to suggest.

GUNS VERSUS CANES?

A common theme throughout the intergenerational equity movement is that the elderly are not only numerous but also expensive: The high cost of Social Security, amounting to about 20 percent of the federal budget, is juxtaposed against a $2 trillion national debt and a massive federal deficit, with the implicit and often explicit message that the costly elderly are a central part of our economic crisis.

As Pollack has noted, however, such equations are misleading at best (14). Social Security, for example, is not a contributor to the deficit and in fact brings in considerably more money than it pays out. Indeed, throughout the 1990s, when the small Depression-era cohort is elderly, the system will bring in literally hundreds of billions more than it will spend (14).

Ironically, the nation's military budget, while a major contributor to the deficit, is virtually excluded from discussions by many analysts of the areas necessary for scrutiny if we are to achieve a balanced budget. AGE President Paul Hewitt indeed has spoken out against a congress which, under pressure from aging interest groups, will "weaken our national defense before it will cut cost of living allowances (COLAs) for well to do senior citizens" (6).

Tendencies by the mass media and others to overlook defense spending in discussions of the costliness of programs for the elderly continues a tradition described earlier by Binstock when he noted that we are taught to think in terms of how many workers it takes to support a dependent old person, but not how many it takes to support an aircraft carrier (16). Citing an OMB fiscal analyst, Binstock further pointed out that classic political economic trade-off, "guns vs. butter," has been reframed "guns vs. canes," in reference to the perceived costliness of the aged population.

In the relatively few years since Binstock's initial analysis, a further reframing has occurred with "canes vs. kids" constituting the new political economic trade-off.

As Kingson et al. (19) have noted, such an analysis assumes a zero sum game in which other possible options (e.g., increased taxes or decreased military spending) are implicitly assumed to be unacceptable (19). It is worthy of note that such traditionally conservative analysts as Meyer and Ein Lewin of the American Enterprise Institute (31) have begun arguing in favor of cutbacks in defense spending as a means of balancing the federal budget without in the process decimating needed social programs. While favoring increased taxation of Social Security and some initial taxing of Medicare benefits, the AEI analysts appear to have come down hardest on the need for massive reductions in military spending if the United States is to cease "protecting sacred cows and slaughtering weak lambs" (31, p. 1).

Still other analysts have urged the closing of tax loopholes for corporations and the rich as a means of redressing huge national deficits. Noting that corporate taxes dropped from 4.2 percent of the GNP in 1960 to 1.6 percent in the 1980s, and that money lost to the treasury through tax loopholes grew from $40 billion to $120 billion over the period 1980-86 alone, Pollack thus has argued that tax breaks for the rich, rather than Social Security COLAs for the elderly, should be viewed as the real culprits in the current economic crisis (14).

Finally, national opinion poll data show overwhelming public support for cutting military spending and closing tax loopholes, rather than cutting programs for the elderly and other population groups as a means of addressing America's economic difficulties (22).

The "canes vs. kids" analytical framework, in short, does not appear to have wide credence in the larger society, and where a hypothetical "guns vs. canes" trade-off is proposed, the American public overwhelmingly supports the latter.

VICTIM BLAMING REVISITED

As noted earlier, the socially constructed "problem" of aging in American society took on added dimensions in the mid-1980s when the costliness of programs like Social Security and Medicare began to be linked by the media, policy makers, scholars, and others to poverty in children and economic hardships among the nation's youth.

The process of drawing such spurious correlations appears to reflect in part a phenomenon alluded to by Ryan (32) in the mid-70s and later described by this author (33) as the new victim blaming. Briefly, the original victim blaming was conceptualized by Ryan as both an ideology and a subtle process applied to American social problems. Through it, problems were identified and those affected were studied to see how they differed from the rest of society. The differences then were defined as the cause of the problem and new government programs were developed to "correct the differences" (32).

Writing in the early 1970s, Ryan noted that the ideology of victim blaming was very different from the "open prejudice and reactionary tactics" of earlier times. Rather, victim blaming was shrouded in humanitarianism and bore "the trappings and statistical furbelows of scientism" (32, p. 7).

By the mid-1970s, and reflecting on Nixon's "New Federalism," Ryan was pointing out that the victim blaming ideology ". . . has become somewhat less prominent in part because it has been superseded by more vicious and repressive formulations" (34, p. 301). While Ryan didn't go on to examine these more recent approaches, they appear to be well demonstrated in recent thinking with regard to the elderly. For as noted earlier, unlike the victim blaming of the 1960s and early 70s, which defined the elderly as a social problem and devised solutions (e.g., expanded Social Security benefits, Medicare and Medicaid) for dealing with that problem, the victim blaming of the 1980s defined these earlier "solutions" as part of the problem. Not only were and are the aged problematic, but ameliorative programs are seen as "busting the federal budget" and in need of massive cutbacks if we are to restore "justice between generations" (7).

The new victim blaming is particularly well illustrated in the application of a market theory perspective to determinations of appropriate resource allocations for the different age groups. Demographer Samuel Preston thus has argued that, "Whereas expenditure on the elderly can be thought of *mainly as consumption*, expenditure on the young is a combination of consumption and investment" (4, p. 49; emphasis added), leaving aside the inaccuracies of such statements from a narrow, worker productivity perspective (since many of the elderly continue to be employed full- or part-time), the moral and ethical questions raised by such an approach are significant. While it is true that the elderly "consume" about a third of all health care in the United States, for example, such figures become dangerous when used to support claims of the differential "costs" of older generations, and the need for the rationing of goods and services on the basis of age (1).

The scapegoating of Social Security and Medicare as primary causes of the fiscal crisis has served to deflect attention from the more compelling and deep-seated roots of the current economic crisis. At the same time, and wittingly or unwittingly fueled by recent mass media and groups like AGE, it has been used as a political tool to stoke resentment of the elderly and to create perceptions of a forced competition of the aged and younger members of society for limited resources. As Kingson et al. have noted, (19, p. 4):

> . . . while the concept of intergenerational equity is seemingly neutral and possesses an intuitive appeal (who can be against fairness?), its application,

whether by design or inadvertence, carries with it a very pessimistic view about the implications of an aging society, which leads to particular policy goals and prescriptions.

These "policy goals and prescriptions" as we have seen, reflect a "new victim blaming" mentality in their suggestion that we must cut public resources to the elderly in order to help youth and to avert conflict between generations.

For as noted elsewhere, to trade the victim blaming approaches of the 1980s for those of the 1960s and 70s is not a solution to problems which ultimately are grounded in the skewed distribution of economic and political power within the society (33). Ultimately, as Pollack has argued, the central issue is not one of intergenerational equity but of income equity (14). Cast in this light, inadequate AFDC payments and threatened cuts in Social Security COLAs which would plunge millions of elderly persons into poverty, are part of the same problem. Programs and policies "for the elderly," like education and health and social services "for youth" must be redefined as being in fact not "for" these particular subgroups at all, but for society as a whole. Conversely, threatened cutbacks in programs for the elderly, under the guise of promoting intergenerational equity, must be seen as instead promoting a simplistic, spurious and victim blaming "solution" to problems whose causes are far more fundamental and rooted in the very structure of our society.

CONCLUSION

In the short time since its inception, the concept of generational equity has become a popular framework for analysis of contemporary economic problems and their proposed solutions. Yet the concept is based on misleading calculations of the relative financial well-being of the elderly *vis-à-vis* other groups and on questionable assumptions concerning such notions as fairness and differential stake in the common good. Predictions that young people, and particularly minority youth, may be increasingly resentful of elderly entitlement programs are unsubstantiated by current national survey data which show strong continued support for these programs across generational and ethnic lines. The reframing of political economic trade-offs in terms of "canes vs. kids" indeed appears to have little credence with the public at large, despite its popularity in the mass media, and with a growing number of scholars, policy makers and new, self-described youth advocates.

Proponents of an intergenerational equity approach to policy have performed an important service in calling attention to high rates of poverty in America's children, and to the need for substantially greater societal investment in youth and in generations as yet unborn. At the same time, however, their tendency to blame the costliness of America's aged for economic hardships experienced by her youth is both misguided and dangerous. The call for intergenerational equity represents a convenient smokescreen for more fundamental sources of inequity in American society. By deflecting attention from these more basic issues, and by creating a false dichotomy between the interests of young and old, the advocates of a generational equity framework for policy analysis do a serious disservice.

REFERENCES

1. Binstock, R. H. The oldest old: A fresh perspective or compassionate ageism revisited? *Milbank Mem. Fund Q.* 63: 420–541, 1983.
2. Longman, P. Age wars: The coming battle between young and old. *The Futurist* 20: 8–11, 1986.
3. O'Connor, J. *The Fiscal Crisis of the State.* St. Martin's, New York, 1973.
4. Preston, S. Children and the elderly in the U.S. *Scient. Am* 251: 44–49, 1984.
5. *Annual Report of the President's Council of Economic Advisors.* U.S. Government Printing Office, Washington, D.C., 1985.
6. Hewitt, P. A Broken Promise. Brochure of Americans for Generational Equity. AGE, Washington, D.C., 1986.
7. Edelman, M. W. Meeting the needs of families and children: Structural changes that require new social arrangements. (Statement before the Consumer Federation of America.) Children's Defense Fund, New York, March 15, 1990.
8. Longman, P. Justice between generations. *Atlantic Monthly*, pp. 73–81, June 1985.
9. Taylor, P. The coming conflict as we soak the young to enrich the rich.
10. Villers Foundation, *On the Other Side of Easy Street: Myths and Facts about the Economics of Old Age.* The Villers Foundation, Washington, D.C., 1987.
11. U.S. Bureau of the Census. Current reports: Poverty in the U.S. Series P 60, No. 163. U.S. Government Printing Office, Washington, D.C., 1989.
12. Bould, S., Sanborn, B., and Reif L. Eighty Five Plus: The Oldest Old. Wadsworth Publishing Company, Belmont, California, 1989.
13. Minkler, M., and Stone, R. The feminization of poverty and older women. *Gerontologist* 25: 351–357, 1985.
14. Pollack, R. F. Generational equity: The current debate. Presentation before the 32nd Annual Meeting of the American Society on Aging, San Francisco, March 24, 1986.
15. U.S. Bureau of the Census, *Statistical Abstract of the U.S.* (109th edition). U.S. Government Printing Office, Washington, D.C., 1989.
16. Binstock, R. The aged as scapegoat. *Gerontologist* 23: 136–143, 1983.
17. Blaustein, A. I. (ed.). *The American Promise: Equal Justice and Economic Opportunity.* Transaction Books, New Brunswick, New Jersey, 1982.
18. Margolis, R. J. *Risking Old Age in America.* Westview Press, Boulder, Colorado, 1990.
19. Kingson, E., Hirshorn, B. A., and Cornman, J. *Ties That Bind: The Interdependence of Generations in an Aging Society.* Seven Locks Press, Cabin John, Maryland, 1986.
20. Bengston, V., Burton, L., and Mangen, D. Family support systems and attributions of responsibility: Contrasts among elderly blacks, Mexican-Americans, and whites. Paper presented at the Annual Meeting of the Gerontological Society of America, Toronto, Canada, November 1981.
21. Pilisuk, M., and Minkler, M. Social support: Economic and political considerations. *Social Policy* 15: 6–11, 1985.

22. Taylor, H. Testimony before the House Committee on Aging, Washington, D.C., April 8, 1986.

23. Rawls, J. *A Theory of Justice*. Belknap Press, Cambridge, Massachusetts, 1971.

24. Callahan, D. *Setting Limits: Medical Goals in an Aging Society*. Simon and Schuster, New York, 1987.

25. Schiffres, M. The Editor's Page, "Next: Young vs. old?" *U.S. news and World Report* p. 94, November 5, 1984.

26. Hayes-Bautista, D., Schinck, W. O., and Chapa, J. *The Burden of Support: The Young Latino Population in an Aging Society*. Stanford University Press, Palo Alto, California, 1988.

27. Longman, P. The youth machine vs. the baby boomers: A scenario. *The Futurist* 20: 9, 1986.

28. Lamm, R. D. *Mega-Traumas, America at the Year 2000*. Houghton Mifflin Company, Boston, Massachusetts, 1985.

29. U.S. Senate Special Commission on Aging. *Aging America: Trends and Projections, 1985–86*. U.S. Department of Health and Human Services, Washington, D.C., 1986.

30. Andrews, J. Poverty and poor health among elderly Hispanic Americans. Commonwealth Fund Commission on Elderly People Living Alone, Washington, D.C., 1989.

31. Meyer, J. A., and Levin, M. E. Poverty and social welfare: Some new approaches. Report prepared for the Joint Economic Committee. American Enterprise Institute, Washington, D.C., 1986.

32. Ryan, W. *Blaming the Victim* (1st edition). Random House, New York, 1972.

33. Minkler, M. Blaming the aged victim: The politics of retrenchment in times of fiscal conservatism. In *Readings in the Political Economy of Aging*, edited by M. Minkler, and C. L. Estes, pp. 254–269. Baywood Publishing, Amityville, New York, 1984.

34. Ryan, W. *Blaming the Victim* (2nd edition). Random House, New York, 1976.

CHAPTER 6

GOLD IN GRAY:
REFLECTIONS ON BUSINESS'
DISCOVERY OF THE ELDERLY MARKET

Meredith Minkler

Almost a decade ago, Estes coined the phrase "the aging enterprise" in reference to the vast array of programs, bureaucracies, providers, interest groups, and industries that serve the elderly but in reality do more to meet the needs of the servicing system of which they are a part. In Estes' words (1, p. 238):

> The social needs of the elderly . . . are defined in ways compatible with the organization of the American economy. The effect . . . is to transform these needs into government funded and industry-developed commodities for specific economic markets, commodities that are then consumed by the elderly and their 'servants.'"

In the ten years since the publication of Estes' landmark book, the concept of an "aging enterprise" appears increasingly to have been prophetic. The elderly population not only is seen as providing serviceable needs to fuel the nation's vast health and social services industries, but indeed is considered the newest exploitable growth market in the private sector.

A sudden plethora of books, and newsletters with titles like "Selling to Seniors" and "The Mature Market Report," are doing a brisk business. *Modern Maturity*, the monthly magazine of the 28 million member American Association of Retired Persons (AARP), has been listed by *Adweek* each year since 1983 as one of the nation's ten "hottest magazines" in terms of advertising growth revenue (2). And in Emeryville, California, gerontologist and entrepreneur Ken Dychtwald receives $25,000 per speech for telling businesses how to profit from an aging population.

The private sector's discovery of the gray market represents a decidedly mixed blessing. On the one hand, business and industry's sudden attention to elderly

81

consumers may provide a welcome contrast to an earlier day when the omission of older people from advertisements and other marketing strategies both reflected and helped reify their exclusion from active participation in the cultural and social mainstream (3).

At the same time, however, current efforts to develop and capture the aging market may sometimes have the effect of creating needs where none exist, reinforcing age separatist policies and approaches, and especially diverting attention from the needs of low income elderly people. The creation of a new image of older Americans as a largely affluent consumer group further may work to support public policies which de-emphasize the provision of needed government programs and services.

This chapter begins with a brief review of the financial status of older Americans, and the private sector's changing image of the elderly population from a negligible consumer group to a $500 billion market (4). The concepts of mainstreaming, consumerism, the social industrial complex, and privatization of care and services for elderly people then are used to help understand the growth and nurturing of the aging market as well as the problems which may accompany this phenomenon. Although both the positive and the problematic aspects of the targeting of older Americans as a potent and neglected consumer population are considered, the attempt primarily is to raise questions about the ethical issues involved in exploiting the new gray market in a heavily consumer-oriented society.

IS THERE 'GOLD IN GRAY'?: THE FINANCIAL STATUS OF OLDER AMERICANS

In 1984, President Reagan's Council of Economic Advisors declared that contrary to myth, elderly Americans were "no longer a disadvantaged group" (5). The poverty rate for the elderly population, they argued, was just 12.4 percent (compared to 14.4 percent for younger Americans) and dropped to just 4 percent if the value of Medicare and other in-kind benefits was taken into account.

In point of fact, the economic situation of the elderly population has improved dramatically over the past two decades, and particularly in relation to younger cohorts. Median adjusted family incomes for families headed by people sixty-five and above thus rose 54 percent between 1970 and 1986, whereas, young families with heads under age twenty-five saw their median adjusted family income fall by 15 percent (6).

The elderly as a group also have impressive financial assets: Some three-quarters of those sixty-five and over own their own homes (compared to a total U.S. home ownership rate of 65 percent), and of the total financial assets held by U.S. families, 40 percent are accounted for by the 12 percent of the population aged sixty-five and above (7).

Of even greater significance from the point of view of corporate America is the fact that people fifty-five and over control about one-third of the discretionary income in the United States and spend 30 percent of it in the marketplace, roughly twice that of households headed by persons under thirty-five (8). Americans fifty-five and over purchase close to 80 percent of all commercial vacation travel (9) and a disproportionate share of many other nonessential commodities as well.

Yet this optimistic picture obscures several important facts. There is tremendous income variation within the elderly cohort, for example, and deep poverty pockets continue to exist. Minority elders and the oldest old (persons eighty-five and above) thus constitute two of the fastest growing and poorest segments of the elderly population. According to the 1980 census, close to 40 percent of aged blacks, 26 percent of elderly Hispanics, and fully 20 percent of persons eighty-five and above lived in poverty (10), and these rates show no sigh of abating in the near future.

As noted in Chapter 5, analyses stressing the low poverty rates of the elderly population also are misleading in their failure to acknowledge that two different poverty lines are used in the United States, one for persons sixty-five and above and the other, 8.5 percent higher, used for all other age groups. [For couples, the differential between the two poverty lines is an even more pronounced 11.2 percent (11).] When the same poverty yardstick is used for all Americans, the percentage of poverty in the elderly population rises to 15.4 percent, giving the aged a higher poverty rate than any other age group except children (11).

Other problems in the measurement of poverty in the elderly population are discussed elsewhere (11–14) and a full analysis of them is beyond the scope of this chapter. Suffice it to say, however, that the new stereotype of the affluent elderly population breaks down when this group is disaggregated and when the methods traditionally used to measure income and poverty levels are examined more closely.

This is not to dispute, of course, that many elderly persons do have substantial assets and discretionary income, but rather to suggest that the overall financial picture of older Americans is less rosy than the mature market analysts would have us believe. Indeed, when it is realized that close to 43 percent of elderly persons live below 200 percent of the poverty line (15), a different and more modest assessment of the economic circumstances of many of the nation's elderly comes into focus.

FACTORS CONTRIBUTING TO BUSINESS' DISCOVERY OF THE NEW OLD MARKET

Although the financial picture of elderly Americans remains a complex one, with millions doing well while millions of others live at or near poverty, the stereotypic images of the aged tend to ignore these complexities. The decade from the late 1970s to the late 1980s witnessed a major shift in the stereotypes of the elderly population from a weak, poor, and deserving subgroup to a wealthy and powerful voting block whose costly entitlement programs were busting the federal budget (16).

In part, of course, this change in image was a function of the earlier-mentioned real and impressive financial gains made by elderly people as a group in the 1970s. A 20 percent increase in Social Security payments in 1972 and the tying of these benefits to the Consumer Price Index to protect them against high inflation thus had the effect of dramatically decreasing poverty rates among the elderly population. Subsequent governmental proclamations that elderly people were "no longer poor" and indeed were financially better off than other Americans helped cement new images of the economically secure aged, while gingerly raising questions as to whether government entitlements for this privileged group shouldn't perhaps be scaled back.

Other analysts were more outspoken on this topic, among them the new non-profit, nonpartisan coalition, Americans for Generational Equity (AGE). Founded in 1985 under the leadership of Republican Senator Dave Durenberger and Democratic Representative Jim Jones, AGE described its mission as that of building a national movement to promote the interests of younger and future generations in the political process (17). Arguing that young families had become "indentured servants" in part as a consequence of bloated entitlement programs for the aged (18), AGE advocated major reforms in Social Security and Medicare and has received impressive corporate backing and media attention for its efforts.

Several leading academic figures also have helped bolster and shape the new image of elderly people as a costly and financially secure population group. Preston, former head of the Population Association of America, received national attention in 1984 for his *Scientific American* article in which he stressed that the nation's comfortable elderly population was in direct competition with youth for scarce resources (19). Skyrocketing rates of poverty and other problems plaguing America's children, according to Preston, were in part a consequence of the country's skewed priorities in putting elders' needs ahead of youths'.

Concurrent with the attempts of such analysts to argue that the elderly population was no longer disadvantaged economically were other efforts to shape a new image of the elderly as a vigorous and independent new generation which also constituted a new and lucrative consumer market. Age-Wave Inc. in Emeryville, California is perhaps the best known contributor to this new image of the elderly population as an untapped gold mine for business and industry. With a substantial consulting business and products like an $1100 resource book for hospitals on how to capture the aging market, Age-Wave Inc. and its founder, Ken Dychtwald, have received extensive national publicity for their vision of the "tinting of America" and its meaning for society in general and business in particular (20).

Another contributor to the new image of the elderly population as a dynamic generation and potent consumer market is, of course, the senior lobby itself. For senior membership and advocacy organizations, however, projecting a new image of elderly people to business and the general public often involves a delicate tightrope walk. The AARP, for example, has found itself in the position of aggressively lobbying Congress against a freeze on Social Security Cost of Living Adjustments (COLA's) at the same time that it has been sending to the business community a different image of elderly people as a healthy, vigorous and financially lucrative market. A media kit promoting AARP's magazine, *Modern Maturity*, to potential advertisers thus describes its constituency as "Affluent. . . Aware. . . Active Buyers with over $500 billion to spend" and goes on to proclaim (4):

> 50 & Over people are putting into practice the credo of Living for Today. They're spending on self-fulfillment *now* (Hedonism vs. Puritanism) rather than leaving large sums behind.

Critics such as Samuelson have branded as hypocritical the tendency of groups like AARP to change the image they evoke of elderly people from destitute widow to wealthy and hedonistic consumer depending on whom these organizations are targeting and toward what end (21). Other analysts, such as gerontologist Tòrres-Gil, have been more generous, however, in viewing this duality as a logical, if problematic, outcome of a pluralistic society (22): Interest groups like the senior lobby must continue to put forward images of elderly people as needy and deserving to garner resources, while at the same time working to improve the public's image of elderly people by breaking down negative stereotypes.

A variety of factors, in short, are contributing to business' discovery of the aging market, among them real changes in the overall financial status of the aged, government and other analysts' arguments that elderly people are "no longer poor," entrepreneurs who have recognized the profits to be made from selling businesses on selling to seniors, and a gray lobby which increasingly has projected positive images of the new old age. Yet beneath all these contributing factors may be seen to lie several key values and historical developments that helped make the business community ripe for the discovery of the gray market.

The development of a geriatric "social industrial complex," through programs like Medicare and Medicaid (23), introduced the health care industry early on to the profits to be made in aging. Defined by O'Connor as a vast service industry born of the merger of private enterprise and public capital, the social industrial complex ideally brought together the best of both worlds to benefit those in need. In reality, however, the primary beneficiaries of such mergers have tended to be instead the providers (1, 23), and this frequently is not an unintended outcome. As McKnight has noted, in times of declining natural resources and overseas market, a new exploitable commodity often is people and their serviceable needs (24). The client often is "less a person in need than a person who is needed." His or her function becomes one of meeting the needs of servicers, the servicing system, and the national economy.

Viewed in this context, the proclaimed crisis of the elderly in the 1970s was less a function of the inherent needs of this group and more one of the demands of a service-based economy in times of economic recession. As Estes has suggested, the elderly population and their needs became the raw materials fueling the expansion of one of the few growth sectors in the economy, that is, aging and gerontology (1).

For the elderly medical care client, this analysis seems particularly apt. Medicare and Medicaid had, for example, helped revitalize small and rural hospitals and indeed enabled the hospital industry overall to emerge as one of the nation's key growth areas. Expenditures on hospital care grew from $14 billion in 1965 to $167 billion in 1985 (25). When inflation is corrected for, the rate of growth still represents a three-fold increase over this period, much of it a direct consequence of the Medicare payment system (26).

In pointing out that the hospital industry profited substantially from Medicare, the author does not mean to detract from the importance of this legislation in increasing the elderly population's access to medical care. As Brown has noted, the nonpoor elderly population had substantially more physician visits in the year prior to Medicare's introduction than did their low income counterparts (27). By 1978, however, that gap had been cut in half, dropping from 22 percent to 10 percent. Utilization differences between elderly blacks and whites also were markedly reduced as a consequence of the legislation and differences in use between poor and nonpoor chronically ill elderly people all but disappeared (27). Yet Medicare's other role in bolstering profits in the hospital and medical care sector should not be overlooked.

Bergthold et al. (28), Estes (29), and Schlesinger et al. (25) have examined in more detail the commodification of care for the elderly population, and particularly the recent role of privatization in making health care for the aged one of the fastest growing businesses in the United States. Briefly, although the term privatization is used in reference to the reduction in state provision of some goods or services, it frequently also is "a euphemism for cuts in the total amount of public expenditures" in health and other areas (28). As Bergthold et al. have noted (28):

> . . . because of the introduction of market criteria, distribution of services becomes based in large part on the ability to pay. After privatization, therefore, the distribution of resources is not likely to reflect the same order of social priorities as under a predominantly public system.

Decreased public provision of health services for elderly people, and the private sector's discovery of a fertile new market (with elderly people accounting for one-third of all health care expenditures, and Medicare covering only about 44 percent of the bill) (30, 31), in fact, may be viewed in retrospect as a portent of things to come. By the late 1970s business was discovering that elderly people were good, or potentially good, consumers not only of hospital and nursing home beds and of denture creams, but of a huge array of goods and services in almost every market sector.

Moreover, as early as the mid-1970s, a new strategy of "recapitalizing capitalism" was leading to a renewed emphasis upon both individual consumption and corporate profits (32). Particularly under the Reagan Administration, the dramatic lowering of corporate taxes, stepped up deregulation of business, a lessening of inflation and an accent on individual responsibility helped bolster the ideal of consumerism as the heart of the American economy. The notion that the consumption of goods was "the greatest source of pleasure, the highest measure of human achievement . . . the foundation of human happiness" (33) indeed appeared to have received renewed meaning and emphasis in an era that de-emphasized values such as equity, equality, and access and stressed instead individualism, self-reliance, government cost containment, and privatization.

SELLING TO SENIORS: A MIXED BLESSING

As noted earlier, the private sector's discovery of the elderly population market may be seen as having both positive and problematic features. On the plus side, as Beck has noted, it represents an overdue realization that older people increasingly represent "a major force in society, not just a shadow population content to sit on the sidelines" (34).

Whereas some goods and services (e.g., Geritol and burial insurance plans) have, of course, long been targeted to elderly people, the very nature of such products may have served, in retrospect, to reinforce the social distance between elderly persons and the rest of society. By contrast, the 1980s witnessed the increasing appearance of silver-haired models in advertisements for automobiles and other valued social goods. In this way, the private sector's new attention to the elderly population market may provide an important partial corrective for the still pronounced tendency of advertisers to employ predominantly youthful models and to reinforce, through their marketing strategies, the youth bias prevalent in American society.

The significance of this contribution should not be underestimated. Indeed, the concept of mainstreaming or integration into dominant social institutions may be seen as having relevance to the elderly population in some of the same ways that it earlier was important for the mentally and physically disabled. Although the issue here is not mainstreaming through the public schools but rather through advertising and the mass media, some similar principles may apply. As Powell and Williamson have noted, "omission implies lack of value [and] exclusion from active participation in the mainstream of American social life" (3). Such omission further suggests that the needs, opinions, and demands of the group in question "are of no real consequence and can therefore safely be ignored." By turning their attention to the long-neglected elderly population market, business and industry may be conferring visibility and value onto this population group which, in turn, should help improve society's images of and attitudes toward its older members.

The private sector's discovery of the elderly consumer also may work to promote the tailoring of needed products and services to better meet the requirements of an aging population. As Dychtwald has pointed out, the design of everything from door knobs to automobiles should be rethought as America ages, hopefully in the process developing products which take into account the physical as well as some of the social changes that may accompany old age (20). Market surveys, which historically have ignored the population fifty and above, similarly must avoid such ageism if they are to help businesses discover what older consumers want and need, and how best to meet those needs.

There is often a fine line, however, between finding out what a given population group may want or need and creating in that group needs and concerns that didn't exist previously. The newly launched *Lear's* magazine for "women over forty" for example, although designed to boost the image of older women, contains ads for "anti-aging supplements" and other products aimed at creating in women a felt need to look younger than their chronological age (35). To the extent that such appeals exploit the "gerontophobia" or cultural dread of aging pervasive in American society (36), hard questions must be raised concerning the ethics involved in their use to sell products. On a more philosophical level, the extensive use of such appeals may be seen as raising yet again the "embarrassing question" asked by foreign observers since de Tocqueville's day: "Have Americans ever developed an appropriate model of maturity?" (37). In Cole's words (38, p. 94):

> We need . . . to criticize liberal capitalist culture's relentless hostility toward physical decline and its tendency to regard health as a form of secular salvation . . .
> The one-sided drive to alter, ameliorate, abolish, retard or somehow control the biological process of aging intensifies the impoverishment of meaning instead of confronting it.

The fine line between meeting older consumers' needs and artificially creating needs to exploit the gray market also is seen in many of the new appeals to business to aggressively target older Americans as a critical new consumer group. In *Midlife and Beyond: The $800 Billion Over-Fifty Market*, the Consumer Research Center has argued that "What we have, then is potentially a highly receptive market for a wide range of luxury goods, for frills and services and top of the price line merchandise" (7). Note that no mention is made in this statement of meeting elderly people's needs, but rather of selling them "frills and services," "luxury goods," and the most costly, top line merchandise.

It can be argued, of course, that such marketing only is effective if there is a consumer demand for these products in the first place, because the power of the market system really lies in individuals rather than in the businesses and organizations that cater to them. Yet as Galbraith has suggested, this perspective may be more myth than reality (33): a myth promoted by the corporate economy to remove the business sector from accountability ". . . if the goods that it produces or the services that it renders are frivolous" or worse.

In the same way that a fine line exists between meeting elderly peoples' needs and having corporations create and shape their needs for profit, a delicate balance also must be struck between, on the one hand, tailoring goods and services to meet the special needs of the elderly population and, on the other, reinforcing age-separatist approaches.

The rapid growth of resort style life care communities provides a good case in point. Although only about 850 such facilities (with and without nursing homes) were operating in 1986, projections by the Real Estate Research Corporation have suggested that an additional 4,400 are likely to spring up by 1995, creating a $46 billion industry (39). As such facilities become big business, hard questions need to be raised concerning the relative merits of promoting these approaches *vis-à-vis* alternatives that would provide for more age-integrated housing and health care arrangements. In particular, the fact must be confronted that the heavy advertising of life care communities and other age-separatist services may have the opposite effect of the positive mainstreaming role of business mentioned earlier. By buying into the notion of elderly persons as "separate and different" (1) and requiring therefore separate and different housing and basic human services, such business appeals may increase the psychological distance between the elderly population and the rest of society.

A final problematic aspect of the sudden emphasis on affluent older Americans as a vibrant new consumer market is that this development, coupled with privatization and other recent trends, may have the effect of obscuring the very real economic problems faced by the millions of elderly people who do not conform to the new stereotype. As noted earlier, more than 15 percent of elderly people still live in poverty and among women, minorities, and the oldest old these figures are considerably higher.

Marketing appeals which wittingly or unwittingly homogenize elderly people and recast them as a monolithic, $500 billion consumer group (4) present a misleading and incomplete picture of the social and economic situation of older Americans today. And this inaccurate portrait, in turn, is troublesome for two reasons. First, in the proprietary sector, such image creation and reinforcement may render even less audible the demands of low income consumers, a group for whom affordable housing, rather than high-priced condominiums, may represent the most pressing consumer need. Decreased attention to the needs of low-income elderly people presents special problems in areas such as health and social services where privatization, along with serious threats to the viability of nonprofit agencies, are occurring at a rapid rate. As Estes has noted, in fields like home health care and home delivered meals, deregulation and the entry of for-profit providers "are challenging the ability of non-profit agencies to continue serving the low income elderly who may need services, but who cannot afford to pay privately for them" (29).

A second, and potentially even more important problem, however, is that business' creation and reinforcement of a misleadingly homogeneous picture of the affluent older consumer may adversely affect public policy. As low-income elderly persons are rendered less visible through such marketing approaches and imaging, for example, governments may find increasing justification for cutbacks in the programs and services that are most needed by those elderly people who fail to fit the new, affluent stereotype. Further, as the private sector aggressively markets goods and services that ideally government should provide, public pressure for such assistance (and hence government incentives to respond) may be reduced.

Long-term care insurance provides an important case in point: When it is realized that 46 percent of persons seventy-five and above who are living alone spend down to poverty level within just thirteen weeks of institutionalization (40), the critical need for government provision of long-term care coverage becomes clear. By appearing to provide a viable alternative to government support, however, long-term care insurance policies (most of which are prohibitively expensive and many of which have loopholes excluding things like coverage for Alzheimer's disease) may, in fact, be acting to retard movement in this important direction. Privatized services seeking lucrative market niches, in short, may be hurting the elderly population and their families by undermining the provision of needed public services.

CONSUMERISM AND THE THIRD AGE: A FINAL NOTE

The last few years have witnessed a dramatic and for the most part welcome new accent on the positive aspects of aging. Developmental psychologists have begun to view old age as a period of continued growth and development, with Erikson defining the final stage of life as one in which "a sense of integrity," completeness, and personal wholeness help offset the negative psychological effects of inevitable physical decline (41). Literature and humanistic gerontology similarly have helped further a perception of old age as "a period of unique capacity for wisdom, for understanding the experience of a whole lifetime and (therefore) for service to the young" (38). Yet as Cole has cautioned, "so called 'positive' aspects of aging often turn out to be disguised forms of the effort to restore youth, rather than appreciation of growing or being old as a fundamental dimension of human existence" (38). If the latter, richer view of aging is to be achieved, the "Third Age" must be reconceptualized, that period in life from age fifty to seventy-five which is largely roleless (42) and which, in Fahey's words, "we tend to waste through inertia" (43).

Fisher (36), Pifer (42), and others (1, 44) have argued that this period of life should be marked by an appreciation of people intrinsically, and not merely in terms of their role as consumers. Yet it must also be a time of opportunity for contributing, whether through new job options made possible by retraining or by other, nonemployment-related activities in a world where paid work is but one of many organizing principles and legitimating ethics (1, 36).

Viewed optimistically, business' new attention to elderly people as consumers can contribute to a meaningful old age by providing those goods and services that foster autonomy and contribute to a sense of competence, without setting the elderly population apart in the process (8). By helping to mainstream elderly people, giving them greater visibility and legitimacy through the use of older models, the world of advertising similarly can play a key role in improving both society's perceptions of elderly people and older people's images of themselves (45).

Viewed in a less positive light, however, the targeting of elderly people by business and industry may, as noted earlier, lead to distorted images of the actual financial adequacy of older Americans, redirecting attention away from the still sizable proportion of elderly persons who live in or near poverty. It may rob old age of some of its unique meaning by "channeling" the lives of elderly people primarily into "trivialized leisure and the consumption of professional services" (38). In so doing, it may reinforce some of the less desirable aspects of American culture, key among them a valuing of people in terms of their consumption patterns and the exploiting of fears of aging to sell products.

Finally, the growth of privatized goods and services in need of profitable markets may wittingly or unwittingly undermine support for needed public services.

America is a society heavily dominated by consumerism and a "market justice" view of the world in which obligations to the larger society are de-emphasized whereas individual responsibility is assigned a high premium (46). Such a society provides fertile ground for a business orientation stressing profits over need and reinforcing a vision of human worth that values people not "inherently, in terms of their basic humanity, but contingently, in relationship to the market place" (47).

Business and industry are discovering the elderly market and the new age wave which it represents. In making this discovery, they can play an important role in helping to meet the health and social needs of the elderly population. Yet both they and society must grapple with the serious ethical dilemmas posed by the extensive targeting of the new gray market in a heavily consumerist nation.

REFERENCES

1. Estes, C. L. *The Aging Enterprise*. Jossey-Bass Publishers, San Francisco, 1979.
2. Dolliver, M. Personal communication, June 9, 1988.
3. Powell, L. A., and Williamson, J. B. The mass media and the aged. *Social Policy* Summer: 38–49, 1985.

4. Longman, P. *Born to Pay: The New Politics of Aging in America*. Houghton Mifflin, Boston, 1987.
5. President's Council of Economic Advisors. *Annual Report*. U.S. Government Printing Office, Washington, D.C., 1985.
6. Congressional Budget Office. Trends in Family Income: 1970-1986. U.S. Government Printing Office, Washington, D.C., 1988.
7. Consumer Research Center. *Midlife and Beyond: The $800 Billion Over 50 Market*. The Conference Board, Inc., New York, 1985.
8. American Society on Aging. EASE: Education in Aging for Scientists and Engineers. American Society on Aging, San Francisco, 1987.
9. Travelling seniors broaden insurance horizons. *Mature Market Report* 2: 4, January 1988.
10. U.S. Bureau of the Census. *Current Population Reports, Series P–60*. November 134, from *Statistical Abstracts of the U.S.: 1982–1983*. U.S. Government Printing Office, Washington, D.C., 1982.
11. Pollack, R. F. *On the Other Side of Easy Street*. The Villers Foundation, Washington, D.C., 1987.
12. Binstock, R. H., Perspectives on measuring hardship: Concepts, dimensions and implications, *Gerontologist* 26: 60–62, 1986.
13. Kingston, E., Hirshorn, B. A., and Corman, J. *Ties That Bind: The Interdependence of Generations in an Aging Society*. Seven Locks Press, Cabin John, Maryland, 1986.
14. Minkler, M. 'Generational equity' and the new victim blaming: An emerging public policy issue. *Int. J. Health Ser.* 16: 539–551, 1986.
15. U.S. Bureau of the Census. Money income and poverty status of families and persons in the U.S., 1984. *Consumer Income*, Current Population Reports Series, P–60, No. 149 (Aug): 12. U.S. Government Printing Office,Washington, D.C., 1985.
16. Binstock, R. H. The aged as scapegoat. *Gerontologist* 23: 136–143, 1983.
17. Binstock, R. H. The politics and economics of aging and diversity. In *Aging and Diversity*, edited by S. A. Bass, E. K. Kutza, and F. M. Torres-Gil, pp. 73–99. Scott Foresman and Company, Glenview, Illinios, 1990.
18. Hewitt, P. A. Broken Promise. Americans for Generational Equity, Washington, D.C., 1986.
19. Preston, S. Children and the elderly in the U.S. *Scient. Am.* 251: 44–49, 1984.
20. Hartman, C. Redesigning America, *Inc.*, pp. 58–74, June 1988.
21. Samuelson, R. J. The elderly aren't needy. *Newsweek*, p. 68, March 21, 1988.
22. Tórres-Gil, F. Interest group politics. Presentation at the School of Public Health, University of California at Berkely, March 1988.
23. O'Connor, J. *The Fiscal Crisis of the State*. St. Martin's, New York, 1973.
24. McKnight, J. Professionalized service and disabling help. In *Disabling Professions*, edited by I. Illich, I. K. Zola, J. McKnight, J. Kaplan, and H. Shaiken. Marion Boyars, Inc., London, 1978.
25. Schlesinger, M., Bentkover, J., Blumenthal, D., Musacchio, R., and Willer, J. The privatization of health care and physicians' perceptions of access to hospital services. *Milbank O.* 65: 25–58, 1987.
26. Schlesinger, M. Personal communication, June 22, 1988.

27. Brown, E. R. Medicare and Medicaid: The process, value and limits of health care reforms. In *Readings in the Political Economy of Aging*, edited by M. Minkler, and C. L. Estes, pp. 117-143. Baywood Publishing, Amityville, New York, 1984.

28. Bergthold, L., Estes, C. L., Alford, R. R., and Villaneuva, T. Public light and private dark: The privatization of home health services for the elderly. Paper presented at the American Sociological Association, Chicago, Illinois, August 1987.

29. Estes, C. L. Cost containment and the elderly: Conflict or challenge? *J. Am. Geriat. Soc.* 36: 68–72, 1988.

30. Health Care Financing Administration (HCFA). Health care financing review: 20 years of Medicare and Medicaid. (Annual Supplement). U.S. Government Printing Office, Washington, D.C., 1985.

31. U.S. Congress, Senate Special Committee on Aging. *Developments in Aging: 1984*. U.S. Government Printing Office, Washington, D.C., 1985.

32. Miller, S. M. The political economy of social problems: From the sixties to the seventies. *Soc. Probl.* 24: 131–141, 1976.

33. Galbraith, J. K. *Economics and the Public Purpose*. Mentor Books, New York, 1973.

34. Perry, M. J. The two hats of corporate America. *Connections* Dec/Jan: 5–6, 1987–88.

35. Wang, C. Lear's Magazine 'For the woman who wasn't born yesterday': A critical review. *Gerontologist* 28: 5, 1988.

36. Fisher, D. H. *Growing Old in America*. Oxford University Press, New York, 1978.

37. *Christian Science Monitor* December 11, 1987.

38. Cole, T. The spectre of old age: History, politics and culture in an aging America. *Tikkun* 3: 14–18, 93–95, 1988.

39. Lublin, J. Costly retirement home market booms, raising concern for the aged, *Wall Street J.*, October 22, 1986.

40. U.S. House of Representatives, Select Committee on Aging. *America's Elderly At Risk*, p. 20. U.S. Government Printing Office, Washington, D.C., July 1985.

41. Erikson, E. *Vital Involvement in Old Age*. W. W. Norton and Company, New York, 1986.

42. Pifer, A. The public policy response. In *Our Aging Society*, edited by A. Pifer, and L. Bronte, pp. 391–414. W. W. Norton and Company, New York, 1986.

43. Fahey, C. Aging: It has never been this way before. Presentation to the Annual Meeting of Grantmakers in Aging, Cleveland, Ohio, October 1987.

44. Butler, R. *Why survive? Being old in America*. Harper and Row Publishers, New York, 1975.

45. Swayne, L., and Greco, A. The portrayal of older Americans in television commercials, *J. Advertising* 16: 47–54, 1987.

46. Beauchamp, D. Public health as social justice. *Inquiry* 12: 3–14, 1976.

47. Ovrebo, B. Commodification of care of elders. Paper presented at the Annual Meetings of the American Public Health Association, New Orleans, November 1987.

CHAPTER 7

A LAMB IN WOLF'S CLOTHING? THE REALITY OF SENIOR POWER AND SOCIAL POLICY

Steven P. Wallace, John B. Williamson,
Rita Gaston Lung, and Lawrence A. Powell

The unprecedented growth of the elderly population in the United States has been accompanied by increasing public and political attention to the potential power of senior citizens to shape public policy. The media and some academics have questioned whether the elderly may be *too* powerful for the good of the nation. Others contend that the elderly have limited political power except in relation to a few very specific issues. In this chapter, we assess the evidence with respect to how much political power the elderly have today, concluding that the elderly rarely have a determining voice in public policy. We also ask whether there is likely to be significant change in the political influence of the elderly in response to the graying of the age structure that will be taking place in the years ahead. Plausible arguments can be made on both sides of this issue. However, a split between the affluent and the low-income elderly will substantially diminish any potential increase in the influence of the elderly as a group.

Steven Lukes identifies three dimensions of power that we find useful for our analysis of the political influence of the elderly (1). The first dimension involves the traditional type of power involved in electoral disputes. This *situational* power focuses on visible behavior and decisions concerning issues on which there is observable conflict. This analysis of power looks at who wins the decisions and who influences their outcomes.

The second dimension of power is *institutional*, involving control by elites and organizations over the agenda of issues, determining which issues become topics of public debate. Elites have additional power through their influence over the ways that government bureaucracies implement policies. By shaping the policy process behind the scenes, public decisions on policy can be reshaped to serve private interests.

The third dimension of power is *structural*, focusing on the way in which the structure of the polity and economy favors certain interests without recourse to any conscious decisions, agenda setting, or manipulation of policy implementation. This type of power creates a context in which the normal functioning of the society leads to the willing submission of the general population to the needs of dominant political and economic interests. The operation of the system in this manner can be labelled "hegemonic" in that it is built into the system (2).

The following analysis of senior power examines the evidence that older persons have exercised power in their self-interests using each of these three types of power. The analysis of situational power explores the electoral power of seniors and their ability to influence *decisions* about publicly contested issues. The analysis of institutional power focuses on the power of senior organizations to shape the *agenda* and the policy *process*, and how policymaking elites respond to seniors. The analysis of structural power examines the transformation of the social structure and economy that is occurring as a result of the changing age composition of society, thereby changing the policy *context*.

SITUATIONAL POWER: THE POWER OF THE VOTE

"Normal politics" in the United States revolves around the electoral process. It is expected that citizens will vote for candidates who represent their interests, and that those interests will be embodied in appropriate legislation. Since legislation establishes the framework within which social policies are undertaken, influence exerted through the electoral system most directly affects the major decisions that are made about social policies. The power of the elderly in this context lies in their ability to help elect friendly representatives and prevent the reelection of those who fail to serve the interests of the elderly.

The growing number of older persons and their high voting rate make them a potentially potent voting block. In the 1988 Presidential election, persons aged sixty-five and over provided one-fifth of the votes cast (3). Both registration and voting increases with age, multiplying the effect of the senior vote. In 1988, the registration rate was 50.4 percent for persons aged twenty to twenty-four, 69.3 percent for those aged thirty-five to forty-four, and 81 percent for those aged sixty-five to seventy-four. Only 38 percent of those aged twenty to twenty-four voted in the 1988 Presidential election, compared with 73 percent of those aged sixty-five to seventy-four (3). Voting then declines with more advanced age as a result of failing health.

One indicator of the impact of older voters is the extent to which politicians campaign diligently for "the senior vote." Many senators and representatives have staff members assigned specifically to senior constituents. It is now necessary for politicians to speak out on issues that are particularly sensitive for older persons.

President George Bush campaigned on promises that he would not touch Social Security and in his first state-of-the-union address he vowed not to "mess around with Social Security" (4).

In addition to votes, politicians can benefit from large numbers of volunteers during their campaigns. Older Americans who are retired have the most time of any age group for volunteer activities, including stuffing envelopes, walking precincts, and attending caucuses (5). A large number of seniors do volunteer work on a regular basis. Among persons aged sixty-five to sixty-nine, 28 percent report that they engage in volunteer activities (of all types), while another 13 percent report that they do not volunteer but would like to do so. Even among the oldest group, those aged eighty and over, 12 percent report volunteering and 9 percent report that they would like to volunteer (6). There is no reason to believe, however, that most older volunteers are drawn to campaigns specifically because of the stance of the candidate on aging issues rather than because of more general social and economic policies.

Several studies at the local level in Florida question the power of the senior vote on policy decisions. Since Florida has the highest proportion of senior voters in the United States, the power of the senior vote should be considerable. Yet local studies have found that Florida's officials do *not* generally respond to the preferences they perceive to be the primary concerns of the elderly. Indeed, these studies suggest that the elderly are not organized or active enough to have a direct policy impact, even though they are visibly and actively involved in local politics (7, 8). Case studies from Minnesota, Massachusetts, and California, however, show that when well organized, even elderly nursing home and single room occupancy hotel residents can make a difference in the political process (9–11).

The question remains, then, how significant are the elderly in determining policy outcomes? Do seniors use their situational power, and if so, when? Three events provide an opportunity to examine these questions: the Townsend Movement, Seniors for Kennedy, and the passage and repeal of the Catastrophic Coverage Act in 1988.

The Townsend Movement—Seniors Finding Their Voice

The Townsend Movement of the 1930s provides an early illustration of the impact disgruntled older citizens can have. Named after its founder, Dr. Francis Townsend of Long Beach, California, the movement was committed to legislative enactment of a social security scheme known as the "Townsend Plan." The plan proposed that all American citizens over sixty-five receive $200 per month ($150 in the initial version). The elderly recipients would have been required to spend the pension amount within thirty days (a Keynesian type measure to stimulate economic demand) and refrain from participation in the labor force (to reduce unemployment among younger workers) (12).

At its peak in the mid-1930s, The Townsend Movement attracted over a million supporters nationally. The potential political clout of the organization became clear in 1934 when Townsendites in Long Beach successfully defeated an incumbent congressman they considered insensitive to elderly interests. This victory sent an unmistakable signal to elected officials that older Americans were a political force to be reckoned with.

While Townsend and his supporters were ultimately unable to prevail in securing enactment of their preferred plan, public officials across the nation—including the President—were nevertheless forced to notice the increasing political salience of elderly interests in American politics. Seniors working "outside" mainstream politics had demonstrated to incumbent politicians that they ignored the expanding influence of the organized elderly at their own peril. Although the unprecedented economic hardships and social dislocations of the Depression were the major factors behind the enactment of the Social Security Act, there is little doubt that the pressure brought to bear on lawmakers by the presence of an alternative plan with vocal popular support helped hasten Social Security's passage. From then on, the elderly promised to be a significant force in American politics.

Senior Citizens for Kennedy—Entry into Organized Politics

One crucial domain in which the clout of older Americans expanded dramatically during the 1960s and 1970s was their ability to systematically apply organized pressure on political candidates and office holders. Politicians, parties, and the media found themselves paying closer attention to elderly voters as a constituency during welfare state expansion in the post-World War II era, while aging issues increasingly became the focus of national attention. In the 1960 election, the Democratic party created a campaign organization called "Senior Citizens for Kennedy" (within the broader umbrella organization "Citizens for Kennedy") in order to pull older voters into the Democratic camp. The national campaign headquarters of Senior Citizens for Kennedy undertook a variety of political activities— including support for Kennedy's presidential bid, generating publicity in the media, lobbying for age-related causes, and doing educational work within the party. Since Kennedy's margin of victory in the 1960 election was so narrow, party officials believed that appealing to seniors as a special group had been an effective way of obtaining votes (13). When Kennedy won the election, the groundwork was laid for the eventual creation of Medicare.

This symbolic recognition by the Democratic party in 1960 acknowledged that older voters comprised an electoral force of importance. For the first time, seniors were working "inside" the system as an organized block—an important juncture in the advancement of senior clout and political activism that led in subsequent elections to enlarged efforts by political elites to court older voters.

Catastrophic Health Insurance—Seniors Flex Their Muscle

Insurance to protect against catastrophic illness has long been discussed by lawmakers as a possible expansion of Medicare. In 1988, both the White House and the Congress agreed on and passed new medical benefits for the elderly to provide a ceiling on hospital and doctor bills, expand payments for nursing home care, and grant new coverage for prescription drugs. The costs of these new benefits were to have been borne entirely by the elderly in the form of an extra monthly Medicare premium for all recipients, and a surtax for individuals over age sixty-five with incomes above $25,000 a year (14). Politicians failed to take into account the lack of grassroots support for these acute care benefits (15). The primary concern of the elderly was more in protection from the costs of long-term nursing home care. In addition, as discussed in Chapters 12 and 20 of this volume, strong resistance existed against the new tax, especially among the more affluent elderly who were most likely to already have similar benefits from their retirement plans or be paying for private supplemental coverage (16).

The first signs of revolt by seniors came at town meetings in California and Florida and in retirement communities in the Southwest. Discontent was fanned by the National Committee to Preserve Social Security and Medicare, led by the grandson of Franklin Roosevelt. The "Roosevelt group" sent fliers to the elderly urging them to enlist in the campaign to "Repeal the Seniors-Only Income Tax Increase." By soliciting $10 memberships during the repeal campaign, the organization helped boost its membership to five million and its budget to $48 million. Largely as a consequence of their effective organizing, 6,000 members resigned from the AARP to protest AARP support of the legislation (17).

Angry letters and phone calls poured into Congress. By late summer of 1989, legislators who had said the law would never be reversed were starting to change their minds. By Thanksgiving, Congress had repealed the law. As an AARP bulletin notes, "it will be remembered as a law that generated more opposition than support from the people it was supposed to help" (18). Such analyses, however, fail to mention that those who would have been helped the *most* by the legislation—the low-income elderly—were not heard from on either side of the issue.

The examples of the Townsend Movement, the founding of Seniors for Kennedy, and the repeal of catastrophic health insurance each illustrate that the elderly *can* be an important force in shaping the national policy agenda. In each of these cases, the elderly exerted their influence through the political process. The issues involved were ones that affected the aged directly—Social Security and health care—though all elderly were not affected equally.

Perhaps most important in each of the issues examined, the voice of the elderly was channeled to policymakers via effective organizations. The Townsend movement was organized around a charismatic leader, Seniors for Kennedy had organizational support from the Democratic party, and the catastrophic repeal movement was organizationally supported by the National Committee to Preserve Social Security and Medicare. Local studies noted above (7–11) show the same general trend—the elderly were most powerful when their opinions were channeled into a cohesive message by professional organizers. The situational power of the elderly comes from their potential as a group to become active in the legislative process. The importance of organizations in generating actual activity leads us to a consideration of the second type of power.

INSTITUTIONAL POWER—POWER ELITES AND ORGANIZATIONS

From an institutional perspective, the electoral activity of the aged is less important than the power of senior organizations and the (often countervailing) power of nonsenior organizations and elites. This type of power can be particularly important in determining how issues are presented on the public agenda and in shaping the ways public policies are implemented. Both of these processes often occur away from public view. An institutional perspective looks at how the organizations involved work primarily for their own *institutional* benefit, "helping the elderly" being as much an ideological legitimation as a goal of the organization (19). In the same way, elites in government and other institutions try to protect their own interests against the demands of the elderly and others. The following section reviews some of the institutional forces that embody as well as limit senior power.

Social Security and Medicare—Symbolic Gesture, Strategy, and Compromise

The passage and implementation of both Social Security in 1935 and Medicare in 1965 demonstrate the importance of political elites in shaping the terms of the debate over policies for the elderly. The institutional base of the elites also provides them with the power to shape the implementation and day-to-day operation of the policies. When a segment of the public is dissatisfied with existing policies and demands that they be reformed, the skillful orchestration of "symbolic gestures," such as passage of token legislation, serves to reassure the public that the situation is being dealt with. The purpose of symbolic action by elites is to provide evidence that something is being done while in fact postponing (sometimes indefinitely) any genuine policy concessions (20, 21). Although the elderly may have been important in keeping social security and health care as top legislative priorities, one must also consider how income security and health care were defined and implemented by elites in ways that conformed to and reinforced the existing system.

In the early 1930s, a combination of pressures by the elderly and other groups on political elites led to old-age security being placed higher and higher on the legislative agenda. In addition to their concern about electoral consequences, policymakers were driven by the need to deflect escalating demands for radical change (22), a desire to rejuvenate industry by increasing purchasing power (23), and the hope of reducing unemployment by removing older workers from the labor force (24). A central concern underlying the introduction of the Social Security Act was therefore that of regime maintenance in the midst of economic crisis and mounting popular discontent (20, 23). Policy elites, led by President Roosevelt, narrowly defined the legislative agenda concerning income security in old age as a pension issue. Social Security passed as a very limited program for wage laborers primarily in industrial occupations, rather than as a universal income guarantee as envisioned by many grass roots supporters (25) (see Chapter 18).

Medicare provides another example of the power of policy elites to dominate the legislative agenda and shape the outcome of programs for the elderly. A special health care program for the elderly was first discussed as a part of the initial Social Security bill in the 1930s. But fear that opposition from the powerful American Medical Association might imperil the passage of the larger Social Security bill led President Roosevelt to prevent medical care from being part of the bill when it was introduced (26).

Concern with the medical costs of the elderly brought the issue of medical insurance to the forefront of policy consideration again during the late 1950s and early 1960s. Hospital costs were rising, and many of the elderly were unable to meet them. These concerns were managed by elites so that the policy debate centered on reimbursement for medical care, rather than on reforming the medical care system.

The Medicare bill that was passed to address cost concerns was the result of elite strategy and compromise. The Democrats had offered a bill that would only have covered hospital bills and would have been financed by a new social security tax. The American Medical Association supported a Republican alternative that would have covered only physician bills and been financed in part by premiums, like traditional health insurance. The resulting Congressional compromise incorporated the Democratic bill as Part A (hospital insurance) and the Republican bill as Part B (physician insurance) of Medicare (27).

The new program was then implemented according to the needs of the hospital industry and doctors' interests by buying into the existing system. Hospitals and physicians were paid whatever their usual charges were, with limited oversight. The support of the insurance industry was guaranteed by having Medicare contract all claims processing to existing insurance companies (28). While the elderly benefited from the increased ability to afford hospital and physician care, the medical establishment and the insurance industry benefited just as much or more. Hospital and nursing home construction blossomed as a result of the new program, while doctor's charges escalated (26).

The medical example demonstrates how the involvement of senior citizens in the political process can be deflected and used for ends different from those advocated by the elderly. While the establishment of Social Security and Medicare were major accomplishments, policy elites defined the agenda and implemented plans that fell far short of the demands of the most vocal advocates. In part, this process can be explained by the fact that the elderly advocates were "outside" the political system, especially during the 1930s. Recent developments in the politics of aging have created permanent institutional forms that help the elderly wield increased institutional power.

Institutionalizing Senior Power—The Organizations for the Elderly

Following the "quiescent period" of the 1950s, the senior movement managed to build a well-coordinated, broad-based organizational network for social change, characterized by a sophisticated division of labor and a formidable membership base. These resources are used to launch periodic entries into the political process in the form of lobbying and electoral pressures on policymakers. New commissions, legislative committees, and government agencies representing the interests of the elderly were created and some of the senior movement's proposed programs of reform were officially adopted.

The mid-1960s and early 1970s saw several significant developments (29). These included: 1) the development of a coordinated national network of senior advocacy organizations that enabled the elderly to apply continuous electoral and lobbying pressures on lawmakers; 2) the initiation of regular White House Conferences on Aging to periodically air elderly grievances and consider proposals for reform; 3) the creation of a permanent bureaucratic structure, the Administration on Aging, within the executive branch of the Federal government to represent ongoing elderly interests; and 4) the emergence of a nationwide cadre of professionals in a variety of aging-related fields with a vested interest in promoting programs and services for older Americans—a development that Estes has dubbed "the aging enterprise" (19).

Much of the important old-age legislation of the 1960s was probably due less to periodic electoral threats *per se* than to sustained organizational pressures on lawmakers. It was, for example, in the period between elections that two major legislative landmarks of the Great Society—Medicare (1965) and the Older Americans Act (1965)—became law. These reform packages went into effect not during an election year, but some time afterwards. A major force behind the eventual passage of the Medicare proposal was unrelenting pressure from a cohesive national network of labor organizations and elderly interest organizations (29). Without these ongoing senior advocacy organizations to help keep up the pressure on policymaking elites, sporadic electoral threats would have produced few lasting results.

The component groups in the aging network were able to exert pressure on lawmakers because of their organizational cohesiveness and their claim to represent millions of older Americans. In contrast, Depression-era senior movements lacked the organizational stability and institutional contacts that have helped move legislation since the 1960s. The legislative victories of the 1960s— Medicare and the Older Americans Act, as well as the Social Security amendments and cost-of-living increases of the 1970s—were shaped by the intense lobbying efforts of the powerful new "gray lobby" on Capitol Hill (30).

The senior lobby has become increasingly visible in the legislative process. In 1970, the American Association of Retired Persons (AARP), the National Council of Senior Citizens (NCSC), and the Gray Panthers appeared in Congress twenty-one times. By 1980, this number had risen to seventy-five appearances, and in 1989 these groups testified regarding aging issues ninety-seven times (31). Assessing the effectiveness of the senior lobby, one Washington observer commented that "(to) find lobbying skills equal to those of organizations that represent the elderly, you have to go to someone with a gun" (i.e., defense contractors or the National Rifle Association) (32).

The American Association of Retired Persons (AARP) was by far the largest organization to emerge within the post-war senior alliance, with 28 million members, 3600 local chapters, and a staff of 1200 (33). As a national club, it is second in size only to the American Automobile Association (33).

The parent organization, the National Retired Teachers Association (NRTA), was founded in 1947. In 1955 Dr. Ethel Percy Andrus joined forces with New York insurance agent Leonard Davis in order to offer group life insurance to NRTA members. The life insurance was so popular that AARP was founded in 1958 as a way of offering the insurance to retired persons who were not former teachers. The combined organization was known as NRTA-AARP until 1982 when the NRTA became a subdivision of the more general AARP (34). AARP's organizational reason for being, therefore, was to function as a sales vehicle for commercial products aimed at senior citizens. This aspect of the organization is still visible today in the revenues generated by advertising in the organization's monthly magazine (35), and in the organization's continued sponsorship of a variety of commercial products.

The initial attractions of the organization to elderly persons are essentially nonpolitical. Membership does not require a great deal of money or effort. In addition to life and health insurance plans, membership benefits include a monthly magazine—*Modern Maturity*—newsletters, travel benefits, tax counseling, education and training services, prescriptions, auto club and driver re-education. All this for just $5.00 (36), in part because many of the benefits are a part of money-making ventures.

Phenomenal popularity rapidly made AARP one of the largest voluntary organizations represented on Capitol Hill. In recent years, its activities have become increasingly political in emphasis, focusing on opposition to compulsory retirement and efforts to improve pensions and Social Security benefits. With professional rather than labor-based roots, AARP has primarily identified with the issues of concern to white-collar, middle-class, professional-status retirees. In contrast to the more ideologically liberal National Council of Senior Citizens and the radical Gray Panthers, AARP has generally taken nonpartisan stances in national electoral politics. AARP maintained some informal ties with the Republican party, particularly in its early years, but the leadership has generally avoided any implication of close partisan identification. One reason for the neutral stance has been to avoid jeopardizing the organization's tax-free nonpartisan status with the Internal Revenue Service. This nonpartisan approach also helps to retain its membership, which includes large numbers of both Democrats and Republicans. Were it to be viewed as partial to one or the other of these parties, independent of their stands on aging issues, the risk to the size of its membership would be substantial. Finally, maintaining a noncommittal strategy forces both major parties to compete for its favor (37).

Owing primarily to its colossal membership and revenue base, AARP is able to maintain a sophisticated full-time lobbying contingent in Washington. Lobbying groups have also been formed in all fifty states, and AARP has sought to construct a political organization in every congressional district in the United States (37). The organization makes use of its publication, *Modern Maturity*, to notify its membership of important issues. In the case of the Medicare Catastrophic Coverage Act of 1988, the AARP issued several "special reports" and "bulletins" to familiarize the public with the ramifications of the complicated legislation. Such bulletins had generated heavy mail from older constituents to congressional representatives on earlier issues (5). While the organization *reflects* the general interests of the membership, the organization tries to *shape* the opinions of the membership on specific issues. In this way, the organization *per se* is as important as its individual senior members.

The National Council of Senior Citizens (NCSC)—is the second-largest mass-membership group with 4.5 million members and a staff of 120 (33). Although officially nonpartisan, it has generally made its political affinities rather obvious. The NCSC developed out of the Seniors for Kennedy clubs in the 1960 presidential campaign and the early 1960s struggle to pass Medicare legislation. Due to strong initial ties with labor unions, the NCSC has generally been more working-class than professional in orientation and has been (unofficially) pro-Democratic party in electoral politics. The organizational strength of NCSC tends to be concentrated in the unionized heavy industrial states (38). In the early days of the organization, funds were derived largely from labor unions, with Walter Reuther and the United Auto Workers providing organizing assistance (37). More recently, NCSC has also copied the AARP's financially successful marketing of insurance and other products as a way of raising funds for the organization.

Whereas AARP has placed policy emphasis on the issue of eliminating mandatory retirement barriers to elderly professionals, the NCSC has focused on issues of primary interest to low-income retirees, such as protection of Social Security benefits and national health insurance. Effective grassroots lobbying efforts by the NCSC were credited by some as having been critical to the passage of Medicare in the 1960s and to the securing of the 1972 Social Security amendments (29).

The Gray Panthers—is small in comparison to AARP and NCSC, with 50,000 members in 100 local groups and a national staff of six (33, 36). Despite its small size, however, it has probably been the most effective group in raising the nation's consciousness about ageism and the problems of the elderly. From its beginning in 1972, the philosophical scope of the organization has been broad-based, encompassing a variety of interrelated societal concerns and calling for a bold anti-ageist coalition of young and old persons.

In contrast to interest groups like AARP and NCSC, the Gray Panthers have consistently made a point of defining themselves in direct opposition to the political and economic status quo, consciously differentiating themselves from "establishment aging organizations" (34). Initially, the organization shunned such standard practices as dues and formal membership cards, but financial and organizational realities have led to more systematic practices. An organized national network of local groups is now linked by a steering committee, and the Panthers publish a national newsletter called *The Gray Panther Network*.

The charismatic personality of Maggie Kuhn has been responsible for most of the publicity accorded the Panthers over the years. Her primary tactic, and that of the Gray Panthers, has been one of local militant action involving grassroots organizing in support of selected social causes. Given their aversion to hierarchical organization as a matter of principle, the Gray Panthers have not been a consistent, organized Washington lobby group as have AARP and NCSC. The Panthers' accomplishments have generally been sporadic and local in nature, although typically highly publicized. In a sense, their political activities are qualitatively different in that they involve attempts at consciousness-raising through publicized symbolic actions rather than the usual mainstream lobbying tactics practiced by establishment aging organizations (29). It is unclear whether the Gray Panthers will be able to replace the charismatic leadership of Kuhn and retain their visibility in the future.

The Policy Impact of Senior Organizations

There are numerous senior advocacy groups that deal with seniors as consumers, subjects of research, or clients. Many have affiliation with labor groups or are comprised of professionals involved in gerontology. Because of their substantial numbers and broad base, these groups have come to participate in most formal and informal policy processes involving the elderly.

These groups have access to public officials by virtue of lobbies maintained in Washington. This ongoing contact allows representatives of senior groups to have input into policies *before* the issue emerges for public debate (13), and allows the organizations to monitor and advocate for seniors during the process of implementing new programs. What is critical, and unknown, is how important the input of organizations for seniors is when other institutions (e.g., organized medicine and the federal bureaucracy) have opposing interests. This insider power can be more effective than grassroots mobilization because popular mobilization is difficult to maintain over long periods of time and often occurs only after policy elites have defined the parameters of the debate. The large senior organizations have the advantage that they are able to obtain public platforms in the national media even without a public outcry because the organizations claim to represent a large legitimate interest group.

Aging organizations rarely employ the tactics of more militant and radical organizations. Like other bureaucratized groups (39), they are disposed against riots, rent strikes, sit-ins, boycotts, or other disruptive forms of social protest (40). This limits the options available for senior organizations to use to bring pressure on policymakers. On the other hand, their use of more mainstream approaches contributes to the legitimacy of senior protest in the eyes of a public that is also wary of aggressive forms of social protest. As a result, the most effective power of senior organizations today seems to be in their potential for making trouble when cost-conscious lawmakers attempt to cut old-age benefits. Pratt notes that the power of the aging groups seems to be at its zenith when attempting to veto change (34).

When direct income transfers such as Social Security, veterans benefits, or Medicare are involved the aging organizations are able to join together and mobilize their memberships in a unified manner to address the immediate economic concerns of the middle-class and to achieve a common goal (41). They often work with trade associations on these issues, especially the health care organizations with vested interests in the way in which income transfers affect their organizations. The efforts in the area of direct income transfer have resulted in obtaining incremental adjustments in existing programs, such as Social Security cost-of-living adjustments (42).

Contemporary aging organizations have not put forth proposals that would result in programs for redistributing purchasing power to the aged (as Townsend's depression-era plan would have done). While the organizations are generally supportive of policies that would benefit primarily low-income seniors, few expend the same organizational resources on those issues as they do on more middle-class issues. Senior organizations, for example, were supportive of the liberalization and federalization of state welfare programs for the elderly into the new Supplemental Security Income (SSI) program in 1972 [in part because it was included in a package that included a 20 percent increase in the Social Security benefits of all retirees (43)]. On the other hand, the fact that only about 50 percent of eligible poor elderly obtain SSI (44) has not been a major focus of lobbying by senior organizations. Rather than use its political muscle to try and change the SSI program to improve coverage, AARP has established several local programs to provide outreach activities in order to increase the number of SSI recipients (44). While laudable, this low intensity-effort will not change the elements of the program that have led to many poor elderly being left out.

When policies or programs involve funding for training, research, program development, or other social, health, or recreational services such as the Older Americans Act or the National Institutes of Health, the senior advocacy organizations are also less united. The battle shifts between the issues of which organization should be receiving funds and how much each organization should get (45). In other words, when the immediate interests of the elderly are not at stake, senior organizations tend to pursue policies that most benefit the *organization*. These aging organizations have sufficient numbers, wealth, leadership, and legitimacy to continue to exist and pursue their goals but are not likely to correct the economic, social, or medical problems of the disadvantaged elderly. With primarily middle-class memberships, it would be uncharacteristic of them to stray far from the concerns of the middle-class elderly.

STRUCTURAL POWER—THE POWER OF DEMOGRAPHICS AND SOCIETAL STRUCTURE

Structural power is the most complex power concept to understand. When the elderly have structural power, the *normal* operation of the political and economic systems automatically takes their interests into account. Nobody asks if those interests are legitimate because they are assumed to be.

One basis for the structural power of the elderly is their numbers. The relatively small proportion of the elderly in comparison to younger persons in the population may be one contributing factor to the overall lack, during the late 1940s, of the kind of sustained elderly interest group involvement that had fueled the pension reform struggles of the 1920s and 1930s. Pratt calls this quiet period of the senior movement the "dismal years." The primary reason for the pension reform movement's loss of prominence after 1935 was society's successful co-opting of the former's reform agenda. Also important, however, was the change in the composition of the population during the 1940s and 1950s. Because fertility rates affect the age composition of the population, when the birth rate rises the proportion of older Americans falls. Historian David Hackett Fisher has suggested that "it is no accident" that the dismal years of the senior movement "coincided almost exactly" with the baby boom that occurred between 1942 and 1957 (40).

The end of the baby boom has led to an aging of the society. By the year 2030 it is predicted that there will be *more* U.S. residents aged sixty-five and over than aged eighteen and under (46). This changing demography is providing the elderly with increased power through the normal functioning of the social system. Most noticeable in the 1980s was the "discovery" of the senior market by business (35). One consequence of the growing aggregate purchasing power of the seniors is that business is increasingly tailoring its products to meet the preferences and needs of older persons (47). In the auto industry, for example, engineers are modifying designs to compensate for changes in vision, making handles and knobs easy for those with arthritis to handle, and are strengthening door panels to better protect older drivers during accidents. New products are also being marketed that can enhance the quality of life for some seniors with chronic problems, such as adult undergarments that allow incontinent elders to go out in public without worry. No group of elderly had to lobby for these changes. They were initiated as a normal outcome of economic incentives.

Not all of the systemic economic incentives work to the advantage of seniors, however. Businesses are interested in selling products to seniors whether a real need for the product exists or not. Further, elders without sufficient means to purchase the redesigned goods and services are left out (35). Thus, while the demographic shift is working to redesign and innovate many goods and services for the elderly as a group, low-income elderly are least likely to benefit (see also Chapter 6).

The political system is also affected by the changing demographics. Pampel and Williamson found that the size of the aged population is the strongest determinant of welfare spending over time in a sample of eighteen nations (including the United States) (48). As might be expected, the size of the elderly population is of particular importance in allocations for programs that benefit the elderly, such as pensions and medical care (49). This holds true regardless of the class forces and governmental factors present in the different countries considered. Although most of the empirical research relating age structure to public policy focuses on Western nations, particularly the industrial nations, there is every reason to believe that the trend is similar in Eastern European nations as well.

The presence of a sizeable subgroup such as the elderly within a society will naturally shape the society in many ways. Consequently, despite continuing discussion in the mass media of a backlash against the numerous and demanding aged (see Chapter 5), their numbers alone will give the elderly considerable power in the basic operation of the society. A declining proportion of young workers will make older workers more critical, just as the growing number of older consumers is becoming an important market. This increasing structural power will give the elderly the potential to exercise direct power over public policies *if* the aged are able to develop a consciousness and organizational capacity to act as a group. The elderly could exert strong power over public decisions not only by voting, but also be engaging in consumer boycotts, striking at paid and unpaid jobs, withdrawing savings or investments from offending financial institutions, or refusing to pay bills for medical care. All of these actions involve limited physical activity (in contrast to civil rights marches, for example) but build on the structural power of the aged.

WHO IS NOT REPRESENTED BY SENIOR POWER?

The media typically portray the power of the elderly as benefiting all of the elderly equally. In reality, however, most of the power lies with the members of the elderly population who vote, belong to organizations, and have economic resources. Political activity is usually low among the poor elderly (6), as are other forms of social protest among the poor of all ages (39). This means that the situational power of the elderly rests largely with the middle class.

Similarly, the poor are less likely than the middle class to be involved as members of organizations, and the poor are even less likely to lead such organizations (50). Senior activists tend to come from the middle class and focus on issues of greatest concern to themselves, such as Social Security rather than Supplemental Security Income, and Medicare as opposed to Medicaid. To the extent that institutional power is used for the interests of organizational members and the organizations themselves, low-income elderly will typically be marginally represented by this source of power as well. As a result, policies that are most beneficial to the elderly poor generate the least institutional activity.

Finally, much of the systemic power of the elderly is related to their economic clout in the labor force and the marketplace. Low-income elderly are in the least advantaged position in both the labor force and the marketplace because of their more irregular and less skilled occupational experience and their lower purchasing power. While some industries (such as fast foods) are already starting to depend on the elderly as a source of low-waged labor, it is easier to replace an unskilled labor force (with immigrants, for example) than it is to replace a highly trained labor force. Thus, the structural power of the low-income elderly is significantly less than that of middle- and upper-income elderly who command more skills and money. This suggests that the interests and power of the low-income elderly would be maximized by forming coalitions with other low-income and minority groups (51), rather than be depending on the use of a generalized senior power.

CRYSTAL-BALL GAZING—THE POTENTIAL FOR THE FUTURE

This review of the power of older persons over social policy in the twentieth century provides mixed findings. There are many examples of specific issues in regard to which seniors have demonstrated some influence over public policies, but there is no enduring pattern of power comparable to either the power of business over a broad range of issues, nor of labor, the new right, or other groups with more focused policy agendas. Only when proposed policy changes affect a large proportion of the middle-class elderly has it been possible to mobilize the elderly to affect legislation (as with proposed Social Security cuts and catastrophic insurance premiums). The resulting activism, moreover, has been the result of common economic interests rather than common identity as senior citizens.

Although public attention usually focuses on the situational power of the elderly voter, their institutional and structural powers are potentially stronger. The organizational network of senior groups provides a durable system for monitoring and shaping the implementation of public policies, although the network has been most successful at blocking rather than innovating policies. The growing structural power potential of the elderly is just now being felt in the marketplace and political system. In spite of all of the public attention currently given to the power of seniors over public policy, however, the much publicized menace of seniors dominating public policy is no more dangerous than a lamb in wolf's clothing.

The question remains, how powerful will seniors be in the future as their numbers continue to grow? In the future, the elderly will be healthier and better educated, which should contribute to a higher voter turnout (6), especially among those aged sixty-five to eighty-five who already have high voting rates. Volunteering also increases with rising education and income. Among those aged sixty-five and over, the wealthiest group (1981 income of $20,000 and over) volunteered at three times the rate of the poorest group (under $5000). College graduates volunteered three times more often than those with less than a high school education (6). These facts suggest that the potential situational power via the electoral process will rise. The increasing numbers and wealth of the elderly will also increase the potential membership and resource bases for senior organizations.

If seniors continue to be active primarily on economic and other issues that do not rely on an explicit "aged" identity, the future potential of senior power could be fragmented by the increasing wealth of a segment of the older population. The financially secure elderly are more likely to be concerned with issues like keeping private pensions solvent through government insurance and providing universal long-term care benefits. The low-income elderly are more likely to be concerned with government efforts to provide low-income housing, income maintenance (e.g., SSI), and accessibility to medical care. If affluent older Americans split with the low-income elderly over policy issues in the future, the influence of the elderly *as a group* could be significantly neutralized, as happened in the case of catastrophic health insurance. It is possible that we will look back on the reversal of that legislation not so much as an example of the strength of the elderly, but as an example of the emerging strength of the *affluent* elderly, which eventually undercut the influence of the elderly as a whole.

The growth of organizations of the elderly, gerontologists, and others who serve the elderly may provide increased power in the future, but it is most likely to be a conservative power that blocks cutbacks and furthers the specialized interests of the groups. Groups representing aging services, such as congregate meals, for example, would not be expected to be active in advocating for food stamps or SSI payments, even though the latter measures might have the greatest impact on nutrition for poor elders. This type of narrow institutional interest is not unique to aging organizations, so representatives of the "aging enterprise" should not be expected to advocate for the general good of the elderly in the future (19, 45). Aging organizations can be expected to maximize membership by capturing issues that are broadly popular among many elderly persons, such as keeping Social Security solvent. If a variety of large membership organizations channel the opinions of seniors to policymakers, a few specific programs such as Social Security may be protected by senior power for the foreseeable future.

The structural power of the elderly will be most apparent in the mid-twenty-first century when the median age of the population is projected to approach fifty years, and well over 20 percent of the population will be age sixty-five or over. Simply funding basic programs for the aged, such as Social Security and Medicare, will challenge the way the programs are currently operated as the number of elderly doubles in the next forty years (46).

When combined with the rising costs of medical care overall, for example, the growing presence of the elderly population may force a reorganization of the American medical care system. Structural pressures on the medical care system are not a result of any "organized" activity of the elderly, but may instead be caused by the inability of the system to provide the promised type and scope of services within the context of an aging population (52). Similarly, the pressures on the Social Security system, combined with a shortage of young workers, may lead to a redefinition of retirement from one based on age to one based on functional ability. Such a change would be a systemic response to the need for increased labor force participation by the elderly. Late retirement would be a reversal of the early twentieth century trend when retirement began as a response to reduced demand for the labor of the elderly in the changing industrial capitalist system (24). A changing concept of retirement could, in turn, lead to a redefinition of "old age" itself.

Within a strong capitalist system, the power of the wealthy and big business will continue to take precedence over the power of the elderly. Most importantly, improvements in the lives of the aged will likely continue to affect classes differently. For example, elders with secure pensions and investments increasingly have the choice of retiring early or working indefinitely. At the same time, low-income workers may be increasingly compelled to continue work through late life because of financial need or to retire early against their will because of ill health. Consequently, the interests of the aged as a group will continue to be subordinated to class interests and "senior power" will play a secondary role in shaping public policy.

REFERENCES

1. Lukes, S. *Power: A Radical View*. Macmillan, New York, 1974.
2. Alford, R. R., Friedland, R. *Powers of Theory*. Cambridge University Press, New York, 1985.

3. U.S. Bureau of the Census, *Voting and Registration in the Election of November 1980*, Current population reports, P-20, #444. U.S. Government Printing Office, Washington D.C., 1980.

4. *Congressional Quarterly* 48: 349, Feb. 3, 1990.

5. Peirce, N. R., Choharis, P. C. The elderly as a political force—26 million strong and well-organized. *Nat. J.* 14: 1559–1562, 1982.

6. Schick, F. L. (ed.). *Statistical Handbook on Aging Americans*, p. 87. Oryx Press, Phoenix, Arizona, 1986.

7. Rosenbaum, W. A., Button, J. W. Is there a gray peril?: Retirement politics in Florida. *The Gerontologist* 29: 300–306, 1989.

8. Franke, J. L. Citizen input and aging policy. *Res. on Aging.* 7: 517–533, 1985.

9. Meyer, M. H. Political organization of the frail elderly. In *Growing Old in America*, 4th edition, edited by B. B. Hess, Transaction, New Brunswick, New Jersey, 1990.

10. Kautzer, K. Empowering nursing home residents: A case study of 'Living is for the elderly,' an activist nursing home organization. In *Qualitative Gerontology*, edited by S. Reinharz and G. Rowles, pp. 163–183. Springer Publishing Co., New York, 1987.

11. Minkler, M. Community organizing among the elderly poor in the U.S.: A Case Study. *Int. J. Health Serv.* (in press).

12. Holtzman, A. *The Townsend Movement*. Bookman Associates, New York, 1963.

13. Pratt, H. J. *The Gray Lobby: Politics of Old Age*. University of Chicago Press, Chicago, 1976.

14. Christensen, S., Kasten, R. Covering catastrophic expenses under Medicare. *Health Aff.* 7: 79–93, 1988.

15. Binstock, R. H. The "catastrophic" catastrophe: Elitist politics, poor strategy. *The Aging Connection* 11(1): 9, 1990.

16. U.S. General Accounting Office. *Medicare: Comparison of catastrophic health insurance proposals*. U.S. Government Printing Office, Washington, D.C., 1987.

17. Tolchin, M. How the new Medicare law fell on hard times in a hurry. *New York Times*. pp. 1, A10, October 9, 1989.

18. Coleman, B. Looking back. *AARP Bulletin* 30: 11, Dec. 1989.

19. Estes, C. L. *The Aging Enterprise*. Jossey-Bass, San Francisco, 1979.

20. Amenta, Skocpol, T. Redefining the New Deal: World War II and the development of social provision in the United States. In *The Politics of Social Policy in the United States*, pp. 81–122. Edited by M. Weir, A. S. Orloff, T. Skocpol, Princeton University Press, Princeton, New Jersey, 1988.

21. Lipsky, M., Olson, D. J. *Commission Politics*. Transaction Press, New Brunswick, New Jersey, 1977.

22. Olsen, L. K. *The Political Economy of Aging*. Columbia University Press, New York, 1982.

23. Piven, F. F., and Cloward, R. A. *Regulating the Poor*. Vintage Books, New York, 1972.

24. Graebner, W. *The History of Retirement*. Yale University Press, New Haven, Connecticut, 1980.

25. Quadagno, J. S. *The Transformation of Old Age Security*. University of Chicago Press, Chicago, 1988.

26. Starr, P. *The Social Transformation of American Medicine*. Basic Books, New York, 1982.

27. Marmor, T. R. *The Politics of Medicare*. Aldine, Chicago, 1973.

28. Feder, J. M. *Medicare: The Politics of Federal Hospital Insurance*. Lexington Books, Lexington, Massachusetts, 1977.

29. Williamson, J. B., Evans, L., and Powell, L. A. *The Politics of Aging*. Charles C Thomas Publishers, Springfield, Illinois, 1982.

30. Sundquist, J. L. *Politics and Policy: The Eisenhower, Kennedy and Johnson Years*. The Brookings Institution, Washington, D.C., 1968.

31. *Congressional Information Service Annual*, 1970-. Congressional Information Service, Washington, D.C., various years.

32. Fisher, D. H. The Politics of Aging: A short history. *J. Inst. Socio. econ. Stud.*. 4: 55–66, 1979.

33. Burek, D. M., Koek, K. E., and Novallo, A. *Encyclopedia of Associations-1990*, 24th edition, Gale Research, Inc., Detroit, 1989.

34. Pratt, H. J. National interest groups among the elderly: Consolidation and constraint. *Aging and Public Policy*, edited by W. Browne and L. Olson. Greenwood Press, Westport, Connecticut, 1983.

35. Minkler, M. Gray in gold: Reflections on business' discovery of the elderly market. *The Gerontologist* 29: 17–23, 1989.

36. Knoke, D. Incentives in collective action organizations. *Am. Soc. Rev.* 53: 311–329, 1988.

37. Binstock, R. H. The aging as a political force: Images and resources. In *Aging: A Challenge to Science and Social Policy*. Vol. 2, Medicine and Social Science, edited by A. J. J. Gilmore, et. al.. Oxford University Press, London, 1981.

38. Lammers, W. *The Politics of Aging*. CQ Press, Washington, D.C., 1983.

39. Piven, F. F., and Cloward, R. A. *Poor People's Movements: Why They Succeed, How They Fail*. Pantheon Books, New York, 1977.

40. Fisher, D. H. *Growing Old in America*. Oxford University Press, New York, 1978.

41. Binstock, R. H. Interest group liberalism and the politics of aging. *The Gerontologist*, 12: 265–280, 1972.

42. Binstock, R. H. Aging and the future of American politics. *Ann. Am. Ac. Pol. Soc. Sci.* 415: 199–212, 1974.

43. Burke, V. J., and Burke, V. *Nixon's Good Deed: Welfare Reform*. Columbia University Press, New York, 1974.

44. U.S. Senate, Special Committee on Aging. *Developments in Aging: 1988. Vol 1*, pp. 121–122. U.S. Government Printing Office, Washington, D.C., 1989.

45. Williamson, J. B., Shindul, J. A., and Evans, L. *Aging and Public Policy: Social Control or Social Justice?* Charles C Thomas Publishers, Springfield, Illinois, 1985.

46. U.S. Senate, Special Committee on Aging. *Aging America: Trends and Projections*. U.S. Government Printing Office, Washington, D.C., 1989.

47. Hartman, C., Redesigning America. *Inc.* June: 58–74, 1988.

48. Pampel, F. C., and Williamson, J. B. Welfare spending in advanced industrial democracies, 1950–1980. *Am. J. Soc.* 93: 1424–56, 1988.

49. Pampel, F. C., and Williamson, J. B. *Age, Class, Politics and the Welfare State*. Cambridge University Press, New York, 1989.

50. Olsen, M. E. Social and political participation of blacks. *Am. Soc. Rev.* 35: 682–697, 1970.
51. Piven, F. F., and Cloward, R. A. *The New Class War: Reagan's Attack on the Welfare State and Its Consequences.* Pantheon Books, New York, 1982.
52. Wallace, S. P., and Estes, C. L. Health policy for the elderly. *Society* 26: 66–75, 1989.

PART III. APOCALYPTIC DEMOGRAPHY AND THE BIOMEDICALIZATION OF AGING

The social construction of aging as a medical problem has profoundly influenced not only the nature of our therapeutic interventions for the elderly, but the very way we define and approach the process of growing old. By equating old age with sickness and pathology, we effectively disempower the old, increasing their dependency and facilitating their social control through medical definition, management, and treatment.

This section begins with Estes and Binney's examination of the "biomedicalization of aging," in terms of both the construction of aging as a form of pathology or abnormality, and the praxis of aging as a medical problem.

In the scientific arena, this biomedicalization is seen to heavily influence what research gets funded and what doesn't. In the professional arena, it has critically shaped the training afforded clinical personnel, and consequently many of the attitudes held by geriatric practitioners. In policy, the influence of the biomedical paradigm is evident both in the policy process and in the context of multiple and diverse policy arenas. Finally, a significant and overlooked aspect of the biomedicalization of aging involves its influence on public opinion and the manner in which it fosters negative images of aging as a process of decline, disease, and decay.

Estes and Binney make a strong case for recognizing and addressing the problems posed by the biomedicalization of aging noting in particular that the continued hegemony of this perspective will prevent us from understanding and confronting the broader complexities of aging both as individuals and as a society.

The biomedicalization paradigm is further examined in Chapter 9, where it is applied specifically to the problem of Alzheimer's disease. While careful to point out the very real health and medical aspects of this tragic social problem, Robertson nevertheless goes on to demonstrate that Alzheimer's disease is not merely a clinical but, equally important, a political and ontological construct as well. The sudden explosion of interest in Alzheimer's disease among policymakers, professionals, the mass media, and the general public indeed is seen as reflecting a political process more than a biomedical one.

Chapter 9 uses the social construct of Alzheimer's disease as a means of exploring a related phenomenon, namely the increasing prevalence of catastrophic projections of the burden to society posed by an aging population. Termed by Robertson, "apocalyptic demography," this "bankruptcy hypothesis of aging" scapegoats the elderly for rising health care costs, feeds into arguments for "generational equity" and further supports proposals for the rationing of health care resources on the basis of age. By contributing to the creation and expansion of a diagnostic category of uncertain boundaries and to the biomedicalization of old age, the politics of Alzheimer's disease indeed represents a classic case study in "apocalyptic demography."

CHAPTER 8

THE BIOMEDICALIZATION OF AGING:
DANGERS AND DILEMMAS

Carroll L. Estes and Elizabeth A. Binney

It can be said that, as a discipline and a "world view," medicine has been one of the most important and powerful forces in the twentieth century. Certainly much has been written about its institutional, scientific, and social influences—criticism as well as praise. This chapter examines the role of the "biomedical model," a paradigmatic perspective which focuses on individual organic pathology, physiological etiologies, and biomedical interventions, in aging and the proposition that the "biomedicalization of aging" is a dynamic, complex and multidimensional process.

We define the "biomedicalization of aging" and then consider some of the theories employed to explain the dominance of the medical profession and the biomedical model of illness and disease. Two dimensions of the biomedicalization phenomenon are examined: the social construction of aging as a medical problem and the praxis of aging as a medical problem. Primary attention is given to praxis, because it has significant consequences for the development of knowledge and the science of aging, the structure of the professions and occupations in the field, the public policy agenda, and the understanding of the lay public concerning aging. The chapter concludes with an examination of what we see as the contemporary crisis facing the biomedical paradigm.

TWO ASPECTS OF THE BIOMEDICALIZATION OF AGING

The biomedicalization of aging has two closely related aspects: 1) the social construction of aging as a medical problem (thinking of aging in terms of a medical problem) and 2) the praxis (or practice) of aging as a medical problem (behaviors and policies growing out of thinking of aging as a medical problem). The praxis has at least four different dimensions related to aging: a) the scientific (or consequences for the overall shaping of the discipline and knowledge base), b) the professional (consequences for the various related professions including status, training, and organization of work), c) the policy arena (impact on public policy formation including research and training), and d) the lay or public perceptions and their consequences. Although we examine each of these dimensions separately, they are inextricably linked to one another. Each dimension cannot and does not stand alone but rather acts in a dialectical relationship with every other, a fact that makes it difficult to isolate cause and effect. Nonetheless, it is precisely this complex set of relations between the social construction of aging as a medical problem and the various dimensions of its practice that makes the biomedicalization of aging such a powerful and pervasive process.

THE SOCIAL CONSTRUCTION OF AGING AS A MEDICAL PROBLEM

The construction of aging as a medical problem focuses on the diseases of the elderly—their etiology, treatment, and management—from the perspective of the practice of medicine as defined by practitioners. This means that the elements of the medical model—with its emphasis on clinical phenomena—take precedence over, and in many cases define the basic biological, social, and behavioral processes and problems of aging. This, in turn, has a number of profound implications for the role of academia and the professions, public policy formation, popular perception, and ultimately the development of scientific knowledge.

Put more generally, the dominance of the biomedical model has not only placed the emphasis on "more sophisticated diagnosis, pursuit of underlying mechanisms, therapeutic intervention or prevention, [and identification of] . . . modifiable biological markers" (1), but also has influenced everything else— other research, policymaking, and the way we come to think about aging and even science as it is defined and evaluated in terms of a biomedical structure of thought. Indeed, the biomedical model has become the "institutionalized thought structure" of the field (2). It is noteworthy that this has occurred despite an increasing array of evidence concerning the importance of social and behavioral factors in explaining health and aging (3, 4).

The equation of old age with illness has encouraged society to think about aging as pathological or abnormal. The "undesirability" of conditions labeled as a sickness or illness also transfer to those who have those conditions, shaping the attitudes of the persons themselves, and those of others toward them (5, 6). Sick role expectations may result in such behaviors as social withdrawal, reduction of activity, increased dependency (7–9), and the loss of effectiveness and personal control (10)—all of which may result in the social control of the elderly through medical definition, management, and treatment (11).

THE PRAXIS OF AGING AS A MEDICAL PROBLEM

Scientific Knowledge Base

A contribution of the sociology of knowledge is the understanding that scientific knowledge is socially produced and reproduced—that knowledge is not inherently unbiased, objective, or politically neutral—as it is often represented. In the case of the biomedical paradigm, this means that the processes of knowledge generation (scientific inquiry, interpretation, and validation) are shaped by (and in fact are themselves) important social, economic and political influences on the larger social order, as distinct from the scientific questions—"puzzles"—that they address. As the knowledge base is constructed and accepted, becoming part of the collective stock of knowledge (12), it then becomes a force of its own with social, political, and economic consequences.

One of the most significant and influential features of the biomedical paradigm is its success in aligning and legitimating itself through its close association with science—a dominant and very powerful mode of thought in Western industrialized societies. As a result, the biomedical paradigm has been highly successful in achieving unquestioning trust and acceptance as our society's basic approach to the definition, study and solution to the multiple problems of everyday life (13, 14).

In aging, the biomedical model has defined old age as a process of basic, inevitable, relatively immutable biological phenomena (3, 15). Historically this has been cast in terms of the relatively inevitable decline, disability, degeneration and death, resulting in an approach called "normal aging" that implies a relatively stable and homogeneous set of biological and psychological processes associated with old age. This approach has fostered research on the isolation, etiology and intervention of these processes, particularly on the cellular level or below.

It has also contributed to a trend toward individualization as one form of reductionism. Methodological individualism (a strategy of theory construction and investigation which seeks to explain any social institution or phenomenon using individuals as the unit of analysis), growing out of an interest in individual diagnosis, disease course, and response can be quite effective on an individual doctor-patient basis. However, it limits the degree to which larger social and environmental factors are considered because the primary focus is on illness as an individual problem with individual cause and individual solutions. For the elderly who are labeled by virtue of their age as diseased and disabled, individualism may contribute to a "blame the victim" mentality as well as to social control through the medical management of their problems (e.g., through drugs or institutionalization) since such decisions are usually made in individual structural situations of vastly unequal power relations between physician and patient.

Likewise, reductionism (a process of reducing phenomena to their smallest units) has many advantages for the deduction, derivation, and the understanding of "fundamental" processes. But its practice too, has the consequence of not only being unable to consider larger social processes, statuses, and interactions, but also further victimizing the individual by considering only part of what makes her/him human. The result is a form of anti-holism that equates an elderly person with his/her disease category (e.g., "the Alzheimer's in room 302"), rather than as a whole, living person.

However, colleagues from the basic biomedical sciences are quick to point out that this emphasis on biology and other basic sciences in biomedicine tends to exist only with reference to what Foucault has called the "clinical gaze" (16). Through the "clinical gaze," problems, phenomena, and people are seen and conceptualized as clinical problems or as relating to clinical issues. With it, the value of basic biological research is recognized but primarily or only for its utility in helping to address medical/clinical problems. This has created a situation in which biology has in some ways become the "new handmaiden" of medicine, losing some of its autonomy as a discipline with its own agenda and priorities. According to a recent past president of the Gerontological Society of America, this has resulted in a defunding of basic biological research relative to biomedical funding, and an emphasis on funding basic research which focuses on the afflictions of old age rather than the basic processes and phenomenology of aging (1).

Our point is that the biomedical model has had major impact on all phases of knowledge development—from the organization of research priorities, the production and reproduction of lay knowledge, the structure of the professions and occupations, and the public policy agenda around aging. A 1988 press release by the Senate Special Committee on Aging bears witness to the power of this trend (17). In a statement entitled "Aging Research: An Investment, Not Expense," Senator John Melcher, Chair of the Senate Committee, decried the lack of a cohesive biomedical research policy and the low levels of federal spending on diseases of the elderly (e.g., Alzheimer's and Parkinson's). The press release focuses on the need for "aging research" described solely from a disease orientation. Hence, biomedical research is equated with aging research, and successful and happy aging are attributed to and contingent upon the continuation of biomedical research. This illustrates the power of the biomedical paradigm both to define the phenomena of aging in biomedical terms and to persuade policymakers that the "solutions" to the aging problem are ones that perpetuate the control by biomedicine. The dominance of the medical model also has a broad effect on the definition of "science" and good scientific practice. This, in turn, has affected the field of aging which has, in the opinion of some, become more "scientific" in its self-representation (18). Whether or not a case can be supported for the increased "scientific" content in aging research, it is certainly true that gerontology has attempted to popularize its image in the academic community through an association with biomedical interests and their popular characterization as "hard" science.

Nevertheless, in an important piece on the history of the development of gerontology, Achenbaum calls into question the legitimacy of gerontology's claim to be a "science" in the established sense of science as a process of systematic model-building and testing. As he states (18, p. 3):

> although we engage in more sophisticated discourse about esoteric theoretical and methodological matters than ever before, in fifty years gerontologists have not yet developed a satisfactory paradigm or established a uniform code of professional standards. Despite the fact that we have grown admirably more "scientific" in our study of aging, gerontology surely has not yet become a science.

In fact, the roots of the construction of old age as a "problem" go back to the late 1930s, to the early days of gerontology, which intersected with major social events of the time and resulted in mass public interest in both academic research and public policy initiatives to help identify and solve the "problem" of aging. However, the lack of academic models to approach complex interdisciplinary topics resulted in academic researchers' falling back on familiar models of "puzzle solving," remaining isolated from other such puzzle solvers (18). According to Achenbaum, a major problem inhibiting the elevation of gerontology to the level of a science is the lack of a generally accepted paradigmatic perspective (and even a concept of what "aging" is) that is generalizable between and across disciplines. This has served to further institutionalize the fragmentation of gerontology and drive researchers back to the disciplinary networks with which they are most familiar.

If it is true that this "Balkanization" of gerontology has resulted in young scholars' attempting to make their mark through research on ever-smaller problems within narrow disciplinary boundaries, it is also true that a vacuum has been created. The space created is one into which biomedicine has entered and flourished, but with its own interests and priorities, selecting from the results of this institutional segmentation to support its own needs and viewpoints.

Professional

The biomedicalization of aging has affected and been affected by the content of professional training; it has shaped an orientation toward medical education—and within that—an orientation to research which deals in biomedical terms with an aging population. As previously discussed, this involves a focus on illness, disease, disability and physiological/psychological decline—states which include some but certainly not all aging individuals. Moreover, the biomedical-clinical orientation is premised on an acute care model of medicine, a model which is in direct conflict with the majority of illnesses and conditions which afflict the elderly (i.e., chronic illness).

The weak status and stature of geriatrics within medicine are reflected in the institutional and professional struggles around whether geriatrics merits the legitimacy of specialty or even subspecialty status. This status of geriatrics within medicine most probably reflects the relatively strong emphasis that geriatrics has given to clinical care and to chronic illness care, as opposed to the more traditional acute care and the approved biomedically driven research careers pursued by the faculty of the elite medical institutions. One result has been that in the realm of medicine, geriatrics suffers from low status and prestige, inhibiting new entry to the field, recruitment of the "best and brightest," and the attraction of research funding and other resources. The lack of professional status of geriatrics within medical schools has also caused geriatric education to be devalued in terms of time and attention, with less than 10 percent of U.S. medical schools reported requiring geriatrics as recently as 1985 (19).

In response to status and recruitment problems within medicine, proponents of geriatric medicine have taken three tactics. They have sought: 1) to increase the biomedical content of medical education and research on aging; 2) to use the professional dominance of the field of medicine to shape and control (whenever possible) public policy concerning all aspects of aging through a fusion of health with aging; and 3) to allow the incorporation of geriatrics into other speciality areas such as internal medicine and family practice, reinforcing the norms and models of scientific thought of other branches of medicine.

Clinical geriatric practice has been pushed further and further away from holistic approaches and those appropriate for chronic disease toward those generated by the micro perspectives of biomedicine.[1] This process has brought pressures for the narrowing of its interdisciplinary focus, for increased specialization (e.g., in a particular disease of the elderly such as Alzheimer's), reliance on high-tech diagnostic procedures, and the adoption of econometric premises and modeling in the care of the elderly. In spite of the relative weakness of geriatric medicine within the larger arena of medicine, it has been extremely successful in insinuating itself into almost exclusive control of the domain of education and training in aging.

A content analysis of the four major study reports appearing on the topic of educational needs for an aging society in the 1980s is illustrative.[2] First is the study on geriatric manpower needs by Robert Kane et al. (1980) which estimates that 900 to 1600 full-time academic medical faculty (1300 basic scientists and 450

---

[1] The American Board of Internal Medicine and the American Board of Family Practice conducted the first joint examination for a certificate of added competence in geriatric medicine in the spring of 1988.

[2] Two are administrative documents prepared by the National Institute on Aging (Report on Education and Training in Geriatrics and Gerontology (21), and Personnel for Health Needs of the Elderly through the Year 2000 (22), and one, a report of a committee convened by the Institute of Medicine (23).

geriatric psychiatrists) are needed, assuming doctors "delegate" moderate responsibility to nurse practitioners, physician assistants, and social workers (20). The second is a report, *Education and Training in Geriatrics and Gerontology* (1984), prepared by the National Institute on Aging (NIA) to develop a clear plan of action to improve and expand training in geriatrics and gerontology (21). This federal report concludes that "Faculty members with special preparation in aging are in very short supply, ranging from 5 to 25 percent of the number required in different fields." However, of the eighty-three pages devoted to the topic, only two pages address the combined category of "biomedical, behavioral and social scientists." Curiously, the section on barriers to developing sufficient numbers of biomedical, behavioral, and social scientists concludes that the barriers are: insufficient incentives to attract young physicians, the large debts of medical and other advanced degree graduates, and the detailed requirements of specialty boards, among others. The report clearly envisions that medicine will play the central role in the biomedical, behavioral and social science work that is needed.

The third report, *Personnel for Health Needs of the Elderly through the Year 2000*, is specifically devoted to the health professions and makes little mention of the social or behavioral sciences except for the need for clinical psychologists (22). The fourth—an Institute of Medicine (IOM) report in 1987, *Academic Geriatrics for the Year 2000*, prepared by eight physicians and biomedical scientists—argues that the growth and excellence of geriatrics depend upon the leadership of a small number of "centers of excellence" which would "emphasize the training of [physician] geriatricians in . . . [an] environment of model teachers, varied basic and clinical research and diverse clinical opportunities" (23, p. 1428). This Institute of Medicine report is astonishing in the omission from its recommendations of any real indication that aging is an interdisciplinary field.

Our conclusion is that the weight of the policy documents now being developed, within both the federal government and the most prestigious private organizations in the United States, uniformly reflects biomedical constructions of the problems of an aging society. Our most respected medical colleagues, many of whom have long espoused aging as an interdisciplinary endeavor, have produced the documentation for our nation's future policy agenda on education and research almost exclusively from the perspective of the biomedical paradigm. It is our prediction that, when the policy environment becomes receptive to new federal and private funding initiatives, the biomedicalization of research and education in aging will reach full maturity.

Policy

The influence of the biomedical paradigm is evident both in the policy process and the content of multiple and diverse public policy arenas, including health policy and research and training policy. As policy is influenced by the institutionalized biomedical thought structure, the characteristics that define the model have also come to define policy priorities.

Health policy—The most visible and vital sign of the power of medicine is imprinted in our nation's health policy. Presently costing more than $70 billion annually, the Medicare program is essentially an acute care program, covering a decreasing share of hospital and physician services for the elderly. The stark fact that Medicare covers less than 45 percent of the health care costs of its beneficiaries points to the major omission of the program—the lack of coverage of long term care, i.e., chronic illness care such as personal care, homemaker services, or even nursing home or home health care (except on a very limited basis).

One of the major compromises of the original Medicare legislation in 1965 was to institute policies that would ensure for physicians that existing patterns of practice and payment for medical care would not be altered; nor would doctors be threatened by the independent judgment of other health professions in the provision of any types of care offered under Medicare such as home health care. Hence, Medicare incorporated "usual, reasonable, and customary" fee-for-service payments for physicians, with permission for doctors to bill patients more than the "reasonable charges" set and reimbursed by Medicare. Further, in virtually every area of Medicare policy since its inception, the ultimate gatekeeping function of the physician has been preserved. As recently as the 1988 Medicare Catastrophic Coverage Act, physicians were the sole health professionals authorized to certify the need for respite care by chronically dependent individuals. Thus, Medicare and other health policies for the elderly (e.g., Medicaid), from their origins to the present day, reflect medicine's monopoly in the control and management of the aging.

Research—The Research on Aging Act of 1974 created the National Institute on Aging (NIA) as the eleventh institute in the National Institutes of Health (NIH). The goals of the Act specified a broad range of medical and social problems for which scientific advances were needed, and a separate unit on Social and Behavioral Research was established at NIA and, through appointment of its own prestigious Associate Director, given parallel status with the other extramural programs (on Biomedical Research and Clinical Medicine). Nevertheless, NIA priorities and funding have historically tended to favor medically defined problems, approached from the perspective of the scientific concerns of biology, chemistry, immunology, and other "hard" sciences.

More specifically with regard to NIA's role in the biomedicalization of aging, three lines of argument may be made: First, some have argued that NIA is biased against the basic sciences of all types (e.g., the biological as well as social sciences), while giving preference to the more applied problems of health and aging as defined from the clinical position of academic medicine (1). According to Adelman, this bias toward a medical-clinical model has created such an inequity between research resources allocated to medical questions and those allocated to basic scientific questions that the percentage of NIA funding concentrated on medically defined problems has increased from 25 percent to 60 percent of the steadily increasing NIA budget, with a resulting major proportional decline for the basic biological and social sciences—despite NIA's growing overall budget.

The second line of argument is that, within NIA, the social and behavioral sciences have been disadvantaged from the start in relation to the other "hard sciences" and this has only been compounded by NIA's increasing attraction to a disease orientation and other clinical problems. Third, *within* the social and behavioral sciences, those which are more quantitative, positivistic and behavioral, (measured on an individual basis), are more favored than those which are either qualitative or focused on sociostructural and system-level problems.

Two aspects of NIA experience illustrate further difficulties of the social sciences. First, the name of the Social and Behavioral Sciences Program was changed in the early days of the Reagan administration. The term "social" was removed from the program name—indicating the potential liability of NIA's harboring a program of "social" science research in the early 1980s. The name change, to the "Behavioral Sciences Research Program," also reflected the legitimacy problems of the social sciences within the host environment of the National Institutes of Health. Although the program was renamed again in 1987 as the Behavioral and Social Research Program (restoring the word "social"), it continues to operate in the context of an advisory and review committee structure that is dominated by the biomedical sciences and disciplines.

The dominance of a biomedical model in aging is both reflected in and shaped by the composition of various advisory councils, study sections, and review committees which constrain the policy, research goals and agendas in aging, as well as determine which research is supported and legitimated. The disciplinary and paradigmatic interests of the majority members of such committees thus reflect and replicate these dominant views and interests. For example, the National Advisory Council on Aging roster from NIA dated May 1988 shows the extent to which the dominance of biomedicine has been institutionalized. Of the nineteen regular members, nine are MDs, three are health business foundation interests, and one is a nurse. Of the six remaining (five of whom are Ph.D.s), two are in the biological sciences, leaving the entire social and behavioral sciences represented by three members (one of whom is a health statistician). This situation had deteriorated even further when the Council was reconstituted in September 1988, and it is replicated in the NIA gerontology and geriatrics review committees where members from the medical, clinical and biological disciplines deeply overshadow the representation of the social and behavioral disciplines.

Second, the adoption of the concept of "behavioral medicine" appears to have been another strategy employed in an attempt to preserve (and hopefully extend) the social and behavioral sciences at NIA, although it has been a difficult umbrella under which a number of these researchers have struggled to fit. Unnamed NIA insiders have long lamented the necessity to camouflage or "dress up" social science problems in medical or clinical garb to legitimate them.

Difficulties for the social sciences have intensified in the current era of austerity and conservatism, as the ideology of biomedical positivism has increased. Moreover, the definition of clinical problems as the primary rationale for and thrust of NIA's aging research agenda has contributed to the usurpation of all applied problems in aging by medicine. This means that problems such as housing, income, and retirement must be justified as NIA research areas by being linked to health (or even better, to disease). Indeed, both policymakers and the public have been so conditioned that problems which cannot be defined in medical or clinical terms or directly linked to them are not likely to be accorded significance. With the phenomena and problems of aging defined and conceptualized in such terms, the biomedical paradigm achieves hegemonic status.

A recent examination of federal funding patterns is illustrative of the continuing and growing strength of biomedicine. A study by the Association for Gerontology in Higher Education (AGHE) has documented the resource allocations of the major federal agencies for research and education in aging for the decade, 1976 to 1986 (24). Major trends of note are that:

1. As a result of budget cuts between FY 1980 and FY 1982, there were dramatic reductions in the combined funding of research and training by the Administration on Aging. There was a 62 percent decrease in these Title IV funds, while total Older Americans Act funds increased more than 63 percent in FY 1986 constant dollars. The reductions in research funding are so severe that they are tantamount to the extinction of the Title IVB research program (25). The substantial decline in total Title IV federal dollars (from an absolute level of $54.5 million in FY 1980 to $23.9 million in FY 1986) represents a significant loss to the social and behavioral sciences because AoA funding was the initial (and until the implementation of the NIA in 1976, the only) federal source of social science research and training.

2. The National Institute on Aging (NIA) is the primary source of federal funding to support social and behavioral research. According to the AGHE study, NIA support for the Behavioral Sciences Program (BSR) has never exceeded more than 18 percent of the Institute's total budget, while the Biomedical Research and Clinical Medicine Program (BRCM) received almost 60 percent of NIA's total funding in the ten-year period studied (24, 26); nevertheless, NIA funding of BSR did increase in constant (inflated) dollars between 1978 and 1986 (from $6.7 million in 1978 to $14.9 million in 1986, or 120 percent). Simultaneously, NIA funding for the biomedical research and clinical medicine program (BRCM) increased in constant dollars approximately 168 percent (from $19.4 million to $52 million)—supporting the conclusion that there is a growing gap between NIA support for research on the social and behavioral versus the biomedical/clinical aspects of aging.

Beginning in 1986 and every year since, NIA has been specifically mandated by Congress to undertake work on Alzheimer's disease. For example, Title IX of the 1986 Omnibus Health Act mandated the establishment of an Alzheimer's Disease Education Center and the 1987 amendments to the Older Americans Act Title III (Sec. 301 [a])—in a dramatic departure from the Act's traditional commitment to services and applied policy solutions—gave NIA authority for clinical trials related to Alzheimer's disease. In FY 1989, NIA received a major appropriation of $20 million earmarked for research on Alzheimer's disease. NIA's attention and resource commitments to Alzheimer's disease have intensified and a reorganization in the agency has been effected to reflect this priority. A new Program on Neuro-psychology and Neuroscience of Aging (NNA) has been created, and approximately two-thirds of NIA's psychological research funding has been transferred to it from the Behavioral and Social Program (BSR). The full implications of NIA's growing commitment to Alzheimer's disease remain unknown. However, what is apparent is that there has been a biomedicalization of dementia (27, 28), and it is reflected in NIA. The commitment to Alzheimer's disease reflects the impressive strength of the "disease approach" to the field of aging in preference to other approaches that emphasize the basic social, behavioral, or even biological processes. Further, the bifurcation of psychological research into two separate programs has divided what once was a unified social and behavioral sciences program and diminished the funding base of the BSR program, and a significant proportion of psychology research has been "biomedicalized" as it has been redefined as "neuropsychology."

Training—As is the case with federally supported research, the bulk of federally supported training in aging is in the area of health. Priority is clearly given to the training of health professionals, and medicine heads the list of this category of funding. Those national programs of training which have given some attention to the social and behavioral sciences are located in two federal agencies, AoA and NIA. It is to these programs that we now turn our attention.

The "gutting" of the AoA Title IV program funding has already been described. From the inception of the Older Americans Act in 1965, multidisciplinary training for social and behavioral scientists as well as for social workers was an important focus of AoA activity. However, by the late 1970s priorities within the agency's training strategy had increasingly shifted to health-related problems and services as the agency began funding geriatric fellows (medical residents) and established long term care centers. The negative impact of Title IV funding reductions on the development of both social and behavioral science research and training programs in the nation's universities was compounded by AoA's administrative decision to fund the education and training of health professionals instead of social scientists in the late 1970s (29). As a consequence, there was, first, a "medicalization" of AoA training. Following this in 1981, AoA adopted an intentional strategy to obliterate main-line university training as the Reagan Administration repeatedly requested no authorization (zero appropriations) for funding of Title IV. Although Congress rejected this move, Title IV training funds were cut so dramatically that the career preparation funds decreased 64 percent (from $7.8 to $2.5 million between 1980 and 1982) and the number of institutional recipients of training funds plummeted from 88 to 33 institutions (more than a 60 percent decline). By 1985, career preparation funding had sunk to $2.1 million (30), ending almost fifteen years of federal commitment to gerontological education and training (25).

NIA's major training initiatives are for research training and most of the specific programs offer support to researchers in the health professions, clinical investigations and/or biomedical research, while those open to the social and behavioral sciences are more limited. For example, both the Postdoctoral Fellowships and the Career Development Awards heavily favor the biomedical sciences. The Biomedical Research and Clinical Medicine (BRCM) and Neuropsychology and Neuroscience (NNA) programs combined received 81.5 percent of all postdoctoral fellowships and 91.6 percent of all career development dollars. Not only are there more award mechanisms for MDs than for PhDs, but also they are funded at higher stipend levels. When we examined the total amount of funding for NIA Institutional Training Grants, Postdoctoral Fellowships and Career Development Awards, which support institutions and individuals and are available to all fields, it was apparent that almost three-quarters (74.8%) of these NIA training funds are committed to the two more biomedically oriented programs (NNA and BRCM). One can only draw the conclusion that federal support for social science training is extremely limited and the potential for significant future expansion is not being realized, even as the fortunes of NIA have risen.

Lay (Public)

The biomedicalization of aging has influenced more than academia and the professions. The lay public has contributed to and helped shape the process in a number of ways, as well as acting in other ways to resist it. One of the most significant aspects of the biomedicalization of aging has been its influence on public opinion and its tendency to view aging negatively as a process of inevitable decline, disease, and irreversible decay (as opposed to the reversible, remediable, and socially constructed aspects of aging). The public appears to have been convinced of the primary and rightful place of medicine in the management of the "problem" of aging. This process of hegemony extends to the individual and subjective experiences in which the biomedical view of aging is reinforced by family, friends, and personal contact with the medical profession and by one's own belief system. Alternative views of aging become inconceivable.

Most important for the lay public are the consequences of the dominant construction of reality for the persons so labeled, in this case, the elderly. We know that perceptions of old persons as dependent, sick, and helped only by high-cost, high-tech medical services may actually "teach" older persons to become dependent and sick, encouraging them to act the part while simultaneously reaffirming the power of the medical model to define what is real and what is important (5). The consequences for the elderly, their families, and the larger public are that they "buy into" the belief that the problems of aging are primarily biological and physiological, while ignoring the socially produced nature of many of these and other problems that occur in old age, e.g., fixed income by forced retirement. Convinced that only biomedical science can save them, the solutions to the problems of aging appear resolvable by the purchase and consumption of more and more high-cost medical services and technology.

The interpretation of public issues as private troubles, and the resulting social construction and production of helplessness and dependency, are then bolstered by public policy which does little to redress these issues. In fact, the biomedicalization of aging and the cost of policies developed from it have contributed importantly to the tendency to blame older persons for the largely "social" problems of demographic aging and a society that cannot provide enough work for its working-age population. Older persons find themselves blamed for the health care crisis (and indirectly, for larger economic crises of the state), as well as the poverty of children, which is blamed on social security, medical care, and other costs (31, 32). With this crisis construction, the elderly are blamed for many of the major ills of society, a blame that is due in no small part to the unwillingness of the proponents of the biomedical model of aging to relinquish its power or control, while the model remains inappropriate to (and hence ineffective in) addressing the inherently "social" phenomenon of the problems attendant to an aging society.

In addition to the public policy ramifications of support for huge outlays for medical care research, technologies and services, another result is the creation of a huge demand for products and services that promise to delay or eliminate the supposed physiological effects of aging, including a multi-million dollar cosmetic industry, vitamins and dietary supplements, prostheses, and growing cosmetic surgical specialties. Thus on a broader societal level, the biomedicalization of aging, like the continued medicalization of many aspects of everyday life, has contributed to the continuation and growth of a multi-billion dollar medical-industrial complex (33, 34) and the expansion of the power and influence of the medical profession. These interests depend in large part on the public acceptance of the authority and legitimacy of medicine. Industry representatives, the medical profession, and the media have each been quick to reinforce public acceptance of this view by emphasizing dramatic "breakthroughs," legislative lobbying and vigorous marketing of products to the elderly.

SOURCES OF RESISTANCE TO THE BIOMEDICAL MODEL

The end result is the solid and widespread public acceptance of the biomedical paradigm. Nevertheless, there are also sources of resistance to the model, its assumptions and practices, that directly or indirectly challenge the dominant conceptualization and produce some alternative models. One source is the ever-expanding population entering their "older years," healthy, active, and with the expectation of an increasing life-expectancy approaching two or more decades. Accompanying this trend is improved awareness about nutrition, exercise, and other lifestyle modifications that also challenge notions of the inevitability of disease, disability, and decay in old age. More important, a number of organizations, ranging from the moderate to the radical, are promoting different images of aging as they advocate for the elderly. Not only are groups like the Gray Panthers, the American Association of Retired Persons, and the Older Women's League serving as role models for vibrant, active and intelligent elders, they are working on issues such as income, housing, intergenerational interdependence, retirement policies, spousal impoverishment, and health insurance, that belie the biomedical construction of aging.

CRISES OF THE BIOMEDICAL PARADIGM

This chapter has developed the notion that aging and aging research have been profoundly affected by "biomedicalization," a process that is predicted on the dominance of the medical model and its encroachment on many aspects of human existence. Although its power is substantial, two major problems currently challenging this dominant model need to be addressed:

The first is that the developments which have extended longevity have not resolved the problems of an increased illness burden and the shift from acute to chronic illness. One major difficulty is how society can deal with the increasing longevity without either challenging the basic premises of medicine or losing faith in the ability of biomedicine to extend a quality lifespan. The medical premise supports the extension of life at all costs and implicitly promises we will all be better off as a result. The crisis is that medicine has used science and technology to extend physical life, yet it has not been able to extend that life with either the quality or reasonable cost in ways that are desirable and practical. Callahan argues that we have the ability to extend life, but since the elderly do not have a reasonable chance for a productive life and society as a whole does not have (or wish to allocate) the resources necessary to aggressively treat the elderly indefinitely, an age-based rationing of medical care is the fairest way to allocate those resources (35). Such an argument is consonant with the debate over the "intergenerational war" (36) and other constructions of crisis around the elderly (11), and it reflects crisis tendencies confronting the biomedical model and its promised lengthened longevity.

The second crisis for the biomedical paradigm is the continuing inability of the biomedical model to address macrostructural problems implicated in the etiology of ill health (e.g., environmental, social, and economic causes). Medicine's response has been to focus attention on individual health behaviors and life styles, making the individual responsible for illness. In contrast, social and behavioral sciences research and the success of the life-course perspective in aging point to the inadequacy of the biomedical model based on unicausal, homogeneous, and inevitable biological processes. Life-course theories point out the fallacies of such a model by demonstrating the importance of cohort and period effects of social, economic, and political phenomena in the environment for the aging process and for health in old age (37).

CONCLUSION

This chapter has discussed some of the parameters of the increasing trend toward the biomedicalization of aging. For a number of reasons, we see a great danger in this trend. In many ways, the demographics and the trends in research and education appear to be working at cross-purposes. Demographers warn that, as we approach the turn of the century, there will be more older persons and more of the oldest-old in the population than ever before. This means there will be more people with problems of chronic illness than ever before. But it also means that there will be more people attempting to deal with all aspects of old age than at any time in our history—well people, ill people, people in need of housing, adequate income, social support and services, and various kinds of care, of which medical care is only one. In many ways we are likely to be needlessly unprepared to address the issues that confront us in an aging society. By "biomedicalizing" aging and devoting fewer resources to understanding the basic social and biological phenomena of aging, we may be tempting the folly so aptly described by John McKinlay.

In a classic essay, McKinlay warns of the danger and ultimate futility of using all of one's time, energy, and resources in pulling a seemingly endless parade of people out of a rushing stream without investigating who is upstream pushing them in (38). The parallels in the field of gerontology are perilously similar. As we expand and support the biomedicalization of aging and its medical "solutions," we abandon the "search upstream" and run the danger of replicating the same problem that McKinlay has described.

The pitfalls of a "gerontology in medicine"—in which the interests of medicine direct the nature and scope of inquiry—are likely to approximate those already identified for the "sociology in medicine" (39), including the proclivity to employ individualistic and reductionist thinking, and to equate the needs of physicians and the medical profession with the needs of society. "Gerontology in medicine" not only subordinates gerontology to the power of the medical model when it is not always most appropriate, but also creates and supports a "magic bullet" mentality, retarding progress in other areas that have promise. Further, it diverts us from the serious pursuit of a national research agenda that is attentive to the much-needed advances in scientific knowledge concerning the basic process of aging, the consequences of life-course choices and life styles on the process of aging, and the social and environmental conditions that shape, structure or limit this process and these choices.

Biomedicine merits a respect and an honored place for its contributions to our health and well-being. But its extension to and control over all aspects of life diminish not only its own effectiveness, but inhibit society from understanding and addressing complex issues in the appropriate and innovative ways necessary. For the sake of the elderly and for those who will age, the biomedicalization of aging must be resisted.

REFERENCES

1. Adelman, R. The importance of basic biological science to gerontology. *J. Geron.* 43: 1, B1–2, 1988.
2. Warren, R., Rose, S. M., and Bergunder, A. *The Structure of Urban Reform.* D. C. Heath and Co., Lexington, Massachusetts, 1974.
3. Riley, M. W. Health behavior of older people: Toward a new paradigm. *Health, Behavior and Aging: A Research Agenda,* Interim report, No. 5. Institute of Medicine, Washington, D.C., 1981.
4. Ory, M. G., and Abeles, R. P. (eds.) *Aging, Health and Behavior.* Johns Hopkins University Press, Baltimore, Maryland, 1989.
5. Estes, C. L. *The Aging Enterprise.* Jossey-Bass, San Francisco, 1979.
6. Conrad, P., and Schneider, J. W. *Deviance and Medicalization: From Badness to Sickness.* Mosby, St. Louis, 1980.
7. Parsons, T. Social structure and dynamic process: The case of modern medical practice. In *The Social System,* pp. 428–479. The Free Press, New York, 1951.
8. Arluke, A., and Peterson, J. Accidental medicalization of old age and its social control implications. In *Dimensions: Aging, Culture and Health,* edited by C. L. Frye. Bergen, Brooklyn, 1981.
9. Walker, A. The social creation of poverty and dependency in old age. *J. Soc. Pol.* 9: 49–75, 1980.
10. Rodin, J., and Langer, E. Aging labels: The decline of control and the fall of self-esteem. *J. Soc. Iss.* 36(2): 12–29, 1980.
11. Estes, C. L., Gerard, L., Zones, J. S., and Swan, J. H. *Political Economy, Health and Aging.* Little-Brown, Boston, 1984.
12. Berger, P., and Luckmann, T. *The Social Construction of Reality.* Anchor, New York, 1966.
13. Zola, I. K. In the name of health and illness: On some socio-political consequences of medical influence. *Soc. Sci. and Med.* 9(2): 83–87, 1975.
14. Zola, I. K. The medicalization of aging and disability: Problems and prospects. In *Toward a Unified Agenda: Proceedings of a National Conference on Disability and Aging,* edited by C. W. Mahoney, C. L. Estes, and J. E. Heumann: Institute for Health & Aging, University of California, San Francisco, 1986.

15. Campbell, R. T., Abolafia, J., and Maddox, G. L. Life course analysis in social gerontology: Using replicated social surveys to study cohort differences. In *Gender and the Life Course*, edited by A. S. Rossi. Aldine, New York, 1985.

16. Foucault, M. *The Birth of the Clinic: An Archaeology of the Human Sciences*. Vintage, New York, 1973.

17. United States Senate Special Committee on Aging. Press release: "'Aging research: An investment, not expense,' Senator John Melcher says." May 11, 1988.

18. Achenbaum, A. Can gerontology be a science? *Journal of Aging Studies* 1(1): 3–18, 1987.

19. Williams, T. F. A perspective on training for academic leadership in geriatrics. *J. Am. Geria. Soc.* 33: 163–166, 1985.

20. Kane, R., Solomon, D., Beck, J., Keeler, E., and Kane, R. The future for geriatric manpower in the U.S., *New Engl. J. Med.* 302: 1327–1332, 1980.

21. National Institute on Aging. *Report on Education and Training in Geriatrics and Gerontology*. DHHS, Washington, D.C., 1984.

22. National Institute on Aging. *Personnel for Health Needs of the Elderly Through the Year 2000*. DHHS, Washington, D.C., 1987.

23. Rowe, J. W., Grossman, E., and Bond, E. Academic geriatrics for the year 2000: An Institute of Medicine report. *New Engl. J. Med.* 316(22): 1425–1428, 1987.

24. Association for Gerontology in Higher Education (AGHE). *Public Policy and the Future of Aging Education*. AGHE, Washington, D.C., 1988.

25. Estes, C. L. The challenge to gerontological education in an era of austerity. *Edu. Geron.* 12: 495–505, 1986.

26. Kerin, P., Estes, C. L., and Douglass, E. Federal funding and aging education: An era of expansion or contraction? *The Gerontologist* 29(5): 606–614, 1989.

27. Lyman, K. Bringing the social back in: A critique of the biomedicalization of dementia. *The Gerontologist* 29(5): 597–605, 1989.

28. Fox, P. Alzheimer's Disease: The Social Construction of Senile Dementia. Unpublished Ph.D. dissertation, University of California, San Francisco, 1988.

29. Craig, B. Weighing the issues and consequences of federal program termination: AOA support for career preparation. *Geron. and Ger. Ed.* 3(2): 92–137, 1977.

30. Consortium of Social Science Associations (COSSA). *Washington Update* 5(3): 1–31, 1986.

31. Hewitt, P. *A Broken Promise*. Americans for Generational Equity, Washington, D.C., 1986.

32. Preston, S. H. Children and the elderly in the U.S. *Scien. Am.* 251(6): 44–49, 1984.

33. Ehrenreich, B., and Ehrenreich, J. *The American Health Empire*. Vintage, New York, 1970.

34. Relman, A. S. The new medical-industrial complex. *New Engl. J. Med.* 303(17): 963–970, 1980.

35. Callahan, D. *Setting Limits: Medical Goals in an Aging Society*. Simon and Schuster, New York, 1987.

36. Binney, E. A., and Estes, C. L. The retreat of the state and its transfer of responsibility: The intergenerational war. *Int. J. Health Serv.* 18(1): 83–96, 1988.

37. Riley, M. W., Foner, A., and Waring, J. Sociology of age. In *Handbook of Sociology*, edited by N. J. Smelser. Sage Publications, Newbury Park, California, 1988.

38. McKinlay, J. B. A case for refocusing upstream: The political economy of illness. In *The Sociology of Health and Illness: Critical Perspectives*, edited by P. Conrad and R. Kern. St. Martin's, New York, 1981.
39. Strauss, R. The nature and status of medical sociology. *Am. Soc. Rev.* 22: 200–204, 1957.

CHAPTER 9

THE POLITICS OF ALZHEIMER'S DISEASE: A CASE STUDY IN APOCALYPTIC DEMOGRAPHY

Ann Robertson

Catastrophic projections of the burden to society of an increasing aging population abound (1–3). The prevailing belief is that an increasing aging population means increasing demands on the resources of society, including health care resources, in the face of competing interests and diminishing, or at best finite, resources. According to this scenario, it is not just the increase in the numbers of people over sixty-five that is the problem; it is also that as more people live to older ages, there will be significant increases in the morbidity in the elder population. In other words, people will live longer but sicker (4, 5). This greater morbidity of increasing numbers of elders, so the argument goes, will drive up health care costs. This "bankruptcy hypothesis of aging" in which "oncoming hordes of elderly" (6) deplete national health care budgets constitutes "apocalyptic demography."

Several authors, from various disciplines, have contested the assertions of apocalyptic demography by critiquing different components of this position. There have been challenges to the "living longer sicker" argument (7–9), as well as to the increased utilization argument (6–12). Some authors have critically examined "intergenerational inequity" (13–16), while others have demonstrated that the "burden of support" argument does not hold up under careful scrutiny (17–20). Finally, others have demonstrated that it is, in part, the response of the health care system to the increasing numbers of elders that has been responsible for the rise in health care costs (6, 21–23).

This chapter discusses the politics surrounding the emergence of Alzheimer's disease (hereafter referred to as AD) as the currently most publicized health problem in old age. By demonstrating how morbidity among elders itself may be socially constructed, this chapter offers another challenge to apocalyptic demography. In addition, by linking the social construction of AD at the micro-level to

135

aging policy at the macro-level, this chapter is intended as a contribution to the political economy of aging.

THE POLITICS OF ALZHEIMER'S DISEASE

In the last decade, AD has emerged as the "fourth or fifth leading cause of adult deaths in the United States." Estimates of the prevalence of AD in the over sixty-five population range from less than 5 percent to slightly more than 11 percent with estimates of the prevalence in those over 85 averaging between 15–20 percent but reaching as high as 47 percent (24). Numbers such as these justify concerns that AD has reached "epidemic" proportions.

But do the upward adjustments of the prevalence rates of AD have anything to do with real underlying disease rates in the population, or is something else going on? This section will demonstrate how "the politics of Alzheimer's" has contributed to the creation and expansion of a diagnostic category of uncertain boundaries.

In order to discuss what is meant by "the politics of Alzheimer's" two conceptual frameworks are used: the biomedicalization of old age and the social construction of disease.

Extending the "Clinical Gaze": The Biomedicalization of Old Age

The view that the "problem" of aging is primarily one of physiological decline medicalizes old age; that is, the phenomenon and experience of aging is brought within the medical paradigm as individual pathology to be treated and cured. Estes and Binney (Chapter 8) argue that the biomedical view of aging has become predominant, in part, because "medicine has come to occupy a privileged role in society and the biomedical model a dominant place," largely as a result of medicine's success in "controlling expertise and knowledge that others cannot evaluate." (For a more detailed explication of the "biomedicalization of old age," see Chapter 8).

By framing the "problems of aging," and therefore, the solutions as biomedical, this view of aging ignores nonmedical issues—such as poverty, isolation, the loss of role and status—and, thus, effectively depoliticizes the problems of aging. Ironically, this "biomedicalization of old age," with its emphasis on costly physician, hospital and "high-tech" services, has been the primary cause of the high costs of health care (25), so that the earlier solution has become, in effect, the current problem (Chapter 5, this volume). In addition, this view of old age ignores the day-to-day lived experience of aging.

Accompanying the biomedicalization of old age is a "gerontologization" of the experience of aging itself. With their search for scientific laws and theories about aging, their emphasis on the physical and psychological aspects of aging, and their adherence to scientific methodology in investigating aging, the disciplines of gerontology and geriatrics constitute old age as observed phenomenon rather than lived experience, and old people as objects of study. As a result, the lives of elders, individually and collectively, increasingly are subjected to professional scrutiny, definition and management—an extension of Foucault's "clinical gaze" (26).

The currently fashionable study of the morbidity and chronic illness that often accompany aging can be seen as a further extension of the "clinical gaze." In his book, *The Political Anatomy of the Body*, David Armstrong (27) applies Foucault's concepts of "clinical gaze" and panopticon—a conceptual device for the surveillance and control of individuals and society (28)—to an analysis of the political economy of community medicine and public health. About the "discovery" of chronic illness, he says, "it would be mistaken to ascribe [the shift from acute to chronic illness] to technological advance and the elimination of acute illness. . . . The problem is as always, a political one" (27, p. 87). Armstrong contends that "geriatrics was a specialty born of the [community] survey" (27, p. 85), which uncovered large amounts of chronic disease in the community, thereby legitimizing the extension of the "medical gaze" over the domestic and social lives of elders. In addition, with the growth in medical technology, such as the imaging technology used in the investigation of AD (CT scanners and MRI), the "panoptic gaze" focuses on ever more detailed examinations of the experience of aging, including brain function. This kind of technology, combined with the technology of cognitive and psychological testing, has been partly responsible for the recent focus on AD.

A Disease in the Making: The Social Construction of Alzheimer's Disease

> What will count in a society as "sin," "crime" or "disease" depends on a variety of conditions such as the intellectual division of labour and the separation of areas of knowledge by professional specialization. The emergence of "disease" as a special category is the product of professional dominance and secularization (29, p. 4).

Before discussing the social construction of the particular phenomenon of AD, it will be helpful to examine very briefly the general notion of disease as a social construct. The biomedical model of disease, based as it is on the Cartesian notion of the separation of mind and body, spirit, and matter, the personal and the social, views disease as a definitive biological entity, a "thing" out there in the world to be discovered, investigated and ultimately conquered. Another view of disease, emerging from the critical medical sociology and medical anthropology literature, is that disease is a social construct (27, 29–33), that is, a way of looking at human experience, a way of organizing "reality." In this view (32, p. 140):

> By interpreting illness as a social as well as a biological fact, and symptoms as a cryptic language of distress, we can see that illness meanings are stable, negotiated and contested. They are not reducible to fixed diagnostic categories (emphasis added).

It is beyond the scope of this chapter to explore the "bottomless pit of deconstructionism" (34) surrounding the debate about the "reality" of the body and the experience of illness. Briefly, however, along with Bryan Turner's (29) interpretation of the body, this discussion starts with the premise that there is a biological reality to the body and its experience of illness, but also acknowledges that "we can never regard an illness as a state of affairs which is dissociated from human agency, cultural interpretation and moral evaluation" (29, p. 4). In other words, "disease" can be seen as a social construct overlaid on a biological substratum; as such, "illness symptoms are . . . coded metaphors that speak to the contradictory aspects of social life, expressing feelings, sentiments, and ideas that must be otherwise kept hidden" (32, pp. 138–139).

In examining the social implications of the "sick role," Talcott Parsons declared that much of illness was sociogenic in origin, that is, caused by the stresses and strains in the prevailing social and economic order (35). Epidemiological investigations of the relationship of stress to illness are providing empirical evidence for the social origins of disease (36–40). Parson's insight into the "sick role" was that, in addition to disabling the ill person, it also exempts that person from social involvement and responsibility. As Scheper-Hughes and Lock say, "whatever else it is . . . assuming a sick role (especially the chronic sick role) signifies a refusal to endure, to *cope*. It says 'I will not any longer' " (32, p. 139).

Parsons recognized that this refusal was a threat to the moral and social order, and that one of the major roles of medicine was to defuse this threat by firstly, defining this refusal as deviance, and, secondly, controlling it through the legitimizing concept of disease. Thus, human distress is "medicalized and individualized rather than collectivized and politicized" (33, p. 10). To put it another way, in a variation on C. Wright Mill's theme, the concept of "disease" constitutes what are really "public issues" as "private troubles" (41).

These and other theorists contend that in order to fully understand the origins and nature of disease it is not enough to look only to biological explanations. We must also analyze factors in the social, political, and economic context— individual and collective—within which people live their everyday lives and experience their illnesses. The following discussion is an attempt to apply this kind of analysis to the phenomenon of AD.

Before proceeding to consider the ways in which AD could be said to be socially constructed, a final caveat about human suffering should be added. The present analysis of AD is in no way intended to ignore or diminish the anxiety, pain, and distress experienced by persons diagnosed with Alzheimer's disease (hereafter referred to as PDWADs) and their families; nor is it intended to dismiss the efforts on the part of those professionals, family members, and social organizations dedicated to alleviating that suffering. The present analysis, which presents an alternative view of the nature of AD, is offered as a contribution to those efforts.

dehumanizing
terminology

This next section examines AD as a construct on three levels, all of which are interrelated: a political level, a clinical level, and an ontological level.

AD as a Political Construct

> The "discovery" of Alzheimer's disease has involved a political process more than simply biomedical discovery (42, p. 597).

Fox argues that current perceptions of AD as the "fourth or fifth leading cause of death in the United States" can be understood in terms of the "salient social structural conditions that influenced the emergence of AD as a social problem which resulted in the creation of a social movement" (43, p. 8). Using a historical and detailed ethnographic approach, Fox described and illuminated the crucial factors in the success of this social movement.

Biomedical — Because of the development of biomedical technology, principally the electron microscope, investigators were able to demonstrate post mortem histological similarities between presenile dementia of the Alzheimer's type (with symptom onset between forty and sixty years of age) and senile dementia (with symptom onset after sixty-five years of age). Previous to this discovery, senile dementia had been regarded as a concomitant of "normal" aging.

These discoveries had two significant results, which as Fox says "provided crucial conditions that facilitated the emergence of the disease as a social and health problem" (43, p. 8): aging and "senility" were conceptually separated, with "senility" now being regarded as a specific disease process; and the elimination of age as the primary criterion for AD resulted in the expansion of this diagnostic category to include all those over sixty-five who had previously been diagnosed with "senile dementia." This enlarged constituency was essential to the perception of AD as a significant health and social problem about which something had to be done by somebody. That "somebody" turned out to be the National Institute on Aging (NIA).

Organizational — Newly established in 1974, NIA was attempting to establish its credibility within the ranks of the National Institutes of Health (NIH). AD provided NIA with a strategic issue for doing so. As Fox states, "the necessity of raising scientific and public awareness of Alzheimer's disease was based on an understanding of *the importance of a categorical disease focus for increasing biomedical research funds* from Congress" (43, p. 1, emphasis added). Once again the dominance of the biomedical model is demonstrated.

As Fox tells the story, it was NIA's successful facilitation of a large and powerful national advocacy organization, the Alzheimer's Disease and Related Disorders Association (ADRDA), recently renamed the Alzheimer's Disease Association, which ultimately brought the issue of AD to national prominence.

This resulted in considerable funds being allocated to primary research on AD, as well as to the establishment of a care, support, and information infrastructure. As a result of these efforts, by the late 1970s, a "public culture" had grown up around AD (31). This "public culture" represented a coalition of primary investigators, clinicians, service providers, care settings, community agencies, and the families of PDWADs and their support networks.

Armstrong's observation about the establishment of the discipline of geriatrics as a new "medical space" could equally well be made about this public culture surrounding AD (27, p. 87):

> The medical gaze has established a domain of medical reality and with it the surveillance apparatus of support groups and social networks which act both to sustain and monitor the new temporally ordered medical space (emphasis added).

Along with and supporting AD as a political construct, there must also be an acceptance of AD as a construct at the clinical level.

AD as a Clinical Construct

> Alzheimer's is factually established, publicized, taught, and shared . . . (31, p. 29).

At the clinical level, AD has been characterized as a progressive abnormal cognitive impairment, manifesting as a loss of memory, language, and other intellectual capabilities, accompanied by a general diminishment of competence and resulting ultimately in death. AD is a problematic diagnosis at best. Diagnosis of AD is by exclusion of other diseases which resemble AD, and confirmation of the diagnosis occurs only with the post mortem examination of brain tissue for the presence of the neurofibrillary tangles and plaques believed by many to be the determining neuropathological sign of the disease.

In a detailed analysis of the social construction of AD, Gubrium examines the role that the "facts" of AD have played in shaping AD as a clinical construct (31). Gubrium demonstrates how the multiplicity of symptoms, the inconclusiveness of diagnosis, and the uncertainty of prognosis are all brought to heel to comply with biomedical notions of single disease entities. This is achieved through a process of negotiation and elaboration on the part of clinicians and primary investigators, which achieves what Gubrium calls a "unity in diversity," that is "a disease code in . . . the varied experience of age-related troubles" (31, p. 3). As a result of this effort, AD is represented to the public as a unitary clinical construct, such that, as Gubrium says (31, p. 133):

> the scientific discourse [surrounding AD] that pervades the public culture does not reveal the conceptual, analytic, and epistemological concerns of those who engage in the tasks of establishing basic facts and elaborating the

disease. It is not that these are hidden from the public . . . but that . . . the implicit trust in science as the court of last resort stands firm.

As discussed above, the "public culture" of Alzheimer's includes not only the family of PDWADs but also the entire professional, service, and support community that has been established in response to the "discovery" of AD. The general public could also be included as a result of the information which filters out through the media (44, 45). In all of these domains, the individual disturbances and difficulties which beset PDWADs and their families are represented in terms of a discrete disease entity, with a discrete pathology, course, and outcome. Alternative ways of conceptualizing disturbances and difficulties—in either sociopolitical or ontological terms—are few.

Lyman takes issue with the "biomedical model of dementia," which clinically constructs this picture of AD (42). According to Lyman, this model is comprised of three major features:

1. The distinction between normalcy and pathology;
2. The assumption of universal stages of progressive deterioration;
3. The legitimation of medical control over persons with dementia.

The neuropathology of AD is far from conclusive. In the first place, post mortem examination of the brain tissue of persons who displayed no symptoms of dementia behavior have been found to contain the neurofibrillary tangles and plaques asserted to be associated with AD. In addition, it appears that the pathologic criteria of AD—the number of neurological lesions indicative of the presence of disease—varies with age (42, p. 600) and with "known" clinical symptoms (31, p. 62), so that a "fit" is often constructed retrospectively between the neuropathology and the clinical symptoms for any given person. As Lyman says (42, p. 600):

> If even the diagnosis and neuropathology of dementia is subject to such negotiation and interpretation, pathology must be framed within a sociocultural as well as a biomedical definition.

The behavior of PDWADs is interpreted—again, often retrospectively—to fit the notion of progressive disease stages, although there is very little epidemiological evidence to support the notion that AD progresses through universal predictable stages (42). The problem with this way of thinking about AD, according to Lyman, is that potentially everything about the person so diagnosed becomes "evidence" for the presence of pathology, thus reinforcing the notion of AD as a definitive clinical construct.

Finally, Lyman contends that the biomedicalization of dementia places the treatment and management of AD under medical authority, effectively individualizing the "disturbed" behavior of PDWADs and, thereby, depoliticizing the power relationships between PDWADs and their families or professional caregivers (42). The ready acceptance of the clinical construct of AD can be attributed to its efficacy in creating order out of chaos for both clinicians and families; a "disease" construct serves to normalize and render manageable the "disturbing" and "disruptive" behavior of the PDWAD. The "biomedical model of dementia," ultimately fails to take into account any notion of the extent to which AD may be socially produced and reproduced.

In order for AD to be accepted as a clinical construct, it must also be perceived to constitute what the PDWAD has become, what he or she now is; in other words, it must be accepted as an ontological construct. *(accepted as reality)*

AD as an Ontological Construct

> In short, the societal and cultural responses to disease create a second illness in addition to the original affliction, what we are calling the "double": the layers of stigma, rejection, fear, and exclusion that attach to particularly dreaded diseases. . . . The disease and its double force the patient, now twice victimized, further into the cage of his or her illness: shunned, silenced and shamed in addition to being very sick (32, pp. 137,–138, original emphasis).

The diagnosis of Alzheimer's is both a stigmatizing label and a sentence. PDWADs are almost always referred to in passive terms such as "victims" and "patients;" AD itself is referred to as a "slow death of the mind," a "never ending funeral," the "brain killer."

According to Goffman, the internalization of the stigmatizing label at the personal level is a crucial step in the process of stigmatization (46). The hopelessness, depression, and despair which may result from the acceptance and internalization of the diagnosis of AD may result in "a self-fulfilling prophecy of impairment" (42, p. 599). Accepting the Alzheimer's label consigns the PDWAD to an ontological position of increasing helplessness and dependency. This notion has gained some legitimacy from empirical studies of the institutionalized elderly, which indicate that dependency and "learned helplessness" (47) result in a "mindlessness" (48, 49), ultimately leading to disability and death (50–58).

As Lyman points out, very little is known about AD from the perspective of the person diagnosed with the disease (42). It is as if no one has thought to ask these people about the nature and experience of their illness. Indeed, much of the literature on AD considers the real "victims" of AD to be, not the PDWADs themselves, but their families. As such, the PDWAD has become the agent in the epidemiological triangle of host, agent, and environment; in other words, the PDWAD *is* the pathogen.

In Armstrong's formulation, this represents a shift in thinking from the nineteenth century notion of disease as localized in specific sites in the body to the twentieth century notion of disease as localized in the social spaces between people (27). As such, it legitimizes the medicalization of social relationships, including family relationships (59). The treatment for Alzheimer's typically consists of treatment, in the form of respite care and support, for the family of PDWADs. In addition, a unidirectional causality is assumed, so that (42, p. 603):

> Changes in the caregiving relationship are traced to disease progression, rather than examining disease progression as a consequence of changes in the caregiving relationship.

Finally, little attention is paid to the ways in which AD may be socially produced and reproduced by the unequal power relations between PDWADs and family members, service providers, care settings, and the entire public culture that has grown up around AD. The loss of autonomy and structured dependence, as well as the expectations on the part of others of inevitable increasing cognitive impairment, place the PDWAD in a no-win position. This is not just a theoretical issue. The work with institutionalized elderly, referred to above, has demonstrated that dramatic improvements in functioning and reductions in mortality result from increasing the sense of control that these elders have over certain aspects of their lives (48–58).

As constructed, AD is a fearsome disease. Surrounding it are images of loss— loss of memory, loss of intellectual function, loss of language, loss of bodily control, and, finally, the loss of connectedness to other people; in other words, AD represents the loss of all those qualities by which we have come to define our humanness. PDWADs are living reminders of our human frailty and our mortality; like Cain they bear the mark of some angry God (30, p. 1):

> It is the fear of collapse, the sense of dissolution, which contaminates the Western image of all disease, including elusive ones such as [AD]. But the fear we have of our own collapse does not remain internalized. Rather, we project this fear onto the world in order to localize it, and indeed to domesticate it. For once we locate it, the fear of our own dissolution is removed. Then it is not we who totter on the brink of collapse, but rather the Other. And it is an Other who has already shown his or her vulnerability by having collapsed.

Perhaps the PDWADs themselves, like persons who have been diagnosed with AIDS, have something to tell us about what it means to be human in the face of such dissolution, if we but ask and listen. In his haunting fictional account of a descent into dementia, J. Bernlef has his protagonist say about his ontological isolation (60, p. 140):

> they understand nothing of what I say . . . the thought of an interpreter doesn't occur to them . . . I am the only survivor of my own language.

Alzheimer's Disease: Normal Aging or Pathology?

The headlines of a front page story in the New York Times proclaimed that "Study Finds Alzheimer's Disease Afflicts More Than Was Estimated" (45). The study itself, which was the result of intensive cognitive testing of a community sample, reported a prevalence of AD in the over eighty-five population of 47.2 percent (24). AD, the investigators concluded, is "a common condition in this community population of persons over the age of sixty-five" (24, p. 2556). A month later, Newsweek reported that "47 percent of those over eighty-five have the disease" as if this were everywhere an established and accepted prevalence rate (44).

An editorial, which appeared in the same issue of JAMA in which this community study was reported, made the observation that clinical diagnosis of AD was made solely on the basis of performance on cognitive tests (61). There was no attempt made to assess the functional ability of those clinically diagnosed with AD; in other words, there was no way to tell how their "dementia" interfered with their day-to-day lives. So, of what practical use is the diagnosis?

As discussed previously, the successful emergence of AD as the most prominent and publicized disease of old age was facilitated by the distinction of senile dementia from normal aging. In light of the above observations, however, Lyman's question "if senile dementia is a pathological condition, what is normal?" (42, p. 600) is especially apt. In other words, at what point does a disease like AD become so "common" that it no longer serves to distinguish between what is pathology and what is "normal?"

Indeed, Gubrium observed a "descriptive tension" in distinguishing AD from normal aging, "revealed in a common caveat, namely, that all the symptoms of Alzheimer's disease may be found, to some degree, in the normal and healthy elder" (31, p. 78). In addition, as Lyman correctly observes, how is it possible to "distinguish mental disorder from behavioral quirks and eccentricities developed over a lifetime" (42, p. 600)?

The social construction of AD as a major disease of old age has succeeded in expanding the diagnostic boundaries of this disease category, and, thereby, shrinking the range of what is considered to constitute normal aging. At some point, the distinction between AD and normal aging must ultimately collapse (31).

many reversible conditions masquerade as AD —

ALZHEIMER'S DISEASE AND APOCALYPTIC DEMOGRAPHY

Apocalyptic demography represents the social construction of catastrophe. As stated in the introduction, this argument postulates that an increasing aging population, with its multitude of health problems, will place major demands on health care resources. Apocalyptic demography scapegoats elders by blaming them for rising health care costs (6, 15, 62–64), fuels "intergenerational inequity" arguments (13, 14, 16, 65), and provides the rationale for current proposals for age-based rationing of health care (66–69). The preceding discussion about the social construction of AD indicates that the response of the health care system to the increasing numbers of elders itself needs to be investigated.

Changing Patterns of Professional Practice

Per capita costs of health care are increasing, and they are increasing at a faster rate for older age groups than for younger age groups. However, recent Canadian studies indicate that the impact of aging per se on the use of health care resources is, in fact, quite small (70, 71). Projecting forward the changing structure of the Canadian population and assuming unchanging age and gender specific utilization rates, it turns out that the "aging of the population" accounts for only a 1 percent per year increase in the per capita use of all health care services for the whole population over the next forty years (6). For physician services, the demographically based rate of increase is at 0.3 percent per year. Historically, however, the real per capita increases per year from 1971 to 1984 have been 2.6 percent for hospital services and 1.5 percent for physician services. These increases have been at a higher rate for the over-sixty-five population.

The fact that the rate of increase in the greater relative use of health care resources by elders is itself increasing indicates that those over sixty-five are being serviced by the health care sector with increasing intensity. It could be argued that advances in diagnostic technology have resulted in higher rates of case-finding; likewise, advances in treatment technology may account for the increasingly higher use rates by elders. On the other hand, it could be that with reductions in use rates by younger population groups and for acute conditions, the health care sector has turned its attention to the new market created by an increasing aging population with chronic health problems.

What may be happening, then, is a change in the way the health care system—hospitals and physicians—respond to and treat the health needs of elders. In other words, we may be witnessing an increase in the extent to which the over sixty-five population is "serviced," or in health economics terms an increase in "provider-induced demand" for health care services. Studies at the University of British Columbia, using longitudinal data to analyze hospital and physician services to the over-sixty-five population between 1969 and 1986, provide support for this notion (21, 22, 72). These studies indicate that there has been, overall, a transfer of hospital days and physician visits from younger age groups to older age groups. How much of this is a system response to changing patterns of morbidity is inconclusive.

One of these studies indicates that increases in hospital use by those over sixty-five were spread over a small number of diagnostic categories (22). Between 1969 and 1985/86, 500,000 patient days of increase to the over-sixty-five population were attributable to behavioral, thought and mood disturbances (lumped together in the diagnostic category "dementia"), and 80 percent of those days of increase were for women over sixty-five. The authors juxtapose this information against the finding that in the same time period, there was no evidence for an increasing temporal trend in the prevalence of dementia.

We may be observing with the increase in the use of the diagnostic category "dementia," and also with the expansion in the diagnostic boundaries of

AD, the creation and extension of a new "medical space" (27) over which presides a professional dominance. Clearly, there has been a shift in health care resources towards the older population, creating what has been called an "aging enterprise" (73).

Aging: Everybody's Business?

Constituting the "problems" of old age in terms of individual pathology leads to individualistic solutions. National policies, which might address more fundamental structural factors, are ignored in favor of policy interventions aimed at the individual level, often in the form of local, fragmented, often stop-gap service measures. The main thrust of these interventions has been to create and fund agencies, professionals, and organizations to develop and manage services and programs for elders. Old age has become literally and figuratively everybody's business (74)!

Critics of this approach argue that it has done little to help elders directly (62, 64, 65, 73). Much effort goes into professionally defining the "needs" of older people, and then meeting those "needs" within the framework of professional expertise and particular institutional arrangements. Money does not go directly to elders but to people paid to help elders meet their "unmet needs" through various services and programs.

> The provider of service receives reimbursement under all of these programs, while the elderly are defined as "recipients," clients, or patients of service. Thus, the helping professions share—and benefit from—the individualized conception of aging, which is implemented through policies in ways that contribute to the further dependency of the aged (65, p. 245).

As argued elsewhere in this volume, much of the dependency of elders can be said to be a "structured dependence" in that dependency is created and fostered by individualized professional interventions. Engendered, in part, by advocates of elders, this "compassionate ageism" is vulnerable to withdrawal in times of economic constraint (62). A stronger critique of this kind of policy approach claims that much of the dependency of elders has been structured as a form of social control. Many professionals, so the argument goes, rather than seeking to enfranchise or empower elders, in fact, either wittingly or unwittingly, collude in the creation of this "structured dependence" (75–78).

The above indicates that "the care of the elderly has become the new growth sector in the health care system" (6, p. 860). It also appears that the health care system's response to the growing numbers of elders is to constitute as "health" problems what may well not be health problems at all (21, 22).

CONCLUSION

> Some individuals and groups have much greater power than others to influence the definition of social problems and to specify the policy interventions that address these problems (65, p. 241).

This chapter has been intended as a challenge to the notion of apocalyptic demography, which asserts that the increasing numbers of elders will bankrupt us. Starting with the concept of the "biomedicalization of old age," and discussing how one disease of old age, AD, may be seen to be socially constructed, it has been demonstrated that the response of the health care system itself to the increasing older population is, in part, responsible for this catastrophic view of aging. It is hoped that the perspective developed here will help shift future policy initiatives away from elders themselves and towards the context within which people grow old.

We need not believe ourselves to be at the mercy of blind forces, such as demographic and economic imperatives, as if these existed outside of the realm of public discussion and debate. Rather, we must acknowledge that it is "politics, not demography, [which] now determines the size of the elderly population and the material conditions of its existence" (19, p. 175).

REFERENCES

1. Kingson, E. R., and Scheffler, R. M. Issues and economic trends for the 1980s. *Inquiry* 18: 197–213, 1981.
2. Waldo, D. R., and Lazenby, H. C. Demographic characteristics and health care use and expenditure by the aged in the United States: 1977–84. *Health Care Finance Rev.* 6: 1–28, 1984.
3. Brody, J. A., Brock, D. B., and Williams, T. F. Trends in the health of the elderly population. *Anna. Rev. Public Health* 8: 211–234, 1987.
4. Schneider, E. L., and Brody, J. A. Aging, natural death and the compression of morbidity: Another view. *NEJM* 309(14): 854–855, 1983.
5. Verbrugge, L. Longer life but worsening health? Trends in health and mortality of middle-aged and older persons. *Milbank Mem. Fund Q.* 62: 475–519, 1984.
6. Barer, M. L., Evans, R. G., Hertzman, C., and Lomas, J. Aging and health care utilization: New evidence on old fallacies. *Soc. Sci. Med* 24(10): 851–862, 1987.
7. Fries, J. F., and Crapo, L. M. *Vitality and Aging: Implications of the Rectangular Curve.* W. H. Freeman, San Francisco, 1981.
8. Fries, J. F. The compression of morbidity. Milbank Mem. Fund Q. 61(3): 397–419, 1983.
9. Palmore, E. B. Trends in the health of the aged. The Gerontologist 26(3): 298–302, 1986.
10. Roos, N. P., and Shapiro, E. The Manitoba longitudinal study on aging: Preliminary findings on health care utilization by the elderly. *Med Care* 19(6): 644–657, 1981.
11. Roos, N. P., Shapiro, E., and Roos, L. L. Aging and the demand for health services: Which aged and whose demand? *The Gerontologist* 24(1): 31–36, 1984.
12. Roos, N. P., Montgomery, P., and Roos, L. L. Health care utilization in the years prior to death. *Milbank Mem. Fund Q.* 65(2): 231–254, 1987.
13. Binney, E. A., and Estes, C. L. The retreat of the state and its transfer of responsibility: The intergenerational war. *Int. J. Health Serv.* 18(1): 83–96, 1988.

14. Kingson, E. R., Hirshorn, B. A., and Cornman, J. M. *Ties That Bind: The Interdependence of Generations.* Seven Locks Press, Washington, D.C., 1986.
15. Minkler, M. Blaming the aged victim: The politics of retrenchment in times of fiscal conservatism. In *Readings in the Political Economy of Aging*, edited by M. Minkler and C. L. Estes, pp. 254–269. Baywood Publishing, Amityville, New York, 1984.
16. Minkler, M. "Generational equity" and the new victim blaming. *Int. J. Health Serv.* 16(4): 539–551, 1986.
17. Denton, F. T., and Spencer, B. G. Canada's population and labor force: Past, present, and future. In *Aging in Canada: Social Perspectives*, edited by V. W. Marshall, pp. 10–26. Fitzhenry and Whiteside, Don Mills, Ontario, 1980.
18. Friedmann, E. A., and Adamchak, D. J. Societal aging and intergenerational support systems. In *Old Age and the Welfare State*, edited by A. Guillemard, pp. 53–73. Sage Publications, Beverly Hills, 1983.
19. Myles, J. F. Conflict, crisis, and the future of old age security. In *Readings in the Political Economy of Aging*, edited by M. Minkler and C. L. Estes, pp. 168–176. Baywood Publishing, Amityville, New York, 1984.
20. Calasanti, T. M., and Bonanno, A. The social creation of dependence, dependency ratios, and the elderly in the United States: A critical analysis. *Soc. Sci. Med.* 23(12): 1229–1236, 1986.
21. Barer, M. L., Pulcins, I. R., Evans, R. G., Hertzman, C., Lomas, J., and Anderson, G. M. Diagnosing Senescence: The Medicalization of British Columbia's Elderly. Health Policy Research Unit, University of British Columbia, 1988.
22. Hertzman, C., Pulcins, I., Barer, M. L., Evans, R. G., Anderson, G. M., and Lomas, J. Flat on Your Back to Your Flat: Sources of Increased Hospital Services Utilization among the Elderly in British Columbia. Health Policy Research Unit, University of British Columbia, 1989.
23. Rice, T. Physician-induced demand for medical care: New evidence from the Medicare Program. *Adv. in Health Econ. and Health Serv. Res.* 5: 129–160, 1984.
24. Evans, D. A., Funkenstein, H. H., Albert, M. S., et al. Prevalence of Alzheimer's disease in a community population of older persons. JAMA 262(18): 2551–2556, 1989.
25. Hertzman, C., and Hayes, M. Will the elderly really bankrupt us with increased health care costs? *Can. J. Publ. Health* 76: 373–377, 1985.
26. Foucault, M. *The Birth of the Clinic.* Vintage, New York, 1975.
27. Armstrong, D. *The Political Anatomy of the Body: Medical Knowledge in the Twentieth Century.* Cambridge University Press, Cambridge, 1983.
28. Foucault, M. *Discipline and Punish: The Birth of the Prison.* Vintage Books, New York, 1979.
29. Turner, B. *The Body and Society.* Basil Blackwell, Oxford, 1984.
30. Gilman, S. L. *Disease and Representation: Images of Illness from Madness to AIDS.* Cornell University Press, Ithica, 1988.
31. Gubrium, J. F. *Oldtimers and Alzheimer's: The Descriptive Organization of Senility.* JAI Press Inc., Greenwich, Connecticut, 1986.
32. Scheper-Hughes, N., and Lock, M. M. Speaking truth to illness: Metaphors reification, and a pedagogy for patients. *Med. Anthro. Q.* 17(5): 137–140, 1986.
33. Scheper-Hughes, N., and Lock, M. M. The mindful body: A prolegomenon to future work in medical anthropology. *Med. Anthro. Q.* 1(1 March): 6–41, 1987.
34. Lock, M. M. The Social Construction of Menopause in Japan. Lecture, University of California, Berkeley, January 31, 1989.
35. Parsons, T. The sick role and the role of the physician reconsidered. *Milbank Mem. Fund. Q.* 53: 257–278, 1975.

36. Marmot, M. G., Rose, G., Shipley, M., and Hamilton, P. J. S. Employment grade and coronary heart disease in British civil servants. *J. Epid. and Comm. Health* 3: 244–249, 1978.
37. Matthews, K. A., and Haynes, S. G. Type A behavior pattern and coronary disease risk. *Am. J. Epidem.* 123: 923–961, 1986.
38. Syme, S. L., and Berkman, L. F. Social class, susceptibility and sickness. *Am. J. Epidem.* 104: 1–8, 1976.
39. Syme, S. L. Social determinants of health and disease. In Public Health and Preventive Medicine, edited by J. M. Last. Appleton-Century-Crofts, Norwalk, Connecticut, 1986.
40. Syme, S. L. Control and Health: An Epidemiological Perspective. Presentation at Pennsylvania State University Gerontology Conference, October 17–18, 1988.
41. Mills, C. W. *Power, Politics and People: The Collected Essays of C. Wright Mills.* Basic Books, New York, 1963.
42. Lyman, K. A. Bringing the social back in: A critique of the biomedicalization of dementia. *The Gerontologist* 29(5): 597–605, 1989.
43. Fox, P. From senility to Alzheimer's disease: The rise of the Alzheimer's disease movement. *Milbank Mem. Fund Q.* 67(1): 58–102, 1989.
44. The Brain Killer. *Newsweek* 54–63. December 18, 1989.
45. Leary, W. E. Study finds Alzheimer's disease afflicts more than was estimated. *New York Times*, November 10, 1989.
46. Goffman, E. *Stigma: Notes on the Management of Spoiled Identity.* Prentice-Hall, Englewood Cliffs, New Jersey, 1963.
47. Seligman, M. E. P. *Helplessness: On Depression, Development and Death.* Freeman Publishers, San Francisco, 1975.
48. Langer, E. J. Old age: An artifact? In *Aging: Biology and Behaviour*, edited by J. L. McGaugh and S. B. Kiesler, pp. 255–281. Academic Press, New York, 1981.
49. Piper, A. I., and Langer, E. J. Aging and mindful control. In *The Psychology of Control and Aging*, edited by M. M. Baltes and P. B. Baltes, pp. 71–89. Lawrence Erlbaum Associates, Hillsdale, New Jersey, 1986.
50. Langer, E. J., and Rodin, J. The effects of choice and enhanced personal responsibility for the aged: A field experiment in an institutional setting. *J. Pers. and Soc. Psych.* 34(2): 191–198, 1976.
51. Langer, E. J., Rodin, J., Beck, P., Weinman, C., and Spitzer, L. Environmental determinants of memory improvement in late adulthood. *J. Pers. and Soc. Psych.* 37(11): 2003–2013, 1979.
52. Langer, E. J., Beck, P., Janoff-Bulman, R., and Timko, C. An explanation of the relationships between mindfulness, longevity, and senility. *Am. Psych. Bull.* 6: 211–226, 1984.
53. Rodin, J., and Langer, E. Long-term effect of a control-relevant intervention. *J. Pers. and Soc. Psych.* 35: 897–902, 1977.
54. Rodin, J. Aging and health: Effects of the sense of control. *Science* 233 (19 September): 1271–1276, 1986.
55. Rodin, J. Health, control, and aging. In *The Psychology of Control and Aging*, edited by M. M. Baltes and P. B. Baltes, pp. 139–165. Lawrence Erlbaum Associates, Hillsdale, New Jersey, 1986.
56. Schultz, R. Effects of control and predictability on the physical and psychological well-being of the institutionalized aged. *J. Pers. and Soc. Psych.* 33: 563–573, 1976.
57. Schultz, R., and Hanusa, B. H. Long-term effects of control and predictability-enhancing interventions: Findings and ethical issues. *J. Pers. and Soc. Psych.* 36: 1194–1201, 1978.

58. Schultz, R. Aging and control. In *Human Helplessness: Theory and Application*, edited by J. Garber and M. E. P. Seligman, pp. 261–277. Academic Press, New York, 1980.
59. Foucault, M. The politics of health in the 18th century. In *Power/Knowledge: Selected Interviews and Other Writings 1972–1977 by Michael Foucault*, edited by C. Gordon. Pantheon, New York, 1976.
60. Bernlef, J. *Out of Mind*. David R. Godine, Boston, 1989.
61. Larson, E. B. Editorial-Alzheimer's disease in the community. *JAMA* 262(18): 2591–2592, 1989.
62. Binstock, R. H. The aged as scapegoat. *The Gerontologist* 23(2): 136–143, 1983.
63. Binstock, R. H. The oldest old: A fresh perspective or compassionate ageism revisited. *Milbank Mem. Fund Q.* 63(2): 420–541, 1983.
64. Binstock, R. H. Reframing the agenda of policies on aging. In *Readings in the Political Economy of Aging*, edited by M. Minkler and C. L. Estes, pp. 157–167. Baywood Publishing, Amityville, New York, 1984.
65. Estes, C. L. Austerity and aging: 1980 and beyond. In *Readings in the Political Economy of Aging*, edited by M. Minkler and C. L. Estes, pp. 241–253. Baywood Publishing, Amityville, New York, 1984.
66. Callahan, D. Health care in the aging society: A moral dilemma. In *Our Aging Society*, edited by A. Pifer, and L. Bronte. W. W. Norton, New York, 1986.
67. Callahan, D. *Setting Limits: Medical Goals in an Aging Society*. Simon and Schuster, New York, 1987.
68. Clark, P. G. The social allocation of health care resources: Ethical dilemmas in age-group competition. *The Gerontologist* 25(2): 119–125, 1985.
69. Kilner, J. F. Age as a basis for allocating lifesaving medical resources: An ethical analysis. *J. Health Polit. Poli. Law* 13(3): 405–423, 1988.
70. Boulet, J. A., and Grenier, G. Health Expenditures in Canada and the Impact of Demographic Changes on Future Government Health Insurance Program Expenditures. Economic Council of Canada, Ottawa, 1978.
71. Woods Gordon Management Consultants, *Investigation of the Impact of Demographic Change on the Health Care System in Canada-Final Report*. Task Force on the Allocation of Health Care Resources, Toronto, 1984.
72. Evans, R. G., Barer, M. L., Hertzman, C., Anderson, G. M., and Pulcins, I. R. The Long Good-Bye: The Great Transformation of the British Columbia Hospital System. Health Policy Research Unit, University of British Columbia, 1988.
73. Estes, C. L. *The Aging Enterprise*. Jossey-Bass, San Francisco, 1979.
74. Minkler, M. Gold in gray: Reflections on business' discovery of the elderly market. *The Gerontologist* 29(1): 17–23, 1989.
75. Evans, L., and Williamson, J. B. Social control of the elderly. In *Readings in the Political Economy of Aging*, edited by M. Minkler, and C. L. Estes, pp. 47–72. Baywood Publishing, Amityville, New York, 1984.
76. Townsend, P. The structured dependency of the elderly: Creation of social policy in the twentieth century. *J. Age. and Soc.* 1(1): 5–28, 1981.
77. Walker, A. Social policy and elderly people in Great Britain: The construction of dependent social and economic status in old age. In *Old Age and the Welfare State*, edited by A.-M. Guillemard, pp. 143–167. Sage, Beverly Hills, California, 1983.
78. Walker, A. Community care and the elderly in Great Britain: Theory and practice. In *Readings in the Political Economy of Aging*, edited by M. Minkler and C. L. Estes, pp. 75–93. Baywood Publishing, Amityville, New York, 1984.

PART IV. CRITICAL PERSPECTIVES ON MARKET ECONOMY HEALTH CARE

The medical-industrial complex is one of the largest employers in the nation and health care is absorbing an ever-increasing percentage of the gross national product. Debate on the causes of soaring health costs continues between individuals and insurers, hospitals and doctors, nonprofit and proprietary interests, and the public and private sectors. Questions of access, rationing, quality of care, regulation, and the public interest are inevitably tied to the rise of market economy health care. An understanding of the U.S. health care system requires untangling the interrelated and conflicting priorities of patient and professional requirements for service, industry focus on profit, and government and public interest in cost containment. This section uses the nursing home industry, the mental health system, and recent health legislation as examples of market economy influences on health care.

Chapter 10 examines the market forces that compromise quality of care in the multibillion-dollar nursing home industry. Harrington argues that although regulatory efforts are essential to the improvement of nursing home care, broader structural reforms will be necessary to assure safety, required services, rights, and an acceptable quality of life for residents. As demand and the complexity of care increase and the supply of beds, staff, and financing are stretched, industry, government, consumers, professionals, and special interest groups will be struggling to resolve the resulting conflicts.

Refuting human development models of aging, which emphasize differing generational roles and assign the tasks of disengagement, adjustment, and coping to the aged, Binney and Swan in Chapter 11 analyze the broader societal causes and treatment polices for mental illness in the elderly. The political economy perspective on the production and treatment of mental illness in western capitalist society examines the role of technology, the change in old age from productive worker to consumer in the "gray market," institutionalization, and social control. Mental health trends affecting the elderly are the growing Alzheimer's "enterprise," tensions between consumer need for government responsibility and political calls for "informalized" family care, and increasing pressures on the mental health delivery system. Mental health politics in this country are contrasted with French and Italian anti-psychiatry movements.

Although long term care services are the primary health-related need of elderly citizens, legislation and government programs persistently make acute care a priority. In Chapter 12, Holstein and Minkler trace the development, passage, and repeal of the most recent health insurance legislation. The drama of the failed Medicare Catastrophic Coverage Act raises moral economy questions of fairness in taxation and illustrates the lack of homogeneity in the aged population. Not a simple case of interest-group politics, the history of this act viewed from a political and moral economy perspective presents a case study of the pitfalls of partial solutions to broad structural problems.

CHAPTER 10

THE NURSING HOME INDUSTRY:
A STRUCTURAL ANALYSIS

Charlene Harrington

The poor quality of care provided in U.S. nursing homes has long been a matter of concern to consumers, professionals, and policymakers. Recently, the General Accounting Office reported that over one-third of the nation's nursing homes are operating at a substandard level, below minimum federal standards during three consecutive inspections (1). Among the findings were evidence of untrained staff, inadequate provision of health care, unsanitary conditions, poor food, unenforced safety regulations, and many other problems (1, 2). No other segment of the health care industry has been documented to have such poor quality of care. Despite a large infusion of public funds into the nursing home industry over the past twenty-five years, investigations and exposés continue to find inadequate care and patient abuse (1).

In 1986, the Institute of Medicine's Study on Nursing Home Regulation reported widespread quality-of-care problems and recommended the strengthening of federal regulations for nursing homes (2). These recommendations, as well as the active efforts of many consumer advocacy and professional organizations, in 1987 resulted in Congress passing a major reform of nursing home regulation, the first significant changes since Medicare and Medicaid were adopted in 1965 (3). Congress has made enhanced regulatory efforts a priority, in spite of the costs associated with regulation, in an effort to improve quality of care and to protect residents from abuse.

This chapter examines the structural features of the nursing home market and the industry itself in an effort to identify factors related to poor quality of care. We argue that regulatory efforts, while essential, are not sufficient to improve the overall quality of nursing home care. Rather, efforts to develop structural reforms will be seen as necessary to make nursing home care safe, to ensure high quality of care, to preserve the basic rights of residents, and to promote an acceptable quality of life for residents.

✓ INCREASED DEMAND

The quality of nursing homes is receiving national attention as the demand for nursing home services is growing with the increasing numbers of individuals who are aged and chronically ill. In 1987, about 30 million Americans were aged sixty-five and older, and this number is projected to increase to 51 million in 2020 (4). As the population ages and develops chronic illnesses, the need for long term care, including nursing home services, increases.

The adoption of prospective payment systems for hospitals by Medicare in 1983 resulted in shortened hospital stays and increases in the demand for nursing home care. This policy change resulted in increased numbers of referrals and admissions to nursing homes from hospitals, as well as increased acuity levels of residents in nursing homes (5). At the same time, the new 1988 Health Care Financing Administration (HCFA) Medicare guidelines to the fiscal intermediaries liberalized Medicare coverage for nursing homes (6). These changes encourage the demand for and use of nursing homes and other long term care services.

✓ INCREASED COMPLEXITY OF CARE

The demand for increasingly complex services in nursing homes is growing with the aging and disability level of residents. While only 4 percent of the nation's elderly are currently in nursing homes, 88 percent of nursing home residents are aged sixty-five and older (7). The population in nursing homes is aging so that the median age is eighty-two (7). The proportion of residents who were eighty-five years and older rose from 30 to 40 percent between 1976 and 1985 (7) and is continuing to rise.

The disability level of nursing home residents is increasing. Between 1976 and 1984, the number of residents who were totally bedfast rose from about 21 to 35 percent of the discharges and the number dependent in mobility and continence increased from 35 to 45 percent (8). The average resident has about four of six limitations in activities of daily living, and 66 percent have some type of mental impairment or disorder (7).

As the acuity level of nursing home residents increases, medical technology formerly used only in hospitals is now being used in nursing homes. Thus, the "performance of duties" has become an even more complex task for personnel. The use of intravenous feedings and medication, ventilators, oxygen, special prosthetic equipment and devices, and other technologies has made patient care management more difficult and challenging (9, 10). The appropriate use of technology, the training and skill levels needed by nursing home personnel, and the need for emergency back-up procedures are problems caused by the use of high technology. Thus, changes in the characteristics of residents are placing greater demands on nursing home providers—demands that are frequently beyond the capacity of the current financing and delivery system.

√ CONSTRAINED SUPPLY

While the demand for increasingly complex nursing home care is growing, the supply of nursing home beds is not keeping pace. The 1985 National Nursing Home Survey reported approximately 19,100 facilities providing care for 1.5 million residents, including hospital-based facilities and residential facilities (7). About 75 percent of these nursing homes were certified to provide services under Medicare and Medicaid programs. The number of beds grew rapidly after the development of Medicare and Medicaid in 1965 until the 1980s, when the growth slowed to a level below the rate of growth of the aged population (11). As the supply of beds has been constrained (except in the Southwest), the average occupancy rate has increased to 92 percent nationally (7). The slowing of growth is the result of complex market factors, including the high costs of capital construction, problems with the labor market, recent lowering of profit rates over previous high levels, and in some states, limits on construction by state regulations.

This limited supply and the high demand for services has created a situation in which nursing homes are able to select the residents they admit. Because they can obtain private-paying residents who can be charged higher daily rates than publicly paid residents, nursing homes prefer private clients and frequently discriminate against those who are on Medicaid (12). Nursing homes also tend to "cream" or select the least sick patients or those for whom they can provide the most cost-effective care. In some situations, this practice reduces access for individuals with the greatest need and limits consumer choice and the competitive market for services.

√ HIGH COSTS

The cost of nursing home services is growing rapidly. The nation spent $49 billion on nursing home services in 1989 (8 percent of its total health expenditure) and expects to spend $54.5 billion in 1990, making this segment of the health industry third only to hospitals and physicians (13). Although the growth in nursing home cost has slowed somewhat, the increase in 1989 was 11.2 percent over the previous year, well beyond the 5 percent rate of inflation (13).

The growing cost of nursing home care has negative consequences for consumers and public payers. Of the total amount spent, one-half of the revenues come from public sources and one-half from out-of-pocket sources. Medicare pays for less than 2 percent of the public expenditure and Medicaid (for those with low incomes) pays most of the remainder. Because of these costs, most public policy efforts, particularly by state Medicaid programs, are focused on controlling or reducing spending.

Since private insurance for nursing home services is virtually unavailable and currently pays less than 1 percent of the cost, most individuals who require nursing home services for any extended period of time are forced to spend their life savings before they become poor enough to qualify for Medicaid services, which then pay for care. The average annual cost of $29,000 (in 1987) forces many individuals to spend their assets within thirteen weeks of admission to a nursing home (14). The high cost of care results in inequities, with the greatest access for those with the highest income and limited access for the poor. This situation has fueled the demand for a national health care program for long term care services.

OWNERSHIP

chains fit for profit

The nursing home industry has more proprietary ownership and chain ownership than any other segment of the health system, with the exception of the drug industry. In 1985, 75 percent of all nursing homes were profit making, 20 percent were nonprofit, and 5 percent were government owned (7). A growing number of nursing homes are chain-owned or operated, this segment of the industry having increased its control of the total market dramatically. In 1973, the three largest chains owned 2.2 percent of the beds, but by 1982, they controlled 9.6 percent of the beds (15). By 1985, chains owned 41 percent of the facilities and 49 percent of the nation's nursing home beds (7).

Many U.S. for-profit health care chain corporations have become multinational, owning companies in other countries. In 1988, eleven U.S. investor-owner hospital companies owned and operated 116 hospitals with 12,560 beds in seventeen foreign countries and managed another twenty-four hospitals with over 5,000 beds (13). The large nursing home chains also owned many facilities in foreign countries.

Several factors have contributed to the growth in chain operations. As Hawes and Phillips notes, capital reimbursement policies encourage the sale and resale of facilities, and other real estate manipulations favor more sophisticated operators (15). Increased demand for services, constrained bed supply, high profitability, and the increased complexity required to meet federal certification standards and to obtain public reimbursement also encourage growth.

Nursing home corporations have traditionally been very profitable. For example, Beverly Enterprises had stock price gains of over 700 percent between 1978 and 1981 and National Health Enterprises of 900 percent (15). Returns on net equity for facilities in California ranged from 58 to 154 percent in 1983 and 1984 (15).

Nursing home profits continued to grow until 1987, when some chains experienced losses. Beverly Enterprises, the largest chain with 16,000 beds, had a loss of $30.5 million in 1987 and continued to lose money through the end of the decade

(16, 17). Beverly experienced losses because it incurred large debts from its aggressive expansion policies, but other nursing home chains such as Manor Care and National Medical Enterprises continued to be profitable with 14 to 17 percent returns on equity in 1989 over the previous year and 13 to 22 percentage earnings per share for the past ten-year period (17).

Nursing home chains have primarily relied on growth through acquisition, which drove bed prices so high that earnings growth did not keep pace with the cost of expansion and which caused high debt-to-capital ratios. Many of these chains have recently been hurt by the expansion of nursing home beds in hospitals, particularly for Medicare patients. Other chains have been affected by the nursing shortage and are reported having to increase their wages. Even so, the industry remains profitable, although little new capital is being infused into the market at this time.

One of the major debates in research, policy, and consumer advocacy circles is whether the proprietary nature of the nursing home industry negatively affects access, costs, and quality of care. Access to services is limited to those who can pay privately because proprietary facilities provide little uncompensated care. Costs of care are driven up by the increasing demand for short-term profits (15). The effect on quality of care has been disputed. A review of research studies on ownership and quality indicates that the preponderance of the evidence suggests the superiority of nonprofits, particularly church-related nonprofits (15).

✓ STAFFING AND LABOR ISSUES

The staffing and educational levels in nursing homes are low. There are only 5.1 full-time equivalent (FTE) registered nurses (RNs) per 100 patients in nursing homes in contrast with a ratio of 1 RN for every 4.5 patients in hospitals (18). There are 7.4 FTE licensed practical nurses (LPNs) and 30.8 FTE nursing attendants per 100 patients in nursing homes (18). Current attendant ratios are sometimes as low as 1 per 15 patients during the day, 1.25 in the evening, and 1.40 to 1.50 at night (19). Registered nurses spend little time with nursing home residents in direct care. In a recent study, RNs in hospitals spend an average of forty-five minutes per patient per day compared to less than twelve minutes for RNs in nursing homes (20). Nearly 40 percent of the 7,402 nursing homes in the survey reported six minutes or less of RN time per patient per day and 60 percent reported no RN hours during the past week (20). Staffing levels are directly associated with ownership, with proprietary facilities having lower staffing levels (20).

Although the 1987 federal nursing home legislation (OBRA) required additional registered nurses, facilities are still not required to have twenty-four-hour a day registered nursing coverage and the legislation is having only a small impact on nurse staffing levels (3). The major barrier to improved staffing is the cost to nursing homes, which in turn would necessitate raising Medicaid nursing home reimbursement rates.

Not surprisingly, higher staffing levels in nursing homes have been associated with better nursing care. Spector and Takada, in a study of 2,500 nursing home residents in eighty nursing homes in Rhode Island, found that low levels of staffing in homes with very dependent residents was associated with reduced likelihood of improvement (21). High catheter use, a low percent of residents receiving skin care, and low participation rates in organized activities were also associated with reduced outcomes, in terms of functional decline and death (21).

Higher staffing levels could not only improve quality, but could also reduce the cost of hospitalization. A recent study of nursing home residents found that 48 percent of the hospitalizations could have been avoided. Factors such as an insufficient number of adequately trained nursing staff, the inability of nursing staff to administer and monitor intravenous therapy, lack of diagnostic services, and pressure for transfer from the staff and family were found to contribute to hospitalization (22). The investigators estimated that the 216,000 nursing home residents who are hospitalized might be treated in nursing homes, for a cost savings of $.9 billion in the United States (22).

Wages and Benefits

Wages and benefits for nursing home employees are scandalously low. Nursing home salaries are estimated to be 20 to 40 percent below the levels for comparable positions in hospitals (19). Nursing assistants or attendants, who make up 63 percent of all nursing home direct care personnel, generally work for minimum wages and few have benefits.

Low wages and benefits are directly reflected in the high turnover rates for nursing home personnel. The overall nursing personnel turnover rates in nursing homes are frequently as high as 55 to 100 percent per year (19). A number of studies have identified poor working conditions, combined with heavy resident workloads, inadequate training and orientation, and few opportunities for advancement among the factors that contribute to high turnover rates in some facilities (23). High registered nurse turnover is associated with decreased likelihood of functional improvement (21). Although high turnover rates are considered undesirable in terms of quality outcomes, nursing homes, like other health facilities, have some economic incentives to encourage high turnover rates to keep wages low. Higher nursing staff turnover rates are associated with proprietary institutions (20).

Education and Specialty Training of Staff

Nurses working in nursing homes have less education than hospital nurses. Fifty-six percent of all RNs working in nursing homes are diploma prepared nurses, and less than 3 percent have master's degrees (18). Many nursing homes are unwilling to pay the higher wages required to attract better prepared nurses, yet evidence suggests that gerontological nursing specialists may be cost effective.

Several geriatric nurse practitioner (GNP) demonstration projects examined the effect of GNPs in the practice setting. One evaluation, which compared thirty nursing homes employing GNPs with thirty matched control homes, found that the use of GNPs resulted in favorable changes in two of eight measures of activities of daily living; five of eighteen nursing therapies; two of six drug therapies; and six of eight tracers (24). The study also reported some reduction in hospital admissions and total days in geriatric nurse practitioner homes (24).

The Robert Wood Johnson teaching nursing home demonstration project was designed to bring nursing schools together with nursing homes to improve nursing education and patient care (25). In these projects, nurse clinicians and faculty provided direct care to patients and worked as consultants and advisors to staff. The preliminary results find positive outcomes in terms of improving both the process of care and the outcomes of care (25).

At one demonstration project, the presence of master's prepared nurses resulted in decreases in decubiti, incontinence, dependency, and use of physical restraints, catheters, psychotropic drugs, enemas, and laxatives (26). Initial results, however, were confounded by a reversal in some of the same outcomes in subsequent years. Another study reported a gradual decline in emergency room visits, hospital admissions, infections, and falls (27). One study related the presence of clinical specialists with a decrease in nosocomial infections and the use of pharmacologic agents (28). Although the results of the demonstration projects appear to be positive, foundation support for the teaching nursing homes cannot fund such programs indefinitely. It is hoped that nursing homes will use the research findings to inform changes in the types of nursing personnel they utilize.

PUBLIC INFORMATION

Public information about the quality of nursing home care, such as nursing home guides or rating systems, is also helpful in improving quality. Consumers requiring nursing home services are vulnerable and lack information on which to base informed choices about which facilities would best meet their needs. Many individuals rely on hospital discharge planners, physicians, and other health professionals for assistance in making plans and decisions regarding nursing home services. Evidence suggests that the discharge planning process is complex and not always operating effectively (29). Discharge planners and other health professionals frequently have inadequate information on nursing homes and other long term care provider options, particularly facts on the quality of providers. Public disclosure of administrative information, consumer guides, and rating systems are methods for assisting consumers and health professionals in making more informed decisions in the marketplace.

Expanding public information about nursing home quality may also be valuable in stimulating nursing homes to improve their services. Hospitals compete, to some extent, on the basis of the quality of their nursing services, but nursing homes have generally not done so. The lack of competition is exacerbated by the short supply of nursing homes in some areas of the country (11). The Institute of Medicine Committee to Study Nursing Home Regulation recommended the development of nursing home rating systems based on quality indicators as one method of pressuring facilities to improve services (2). Such approaches, which aim to give consumers and professionals greater choice in making informed decisions, are attractive but difficult to develop.

REGULATORY APPROACHES

The 1987 OBRA nursing home reform legislation was the first major legislative improvement in the federal regulation of nursing homes since 1965 (3). The legislation mandates comprehensive assessments of all nursing home residents after admission and periodically so that nursing homes can define the functional, cognitive, and affective levels of residents initially and over time. The legislation requires the development of quality indicators that are more outcome-oriented than process-oriented. Outcome measures include resident behavior, functional and mental status, and resident conditions (such as incontinence, immobility, and decubitus ulcers). More detailed and prescriptive regulations have been drafted to implement the OBRA legislation. For example, the draft regulations establish criteria for and prohibit the use of "unnecessary drugs." The OBRA legislation also requires changes in the federal survey procedures to orient them more toward the rights of residents and enforcement of the law.

The new regulation and enforcement effort should bring about substantial improvements in quality of care. The OBRA regulations appear to have had some beneficial effects already in reducing the use of physical restraints, which are used to tie nursing home residents to beds or chairs. Because the regulations do not allow the inappropriate use of restraints, a number of nursing homes are now reporting new efforts to train staff not to use such restraints and to move toward restraint-free facilities (30).

SPECIAL INTEREST GROUP POLITICS

Three key special interest groups are involved with nursing home issues: 1) the industry, which is represented by the American Health Care Association and the American Association of Homes for the Aging; 2) the government, with interests split between quality regulators and fiscal agents who pay for services; and 3) the consumer interests, primarily represented by National Citizens' Coalition for Nursing Home Reform (NCCNHR). Both the American Medical Association and the American Nurses' Association have interests in nursing homes, but neither organization has considered these nursing home regulatory issues to be a priority. Although nursing organizations have advocated for improved nursing staff levels and wages and benefits in nursing homes, few nurses working in nursing homes are active members of major nursing organizations. This lack of representation translates into a low organizational priority on nursing home lobbying efforts when organizational resources are limited.

Unfortunately, the special interests of the three major groups are often conflicting and frequently lead to stalemate. The industry is primarily interested in minimizing government regulation of quality and access, while obtaining high government reimbursement rates with minimal strings attached to the funds. The industry wants to increase reimbursement rates substantially, but generally opposes efforts to guarantee that rate increases would be passed on to employees. While government monitoring systems, such as improved financial reporting and increased numbers of audits, could be developed to ensure greater financial accountability, the industry would fight such efforts. Because substantial amounts of public funds to nursing homes traditionally have been used to finance excessive administrative costs, high profit rates, and the expansion of chain operations, there is a legitimate distrust of the industry and an unwillingness on the part of government to spend more money.

Government is struggling to balance its interests in ensuring minimum levels of quality while at the same time controlling costs and operating under severe fiscal constraints. Consumer representatives primarily want to ensure quality and access to appropriate services through greater governmental regulation of the industry and improved enforcement efforts.

There is an unequal distribution of power between the industry and consumers. The nursing home industry is well-represented by highly paid professionals with extensive organizational resources for lobbying government. Consumer groups have less funding and resources and must operate primarily through commitment and volunteer efforts, but nevertheless have a strong presence in Washington through NCCNHR. If professional groups (particularly those of nurses and physicians) would form a coalition with consumer groups and be willing to allocate resources to representing the public interest, they could shift the power base to favor consumer interests.

Consumer groups, particularly the National Citizens' Coalition for Nursing Home Reform, have worked extremely hard to have legislation passed and to develop new regulations and survey procedures (31). Nursing home industry representatives, while generally cooperating with the new legislation, have made efforts to weaken its implementation and to use it as a means of increasing Medicaid reimbursement rates.

The current struggles between the industry and the consumers are focused on the development of new regulations and enforcement to improve the quality of regulation. Stronger support by nursing and other professional organizations would give greater weight to consumer groups in their effort to prevent the watering down of regulations by industry officials. In addition, a coalition of consumers and professionals supporting greater allocations of federal funds by Congress and the Administration to implement state survey procedures would serve to protect the public interest.

SUMMARY

The nursing home industry is growing in size and importance as a provider of long term care. The major quality and access problems of the nursing home industry are likely to grow in magnitude as demand increases and supply is relatively inelastic. Regulatory efforts are the highest priority for improving quality of care. At the same time, renewed efforts are needed to improve wages, benefits, and staffing levels for the professionalized staff of nursing homes. This effort will entail substantial increases in public funds but is essential to the improvement of the system. Methods are needed to ensure financial accountability on the part of nursing homes. Maximum limits on nursing home administrative costs, profits, and capital expenditures are crucial. Finally, methods for reducing the trend toward proprietary ownership and the consolidation of the industry should be quickly examined in order to stimulate ownership and management by government and nonprofit corporations.

REFERENCES

1. U.S. General Accounting Office (GAO). *Medicare and Medicaid: Stronger Enforcement of Nursing Home Requirements Needed.* Report to the Chairman, Subcommittee on Health and Long Term Care, Select Committee on Aging, House of Representatives. U.S. GAO, Washington, D.C., 1987.
2. Institute of Medicine (IOM) Staff and National Research Council Staff. *Improving the Quality of Care in Nursing Homes.* National Academy Press, Washington, D.C., 1986.
3. Omnibus Budget Reconciliation Act (OBRA) of 1987. Public Law 100-203. Subtitle C: Nursing Home Reform. U.S. Government Printing Office, Washington, D.C., 1987.
4. U.S. General Accounting Office (GAO). *Long Term Care for the Elderly: Issues of Need, Access, and Cost.* Report to the Chairman, Subcommittee on Health and Long Term Care, Select Committee on Aging, House of Representatives. U.S. GAO, Washington, D.C., 1988.
5. Guterman, S., Eggers, P., Riley, G., Greene, T., and Terell, S. The first 3 years of Medicare prospective payment: An overview. *Health Care Fin. Rev.* 9(3): 67–77, 1988.
6. Scanlon, W. Delivery of long term care services: Latest developments in nursing homes and housing. Commissioned paper for meeting on The Economics and Politics of Long Term Care, sponsored by the University of California, Irvine and the FHP Foundation, p. 5, 1989.
7. National Center for Health Statistics, Hing, E., Sekscenski, E., and Strahan, G. National Nursing Home Survey: 1985 Summary for the United States. *Vital and*

Health Statistics, Series 13, No. 97. DHHS Pub. No. (PHS) 89-1758. U.S. Government Printing Office, Washington, D.C., 1989.

8. National Center for Health Statistics, and Sekscenski, E. Discharges from nursing homes: Preliminary data from the 1985 National Nursing Home Survey. *Advance Data from Vital and Health Statistics*, No. 142. DHHS Pub. No. (PHS) 87-1250. Public Health Service, Hyattsville, Maryland, 1987.

9. Harrington, C., and Estes, C. L. Trends in nursing homes in the post-Medicare prospective payment period. Unpublished. Institute for Health and Aging, San Francisco, California, 1989.

10. Shaughnessy, P. W., and Kramer, A. M. The increased needs of patients in nursing homes and patients receiving home health care. *New Engl. J. Med.* 322(1): 21–27, 1990.

11. Harrington, C., Swan, J. H., and Grant, L. A. Nursing home bed capacity in the states, 1978–86. *Health Care Fin. Rev.* 9(4): 81–111, 1988.

12. Phillips, C. D., and Hawes, C. *Discrimination by Nursing Homes Against Medicaid Recipients: The Potential Impact of Equal Access on the Industry's Profitability*. Research Triangle Institute, Research Triangle Park, North Carolina, 1988.

13. International Trade Administration. Health and medical services. In *U.S. Industrial Outlook 1990*. Department of Commerce, Washington, D.C., 1990.

14. U.S. Department of Health and Human Services (DHHS). Task Force on Long Term Care Policies. *Report to Congress and the Secretary: Long Term Health Care Policies*. U.S. Government Printing Office, Washington, D.C., 1987.

15. Hawes, C., and Phillips, C. D. The changing structure of the nursing home industry and the impact of ownership on quality, cost, and access. In *For Profit Enterprise in Health Care*, edited by B. H. Gray, pp. 492–538. National Academy Press, Institute of Medicine, Washington, D.C., 1986.

16. Wagner, L. Nursing homes buffeted by troubles. *Mod. Health Care*, 18(12): 33–42, 1988.

17. Forbes. Health. *Forbes*, pp. 180–182, January 8, 1990.

18. National Center for Health Statistics, and Strahan, G. Characteristics of registered nurses in nursing homes: Preliminary data from the 1985 National Nursing Home Survey. *Advance Data from Vital and Health Statistics*. No. 152. DHHS Pub. No. (PHS) 88-1250. Public Health Service, Hyattsville, Maryland, 1988.

19. Harrington, C. Nursing home reform: Addressing critical staffing issues. *Nurs. Out.* 35(5): 208–209, 1987.

20. Jones, D., Bonito, A., Gower, S., and Williams, R. *Analysis of the Environment for the Recruitment and Retention of Registered Nurses in Nursing Homes*. U.S. Department of Health and Human Services, Washington, D.C., 1987.

21. Spector, W. D., and Takada, H. A. Characteristics of nursing homes that affect resident outcomes. Paper presented at the Gerontological Society of America, Annual Meeting, Minneapolis, Minnesota, 1989.

22. Kayser-Jones, J., Wiener, C., and Barbaccia, J. Factors contributing to the hospitalization of nursing home residents. *The Gerontologist* 29(4): 502–510, 1989.

23. Wagnild, G. A descriptive study of nurse's aide turnover in long term care facilities. *J. Long Term Care Admin.*, pp. 19–23, 1988.

24. Kane, R., Garrard, J., Skay, C., Radosevich, D., Buchanan, J., McDermott, S., Arnold, S., and Kepferle, L. Effects of a geriatric nurse practitioner on process and outcome of nursing home care. *Am. J. Pub. Health* 79(9): 1271–1277, 1989.

25. Mezey, M., Lynaugh, J., and Cartier, M. Reordering values: The teaching nursing home program. *Nursing Homes and Nursing Care: Lessons from the Teaching Nursing Homes*, pp. 11–12. Springer, New York, 1989.

26. Joel, L., and Johnson, J. Rutgers, the State University of New Jersey and Bergen Pines County Hospital. In *Teaching Nursing Homes, the Nursing Perspective*, edited by N. Small and M. Walsh. National Health Publishers, Owings Mill, Maryland, 1988.

27. Dimond, M., Johnson, M., and Hull, D. The teaching nursing home experiences, University of Utah College of Nursing and Hillhaven Convalescent Center. In *Teaching Nursing Homes, the Nursing Perspective*, edited by N. Small and M. Walsh. National Health Publishers, Owings Mill, Maryland, 1988.

28. Wykle, M., and Kaufmann, M. The teaching nursing home experiences, Case Western Reserve University, Frances Payne Bolton School of Nursing and Margaret Wagner House of the Benjamin Rose Institute. In *Teaching Nursing Homes, the Nursing Perspective*, edited by N. Small and M. Walsh. National Health Publishers, Owings Mill, Maryland, 1988.

29. Wollock, I., Schlesinger, E., Dinerman, M., and Seaton, R. The posthospital needs and care of patients: Implications for discharge planning. *Soc. Work Health Care* 12(4): 61–76, 1987.

30. Lewin, R. Nursing homes rethink tying aged as protection. *New York Times*, p. A1, December 28, 1989.

31. National Citizens' Coalition for Nursing Home Reform (NCCNHR). *Consumer Statement of Principles for the Nursing Home Regulatory System—State Licensure and Federal Certification Programs*. NCCNHR, Washington, D.C., 1983.

CHAPTER 11

THE POLITICAL ECONOMY OF MENTAL HEALTH CARE FOR THE ELDERLY

Elizabeth A. Binney and James H. Swan

Nowhere in the field of aging has the news of the imminent "demographic revolution" had a greater impact, nor caused a greater furor, than in the arenas concerned with the provision of health care to the elderly (1–3). With the predictions of massive growth in the elderly population in the next century, increasing attention has been paid to the potential impact of mental health problems on this population. In fact, the use of "apocalyptic demography," as described by Robertson in Chapter 9 is well illustrated in the construction of Alzheimer's disease as the "Disease of the Decade," complete with dramatic and desperate calls for massive increases in basic and clinical biomedical funding to halt the devastating results that will otherwise occur. Yet the multiple issues and changing context of the mental health needs of the elderly remain underaddressed, mired in narrow disciplinary battles dominated by the hegemony of biomedicine (Chapter 8). To uncover and unpack these issues and begin to address these complex problems, new models and approaches are required. This chapter outlines one such model.

The overview of aging, mental health, and public policy in this chapter uses a political economy model. It begins from a vantage point not typically taken, that is, the "understanding that mental illness in a class society has a class character" (4) and that the institutions and policies that support it also have a class character. Therefore, the chapter begins with a brief discussion of models of mental illness and contrasts them with current gerontological models, reflecting both the dominance of particular types of models and the inherent ideological and political nature of such models. An analysis of the production of mental illness in the elderly in western capitalist society includes a discussion of how aging and mental illness are socially and politically constructed to meet the needs of capital and the state, as well as the class, gender, and race issues inherent in such constructions. The dual processes of institutionalization and deinstitutionalization affect the elderly mentally ill in ways that are different from younger cohorts. Such differences highlight the importance of analyses that attempt to understand the uniquely age-related aspects of mental illness.

The treatment of mental health problems in the elderly, including the delivery of services, financing, and policymaking, remains a problem in our society. An important issue concerns the role of the "Alzheimer's Enterprise" and its potential for distorting policy and treatment for the mentally ill elderly. The "Alzheimer's Enterprise" and its relationship to broader structural interests is discussed, as is the link of these trends to the social and cultural reproduction of mental health problems. Finally, policy issues pertaining to mental health and aging, in particular, the effects of the Reagan years and decentralization policies, and some of the most important provisions of OBRA 1987 legislation are critically analyzed.

MENTAL HEALTH AND THE ELDERLY

Estes notes in Chapter 2 that multiple social constructions of aging dominate not only our attitudes toward the elderly, but public policies as well (5). These constructions of reality (6) include three sets of perceptions that are pertinent to the issues of mental illness and the elderly:

- The aging process brings with it inevitable physical and psychological decline, decay, and degeneration considered part of "normal aging;"
- While some elders are seen as more deserving than others, in general, most elders have lived out their useful lifespan and are thus less deserving (of time, attention, and especially resources) than younger persons; and
- Older persons, however, have both accumulated and demanded through public policy, more than their share of scarce resources and are thus jeopardizing the future of younger generations (5, 7).

These constructions have distinct consequences for the treatment and care of the elderly. Despite the general acceptance of first construction described, physical and especially psychological decline are *not* inevitable parts of aging. Nor is it necessarily true that problems of mental illness experienced by the elderly are directly or solely related to the aging process itself. Drug misuse or interaction, physical illness, stress-related etiologies, societal factors including the individual life experiences of people, and many other factors can cause or greatly contribute to psychological problems in the elderly (8, 9).

This is not to say that the mental health problems of the elderly are not real. On the contrary, many studies cite the probability of underreporting of psychological problems among the elderly, due to factors such as stigma, fear, lack of assessment, and lack of information and training on the part of providers dealing with the aged. However, even with this underreporting bias, the epidemiology of mental illness in late life documents a considerable prevalence in the elderly population (10).

Much disagreement remains about the prevalence of conditions of depression, a major mental health problem among the elderly. Median prevalence rate across studies for depressive disorders in those 65 and over is 3.75/100 and for significant dysphoria, 14.75/100. Although a significant proportion of the elderly reported numerous symptoms of depression, only 4-5 percent met criteria for major depressive illness (10). While different measures result in different rates, it is significant that there are especially low rates among the old as a result of the use of DSM-III criteria that emphasize specific psychiatric disorders and operationalize diagnostic (biomedicalized) criteria. One important issue raised by these authors is the possibility of cohort effects. Rates of depression tend to be significantly lower among the elderly than younger people, and risk factors include gender, social class, marital status, and physical illness. Rates are higher for women, even controlling for all other variables. Some studies show that gender differences remain into older ages, but are somewhat less pronounced.

Across age strata, and whether defined by occupation, education or income, people of low social class are at significantly greater risk for depression (10). For the elderly, the importance of marital status is great, with separated, divorced, and widowed persons at greater risk for depression. The only factor that emerges in all studies as a significant predictor of depression is poor health, particularly in late life. Thus, depression may be less prevalent in elderly than in younger population groups, but it may have greater consequences. For example, higher mortality and morbidity rates may result because of sensitivity to psychotropic drugs, and the lack of alternative treatments. As mentioned above, the special features of clinical presentation of depressive symptoms by the elderly may lead to a misdiagnosis/treatment by health care professionals.

In the important area generally termed senile dementia, the studies indicate that prevalence varies by different types: Alzheimer's disease, vascular/multi-infarct, secondary to alcoholism, and acute (reversible). The best studies result in prevalence results varying between 2.6–23.3 percent (median 11.5 percent) in the elderly population (10). However, in almost all studies, prevalence appears to increase dramatically over the lifespan.

In old age, the prognosis tends to be one of irreversibility, diminishing functional capacity, behavioral problems, and significantly reduced life expectancy. Just as importantly, there is a major family impact. Most patients are cared for at home by family members (11, 12), and this care is often accompanied by extreme stress and burden (13, 14).

Substance abuse and misuse account for a significant proportion of the mental health problems of the elderly, including a great deal that remains unreported and untreated. Typically thought of as young adult issues, both drug and alcohol are problems for a significant proportion of the elderly. Two major groups of special elderly cases are life long alcoholics and drug users, and those that begin use in late life, presumably due to special life stressors. In addition, a category of elders not yet enumerated is, by virtue of complex and unregulated drug use, experiencing psychological as well as physical problems. These complicating problems include, for example, balance disorientation leading to a fall, leading to a fractured hip, leading to institutionalization, leading to disorientation and agitation, leading to the use of further (often psychotropic drug) therapies.

MENTAL HEALTH AS A POLITICAL ISSUE

Reviews of the gerontological and geriatric literature on aging and mental health rarely examine the political context and content of the issues. In fact, the issues of class, race, gender, and age are distinct from much of the current work in mental health and aging. A political perspective, defined in classic work by Laswell (15), characterizes politics as the process of "who gets what, when, how" (16). In the environment of post-industrial capitalism in the United States, the political arena is a central battleground for the medical-industrial complex (17, 18) including mental health. Because of the dominance of public funding for mental health services and research, this area may be even *more* subject to political dealings and negotiation than others (16). However, attention to the political processes alone gives only a partial understanding of the political nature of mental health care because such a perspective tends to stress the distributive aspects of benefits and burdens in a system (16) without equal attention to the productive and reproductive elements also inherent in the process. In part, this is the "economic" part of a "political-economic" perspective although the two elements are not neatly or easily separable. Clarity is especially elusive since the "system" is a varied and fragmented amalgamation set in the broader context of a nearly $600 billion medical-industrial complex operating in an environment of federal, state, and local venues with public and private funders, providers, and consumers (18).

The political economy analysis of health and aging is relatively new. Political economy is ultimately concerned with the social relations of production rather than with individuals or technology as primary causal forces in society (19). Political economy analyses of aging have commonly addressed ways in which the needs of capital accumulation affect the lives of older people, such as pushing them out of the labor force as part of regulation to maximize profits (20, 21). This view presents retirement as a creation of the forces of capital accumulation and the reproduction needs of the capitalist system at a social-structural level rather than as a role or life stage (22). A similar focus in medical sociology examines how the organization of production for profits structures the provision of medical care (17, 23) and the creation of illness (24).

Political economy research in aging has also increasingly focused on the state as a key structural component of advanced capitalism (7) with the policies and institutional arrangements that reinforce the dependent position of the elderly seen as reflecting and reinforcing the prevailing class structure of society (25). The relationship between the state, the needs of capitalism, the structural contradictions of the state in a capitalist system, and the role of ideology are objects for study through health and aging policies of the state (7, 26, 27). In general, political economy analyses are most effective in focusing on social power and inequality. This perspective alters the focus of study from how individuals or society can *adapt* to mental health and aging problems to how political and economic changes can optimize social justice and equality for all ages in society—not only changes in distributive policies, but changes that affect the production and reproduction of mental health problems themselves.

The theoretical perspective chosen leads to the consideration of specific issues and solutions. Dominant paradigms in both medical sociology and social gerontology have traditionally reinforced a focus on medical aspects of illness and the individual pathology (and resulting social problems) of old age. The knowledge that comes from the use of these paradigms is not politically neutral (19). Focusing on particular elements of health and aging makes those elements the primary and legitimate target of social policy to the exclusion of other elements (26).

Paradigmatic approaches to aging and mental health, combine both the hegemony of biomedical particularism and the individuation of most of the dominant gerontological and mental illness/psychological models. What results is a paradigm that both implicitly and explicitly supports notions of individual etiology, illness course, and treatment, with little if any attention paid to the social, economic, political, or environmental factors contributing to causation, maintenance, or exacerbation of mental health problems among the aged.

For example, the policy implications of aging theories are illustrative. Disengagement theory proposes that a "healthy" aging consists of a mutual disengagement of the elderly from the rest of society, yet suggests no policy interventions that aid the withdrawal of the individual and society from each other. In such a framework, retirement policies receive legitimation, as do other separatist approaches (5), but the social isolation, feelings of withdrawal and lack of usefulness, disorientation, and economic hardship that may accompany such disengagement and contribute to psychological problems are not addressed. In contrast, activity theory, which is essentially a classless and universal prescription for continued activity in old age, supports policies that assist in the social integration of the aged. Policies focusing on recreational, exercise, and social activities are among the preferred interventions under activity theory. Similarly, development theories, which are based on the "live and let live" principle, emphasize policies that would enable people to maintain continuity in status throughout the life cycle (26).

Developmental theoreticians endorse highly individualized social policies to meet each individual's needs. All three of these theoretical perspectives provide rationalizations for a purely symbolic policy devoid of class, race/ethnicity, and gender considerations, ignoring the heterogeneity of the aged population and emphasizing individual development, individual problems, and individual solutions. Even the age stratification theory, although attempting to attend to structure via the notions of age cohort and generational succession, has spawned a research tradition focused on differentiating the effects of age, period and cohort but in a manner that still maintains heterogeneous assumptions about the experience of the elderly (26).

Social scientists in the United States have effectively legitimized incrementalist and individualistic approaches to public policy for the elderly. Both health policy and social gerontology in the country reflect this influence. The emphasis on these concepts has spawned a research tradition concerned with social integration, cohort effects, and biomedical models of aging. The biomedical approach in ascendancy determines the research priorities of the major federal research institutes, which seek knowledge of hypothesized biological and physiological sources of decline with age. Biomedical theories not only individualize and medicalize old age, but also overlook the relationship between socioeconomic status, and the economy (Chapter 8). Likewise, dominant models of mental health and the elderly can be categorized as medical or social/psychological models, both of which support individualism, particularism, and reductionism. The medical model views mental health problems as organic in origin, with a discernable progression, and as amenable to medical treatment. This model has become increasingly prevalent, especially in research concerning Alzheimer's disease (28). The social/psychological model acknowledges that causal and/or influential factors may include social, environmental, and psychological elements, and that treatment may include therapeutic interventions not normally considered medical treatment. Nevertheless, both of these models accord central focus to the individual, although human development models of aging emphasize differing roles of the generations, disengagement, adjustment, and coping. Neither model deals with broader societal causes and changes.

The political economy of aging, mental health, and public policy must begin with the understanding that mental illness in a class society has a class character: the 'mental illness' of the owner of the means of production has other causes and forms than the mental illness of those who work on those means (4). The organization of labor, production and reproduction of social relations, and the ideologies underlying this organization contribute to and shape the social and productive relations associated with mental illness in society.

THE PRODUCTION AND TREATMENT OF MENTAL ILLNESS AND THE ELDERLY IN WESTERN CAPITALIST SOCIETY

The production of mental illness in the elderly is intrinsically tied to social and economic relations under capitalism. This is not to deny that some percentage of mental illness among the elderly is organically-based, genetically-predisposed, or otherwise seemingly outside the purview of capitalist origins. But even in those cases, the productive and reproductive mechanisms of mental illness and its treatment in U.S. society inherent in capitalist relations are still major factors in the experience of the problem and care and quality of life the patient may have.

The wage relation (the imposition of labor activity in the commodity form) remains the central antagonistic relation in capitalism, and central to the production of mental illness in the elderly. The "welfare state" represents a transformation (as a result of class and other struggles) as a socialization of the wage relation, particularly to the "surplus labor force," (which the elderly and the mentally ill have both partially constituted), yet the antagonism around this wage relation remains. This transformation has the potential for both the exacerbation of antagonist relations *and* social change (29). On one hand, this socialization has enabled capital to cut labor costs and replace older, possibly less productive workers, thus increasing the potential for profits. At the same time, the state avoids a possible crisis of legitimation (and potential sources of unrest) by providing an alternative source of income to wage labor for a system which widely enforces withdrawal from the paid labor force based on chronological age.

On the other hand, this socialized wage relation can be politically manipulated and conceptualized as a drain on both the state and capital. In health care, this has taken the political form of crisis construction around issues of financing and allocation. Capital claims that it cannot afford the spiraling costs associated with financing health insurance, and the declining rates of profits attributable to providing un- or undercompensated care, while the state asserts that it is spending itself broke by allocating a larger and larger share of its budget to health care and other entitlement programs, premised on the concept of a finite domestic (especially social welfare) budget and inequitable distribution to some segments of the population (30). This transformation of the wage relation, therefore, has the potential to exacerbate antagonisms not only in the capital (and state)/worker relation, but in relations between workers (especially those conceptualized as in "productive" wage relationships and those seen as being in "nonproductive" relations) and sets up segments of the population in opposition to each other in battles over "scarce" resources.

One expression of the antagonism in capital/worker and worker/worker relations is the "Setting Limits" debate. Popularized in the past several years by such groups as Americans for Generational Equity (AGE) and individuals such as former Colorado governor Richard Lamm and ethicist Daniel Callahan (31), this debate centers in the question of the spiraling costs of supporting the elderly with an ever-increasing life span in an era of fiscal austerity. The proposals for "setting limits" on the availability and provision of medical care to the elderly are framed in such a way that the elderly are portrayed as villains, greedily demanding more and more of societal resources at the expense of others, especially children. Increasingly, the mental illness problems of the elderly have taken center stage in this debate, with reports of the catastrophic effects of the aging of the population on health care costs, especially the costs of caring for elders with dementias (2, 3, 32).

Although science and technology appear to be able to dominate both nature and the human body, they have failed to provide solutions to the problem of mental illness in the elderly. Instead, one population group is pitted against another in a politically characterized battle for survival in an age of objective scarcity. An ideology of scarcity and competition is perpetuated for political ends while the roots of the contradiction are ignored—the need for capital expansion and profit accumulation by specific interests (loosely termed the "medical industrial complex," which has utilized the growth, longevity, and now mental health problems of the elderly population for its purposes, versus the debit that occurs when the growing costs for such profit cannot be met by the population, due in part to the transformation of the wage relation for that population.

INSTITUTIONALIZATION AND DEINSTITUTIONALIZATION

The issues of institutionalization and deinstitutionalization have been with us for several decades, although few investigations have examined the specific effects of changing policies on the mentally ill elderly. In one such attempt, Estes and Harrington examine the history of policies that initially increased the institutionalization of the elderly during this century and developed institutions into private profit-making enterprises (33). Because capitalism must maintain a constant supply of labor, groups unable to be part of the workforce—including the mentally ill and the elderly—were labeled as problems, disenfranchised, and assigned to a system of institutions under the control of a new group of professional caretakers (23, 33). Between 1910 and 1970, there was a 267 percent increase in the proportion of the elderly residing in institutions or group quarters of some type. The trends, however, show that the type of institution changed considerably over this period, with a tremendous decrease, especially in the years 1960-1970, of the elderly residing in mental institutions and a significant increase in those residing in nursing homes and residential care homes (33).

The trend toward the deinstitutionalization of the state mental hospital population begun in the mid-1950s had a major effect on the elderly in these institutions. It was argued that the aged were the least likely to benefit from psychiatric treatment and thus could be cared for in less costly, nontherapeutic settings such as nursing homes. A large number of persons were dumped from mental institutions as a result, often with no other place to go (23).

Thus, policies over time first incarcerated the elderly with mental health problems, then decarcerated many of the aged, while reincarcerating others into board and care, inadequate single-room-occupancy hotels, and nursing homes. The likelihood of assignment to a particular care site bears a strong relationship to general cultural values of deservingness and underservingness (7)—values related to class, gender, race, and perceptions of the economic utility of the elderly to the capitalist class and accumulation. Class issues abound. Middle-class, white elderly, especially with sufficient assets to avoid the Medicaid system, are more likely to be institutionalized in a nursing home if mental problems arise. Poor and/or nonwhite elders are more likely to be unable to obtain a nursing home bed. Elders with chronic mental illness, especially if combined with poverty, are likely to be deinstitutionalized (the nursing home population is only 6 percent Black and 1 percent other nonwhite residents), even though low income, social isolation, and lack of social support are all related with increased vulnerability to mental health problems (34–42).

MENTAL HEALTH AND THE NURSING HOME

By the 1960s, due to effects of the Hill-Burton Act and other policies to promote private incentives, there was a tremendous rise in the number of nursing homes, with nearly all growth in the proprietary sector. The institutional and acute care bias of the Medicare/Medicaid program has encouraged nursing home placement rather than other community-based care such as home health care for elders who are sick and living at home (33).

At any given point in time, about 5 percent of the elderly population in the United States are in nursing homes (43–45), and the risk of institutionalization in an individual's lifetime is about 25 percent (44). With advancing age, the risk of institutionalization increases. Data from the National Nursing Home Survey (1985) indicates that 1 percent of those persons 65–74 are institutionalized, while 22 percent of those persons 85 and older were in institutions (46). As the population ages, the current population of more than 1.3 million nursing home residents is expected to more than triple to 4.6 million by 2040 (47), raising with it, the current $40 billion costs of this care.

Data from the National Institute of Mental Health (NIMH) estimates that between 668,000 and 855,270 have serious mental problems (50-60 percent of residents), and at least 72,000 are placed in nursing homes as a result of mental illness with no accompanying physical disorder (48, 49). Nursing homes are thus the largest single site for the care of persons with mental illness (50). In addition, upwards of 70 percent of residents may be suffering from Alzheimer's disease or a related disorder, although only 5 percent have had contact with a mental health professional (49). In general, the elderly, both institutionalized and noninstitutionalized, are greatly under-treated for mental health problems. An estimated 15-25 percent of older Americans have significant mental health problems but receive only 7 percent of inpatient psychiatric services, 6 percent of community mental health center (CMHC) services, and 2 percent of the services provided in private psychiatrist's offices (49, 51).

Despite one of the original goals of the deinstitutionalization movement from state mental institutions, the elderly with mental health problems in nursing homes frequently receive little or inappropriate care for these problems. All too often, nursing home residents with behavior problems are over-medicated with psycho-tropic drugs, causing physical side effects as well as serious psychological effects such as depression, agitation, sedation, and confusion (52). There remains a substantial unmet need for mental health services for the nursing home population, particularly a need for trained nursing home staff to treat mentally ill nursing home residents and for funding of mental health services in nursing homes (53).

The situation of the elderly with mental health problems in nursing homes illustrates the intersection of personal lives, public policy, geriatric practice, and the organization of health and medical care in the United States. Staffing issues, including the nursing shortage, professional turf battles, and the use of staffing patterns to cut costs are also closely related to the situation of the mentally ill elderly. The majority of care for the mentally ill elderly is provided by the least skilled staff in the facility—staff who themselves are likely to be subjected to severe personal and professional stresses. In addition, although little data exists on the extent of mental health interventions in nursing homes, some studies estimated that fewer than 1 percent of all patients with a diagnosable mental disorder receive appropriate interventions of any kind (54, 55).

One barrier to appropriate care is that there are not enough mental health practitioners of any type to meet current or estimated future needs. Further, Medicare policy works in direct opposition to psychiatric involvement in nursing homes. For a patient covered by Part B of Medicare, only an initial consult and two brief follow-up visits are covered, and the out-of-pocket expenses for psychiatry are not covered. There is no coverage whatsoever for persons without Part B. In addition, Medicare "supervisoral" regulation inhibits qualified psychologists from practicing due to the Medicare requirements that mandate physician supervision, placing psychologists in conflict with their professional code of ethics, and further limiting the chances that institutionalized elders with mental health problems will receive adequate care (54).

Unfortunately, one of the most prevalent forms of care for the institutionalized elderly is drug treatment. A recent report by the Inspector General of the U.S. Department of Health and Human Services analyzed the prescription drug use of residents in nursing homes and reported that 61 percent of the institutionalized elderly receive three or more prescription drugs, 37 percent five or more, and 19 percent seven or more. While this may seem warranted by the documented comorbidity of the institutionalized elderly, additional studies show the high rate of antipsychotic drug use in nursing homes—up to 43 percent of residents in one study were receiving antipsychotic drugs, a study that has been replicated by many others (56). It has been found that 21 percent of those receiving a psychotropic drug had no diagnosis of a mental disorder (54, 56).

The inappropriate use of such antipsychotic drugs can cause depression, agita-tion, sedation, and confusion, the precise kind of behaviors for which they were used initially. They can also mask psychological disease, and make depression, anxiety, and confusion difficult to recognize. These drugs also have the effect of subordinating the patient's autonomy to the caregivers, becoming social control agents and raising serious ethical questions (57, 58).

Staffing patterns, labor policies, and governmental regulations also contribute to the overuse and abuse of psychotropic and psychoactive drugs among the elderly in nursing homes and other similar institutions. First, the lack of physician contact (with both patients and nursing staff) and monitoring not only increases the possibility of ineffective and inappropriate drug use, but also increases the chances of unintentional drug interactions. Since only physicians can receive direct Medicare payment for mental health services, between 75-85 percent of mental health services do not come from a mental health professional but un- or under-trained general physicians (59). Physicians who lack specialized training in the mental health problems of the elderly are less likely to know about alternative treatments for geriatric mental health problems, and may create iatrogenic mental health problems. Alternative treatments, when considered, are often rejected because they are not covered by Health Care Financing Administration or fiscal intermediary policies. In addition, collaboration between nurses, physicians, and pharmacists in nursing homes is jeopardized by labor policies and shortages that place a single RN in charge of dozens of patients and make an aide responsible for 15 or more (45). Under such circumstances, even if a patient is known to be anxious or grieving for a lost lifestyle rather than psychotic, drugs may be used for social control, rather than as therapeutic agents. The use of other trained professionals such as nurse practitioners, physician assistants, and pharmacists in "pharmacists as prescribers" programs to monitor the drug regimens of patients in nursing homes could go a long way to alleviate this situation, yet rarely are they used. This problem also extends to community-resident elders who also have very high usage of psychological drugs and have a great risk of unsupervised polypharmacy (the use of multiple drugs) (60, 61).

Again, race, class and gender issues are dominant in determining the risk of institutionalization (and presumably risk of incarceration by the use of chemical and physical restraints). Women make up three-quarters of the nursing home population, and have a far greater risk of institutionalization due to cognitive problems than do their male counterparts, especially in the older cohorts, although several studies indicate that there may not be a significant gender difference in some types of mental disorders (39, 40, 62). Women are, however, much less likely than men to have the social support necessary to maintain themselves in the community (36–38) and are more likely to have chronic impairments (often as a result of a lifetime of multiple generational caregiving, both major factors in the risk of institutionalization in nursing homes.

THE ALZHEIMER'S ENTERPRISE

In many ways, the fragmentation and contradiction inherent in the treatment of the elderly with mental health problems can be represented by the multiple, and often contradictory roles played by what may be termed the *"Alzheimer's Enterprise."* In 1979, Estes coined the phrase the *"Aging Enterprise"* with her description and indictment of the complex of professions and entrepreneurial and bureaucratic interests—the "Geriatric Establishment"—that exists both to serve a specified and in-need population but also to serve the servicing system and further the needs of capitalism itself (5). This classic formulation of the aging enterprise points to the fact that the needs of the elderly are defined in ways that are compatible with the needs of capital, thus transforming the elderly and their needs into state-supported commodities for the use of capital (5, 25), the system of research, professions, services, organizations, and policies dedicated to Alzheimer's disease and its victims can also be viewed similarly as an "Alzheimer's Enterprise,"—an enterprise that is in some important ways distorting policy formation for the mentally ill elderly by crowding out every other type of mental health problem while increasing the biomedical hegemony and control over definition and policy (Chapter 9, 28, 63).

Alzheimer's disease has increasingly gained attention, and an accompanying sense of urgency because of the enormous costs involved in caring for potentially millions of people with the debilitating disorder (3, 64, 65). Estimates of the billions of dollars to be incurred into the next century have fueled public awareness of the "disease of the century." Alzheimer's has been socially created as a crisis of epidemic proportion (63, 66). Major increases in funding allocations for research in search of a cure (and moderate ones for direct service provision) have been legitimated, but have had the detrimental side effect of deflecting attention and resources from many more prevalent and treatable mental and physical conditions of old age.

The biomedicalization of mental health problems has diverted a majority of attention and funds to biomedical Alzheimer's disease research (Chapter 8, 28, 63, 67) and sapped resources from service provision and non-Alzheimer's problems. Voluntary associations of consumers and advocates have sprung up under the umbrella of the national Alzheimer's Disease and Related Disorders Association (ADRDA) (28). This organization, while responsible for an untold amount of positive action, has also in some ways acted to the detriment of the broader issues of mental illness and the elderly. By promoting the case of both organic causation (excluding any label of "mental illness,") and biomedical research as the sole source of "cure," ADRDA has been in part responsive to the acute and medical care bias of current health and social policy. The organization has, at the same time, retarded progress and social action or broader societal factors and issues. It has, perhaps unwittingly, played into the individuation and organicism promoted by biomedicine and its effect on policy, only one consequence of which is the proliferation of what can only be termed "insurance scams" that have left hundreds of thousands increasingly impoverished and still uninsured for the costs of Alzheimer's disease. A diagnosis of Alzheimer's may have the benefit of access to an increasingly specialized service system (e.g., day care, respite care), but this is dependent on many external conditions and may, in fact, limit access to other types of care (i.e., SNFs or Medicare/Medigap coverage). ADRDA has also been a major supporter, along with the government (68, 69) of private policy initiatives and financial support, rather than universalist and federal/state initiatives, to deal with current and future problems of AD. This focus increases the comodification potential of AD for various segments of capital, as well as the likelihood for access differentials for specific segments of the population. Sole attention to the problem of Alzheimer's may limit research into the causes of other, non-AD mental problems including depression, affective disorders, drug overdoses and interactions, and social causation (e.g., lack of social support, fear). This problem is exacerbated further when research into the causes of various types of dementias gives priority to organically caused illness over non-organically caused problems.

POLICY ISSUES: MENTAL HEALTH AND AGING POLICY AS REFLECTIVE OF CLASS INTERESTS

OMNIBUS BUDGET RECONCILIATION ACT OF 1987 AND BEYOND

The passage of the Omnibus Budget Reconciliation Act of 1987 (OBRA) marked a watershed in the development of social policy for the elderly, especially the institutionalized elderly and those with mental health problems. This sweeping legislation affects many segments of the treatment and financing of care for the elderly, and has potentially massive impact on the institutionalized sector of care, especially the nursing home industry. Among the provisions of this legislation are major reforms including requirements for uniform assessment and screening of patients and provisions concerning the use of chemical and physical restraints in institutional settings. Both provisions have major implications for the organization and delivery of care to tremendous numbers of elders in the United States.

The intent of the nursing home screening regulations is positive: to assure the most appropriate placement of elderly patients with mental health problems. However, the policy does not consider the problems of comorbidity, especially the interconnectedness of physical and mental health. The lack of interdisciplinary assessment and coordination remains a major barrier to adequate care. The OBRA 1987 uniform assessment regulations present the possibility that prospective nursing home patients in need of mental health care will be denied physical care because institutions are unable to meet their mental health needs. There is also the possibility that some current residents will lose their places in homes because their mental health needs are deemed too severe to be treated in such facilities. Even if proper referral mechanisms were in place and assured by legislation, the assault on the community-based system of care and on state-funded institutions has rendered many alternative sites and forms of care inadequate or unavailable substitutes.

Many alternative sites, such as board and care homes, are even less prepared to deliver adequate psychological care, yet may, de facto, become the "nursing homes" for the mentally ill elderly denied access to nursing homes.

In addition, the HFCA policy of requiring a board-certified psychiatrist to certify all assessments is another well-intentioned policy that could adversely affect poor, rural, and minority elderly populations. Designed austensibly to accurately assess any physical comorbidity along with mental status (although continuing the dominance of biomedical control and hegemony is also at issue), the unequal geographical distribution of psychiatrists means that many patients are waiting extra days in acute hospital settings. The new assessment policies have caused a furor in the hospital sector with hospitals claiming the new regulations are causing a crisis of hundreds of "unnecessary" hospital days in which "the patient becomes stranded in the hospital and the hospital becomes a holding facility" (70). But little is being said about the greater burden borne by rural, poor urban, and minority clients in settings where certifying psychiatrists are rare or those in states that are interpreting the regulations very strictly, creating lengthy waits for assessment. This state differentiation is a recurrent theme in many aspects of mental health care, especially for the elderly, and remains a critical political-economic issue. Each state is given the leeway to adopt its own assessment technique and procedures, and thus there is no standardization of measures (even though established, standardized measures are available).

Many knowledgeable practitioners and administrators in the field feel that the exclusion of psychologists and other qualified mental health personnel from participating in the screening process further inhibits the accurate and expeditious assessment and placement of patients. The exclusion of such practitioners also plays into a biomedical treatment bias by limiting the potential for behavioral and interdisciplinary treatment modalities, and quite possibly increasing the overuse of psychotropic and psychoactive drugs.

Medicare policy, including the OBRA 1987 regulations, currently work against accurate assessment and diagnosis of mental disorders of residents in nursing homes because institutions may run the risk of being labeled Institutions for Mental Disease, and thus lose their Medicare funding if a sufficient proportion of their population is diagnosed as mentally ill. This contributes to the further medicalization of nursing home care by encouraging all problems to be diagnosed and labeled as physical disorders, discouraging appropriate psychological interventions (54).

The use of both chemical and physical restraints in nursing homes, other institutional settings and in private homes is a complex issue in the treatment and care of the mentally ill elderly. The issue has garnered such attention that another provision of Omnibus Budget Reconciliation Act of 1987 (OBRA 1987(C): Sec. 1819; 1819) addresses nursing home patient rights as they pertain to use of both physical/mechanical and chemical restraints. The Act states that the resident has "the right to be free from physical or mental abuse, corporal punishment, involuntary seclusion, and any physical or chemical restraints imposed for reasons of discipline or convenience and not required to treat the resident's medical symptoms." However, the interpretation and consequences of this regulation is the subject of considerable debate and controversy. A meta-analytic study of physical restraint use (71) indicates that an extraordinary number of older Americans, over a half million daily, are physically restrained to beds and chairs, although there is a surprising lack of literature concerning the practice. Restraint and control practices have been greatly reduced among non-elderly psychiatric patients, but remain common in institutions that serve the elderly. Studies indicate that the incidence and prevalence of use varies by setting and by particular patient characteristics. Evans and Strumpf identify patient predictors of restraint use in the elderly as age, cognitive impairment, risk of injury to self or other, physical frailty, presence of monitoring or treatment device, and need to promote body alignment. They also note that the literature indicates several systemic factors, including administrative pressure to avoid litigation, availability of restraint devices, staff attitudes, and insufficient staffing (71). However, the interaction of these two sets of characteristics is unclear due to the limited amount of data, and no analysis has been done of the interaction and correlation of patient and structural factors. Williams identifies six elements as minimal standards for institutional care: continuity of relationships; opportunities for choices; comfort, safety, and a homelike setting; staff attitude/morale; and special care for people with dementia (72). Yet the majority of institutions continue and defend the use of leg restraints, hand mitts, soft ties, vests, wheelchair safety bars or Gerichairs, limiting the physical autonomy of patients who may also be chemically restrained.

FINANCING, DELIVERY, AND ACCESS: THE POLITICS OF MENTAL HEALTH SERVICES FOR THE ELDERLY

Any political-economic analysis of mental health care for the elderly must eventually consider the politics of financing and delivery. Mental health services, like other forms of health services, depend on financing and reimbursement systems, and are shaped by them. Like the entire U.S. health care system, mental health policy and delivery is biased toward acute rather than chronic care, medical rather than social/psychological care, inpatient and traditional care rather than other alternatives (51). These biases, coupled with the penurious social policies of the late 1970s and 1980s (30), have created not only a fragmented, inequitable, and inefficient system, but one unable to address the changing needs of the elderly requiring mental health services. While the deinstitutionalization of the 1960s through the 1980s, and the reinstitutionalization of many sectors of the elderly with mental health problems due to effects of prospective hospital payment and a lack of resources for community-based services radically changed the environment, and needs for the delivery of mental health services, policy and the organization of care has not kept pace.

The financing of mental health services for the elderly is complicated by the multiple and decentralized sources of payment and reporting systems. On the financing end alone, payment sources include Medicare, Medicaid, Supplemental Security Income, Social Security Disability Insurance, Title XX, private insurance, and out-of-pocket payments (51, 59, 73–75). And as mentioned above, deinstitutionalization and reinstitutionalization have created important changes in the mode and location of delivery of services which have, themselves, affected and been affected by current financing policies.

Reimbursement programs have been the major factor in shaping the mental health "system,"—a fragmented non-system of providers and services—and this is especially true of the sector that provides care to the mentally ill elderly. For the elderly, much of this care is provided by non-mental health providers in settings that do not mainly provide psychiatric care (59, 76, 77). In part because of the reimbursement-driven nature of the system, the elderly underutilize formal mental health system services as compared to other population groups (59).

The U.S. House of Representatives Select Committee on Aging (1980) reported that 25 percent of persons aged 65 and over have significant mental health problems (78), and a recent NIMH study estimates that 9 to 18 percent of the elderly in America have diagnosable mental disorders, with an additional 12 to 18 percent suffering mild cognitive impairment (10). Yet only 5 to 20 percent of persons aged 65 and older with a recent mental disorder made even one mental health visit, even to a general medical practitioner, and the proportion seeking treatment in either a Community Mental Health Center or a private practice setting is even lower (77, 79).

Underutilization of mental health services by the elderly is represented in much of the gerontological literature as a problem of negative attitudes, either on the part of service providers or of the elderly themselves (8, 78–84). Much of the literature focuses on the problem of the elderly's attitudes toward mental health care and mechanisms to change such attitudes (78, 82, 83), there is also some work on the characteristics of providers that predispose them to negative attitudes and treatment of the aged (81).

However, all of these studies share the omission of macro-level factors that would take the analysis beyond the level of the individual. Little systematic attention is paid to the interaction of the dual factors of the general American cultural attitude of negativity and abhorrence toward mental illness and the mentally ill (82) and the ideological factors that have constructed old age in this society, including a set of values and policies creating a "blame the elderly victim" mentality (7, 84, 85). The power and importance of these factors cannot be underestimated in an analysis of the underutilization of mental health services for the elderly. Research indicates that social class has a significant effect on the use of mental health services in at least two ways. First, the social class effect is shown in terms of willingness to accept psychiatric treatment, a psychiatric point of view, and the role as a mental patient (82, 86). Social class is also related to practitioners' attitudes, their perception of the utility and effectiveness of treatment, and the willingness to accept the client for treatment (86, 87). In their classic study, Hollingshead and Redlich document the correlation of age and class in the determination of who will receive psychological care, with lower social classes receiving less care which increases with the age of cohort (87).

But in addition, a number of systemic factors have been identified as being critical, not the least of which is the segregated system of service organization for the elderly as opposed to the general population, and the role of financing and reimbursement in shaping this organization of services. Government programs have played an especially important role in forming the mental health care system, and higher proportions of funding have come from governmental sources than for other forms of health care, largely due to the lack of coverage for such services by private insurers, severely restricted benefits when coverage is offered, and the high rates of uninsurance among populations most at risk (51, 88).

Medicare, the primary source of health financing for most elderly people, covers very little mental health care. Less than 3 percent of the Medicare dollar is spent on mental health (75, 89), reflecting both the underutilization of and lack of access to mental health services by the elderly. Medicare pays for the evaluation of mental illnesses, but its payment for treatment differs from that for physical illness. Under OBRA 1987, the Medicare Part B payment ceiling for mental health care was increased from 50 percent of the first $500 to 50 percent of the first $2,200, placing the payments more in line with those for other chronic illnesses. In addition, a 1984 Medicare ruling excluded patients with Alzheimer's disease and related disorders from the $500 (now $2200) limit (one of the "benefits" of an AD diagnosis). Finally, in the 1989 budget reconciliation, the limit for psychotherapy was lifted although the 50 percent cost sharing was retained (75, 89). Contrasted with the 20 percent cost sharing for other outpatient services under Medicare, this 50 percent cost sharing is much more burdensome to low- and moderate-income elderly people, limiting access and utilization. Under Medicare Part A, there is a lifetime limit of 190 days of paid care in freestanding psychiatric hospitals, and 90 days per benefit period in general hospitals, resulting in the likelihood of uncovered days for chronically mentally ill elderly.

Medicaid has always been more generous with regard to mental health benefits than Medicare, and it accounts for about two-thirds of federal funding for mental health care (51). Yet strong financial incentives in the Medicare program, such as higher spend-down levels for institutionalized patients, encourage institutionalization (90), and federal participation has encouraged states to institutionalize the elderly in nursing homes rather than in state mental hospitals (51). The latitude of state discretion in the Medicaid program causes mental health care coverage to be a patchwork of policies, benefits, reimbursements, and eligibility levels (51, 73). Coverage has increasingly been limited throughout the decade of the 1980s (88), further burdening the states with indigent care, and jeopardizing access to needed care by the poor and near-poor (51). In addition, the advent of prospective payment reimbursement in nursing homes in nearly every state has served to further restrain Medicaid expenditures for nursing homes, possibly further limiting access (51).

The regulations have the potential for limiting access to the major site of care for elders with mental health problems—the nursing home—and although far from perfect, the nursing home remains an important cog in the long term care continuum for many, especially for the elderly with problems of mental illness. Although effects of these regulations are not yet known, if access to this site of care is limited, the further transfer of responsibility to families (informalization) is assured. For the older person with a variety of physical as well as mental health needs, the ability to obtain the needed range of services is increasingly limited.

Efforts to create a rational and responsive mental health policy on aging in the late 1970s were suffocated by Reagan's successful push for OBRA 1981 legislation which effectively cancelled a special community-based program of mental health for the elderly and imposed block grants for mental health services (the Alcohol, Drug Abuse, and Mental Health Block Grant) (89). This legislation not only placed CHMC programs in competition with other social programs, but also increased the competition for service priorities between the (younger) chronically mentally ill and the aged (51). Increasing attention to drug problems, the homeless, and other crises has eroded and occluded the meager attention paid to the elderly with mental health problems. Competition between disenfranchised groups only serves to deflect attention from common issues and common solutions.

CONCLUSION: TOWARD THE DEVELOPMENT OF MARXIST MODELS

It is clear that we need not only new institutions and service delivery structures for the elderly with mental health problems, but new models for thinking about these issues as well. In *Setting Limits*, Daniel Callahan insists that we reconsider and develop a social consensus on the meaning and social significance of aging (31), believing from this reconsideration (which Callahan believes must be based on communal and not individual values), that a truly just social policy for the aged will be found. In Callahan's view, individualism must give way to a community-based and -affirmed notion of the value of the aged in society and an acceptance of limits to health care for the aged. These limits, he contends, will not result in the abandonment of the old because the new social consensus will provide older people with a deep sense of value in the community and also the guarantee that they will receive comfort, care, and relief from suffering (31).

But for the elderly in our society, especially those with mental health problems, this promise is not remotely close to being fulfilled. The project that remains is to develop models of aging and of mental health and illness that radically depart from old conceptions and replace them with values, beliefs, institutions, and structures which affirm, support, empower and serve those in need. Policies and institutions of social, economic, and political reform are required to ensure that true needs of those groups disenfranchised from the mainstream of society are not subsumed under the needs of capitalism. The question is: "How would a truly democratic model of aging and mental illness look, and what kinds of institutions and programs, social and economic responses would be required to put this model into practice?"

One preliminary set of answers to these questions is presented in the work of Italian psychiatrist Franco Basaglia (1924–1980), who has perhaps been most responsible for furthering innovative democratic models and policies and placing them into practice. A young psychiatrist in rural Italy, Basaglia ran a small, 650 bed psychiatric hospital in Gorizia. There he began to dismantle the asylum by abandoning even new "liberal" models of psychiatry (phenomenological, behaviorist, and existential alike) because in them, he recognized the same limitations as in the old organicist models—an inability to cast light on the class nature of illness, and the larger social and political context that determines its expression (91).

> Like psychoanalysis, [these new models] have yet to modify the nature of the object with its inquiry; it keeps [the person who is ill] at a distance in the same objective and a-dialectical dimension to which classical psychiatry has already relegated it (Basaglia, 1967 fn17).

While at Gorizia, Basaglia gradually worked to eliminate the features of the asylum that made it an institution of violence and dehumanization in order to create an environment (rather than an institution) that met the needs of those who, by virtue of their difference, had been punished, disenfranchised, and incarcerated by society.

Utopian visions of mental health care (the perfect asylum, the well-run community, or the territorial system) have shifted in accordance with the changing goals of the social and historical context. Yet their application always falls short of the ideal aspired to and, in the end, generally results in custodialism or a new, more subtle form of domination, and an emergent professionalism is revealed or rediscovered (91). The work of Basaglia marks an epistomological break in the history of western psychiatry by creating a *practical* utopian vision of caring for the mentally ill, wedded to a political praxis (which later resulted in Law 180, a landmark and far-reaching piece of legislation that transformed the old system of psychiatry in Italy) and grounded in its specific historical and social context (91). For Gorizia, this meant not only an "open-door" policy, but increasing patient autonomy in medication policy, the establishment of a paid-work system to replace forced unpaid labor from patients in the name of "therapy," and the assemblee, a daily public meeting where chaotic complaints and demands eventually gave way to a collectivization of responsibility for both leadership and the consequences of behavior (91). This led, eventually not only to an unlocked institution but, unlike the deinstitutionalization of the American mental health system, to a radical transformation of the alternative environments to which these patients returned, including adequate social and medical services, housing, appropriate employment, and a process that began the process of opening up communities to make them more "receptive, responsive, and responsible, and more than just passively tolerant" (91).

It is hoped that the work of Basaglia sketched above and that of similar reformers might serve to inspire creative and critical thinking about the massive problems faced by the mentally ill elderly in our society. In the United States, the use of the mentally ill elderly (and other disenfranchized populations) to help solve the problems of the state and capital have created new organizational forms and new institutionalized responses to control and regulate suffering among the elderly. But these trends have left the major structures of oppression untouched. Basaglia's work offers hope for a simultaneous deinstitutionalization and empowerment to encourage democratic participation and actions that promote autonomy and resistance, even if voiced in a way that may be labeled deviant by much of society (91). The project ahead is to introduce these ideas and ideals to the U.S. context and challenge the social and cultural norms that undergird our treatment of the mentally ill elderly, while changing the structures that help produce and reproduce such problems.

REFERENCES

1. Waldo, D. R., and Lazenby, H. C. Demographic characteristics and health care use and expenditure by the aged in the United States: 1977–84. *Health Care Fin. Rev.* 6: 1–28, 1984.
2. Guralnik, J. M., Yanagishita, M., and Schneider, E. L. Projecting the older population of the U.S.: Lessons from the past and prospects for the future. *The Milbank Q.* 66(2): 283–308, 1988.
3. Schneider, E. L., and Guralnik, J. L. The aging of America: Impact on health care costs. *JAMA* 263(17): 2335–2340, 1990.
4. Dowd, J. J. Mental illness and the aged stranger. In *Readings in the Political Economy of Aging*, edited by M. Minkler and C. L. Estes, pp. 94–116. Baywood Publishing, Amityville, New York, 1984.
5. Estes, C. L. *The Aging Enterprise*. Jossey-Bass, San Francisco, California, 1979.
6. Berger, P., and Luckmann, T. *The Social Construction of Reality*. Doubleday, New York, 1966.
7. Estes, C. L., Gerard, L. E., Zones, J. S., and Swan, J. H. *Political Economy, Health and Aging*. Little Brown, Boston, 1984.
8. Butler, R. N., and Lewis, M. I. *Aging and Mental Health*. The C. V. Mosby Co., St. Louis, Missouri, 1982.
9. Lurie, E. E. The interrelationship of physical and mental illness in the elderly. In *Serving the Mentally Ill Elderly: Problems and Perspectives*, edited by E. E. Lurie, J. H. Swan, et al., pp. 39–60. Lexington Books, Lexington, Massachusetts, 1987.

10. Bliwise, N. G., McCall, M. E., and Swan, S. J. The epidemiology of mental illness in late life. In *Serving the Mentally Ill Elderly: Problems and Perspectives*, edited by E. E. Lurie and J. H. Swan, et al., pp. 1–38. Lexington Books, Lexington, Massachusetts, 1987.

11. Johnson, C. L., and Catalano, D. J. A longitudinal study of family supports to impaired elderly.*The Gerontologist* 23: 612–618, 1983.

12. Moon, M. The role of the family in the economic well-being of the elderly. *The Gerontologist* 23: 45–50, 1983.

13. Brody, E. M. Parent care as normative family stress. *The Gerontologist* 25: 19–29, 1985.

14. Cohen, B., Kennedy, G., and Eisdorfer, C. Clinical Reality of the Family Caring for a Relative with Alzheimer's Disease and Family Management. Paper presented at the Annual Meeting of the Gerontologist Society, San Francisco, 1983.

15. Laswell, H. D. *Politics: Who Gets What, When, How.* McGraw Hill, New York, 1936.

16. Rochefort, D. A. The political context of mental health care. In *Improving Mental Health Services: What the Social Sciences Can Tell Us. New Directions for Mental Health Services*, edited by D. Mechanic, pp. 93–106, no. 36. Jossey-Bass, San Francisco, 1987.

17. Navarro, V. *Crisis, Health, and Medicine: A Social Critique.* Tavistock Publishers, New York, 1986.

18. Estes, C. L., Harrington, C. A., Davis, S., and Binney, E. A. The medical industrial complex. In *Political Economy, Health and Aging*, edited by C. L. Estes et al., forthcoming.

19. Alford, R. R., and Friedland, R. *Powers of Theory.* Cambridge University Press, New York, 1985.

20. Graebner, W. *A History of Retirement.* Yale University Press, New Haven, Connecticut, 1980.

21. Estes, C. L., Swan, J. H., and Gerard, L. G. Dominant and competing paradigms: Toward a political economy of aging. *Age. and Soc.* 2(2): 151–164, 1982.

22. Guillemard, A. M. *Old Age and the Welfare State.* Sage, Beverly Hills, California, 1983.

23. Scull, A. T. *Decarceration: Community Treatment and the Deviant-A Radical View.* Prentice-Hall, Englewood Cliffs, New Jersey, 1977.

24. Waitzkin, H. *The Second Sickness.* The Free Press, New York, 1983.

25. Estes, C. L. The aging enterprise: In whose interests? *Int. J. Health Serv.* 16(2): 243–251, 1986.

26. Estes, C. L., Wallace, S. P., and Binney, E. A. Health, aging, and medical sociology. In *Handbook of Medical Sociology* (4th ed.), edited by H. E. Freeman and S. Levine, pp. 400–418. Prentice-Hall, Englewood Cliffs, New Jersey, 1989.

27. Brown, E. R. *Rockefeller Medicine Men.* University of California Press, Berkeley, 1979.

28. Fox, P. From senility to Alzheimer's Disease: The rise of the Alzheimer's Disease movement. *Milbank Mem. Fund Q.* 67(1): 58–102, 1989.

29. Swan, J. H., and Gerard, L. E. Reimbursement and funding systems. In *Serving the Mentally Ill Elderly: Problems and Perspectives*, edited by E. E. Lurie and J. H. Swan et al., pp. 139–161. Lexington Books, Lexington, Massachusetts, 1987.

30. Estes, C. L. The Reagan legacy: Privatization, the welfare state, and aging. In *States, Labor Markets & The Future of Old Age Policy*, edited by J. Myles and J. Quadagno. Temple University Press, Philadelphia, 1990.

31. Callahan, D. *Setting Limits: Medical Goals in an Aging Society*. Simon and Schuster, New York, 1987.
32. Fries, J. F. The sunny side of aging. *JAMA* 263(17): 2354–2355, May 2, 1990.
33. Estes, C. L., and Harrington, C. A. Fiscal crisis, deinstitutionalization, and the elderly. *Am. Behav. Sci.* 24(6): 811–826, July/August 1981.
34. Wagenaar, H., and Lewis, D. A. Ironies of inclusion: Social class and deinstitutionalization. *J. Health Pol., Polit. and Law* 14(3): 503–522, 1988.
35. Butler, R. N., and Lewis, M. I. *Aging and Mental Health*. The C. V. Mosby Co., St. Louis, Missouri, 1977.
36. U.S. Senate. Special Committee on Aging. *Developments in Aging: 1987*. Vol. 1, U.S. Government Printing Office, Washington, D.C., 1987.
37. U.S. Senate, Special Committee on Aging. *Developments in Aging: 1987*. Volume 2. U.S. Government Printing Office, Washington, D.C., 1987.
38. U.S. Senate, Special Committee on Aging. *Developments in Aging: 1987. The Long-Term Care Challenge*. Vol. 3, U.S. Government Printing Office, Washington, D.C., 1987.
39. Feinson, M. C. Mental health and aging: Are there gender differences? *The Gerontologist* 27(6): 703–711, 1987.
40. Waxman, H. M., Carner, E. A., and Klein, M. Underutilization of mental health professionals by community elderly. *The Gerontologist* 24(1): 23–30, 1984.
41. Webster, D. Women and mental health. In *Women's Health Perspectives: An Annual Review*, Vol. 1., edited by C. J. Leppa, pp. 14–33. Oryx Press, New York, 1988.
42. Snapp, M. B. *Toward Race, Class, and Gender Inclusive Research on Stress, Social Support, and Psychological Distress: A Critical Review of the Literature*. Center for Research on Women, Memphis State University, Memphis, 1989.
43. Liang, J., and E. J.-C. Tu. Estimating lifetime risk of nursing home residency: A further note. *The Gerontologist* 26(5): 560–563, 1986.
44. Palmore, E. Risk of institutionalization among the aged. *The Gerontologist* 16(5): 504–507, 1976.
45. Johnson, C. L., and Grant, L. A. *The Nursing Home in American Society*. Johns Hopkins University Press, Baltimore, Maryland, 1985.
46. Hing, E. Use of nursing homes by the elderly: Preliminary data from the 1985 National Nursing Home Survey. *Adv. Data* 135: 1–12, 1987.
47. U.S. Senate. Special Committee on Aging. *Developments in Aging: 1986*. Vol. 1. U.S. Government Printing Office, Washington, D.C., 1986.
48. Roybal, E. R. Testimony before the Subcommittee on Human Services and the Select Committee on Aging, House of Representatives, U.S. House of Representatives. *Mental Health in Nursing Homes: Barriers and Solutions*. Joint Hearing Before the Subcommittee on Human Services and Select Committee on Aging. 101st Congress. August 3, 1989.
49. Downey, T. J. Testimony before the Subcommittee on Human Services and the Select Committee on Aging, House of Representatives, U.S. House of Representatives. *Mental Health in Nursing Homes: Barriers and Solutions*. Joint Hearing Before the Subcommittee on Human Services and Select Committee on Aging. 101st Congress. August 3, 1989.
50. Saxon, J. Testimony before the Subcommittee on Human Services and the Select Committee on Aging, House of Representatives, U.S. House of Representatives. *Mental Health in Nursing Homes: Barriers and Solutions*. Joint Hearing Before the Subcommittee on Human Services and Select Committee on Aging. 101st Congress. August 3, 1989.

51. Swan, J. H., and Gerard, L. E. Reimbursement and funding systems. In *Serving the Mentally Ill Elderly: Problems and Perspectives*, E. E. Lurie and J. H. Swan et al., pp. 139–163. Lexington Books, Lexington, Massachusetts, 1987.

52. Snowe, O. J. Testimony before the Subcommittee on Human Services and the Select Committee on Aging, House of Representatives, U.S. House of Representatives. *Mental Health in Nursing Homes: Barriers and Solutions*. Joint Hearing Before the Subcommittee on Health Services and Select Committee on Aging. 101st Congress. August 3, 1989.

53. Pacatte, J. Testimony before the Subcommittee on Human Services and the Select Committee on Aging, House of Representatives, U.S. House of Representatives. *Mental Health in Nursing Homes: Barriers and Solutions*. Joint Hearing Before the Subcommittee on Human Services and Select Committee on Aging. 101st Congress. August 3, 1989.

54. Smyer, M. A. Testimony before the Subcommittee on Human Services and the Select Committee on Aging, House of Representatives, U.S. House of Representatives. *Mental Health in Nursing Homes: Barriers and Solutions*. Joint Hearing Before the Subcommittee on Human Services and Select Committee on Aging. 101st Congress. August 3, 1989.

55. Borson, S., Lipzin, B., Nininger, J., and Rabins, P. Psychiatry and the nursing home. *Am. J. Psy.* 144: 1412–1418, 1987.

56. Burns, B. J., and Kamerow, D. B. Psychotropic drug prescriptions in nursing home residents. *J. Fam. Prac.* 26(2): 155–160, 1988.

57. U.S. Senate. Symposium before the Special Committee on Aging, U.S. Senate, *Untie the Elderly: Quality Care Without Restraints*. 101st Congress, December 4, 1989, U.S. Government Printing Office, Washington, D.C., 1990.

58. Hegeman, C., and Tobin, S. Enhancing the autonomy of mentally impaired nursing home residents. *The Gerontologist* 28(Suppl.): 71–75, 1988.

59. Swan, J. H., and McCall, M. E. Mental health system components and the aged. In *Serving the Mentally Ill Elderly: Problems and Perspectives*, edited by E. E. Lurie and J. H. Swan et al., pp. 111–138. Lexington Books, Lexington, Massachusetts, 1987.

60. Avorn, J. Drug policy in the aging society. *Health Affairs* 2(3): 23–32, Fall 1983.

61. Cabana, B. E. Mental health and the elderly: New biopharmaceutic considerations. *Health Aff.* 2(3): 33–38, Fall 1983.

62. Smallegan, M. Level of depressive symptoms and life stresses for culturally diverse older adults. *The Gerontologist* 29(1): 45–49, 1989.

63. Lyman, K. Bringing the social back in: A critique of the biomedicalization of dementia. *The Gerontologist* 29(5): 597–605, 1989.

64. Shanas, E., and Maddox, G. M. Health, health resources, and the utilization of care. In *Handbook of Aging and the Social Sciences* (2nd ed.), edited by R. H. Binstock and E. Shanas. Van Nostrand Reinhold, New York, 1985.

65. Gilhooly, M. L. M., Zarit, M., and Birren, J. E. (eds.). *The Dementias: Policy and Management*. Prentice Hall, Englewood Cliffs, New Jersey, 1986.

66. Gubrium, J. *Oldtimers and Alzheimer's: The Descriptive Organization of Senility*. JAI Press, Greenwich, Connecticut, 1986.

67. Kerin, P. B., Estes, C. L., and Douglass, E. B. Federal funding for aging education and research: A decade analysis. *The Gerontologist* 29(5): 606–614.

68. U.S. Congress, Office of Technology Assessment. *Losing a Million Minds: Confronting the Tragedy of Alzheimer's Disease and Other Dementias*. OTA-BA-323. U.S. Government Printing Office, Washington, D.C., April 1987.

69. Light, E., and Lebowitz, B. D. *Alzheimer's Disease Treatment and Family Stress: Directions for Research.* U.S. Department of Health and Human Services, Alcohol, Drug Abuse, and Mental Health Administration, Washington, D.C., 1989.
70. Salahuddin, M. Hospitals angry over delays in mental health screenings. *HealthWeek* 3(10): 14–15, May 15, 1989.
71. Evans, L. K., and Strumpf, N. Tying down the elderly: A review of the literature on physical restraint. *J. Am. Ger. Soc.* 37(1): 6–14, 1989.
72. Williams, C. C. Liberation: Alternative to physical restraints. *The Gerontologist* 29(5): 585–586, 1989.
73. Scheffler, R. A. Mental health services. *Generations* 9(4): 33–35. Summer, 1985.
74. Taube, C. A., Goldman, H. H ., and Salkever, D. Medicaid coverage for mental illness. *Health Aff.* 9(1): 5–18, 1990.
75. Lave, J. R., and Goldman, H. H. Medicare financing for mental health care. *Health Aff.* 9(1): 19–30, 1990.
76. Shapiro, S., Skinner, E. A., Kessler, L. G., Von Korff, M., German, P. S., Tischler, G. L., Leaf, P. J., Benham, L., Cottler, L., and Regier, D. A. Utilization of health and mental health services. *Arch. Gen. Psy.* 41: 971–978, 1984.
77. Shapiro, S., et al., Measuring need for mental health services in a general population. *Med. Care* 23: 1033–1043, 1985.
78. Woodruff, J. C., Donnan, H., and Halpin, G. Changing elderly persons' attitudes toward mental health professionals. *The Gerontologist* 28(6): 800–802, 1988.
79. Chacko, R. C. Community mental health services to geriatric patients. *The Southwestern*, pp. 53–61, 1990.
80. Poggi, R. G., and Barland, D. J. The therapists' reactions to the elderly, *The Gerontologist* 25(5): 508–513.
81. Ray, D. C., McKinney, K. A., and Ford, C. V. Differences in psychologists' ratings of older and younger clients. *The Gerontologist* 27(1): 82–85, 1987.
82. Lasoski, M. C., and Thelen, M. H. Attitudes of older and middle-aged persons toward mental health intervention. *The Gerontologist* 27(3): 288–292, 1987.
83. Hagebak, J. E., and Hagebak, B. R. Serving the mental health needs of the elderly: The case for removing barriers and improving service integration. *Com. Mental Health J.* 16: 263–275, 1980.
84. Butler, R. *Why Survive? Being Old in America.* Harper Colophon, New York, 1975.
85. Binney, E. A., and Estes, C. L. The retreat of the state and its transfer of responsibility: The intergenerational war. *Int. J. Health Serv.* 18(1): 83–96, 1988.
86. Clausen, J., and Huffine, C. Sociocultural and social psychological factors affecting social responses to mental disorders. *J. Health and Soc. Behav.* 16: 405–420, 1975.
87. Hollingshead, A., and Redlich, F. *Social Class and Mental Illness.* John Wiley, New York, 1958.
88. Sharfstein, S. S., Frank, R. G., and Kessler, L. G. State medicaid limitations for mental health services. *Hosp. and Com. Psy.* 35: 213–215, 1984.
89. Marmor, T. R., and Gill, K. The political and economic context of mental health care in the United States. *J. Health Pol. Polit. and Law* 14(3): 459–476, 1989.
90. Holahan, J., and Cohen, J. W. *Medicaid: The Tradeoff between Cost Containment and Access.* Urban Institute Press, Washington, D.C., 1986.
91. Scheper-Hughes, N., and Lovell, A. M. (eds.). *Psychiatry Inside Out: Selected Writings of Franco Basaglia.* Columbia University Press, New York, 1987.

CHAPTER 12

THE SHORT LIFE AND PAINFUL DEATH OF THE MEDICARE CATASTROPHIC COVERAGE ACT

Martha Holstein and Meredith Minkler

The Medicare Catastrophic Coverage Act (CHI), signed into law in 1988, represented the greatest expansion of Medicare since the program's establishment in 1965. Providing important new benefits for recipients, including a cap ($2,146 in 1990) on the amount beneficiaries are required to pay for hospital and physician care,[1] CHI also introduced a novel and, as it turned out, a vastly unpopular taxing strategy to finance these new benefits. Unlike the previously accepted cross-generational transfers embodied in social insurance, the CHI legislation required older beneficiaries to pay all program costs through an increase in Medicare Part B (physician payments) and a new, income-related supplemental premium.

The Catastrophic Coverage bill, which Congress had overwhelmingly approved and enacted in 1988, was repealed by a similarly large majority the following year, primarily in response to a massive "senior backlash" against the legislation and its unpopular self-financing mechanism (1). Although the nature and extent of the political fallout from these events is yet to be fully appreciated, the short life and painful death of CHI deserves attention.

An interest-group perspective has been employed by Torres-Gil (2) and others (1, 3, 4) to illuminate the immediate decisions made about CHI. The reader is directed to these analyses for an in-depth examination of the legislation's short-term context.

This chapter probes instead some of the underlying conditions that influenced both the passage and the repeal of the legislation. A political economy perspective explicates the economic, political, and related factors that helped shape the Act's

---

[1] The cap CHI placed on hospital and physician fees did not include the fees nonparticipating providers could levy above Medicare's approved rates.

most characteristic features—the self-financing mechanism and the minimal long-term care coverage it provided. Such a theoretical framework helps explain how three underlying factors—the legacy of Medicare, the politics of austerity and the declining political legitimacy of old people in the 1970s and 1980s—combined to heavily influence the form of the new legislation. Similarly, a moral economy perspective provides a deeper understanding of the "senior backlash" that triggered the legislation's repeal. The latter framework illustrates how moral economy concerns with reciprocity, fairness, and just taxation help explain the intensity of the negative reaction of many older Americans against the legislation.

We will begin by considering some of the strengths and limitations of interest-group politics as a conceptual framework for understanding developments like the rise and fall of CHI. A combined political and moral economy analysis is offered as a critical alternative to a classical interest group politics framework and one that illuminates the origins and evolution of the negotiating boundaries or parameters within which interest-group politics are played out legislatively, as in the CHI drama. Following a brief summary of the catastrophic coverage legislation and key events surrounding its passage, we examine the underlying political and economic factors, both historical and contemporary, that determined the parameters within which interest-group politics operated. Next, we turn to the legislation's death, noting the early signals of growing popular discontent and the inattention of legislators and some key aging organizations to this increasingly troubling situation. We draw principally on a moral economy perspective to explain the "senior revolt" as the primary contributor to CHI's repeal. Finally, we consider briefly the implications of the repeal in terms of who lost and who benefitted; the impact of repeal on subsequent state and federal health care policy prospects; changing perceptions of both the legitimacy and the "clout" of the old; and lessons to policymakers concerning the public side of the politics of legislation.

CONCEPTUAL FRAMEWORK

The passage and subsequent repeal of CHI appears at first glance a clear-cut case of interest-group pluralism in action. Within this conceptual framework, interest groups are viewed as putting forward their varied demands within a competitive bargaining environment and competing for access to key political actors and decision-making processes (5). Public policy, then, is seen as "the outcome of pluralistic competition among social groups, each seeking to articulate the private interest of its membership" (5, p. 76).

Although this paradigm provides critical insights into the policy processes including the immediate activities surrounding CHI, it has several important limitations. A full discussion of these inadequacies is available elsewhere (5–8) and is beyond the scope of this chapter. Two points, however, are of particular relevance. First, a pluralistic approach, which vests power primarily in individual and organizational actors, does not address the "classical democratic problem of representation and power" (9, p. 119). Do organizations represent their members? What is the role of leadership in the genesis and content of the policies of voluntary associations (8)? Second, many actors, excluded from the policy table altogether, fail to have their demands heard or negotiated (5). Each of these factors affected CHI deliberations.

In addition to these specific limitations, some of interest-group pluralism's core philosophical assumptions are themselves problematic. Pluralism assumes, for example, that interest groups emerge and survive because they reflect private values shared by large numbers of citizens; as representative groups negotiate their competing interests, the resolution will somehow serve the common good. A pluralist approach thus emphasizes procedural, rather than substantive justice, while sanctioning the continuity of normative assumptions about the basic political structure and the patterns of values, power distribution and interests the structure represents (9).

A political economy framework questions the basic assumptions of pluralism and overcomes many of its limitations. Political economy explores the intersection of political and economic factors in determining how unequal distributions of power occur and examines the interrelationships between the individual and the social structure in influencing such phenomena as how capitalist societies shape social policies. In so doing, political economy highlights the genesis of the operating frame of reference—the existing "rules"—within which interest-group politics operate.

A political economy approach clarifies the socioeconomic and political conditions that shaped distinguishing characteristics of CHI. Although political economy alone cannot explain the "senior revolt" that the legislation triggered, a perspective combining political with moral economy is illuminating. Explained by Kohli (Chapter 17) as "the collectivity shared moral assumptions defining the rules of reciprocity" in which an economic system is embedded, moral economy provides new ways to understand the overwhelming grassroots response to CHI. This theoretical perspective explicates "new arenas of moral conflict" such as entitlement programs for the elderly and resource allocation among different groups. The Catastrophic Coverage Act, which in part reflects changing assumptions regarding reciprocal obligations as they apply to the elderly, provides an excellent case study of a policy development better understood through a combined political and moral economy framework.

THE CATASTROPHIC COVERAGE ACT:
A BRIEF SUMMARY

From its inception, what marked CHI was the cap (set at just over $1,600 in 1989) it placed on an elderly patient's annual hospital and physician costs. Together with the self-financing mechanism, this cap was the only feature of the final legislation contained in the Reagan Administration's original proposal and was the foundation on which public and private- interest groups and Congress constructed the final and greatly expanded CHI bill.

CHI provided for outpatient prescription drug coverage, with a 20 percent coinsurance, for patients who paid a $500 deductible. To assist Medicaid recipients, and to guarantee reinvestment in health care savings created by CHI, the Act mandated a Medicaid buy-in paid by each state to finance Medicare premiums, deductibles, and coinsurance.

CHI also provided an extremely limited expansion of long-term care, including eighty hours of respite care for chronically dependent and homebound patients, elimination of the prior hospitalization requirement for nursing home coverage, and fifty additional days of nursing home care (for a total of 150 days). The bill also added ten homecare days and improved reimbursement for mental health services.

A noteworthy long-term care provision of the Act protected minimal levels of income and assets (up to about $63,000) of the spouse of an elder receiving Medicaid-financed nursing home care. Finally, the Act created the U.S. Bipartisan Commission on Comprehensive Health Care, later known as the Pepper Commission, and charged it with developing recommendations on long-term care and health care for the uninsured. Of the above measures, only the Medicaid buy-in, the spousal protection measure, and the creation of the Pepper Commission survived the repeal of CHI.

As Torres-Gil notes, at least as important as what CHI did cover was what it did not (2). Dental care, eyeglasses, most preventive services, and the vast majority of long-term care were conspicuous in their omission. Consequently, although early Congressional Budget Office estimates suggested that 22 percent of Medicare enrollees would receive higher payments as a result of CHI (10), a substantial portion of an elder's health care bill would remain uncovered. Most significantly, with nursing home costs averaging $29,000 annually (11) and one in three Americans spending some time in a nursing home (12), the failure to cover more than 150 days of nursing home care left the elderly unprotected from one of the most costly health care expenses.[2]

THE CATASTROPHIC COVERAGE ACT:
IMMEDIATE BACKGROUND

Ronald Reagan's election in 1980 was interpreted by the Administration as a "popular mandate" for government to be only minimally involved in health and

[2] The majority of elders who enter nursing homes, of course, have relatively short stays and these frequently are covered by Medicare. Yet the high expenses incurred by those having long stays (three or more months) are substantial enough to make this one of the laragest out-of-pocket health care expenses paid by the elderly as a group.

social services (13). Economic metaphors, policies, and regulations, captured in terms like privatization and competition, combined with tax cuts and greatly increased military spending to create a new framework for policy choices (14, 15). Central to this new framework was the growing budget deficit that further justified cuts in social spending (15). Under these conditions, as Piven and Cloward predicted, the constraints imposed on social spending "tend to become invisible as political issues and instead appear to be merely the limits of the possible" (15, pp. 1, 3, 4).

In this climate of austerity, President Reagan's call for an expansion of Medicare—even a revenue neutral one—was surprising. Some observers have offered partial explanations focused on the President's need to recoup credits lost as a result of his unpopular early attacks on Social Security and his subsequent troubles over the Iran Contra affair (1). Others have stressed the key role played by Department of Health and Human Services (DHHS) Secretary Otis Bowen, who brought to the office he assumed in 1984 a deep personal interest in catastrophic and long-term care, related to his wife's illness and recent death from bone cancer (2). (See Torres-Gil (2) for a comprehensive summary of these events.)

Whatever their relative weights, however, such developments culminated in the President's 1986 State of the Union announcement that he was asking Secretary Bowen "to conduct a one-year study of how government and the private sector could provide catastrophic medical insurance for Medicare recipients and for the general population" (2, p. 14).

While Bowen, with the Reagan Administration's blessings, began work on catastrophic coverage legislation, however, the American public was becoming increasingly aware that the real health financing catastrophe for elders lay not in acute care but in long-term care. The realities of inadequate long-term care coverage had become particularly evident since the 1984 implementation of the diagnosis-related group (DRG) prospective payment system for hospitals. Designed to save the government money by "radically altering" the incentives that heavily shape hospital decisions (16), the DRG system had the effect of moving patients more quickly from a Medicare reimbursed acute care hospital system into a system dominated by informal (unpaid) care and sparsely reimbursed chronic care (17, 18). The consequences of this system in requiring elders and their caregivers to absorb an additional 21 million caregiver days annually (18), further dramatized the inadequacy of America's long-term care system, and helped the latter emerge as a primary and visible symbol of unmet need (2).

Public awareness of this issue was heightened still further through a national political campaign sponsored by the 31 million member American Association of Retired persons (AARP) and a progressive philanthropic organization then known as the Villers Foundation. The campaign, entitled "Long Term Care '88," pressured electioneering politicians to openly support public long-term care coverage. Through extensive media publicity and candidate forums, the campaign raised public consciousness, stimulated public discussion, and very likely contributed to skepticism and dissatisfaction with the new CHI proposal, which claimed to provide protection against catastrophic costs without attending to the high cost of long-term care (2). The effect of DRGs and the long-term care campaign suggested a different focus for new legislation than the direction in which the Administration was moving (2). All of these events—the untoward effects of DRGs, the advocacy of the Long Term Care Campaign, and the President's proposal—also offered new information to the media. The crises in health care became front-page news.

EVENTS SURROUNDING THE BIRTH OF CHI

The plan for catastrophic coverage introduced by President Reagan in his 1987 State of the Union address was far more streamlined than the Bill that eventually passed. Despite the narrowness of the President's proposal, however, many of his conservative supporters, who considered any federal expansion for social programs a betrayal, greeted it with anger. Among opponents, a substantial segment of the commercial insurance industry, led by Mutual of Omaha, and of the pharmaceutical industry, led by the Pharmaceutical Manufacturing Association (PMA), were particularly vocal (2, 3).[3]

Not only did potentially affected business interests and the political right react negatively to the proposed legislation, but political liberals and progressives tended to be equally dissatisfied. The latter opposed CHI as another fragmented response to a larger crisis in health care and objected in particular to the self-financing mechanism and the plan's failure to cover long-term care (4).

Despite criticisms from both the left and the right, Congress and some aging organizations, most notably the American Association of Retired Persons (AARP), seized catastrophic coverage as an opening for a new health agenda. The political appeal of a new and significant benefit, with assured Presidential support, was irresistible. Within this context, a plethora of interest groups worked either to place their imprint on the proposed legislation, or, in the case of the PMA, to undertake a multimillion-dollar lobbying effort aimed at killing the legislation altogether (2–4).

As noted above, a pluralist analysis can explain how interest groups negotiated their agendas within the extant framework of values and power distribution that had established the relatively inflexible boundaries of the CHI discussion. But such an analysis remains incomplete because it misses the underlying historical, political, and economic conditions that kept a substantial long-term care benefit off-limits and forbade broad cross-generational financing. An examination of these underlying contextual factors is critical to a deeper understanding of the CHI experience.

---

[3] In contrast, Blue Cross and Blue Shield among insurers, and generic pharmaceutical interests, were supportive of CHI.

The Medicare Legacy

Although separated by more than two decades, decisions made in the 1960s about the original Medicare program are among the critical historical facts that directly influenced CHI deliberations. Of particular relevance were: the decision to fund a limited old-age entitlement program rather than universal health care; the emphasis on acute, rather than long-term, care; and the failure to impose strict cost controls or to grapple with the fee-for-service, increasingly high-intensity orientation of the medical care system.

Medicare made U.S. elders not only the principal, but the most visible, beneficiaries of direct federal spending for medical care. Ironically, Medicare's very success in reducing by half the gap in physician visits between poor and nonpoor elderly between 1964 and 1978 (19) and the dramatic reduction in poverty among the old (from 24 percent in 1970 to 15 percent in 1983) that was achieved as a result of Social Security improvements (20) combined to provide raw data for the Reagan Administration's argument that the old were "no longer needy" (21). Thus, the high profile of climbing Medicare expenditures offered further ammunition to those who believed the old were already exceeding their fair share of social spending (22). As Gilbert suggests, Medicare and other direct welfare expenditures appear particularly excessive since comparable uncounted welfare state benefits in the form of tax deductions for home mortgages, etc. remain invisible (23). The $312 billion in indirect tax expenditures for individuals and corporations, including large tax subsidies for the employment-based medical plans of generally higher income workers, thus escaped notice (24) while climbing Medicare bills were a visible reminder of the "costliness" of the aged. Such conditions were ripe for blaming the old for busting the federal budget and reaping a disproporiate share of benefits at society's expense (25, 26).

As is discussed below, subsequent efforts to de-legitimate the claims of the elderly as a welfare state constituency (26) helped establish the preconditions for the CHI financing strategy, which burdened middle- and upper-income elders with program costs.

In addition, early political decisions to only minimally interfere with fee-for-service and high intensity medical care, in part to appease the American Medical Association and the American Hospital Association, contributed to ever-escalating program costs. As a result, many decision-makers generalized the experience with Medicare to all publicly financed medical care, either rendering invisible or leaving off-limits the principal inputs to costs. The impact on CHI deliberations is clear. Once again, rather than tackling these and other causes of health care inflation, CHI simply shifted the cost burden; beneficiaries instead of government, would bear program costs.

Lastly, Medicare's exclusions, e.g., long-term care and prescription drugs, together with significant copayments and deductibles, meant that elders still had to shoulder more than 50 percent of their total health care bill (27). These program features also left an important role for the private market. The Medigap industry, which emerged in the late 1960s to cover some of the cost-sharing components of Medicare, thus found a profitable new market in elders' continued concerns about the costs of health care (28).

De-Legitimating the Claims of the Old

During the past two decades, American politics and the political legitimacy of the aged have undergone profound shifts. As Miller suggests, changing perceptions of the economy as it moves from "fat times" to "lean times" have in turn led to a redefinition of perceived social problems and problematic groups like "the aged" in ways that permit contracted, less costly approaches to their "solution" (29). This cyclical nature of social problems has had major consequences for the elderly (25, 26). In times of relative economic prosperity, an activist government that responded, in some measure, to the needs of the citizenry, including the old, was easy to accept. But since acceptance of the fundamental right to have minimum needs met lacks firm grounding in the American political landscape (30), it was also easy to discard when the economy faltered and new realities—in this case "fiscal crisis" and the new "affluence" of the aged—were pronounced (31). Both reactions contributed directly and indirectly to the catastrophic coverage experience.

A perception of the "affluence" of the elderly, particularly when contrasted with the growing poverty of children, has drastically reduced the political legitimacy of the old. As a result, a number of individuals and groups have systematically attacked entitlements for the elderly (20, 22). Such attacks contrasted the steady increase in cost-of-living adjusted Social Security benefits with the decline in real wages for young workers and in expenditures on children and youth (20, 22). By framing Social Security and Medicare as programs serving only the old and raising the specter of widespread intergenerational tension over disproportionate resource allocation, proponents of the "generational equity" thesis sought a rethinking of traditional moral economy notions undergirding support for the old (see Chapter 5).

The conservative political and economic climate that gave rise to concerns over "generational equity" supported the emergence of two corollary assumptions in relation to CHI—that America's elders had sufficient resources to cover self-financing and that intergenerational transfers would be politically unacceptable. The consequent imposition of a surcharge on middle- and upper-income program beneficiaries sharply departed from traditional approaches to taxation and is credited with ultimately leading to the legislation's defeat (1).

The Politics of Austerity

Emerging in the same environment as the de-legitimation of the old was a third key factor that helps explain the particular form CHI took: the politics of austerity.

The 1980s created a peculiar amalgam of deficit reduction politics, generalized attacks on big government and taxation, and a shifting income stratification in which the income gap between rich and poor Americans reached its highest level since World War II (32).

The Reagan Administration contributed to an already mounting deficit through unprecedented military expenditures (amounting to $2,200,000,000,000 over eight years (33)), and supply side economic policies that reduced taxes, particularly for corporations and the more affluent, as a strategy for raising revenues and so managing the deficit. At the same time, the size of the deficit was used to justify major cutbacks in social spending. As Piven and Cloward observe, fiscal austerity appeared under these circumstances not to be politics, but rather "the inevitable adaptation of a responsible government to the constraints imposed by limited resources" (15, p. 134).

President Reagan's insistence on no new taxes, continuing conservative attacks on an expanded government role, and President Bush's campaign slogan "read my lips" reinforced the politics of austerity. But more important, they helped establish a world view which became the prevailing political reality of the 1980s and early 1990s. Translated into a politics of retrenchment, this world view ignored need or defined it away (e.g., by changing the factors considered in the measurement of poverty [25]) and heightening a sense of individualism. The politics of austerity thus sharply constrained the nature and content of deliberations over catastrophic coverage, mandating that any new program be completely self-financed, and determining that catastrophic coverage, and not the more costly long-term care, would be the selected program.

In summary, the shape that CHI took cannot be understood in isolation from the broader sociopolitical and historical factors described above. Medicare's segregation of the elderly, its attention to acute rather than chronic illness, and its maintenance of traditional fee-for-service and high-technology approaches to medical care thus heavily influenced the "seniors only," acute care orientation of CHI. The spiralling medical care costs Medicare engendered lent added legitimacy to the call for a self-financing mechanism.

The politics of austerity and the related redefinition and contraction of social problems to enable less costly "solutions" further contributed to legitimizing circumscribed benefits and the imposition of a surtax to pay for the new measure. Finally, and consistent with the 1980s "war on welfare," (30) the de-legitimation of the claims of the elderly made a self-financing approach to CHI appear not merely politically prudent but within moral and ethical bounds as well. The latter assumption, however, proved highly inaccurate.

EVENTS SURROUNDING THE DEATH OF CHI

Throughout the winter of 1987, early negative signals, in the form of letters to the editor, to Congress, and to organizational newsletters, should have alerted

Congress to the fact that the bill that it was so enthusiastically developing had not created comparable enthusiasm beyond the corridors of Washington (1). Although CHI obtained active support from key groups, such as AARP, aging interest-group support was divided on the financing mechanism, the lack of long-term care coverage, and, for some, the belief that passage of a limited bill would remove the incentive and pressure for more comprehensive health legislation. The Gray Panthers, for example, although historically concerned with the needs of low-income elders (the primary beneficiaries of CHI), actively opposed the bill for all these reasons. Two other aging-based organizations that had originally supported passage—the four million member National Council of Senior Citizens (NCSC) and the National Association of Retired Federal Employees (NARFE)—subsequently switched their positions in the face of the repeal movement (34).

The most vocal and organized public opposition to CHI came from the National Committee to Preserve Social Security and Medicare (NCPSSM), commonly known as the "Roosevelt Group" in reference to the organization's founder, former President Franklin D. Roosevelt's youngest son James Roosevelt. Although this group had opposed the legislation prior to its enactment, chiefly because of the self-financing mechanism, it became most active after CHI's passage, mounting a huge direct-mail campaign to convince elders of what it saw as the law's fatal and costly flaws. Partly in response to the Roosevelt group's campaign, the AARP saw several thousand of its members resign to protest the Association's support of the legislation. Congress too, was deluged with mail, including thousands of the tear-away cards circulated by the Roosevelt organization (1).

Effective as the direct-mail tactics of a political interest group may be, they would not alone have been sufficient to cause Congress to reconsider its actions and undertake the first repeal of social legislation in U.S. history. Congressional representatives took seriously the Roosevelt group's message because it amplified and reinforced what they were hearing from their own constituents, namely angry outcries that CHI was an ill-conceived and grossly unfair piece of legislation that would cost seniors money and give them little in return (35).

In reality, of course, the absence of poll data from representative samples of older Americans made it impossible to accurately determine whether the elderly understood the measure, or the extent to which the most vocal proponents of repeal represented the majority of the elderly. Although AARP had earlier polled its members about the benefits to be included under CHI, for example, it did not seek their reactions to the proposed self-financing mechanism. Nor did the organization poll its members near the time of the repeal to determine whether the majority in fact favored or opposed repeal (34). Conversely, while an ABC poll conducted during the repeal process showed 57 percent of the elderly to oppose repeal (36), it was not preceded by earlier surveys that would have indicated the degree of change or consistency in attitudes of the elderly over time.

In retrospect, the failure of AARP, Congress, and other concerned groups to regularly poll the elderly about their attitudes toward the legislation is recognized as one of the striking errors made during the legislative campaign (34). As Binstock notes, "the Catastrophic Act was not developed with any widespread grassroots understanding and support for its content" (37, p. 9). Consequently, neither Congress nor the aging advocacy organizations were in close enough communication with their constituents to understand the significance or extent of the growing concerns over fairness that were emerging (1).

CONCERNS OVER FAIRNESS

We can hypothesize a number of factors that may have contributed to the sense of profound unfairness conveyed by growing numbers of elders and their advocates. First, after ten years of tax cuts and assertions by President Reagan and later Bush that there would be "no new taxes" CHI initiated a new tax. Called a "surcharge" rather than a tax, it affected less than half of all people sixty-five and over. Older people who paid over $150 a year in taxes would finance 63 percent of the program through a surcharge of $22.50 for each $150 of income tax with a ceiling or cap on income to be taxed. This amount was scheduled to climb to $42 per $150 by 1993.

Not surprisingly, many older people—including many who would not have to pay—reacted negatively. What was the surcharge but a new tax, a tax on old age? Reports soon indicated that while people under sixty-five who earned over $208,000 a year paid a marginal tax rate of 28 percent, people over sixty-five with $50,000 a year in income would pay a rate of 42 percent. Like the 1990 Social Security payroll tax increase, the CHI surcharge was a new, regressive tax. Although the tax rates increased according to income, the surcharge leveled out above $50,000 for a single person and $90,000 for a couple to reflect the Act's cap on total annual premium payments. As the Wall Street Journal pronounced, the hardest hit would be elders making between $30,000 and $50,000 a year (38).

Compounding the sense of unfairness was the fact that taxation for the Catastrophic Coverage Act rested solely on the amount of taxes paid. Thus, the surcharge would minimally affect people who derived their incomes primarily from tax-free bonds or other tax shelters since they pay no tax on those earnings. Once again, as with the tax cuts of 1981, this tax policy affected the middle class most severely.

As discussed below, the structure of CHI taxation also violated moral economy notions of fairness in asking less than 6 percent of America's population to do what was expected of no one else: to pay a special tax for benefits for their age group. Comparable concerns over fairness might have been raised had affluent parents been asked, in the interests of the public good, to pay a special assessment to assure education of high quality in our inner-city schools. Asking the elderly, a relatively small group, to pay a tax for a benefit that many already had may also be analogous to levying a tax on employed Americans for health benefits that duplicate what they have already—but not quite—so that these employees would still have to purchase supplemental coverage at ever-increasing costs.

Moral economy provides a new way to understand why so many older Americans passionately rejected the new CHI taxing strategy. The anger of older people emerged when the rules of taxation suddenly shifted. They were not asked, nor did they give, informed consent to a policy that many perceived as not being in their own long-term best interest (see Chapter 4). In retrospect, it was risky for Congress not to seek the collaboration and commitment of elders, but to expect them to comply passively with a new policy. A moral economy framework helps explicate the shaky ground on which Congressional expectations were based. The current political structure rests on long-held values that have accepted progressive taxation as a way to meet broad social goals and, for over fifty years, have also tacitly accepted an intergenerational compact in which each successive generation contributes to the well-being of its elders. Further, one need only recall that America fought a revolution over tax policy.

Additional grounds for anger lay in the fact that the Bush Administration viewed the surcharge, like the increases in the Social Security payroll tax, as a strategy to reduce the deficit without raising general taxes. Many older Americans astutely perceived Bush's meaning when he resisted repeal arguing not for the importance of the benefits, but rather that repeal would have a damaging effect on meeting deficit reduction targets. The premium would have produced a $4 to $7 billion surplus over the added costs to Medicare (39).

CONCERNS OVER DUPLICATION OF BENEFITS

The questionable tax policies of CHI were sufficient to cause outrage among many elders. Yet, in addition, many CHI benefits replicated those that elders had through retiree health benefits or union contracts. Not only did this redundancy undermine the urgency with which elders experienced a need for the benefit which was ultimately passed, but is also would provide a windfall to corporations that offered such benefits as part of a retirement package. After the first year, employers could seek to eliminate benefits covered by CHI for their retirees. Benefits these retirees already had—at no cost—were to be offered to them, often at a significant cost, while their employers would ultimately realize a savings.

Additionally, more than two-thirds of older Americans had protection through privately funded Medigap policies (40), which, despite the anticipation of catastrophic coverage, projected increased rates. Almost simultaneously with the passage of catastrophic coverage, a number of insurance companies announced increases of up to 75 percent, contending that "increased premiums reflect rises in both the cost and volume of health services, brought on by new medical technologies and an increased volume of medical care because the number of older people is growing" (41). Without CHI, insurers argued that rates would be 10 to

15 percent higher than the newly announced rates. Since CHI covered the end period of an acute illness, like the basic Medicare package, it protected those who already had gained entry into the system. Hence, Medigap policies would remain essential for those elders desiring coverage of initial Medicare deductibles and copayments. Knowing, from a number of Congressional hearings, the tendency of older people to overinsure themselves whether because they feared unanticipated costs or because of the unscrupulous tactic of some insurance salespeople (42), the framers of CHI hardly alleviated uncertainty. The only certainty, based on previous experience, seemed to be an expectation that costs for the new benefit would continue to climb, requiring a steadily larger surtax if the cap was to remain fixed.

The relationship of CHI to Medigap graphically illustrates the confusion that follows from partial solutions to complex problems. As noted above, the initial Medicare program's limitations assured that large areas of need would provide profitable market areas for private solutions. Instead of fully covering the needs that supplemental policies addressed, CHI again chose a partial solution, leaving large segments of the private market untouched. Hence, many older people had a double financing burden: they would pay taxes for CHI and also continue to pay for their private Medigap policies. This fact also provoked a sense of unfairness.

IMMEDIATE AND LONG-TERM IMPLICATION
OF THE REPEAL OF CHI

Although it is still too early to gauge the full extent of the fallout from the repeal of CHI and the events surrounding its repeal, several consequences are already apparent. The very poor in states that did not previously provide a mandatory Medicaid buy-in benefitted from the Congressional decision to salvage the portion of CHI requiring such buy-ins, through which Medicare premiums, deductibles, and copayments would be covered. But the repeal harmed older Americans who are too rich for Medicaid but too poor to afford supplemental insurance. Minority elders, women, and the "oldest old" are disproportionately represented in the latter group.

Women have also been the losers in the repeal of CHI in other ways. The loss of the CHI drug benefit is of particular significance to elderly women, who receive the major share of prescriptions and have less income to pay for them. A recent survey conducted by AARP reinforced the significance of this loss by showing the high cost of medications to be the second main reason for the failure of elders to fill their prescriptions (43). Because women represent 75 percent of all nursing home residents (28), they also are most affected by the loss of expanded (albeit still limited) nursing home coverage under CHI. Weiner (40) estimates that 500,000 people, most of them women, would have had at least part of their nursing home stay paid through CHI provisions by 1993.

The repeal of CHI is also being felt on the state level. First, CHI would have assisted states in covering certain long-term care benefits contained in the Act, as well as long-term acute care. In 1990 alone, for example, Medicaid had to pick up $2 billion that CHI would have covered (40). Both the provisions of CHI for a state Medicaid buy-in for lower income beneficiaries, which survived repeal, and the $2 billion in costs that repeal returned to Medicaid, thus put further demands on already constrained state Medicaid budgets. Second, the repeal adversely affects some state-level plans to improve access to health care coverage. New York's Unicare Plan was designed to provide health insurance to the uninsured in that state, but with the understanding that CHI would pick up many of the costs of expanded coverage for the elderly. With the repeal of CHI, successful implementation of the Plan has become problematic (44).

The negative fallout from the repeal of CHI also includes significant increases in the costs to consumers of Medigap policies, on which elders will pay some $10 billion this year alone (45). The cost of Medigap policies is projected to soar 20 to 30 percent in 1990, and insurance spokespersons claim that half of this increase can be directly attributed to the repeal of CHI (45).

Employers who provide group medical coverage for retired workers also will lose money as a consequence of the repeal. One estimate thus projected employer losses of $750 million to $1 billion annually in the latter's share of increased premiums (40). Finally, American taxpayers (including the elderly) will pay about $10 million annually in hospital, nursing home, and physician bills that CHI would have covered (40).

In addition to the fiscal costs of repeal are the harder-to-calculate shifts in the attitudes and perceptions of Congress and the general public toward the old and programs for the old. On the one hand, as Torres-Gil notes, older Americans lost ground with the repeal, in terms of the automatic legitimacy that had been critical to them over the last thirty years (46). Mass media, policymakers, and vocal critics have used the older Americans' fight for repeal to build on the recurrent theme of generational equity, contributing to the further construction of a reality in which the old are blamed for selfishness and unwillingness to assist others (1).

The automatically accorded legitimacy lost by elders may have been offset by the political power emanating from their demonstration of raw political muscle and the ability to act independently from their organizations. At the same time, however, as Torres-Gil argues, older Americans must recoup some of their lost legitimacy and sympathy or risk being perceived as just another interest group (46). To do this, and to minimize their losses, the elderly thus might use their political strength to further interests that go beyond age—issues such as public education, decreasing the budget deficit, and enactment of a national health program. In this way, as Estes suggests, they can move away from what has been perceived as "selfish separatism" toward broader cross-generational advocacy and action (47).

Although the immediate Congressional reaction to the repeal of CHI suggested that the backlash would harm indefinitely the possibilities of legislation for long-term care and/or for national health coverage (1), both fears appear to be abating. Further, the publicity that the CHI experience afforded to the issue of inadequate chronic care coverage may have had an opposite effect. In the words of AARP legislative director John Rother (48, p. 10):

> If the catastrophic episode did anything it dramatized the need for a long term care program for the American people. Three years ago, this was an issue that people didn't recognize. That is no longer the case.

Additional attention to the long-term care issue has resulted from the CHI-created Pepper Commission, which released its report on long-term care and coverage for the uninsured in March of 1990. The report proposals, particularly on long-term care, were approved by a substantial majority of Commission members, and a number of bills that build upon the Commission's work will be introduced in Congress. As one analyst observes, the Commission may turn out to be the critically important "sleeper" of the whole CHI experience (49).

Opinion poll data continue to demonstrate widespread public support for both long-term care insurance and national health insurance, and the recent support of key business, physician, and consumer groups is making its pressure felt. Clearly, however, Congress will not soon forget the "catastrophe of catastrophic," nor is it likely to adopt new strategies in this area without a far greater measure of public dialogue and informed consent.

As Binstock notes (36, p. 9):

> One lesson may be that, in the contemporary political context, the traditional elitist "top-down" approach to social legislation, exemplified in the Catastrophic Act, needs to be inverted. "Bottom-up" support for public and long term care insurance will have to be genuinely sought from the grassroots, with desires and demands articulated actively in virtually every Congressional district.

If new mechanisms can be introduced to elicit such dialogue and make possible a truly "bottom-up" approach to social legislation, the lessons of the Catastrophic Coverage experience will perhaps have been worth the price.

CONCLUSION

CHI provides a particularly vivid example of how a political and moral economy perspective can transform our perceptions of a complex and troubling legislative experience. Although an interest-group perspective provides vitally important information, the case of CHI graphically displays its limits. As a form of analysis, interest-group politics thus gives us primarily a "slice of time" perspective; a perspective that lacks the historical dimension that political and moral economy provide. Without that long view, the interest-group framework misses the multiple underlying factors responsible for the operating boundaries of CHI—those limiting preconditions which played a determining role in the legislation's demise. As this chapter has suggested, such historical factors as Medicare's segregation of the old, the de-legitimization of the claims of the old as a welfare state constituency in the 1980s, and that decade's recurrent denigration of taxes, are irrevocably bound to policy making around CHI. By divorcing the "senior revolt" from its historical and moral foundations, it becomes relatively easy to condemn rather than to comprehend the responses of many elders who opposed the legislation.

A political and moral economy analysis sharply delineates such factors. The understanding that emerges points the way not only for an alternative understanding of what happened with CHI but also suggests how we might respond differently at comparable future decision points. At a minimum, it should mitigate anger against older Americans, many of whom reacted as a pluralist analysis might have predicted. An understanding of the CHI experience grounded in part in moral economy analysis might also suggest that political leadership must, at least on occasion, be transformative rather than transactional, moving beyond "marketplace leadership" that trades preferences and interests in the present without seeking to transform either those preferences or the structures that house them. Such a perspective may help move closer to the Ciceronian ideal of "an agreement with respect to justice and a partnership for the common good" (50, p. 141). As such, it may help us avoid repetition of the "Catastrophic catastrophe" in other legislative arenas in the years ahead.

ACKNOWLEDGMENTS

The authors gratefully acknowledge Fernando Torres-Gil, John Coster, Christopher Jennings, and Gregory Merrill for sharing their personal insights into the CHI experience. Our sincere thanks also are due Carroll L. Estes, Diane Arnold-Driver, and Ida Red for helpful comments on earlier drafts of this chapter.

REFERENCES

1. Tolchin, M. How the new Medicare law fell on hard times in a hurry. *New York Times*, pp. 1, A10, Oct. 9, 1989.
2. Torres-Gil, F. The politics of catastrophic and long term care coverage. *J. Aging and Soc. Pol.* 1(1/2): 61–86, 1989.
3. Iglehart, J. K. Medicare's new benefits: 'Catastrophic' health insurance. *New Engl. J. Med.* 320(5): 329–335, 1989.
4. Coster, J. M. The relationship between politics and policy in the formation of the Medicare Catastrophic Coverage Act's outpatient drug benefit. Unpublished report. U.S. Congress Office of Technology Assessment, Washington, D.C., 1989.
5. Navarro, P. *The Policy Game: How Special Interests and Ideologues are Stealing America*. John Wiley and Sons, New York, 1984.
6. Olson, M., Jr. *The Logic of Collective Action: Public Goods and the Theory of Groups*. Harvard University Press, New York, 1965.

7. Bachrach, P., and Baratz, M. Two faces of power. *The Search for Community Power* (2nd ed.), edited by W. Hawley and F. Wirt. Englewood Cliffs, New Jersey, 1974.
8. Rogin, M. Nonpartisanship and the group interest. In *Power and Community: Dissenting Essays in Political Science*, edited by P. Green and S. Levinson, p. 119. Vintage Books, New York, 1970.
9. Dolbeare, K. M. Public policy analysis and the coming struggle for the soul of the post behavioral revolution. In *Power and Community: Dissenting Essays in Political Science*, edited by P. Green and S. Levinson, pp. 85–111. Vintage Books, New York, 1970.
10. Christensen, S., and Kosten, R. Covering catastrophic expenses under Medicare. *Health Aff.* 7(5): 79–93, 1988.
11. U.S. Department of Health and Human Services (DHHS), Task Force on Long Term Care Policies. *Report to Congress and the Secretary: Long Term Health Care Politics.* U.S. Government Printing Office, Washington, D.C., 1987.
12. Liang, J., and Tu, E. J. Estimating lifetime risk of nursing home residency: A further note. *Gerontologist* 26: 560–563, 1986.
13. Navarro, V. The 1980 and 1983 U.S. elections and the New Deal: An alternative explanation. *Int. J. Health Serv.* 15(3): 359–394, 1985.
14. Block, R., Cloward, R., Ehrenreich, B., and Piven, F. F. *The Mean Season.* Pantheon Books, New York, 1987.
15. Piven, F. F., and Cloward, R. A. *The New Class War: Reagan's Attack on the Welfare State and Its Consequences.* Pantheon Books, New York, 1982.
16. Davis, K. Paying the health care bills of an aging population. In *Our Aging Society,* edited by A. Pifer and L. Bronte. W. W. Norton, New York, 1986.
17. Shaughnessy, P. N., and Kramer, A. M. The increased needs of patients in nursing homes and patients receiving home health care. *New Engl. J. Med.* 322(1): 21–27, 1990.
18. Estes, C. L. Aging, health and social policy: Crisis and crossroads. *J. Aging and Social Policy* 1(1/2): 17–32, 1989.
19. Brown, E. R. Medicare and Medicaid: The process, value, and limits of health care reforms. In *Readings in the Political Economy of Aging,* edited by M. Minkler and C. L. Estes, pp. 117–143. Baywood Publishing, Amityville, New York, 1984.
20. Preston, S. Children and the elderly in the United States. *Sci. Am.* 251: 44–49, 1984.
21. Annual Report of the President's Council of Economic Advisers. U.S. Government Printing Office, Washington, D.C., 1985.
22. Longman, P. *Born to Pay: The New Politics of Aging in America.* Houghton Mifflin Company, New York, 1987.
23. Gilbert, N. *The Enabling State: Modern Welfare Capitalism in the U.S.* Oxford University Press, New York, 1989.
24. Nelson, G. Re-examining social spending and fair shares. *The Aging Conn.* 10(5): 10, Oct./Nov. 1989.
25. Minkler, M. Blaming the aged victim: The politics of retrenchment in times of fiscal conservatism. In *Readings in the Political Economy of Aging,* edited by M. Minkler and C. L. Estes, pp. 254–269. Baywood Publishing, Amityville, New York, 1984.
26. Estes, C. L. "Equity and Aging Policies: Fiscal Crisis and New Federalism" Presidential Address to the Western Gerontological Society, April 19, 1983.
27. Waldo, D. R. National health expenditures, 1985. *Health Care Fin. Rev.* 8: 93–100, 1986.
28. Gornick, M., Greenberg, J. N., Eggers, P. W., and Dobson, A. Twenty years of Medicare and Medicaid: Covered populations, use of benefits, and program expenditures. *Health Care Fin. Ann. Rev. Suppl.* pp. 13–59, 1985.

29. Miller, S. M. The political economy of social problems: From the sixties to the seventies. *Soc. Prob.* 24(1): 131–141, 1976.

30. Katz, M. B. *The Undeserving Poor: From the War on Poverty to the War on Welfare.* Pantheon Books, New York, 1989.

31. Estes, C. L. Austerity and aging: 1980 and beyond, In *Readings in the Political Economy of Aging*, edited by M. Minkler and C. L. Estes, pp. 241–253. Baywood Publishing, Amityville, New York, 1984.

32. Silk, L. Economics scene—rich and poor: The gap widens. *The New York Times*, May 12, 1989.

33. Erdman, P. Victory in 'losing' the war. *San Francisco Examiner*, pp. A1, A16, June 17, 1990.

34. Personal communication from Gregory Merrill, Director of State Legislation, AARP, June 5, 1990.

35. Personal communication from Christopher Jennings, Senate Select Committee on Aging, May 31, 1990.

36. Binstock, R. H. House repeals Medicare catastrophic law: Accused of giving in to wealthy elderly vote. *Older Americans Report*, p. 382, October 6, 1987.

37. Binstock, R. H. The 'Catastrophic' catastrophe: Elitist politics, poor strategy. *The Aging Conn.* 11(1): 9, 1990.

38. Gottschalk, E., Jr. Is beating the Medicare bite worth it? *Wall Street Journal*, p. C9, March 14, 1989.

39. Levin, C. The deficit's secret weapon. *New York Times*, September 20, 1989.

40. Freudenham, M. Change in Medicare law to be costly. *New York Times*, October 10, 1989.

41. Tolchin, M. Recipients of Medicare also received rise in cost of private insurance. *New York Times*, p. 1, February 12, 1989.

42. Tolchin, M. Concerns about Medigap insurance abuses grow. *Update: Adv. Sen. Alert Proc.* 6(2): 5, 1990.

43. American Association of Retired Persons, AARP National Surveys. *AARP 8th Annual Survey of Older Americans.* AARP, Washington, D.C., December, 1987.

44. Personal communication from Dr. Dan Beauchamp, Deputy Commissioner, Division of Planning, Policy and Resource Development, Department of Health, State of New York, October 24, 1989.

45. Medicap prices on the rise. *Nat. Retired Teachers Assoc. Bull.* 31(3): 1, 20, 1990.

46. Personal communication from Dr. Fernando Torres-Gil, Professor of Gerontology and Public Administration, Leonard Davis School of Gerontology, University of Southern California, March 29, 1990.

47. Estes, C. L. The aging enterprise—in whose interests? *Int. J. Health Serv.* 16(2): 243–251, 1986.

48. Carlson, C. Backlash on the way. *Nat. Retired Teachers Assoc. Bull.* 30(11); 1, 10, 1989.

49. Personal communication from Ed Howard, former Public Policy Coordinator of the Villers Foundation, October 3, 1989.

50. Stout, J. Language of morals. In *Community in America*, edited by C. H. Reynolds and R. V. Norman. University of California Press, Berkeley, 1988.

PART V. RACE, CLASS, GENDER, AND AGING

Much as intergenerational, biomedicalization, and market economy health perspectives contribute to an explanation of the current situation of the elderly in the United States, a comprehensive understanding requires an analysis of the enormous effects of race, class, and gender status on aging and aging policy. Minority status, whether gender, ethnic, economic, or social position, significantly shapes the individual aging process as well as the formal and informal treatment of elderly minority group members. A political economy of aging framework must examine the role of capital and patriarchy in defining minority groups and establishing differential policies based on social definitions and perceptions.

Although women are a demographic majority of the elderly population, they occupy minority status. In Chapter 13, Arendell and Estes argue that the disadvantaged position of old women, although deteriorating in the post-Reagan era, has its origins in the gendered division of labor and socioeconomic stratification over the lifecourse. The economic vulnerability of over half of all old women is related to unpaid family labor and employment discrimination. Many women continue to be unpaid caregivers well into old age, further risking their health and economic resources. The interrelationship between U.S. publicly and privately institutionalized treatment of aging women contributes to their impoverishment, poor health, and race and class inequities.

In Chapter 14, England and associates illustrate how the current U.S. approach to the provision of community care to the elderly interacts with the feminized structure of family caregiving to foster inequities for women, who provide the bulk of unpaid informal care. Present policies to limit eligibility and ration benefits to ill and disabled elders reduce the choices of caregivers, many of whom are already economically disadvantaged. For gender justice, the authors see the need for expanded supports to families and examine the relationship of adequate government support to the capacity of individuals to freely choose the caregiving role.

The "feminization of poverty" concept introduced in the 1970s to describe the increasing pauperization of women and children in the United States holds special relevance for older women. In Chapter 15, Dressel acknowledges the structural and ideological bases of the feminization of poverty approach, but argues that it is politically divisive and, in isolation, distorts and simplifies a complex issue.

Racial stratification is examined as a primary feature of the political economy that differentiates women in old age. The theoretical approach proposed would not dichotomize elders by gender alone, but rather account for the complex interplay of race, gender, and class in the analysis of old age experience and policy. Such an approach has the potential of supporting political alliances among the working poor, the underclass, and other economically vulnerable groups.

In Chapter 16, Wallace examines the role of race in U.S. health policy. An analysis of health care for older blacks assesses the relative importance of class and race as dependent or independent factors. Theories attempting to explain why racial inequality persists in the United States are summarized. The interplay of race and socioeconomic class are detailed at both individual and institutional levels. Public solutions to health care problems reflect the cultural or class theories on which policy is based. The health and the health care of all elderly groups depends on economic justice.

Viewing aging as a structural problem requiring a thorough examination of the interrelationships among polity, economy, and society, the authors of this section illustrate that the vulnerability experienced by the elderly and the ineffectiveness of aging policy are rooted in the class biases of the U.S. socioeconomic system.

CHAPTER 13

OLDER WOMEN IN THE POST-REAGAN ERA

Terry Arendell, * and Carroll L. Estes,

Gender status is central in explaining differences in the economic and health issues that the aged confront. So too is racial minority status. Significantly, the disadvantaged situations experienced by older women are not a direct result of age, but are a consequence of the lifelong effects of gender, racial, and socioeconomic stratification. Thus, the social origins of the disadvantaged status of older women are not mysterious; they reside in the institutional arrangements and processes of the family (the informal sector), the labor market and the state and its social policy (both parts of the formal sector). Each of these areas has received extensive independent study, but in order to grasp their particular consequences for older women, these social institutions must be examined in terms of their complex and often subtle interrelationships (1). Women's family roles, particularly their caregiving activities, directly impinge upon their economic status and labor market involvement. Women's relative economic dependency in the family is reinforced by social policies that buttress the systems of gender stratification characterizing both family and employment. Socioeconomic class status affects access to health care and, as has been shown repeatedly, is directly linked to health status as measures by mortality, disability, chronic illness and institutionalization (2–6).

A more comprehensive and integrated health and social service delivery system is needed by older women as well as by all individuals who provide caregiving within and between the generations in the growing number of three and four generational families. State support of services—access, availability and financing—remains vitally important. However, because of the structural embeddedness and complexity of the arrangements and interrelationships of the family, labor

*Order of authorship is alphabetical.

market, and state, the resolution of older women's economic and health issues cannot be achieved by providing services alone. Changes in service provision solely will do little to redress the effects of the stratified division of labor, shaped by patriarchal tradition and the capitalist mode of production, that has played a pivotal role in creating the precarious situations faced by contemporary older women. The analytical framework proposed here acknowledges the link between income and health status and needs in a lifecourse perspective. Broad-based solutions must be devised that address sex, race, age, and class discrimination throughout society, including the inequities in women's access to occupations, earnings, and income security programs. Women's caregiving activities, carried out across the lifespan, must be revalued.

A primary factor in older women's precarious economic status is their lifelong responsibility for family. Lodged primarily in the family, socially defined as the private sphere, women have been responsible for providing care and nurturing to the very young, very old, and disabled in a social and political context that romanticizes family caregiving activities. Because the labor or caring occurs within the relative isolation of millions of individual family units, it is given little recognition and no financial remuneration. Contributing to the relative invisibility of women's caregiving activities are the historic devaluation, even neglect, of women's labor and the ideological dichotomy between the "public" and "private" spheres in which the family is defined as being personal, autonomous, self-sufficient, and a place of self-sacrifice. Although women have entered the wage labor force in unprecedented numbers over the last two decades, the wage differentials between men and women have not changed significantly; a sizeable proportion of women hold part-time jobs, and a majority of wives remain economically dependent on husbands (7).

In old age, many women discover that the structural conditions and the normative expectations that have promoted and maintained their economic dependence converge, resulting in economic uncertainty, near-poverty, or poverty. Indeed, poverty is the central problem facing older women (8). In contrast to the implications of recent reports asserting the economic gains made by the elderly over the past several decades, the aged are not a homogeneous population. While there has been a decline in the overall rate of poverty among the aged over the past 15 years, major pockets of economic hardship persist (7, 9, 10). Because so many aged persons are near poverty (150 percent poverty level and below), the proportion of aged who are poor and near poor is larger than the proportion of nonaged who are poor and near poor (7). Specifically, well over 50 percent of older women find themselves facing economic hardships.

DEMOGRAPHIC CHARACTERISTICS

The older population is disproportionately female: 59 percent of all Americans 65 years and older are female as are nearly 70 percent of the age 80 and over population. Because wives typically outlive their husbands, fewer than 40 percent of older women are married. In contrast, nearly 80 percent of older men are married and live with their wives. Marital status—especially being widowed but also being divorced or separated—is a primary explanation for the high percentage (41 percent) of older women who live alone (7). Gender differences in marital status and living arrangements are significant because women's economic status in later life, as well as throughout the lifespan, is directly related to marital status.

Life expectancy, both at birth and at age 65, is higher for women than men. In 1986, the total remaining life expectancy for men age 65 was estimated at 14.4 years while that for women was estimated at 18.7 years. For those born in 1986, life expectancy was estimated at 71.3 years and 78.3 years, respectively for men and women. Though improvements in mortality rates have been experienced by both sexes over the last three decades, women have experienced more rapid improvements for most leading causes of death. Yet, proportionately more elderly women are limited in their activities of daily living, visit physicians more frequently, and use more days of hospital and nursing home care than their male counterparts (11). Thus, older women have more acute and chronic conditions than do men; while these diseases limit women's activities, they are seldom life-threatening (12, 13). Women bear the greater burden of health care costs. Older women's health care expenditures constitute 63 percent of the total health care costs of the elderly, although women make up 59 percent of the population (11).

Three-quarters of the 1.3 million elderly persons residing in institutions are women (7). Several factors account for this phenomenon: women live longer, have a higher prevalence of chronic disability, and are less likely to have a spouse from whom to receive care than are men. Persons who are single, divorced, or separated and who live alone have a ten times greater probability of being institutionalized than those who are married (4). Because the majority of older men have living spouses, they typically receive informal care from their wives. However, given the gender differences in marital status, older "females [depend on] care from offspring and relatives" (14). The availability of adult children, particularly daughters, to give care is the significant factor in keeping frail and disabled elderly women out of residential care (15, 16). Indeed, researchers have found that "the critical variable in the elderly's living arrangement was not the degree of the elderly's functional impairment but rather the access to family care" (16).

Given demographic trends, the greatest increase in persons potentially needing long term care will be unmarried women aged 75 and over, with women aged 85 and over making up the most significant proportional increase (14). The oldest old—generally women—will be encumbered, as they are presently, not only by increasing infirmity but also by the outliving of their close relatives.

ECONOMIC STATUS OF THE AGED:
A GENDER STORY

That the old are financially well off and that their economic status has been achieved at the expense of the young are myths. Over half of all older women live marginally close to, if not actually below, the poverty level (7, 17). Furthermore, even with the low official poverty line of 5,447 dollars a year (105 dollars a week for a single individual), older women have almost double the poverty rate of older men (7). While older women were 59 percent of the elderly population in 1984, they comprised 71 percent of its poor (18). Additionally, significant racial differences exist in the economic status of older women. Being old, female, and a member of a minority group represents a "triple jeopardy" (18, 19).

Women's poverty in old age is significantly related to their marital status and to the cumulative effects of unpaid work in the family and wage discrimination in the employment sector. Unmarried women between the ages of 65 and 69 receive approximately 40 percent of the total income of their married counterparts (7). The substantial difference in poverty rates between married and unmarried older women indicates the economic vulnerability of a large majority: most women outlive their husbands and widowhood is accompanied for most by a dramatic decline in overall income.

Women's economic problems are compounded with age. The oldest elderly have the lowest money incomes and, further, medical expenditures increase with age. For example, the oldest elderly were found in 1984 to have an average income that was 36 percent less than the income of people aged 65 to 69, while Medicare costs of persons aged 80 and over were 77 percent higher than those of persons aged 65 to 69 years (20). The "oldest old" tend to be widowed women who are in precarious economic circumstances.

The impoverishment of women is not unique to old age, however. Women of all ages are at risk of being poor as denoted by the popular phrase "the feminization of poverty." Factors in the impoverishment of women include: wage discrimination, occupational segregation, and lack of comparable pay; the increase in numbers of female-headed households; costs of child care, inequitable divorce settlements and extensive noncompliance with support orders; increased health care costs; the inadequacy of and cutbacks in domestic social programs. Contributing also to the impoverishment of women is the rapid increase in the numbers of displaced homemakers. These women are especially disadvantaged in re-entering the employment sector as a result of both ageism and sexism, the "widow's gap" in Social Security, and biases in pension and retirement programs for the aged (21–25).

Women are actively pushed into low income and poverty conditions by various combinations of these social phenomena. Moreover, the feminization of poverty and the economic marginality of older women cannot be fully understood without acknowledging the role of racial status. As Dressel (Chapter 15) has demonstrated, a comprehensive explanation of economic inequality and impoverishment requires attention to the complex interrelations between gender, class, and race. This is particularly important for policy since programs designed to address poverty on the basis of gender alone will be insufficient to address the economic issues of black and other racial-ethnic older women.

FACTORS IN THE ECONOMIC GENDER GAP

Older women's low income status reflects the culmination of a lifetime of secondary economic status. Contemporary wage levels and social policies continue to be based on the underlying assumption that women depend economically on a wage-earning male head-of-household who, theoretically, shares with his wife and other dependents his higher earnings, employment-related benefits, and retirement. The eligibility rules for public entitlement programs reflect men's patterns of labor force participation and the male model of work (26). The nonmeans-tested entitlement programs, such as Social Security, provide men greater access to and higher levels of benefits, rewarding continuous participation in the primary labor force. The means-tested and state-variable social assistance programs, including Supplemental Security Income, are set at penurious levels and primarily support women (27).

Public and private sector policies have contributed to the perpetuation of both the gender-structured wage and public pension systems. Most women are employed in secondary jobs, receiving substantially lower wages than their male counterparts and fewer work-related benefits (for example, health insurance coverage and retirement pensions), and women's earnings continue to average three-fifths of men's. Older women's incomes average even less. Specifically, in 1987 the median income for older men was 11,854 dollars and was 6,734 dollars for older women (7).

Women who commit themselves primarily to the activities of homemaking and caring for children—prescribed women's roles—discover when they divorce, are widowed in mid-life, or become aged, that they are economically penalized for having performed these socially necessary but gender-defined activities. As displaced homemakers or elderly widows, these women often find themselves living in conditions of genuine economic hardship.

The increase in numbers of mid-life and older women who suddenly need to be self-supporting after having been economically dependent in marriage is due largely to the high rate of divorce. Over one-third of the more than one million divorces annually occur between couples married ten or more years, and 20 percent of all divorces involve couples married 15 or more years. The divorce rate among couples of long-term marriages and among those middle aged or older continues to rise (22, 28).

Divorce has profound, often lasting, effects on women's standard of living. Studies show that men recover economically from divorce, and in fact, improve their financial status after divorce. Women, however, generally experience no such recovery unless they remarry, which few women over age 40 do (22, 28, 29). While the economic effects of divorce adversely affect women of all ages, mid-life and older women have even fewer options for reversing the downward mobility prompted by divorce than do younger women (21, 22). "The dramatic increase in divorce, especially in marriages of long duration, predicts an increase in the number of older women living alone and in poverty in the next generation" (8).

Becoming a widow also moves some women into the ranks of displaced homemakers. The average age at which a woman becomes widowed in this country is 56, yet no Social Security widow's benefits are available until age 60 (30, 31). The time between becoming widowed and turning age 60, referred to as the "widow's gap," is one of desperate economic uncertainty for many women. Coupled with the unfavorable labor market for mid-life and older re-entry women, the lack of social programs offering economic protection pushes many widowed women, who were economically secure during marriage, into harsh and unremitting economic conditions.

Essentially no public funds are available for providing temporary support to women without minor children who lose their economic base. Displaced homemakers qualify for no unemployment compensation since their family and home work is unpaid labor. Nor do they qualify for Social Security disability benefits. Despite the increased numbers of displaced homemakers, now estimated at nearly 11.5 million American women, 70 percent of whom are over age 55 (32), no programs have been initiated to ease their economic situations. Federal cuts in employment and training have brought these programs to their lowest funding levels in fifteen years (33), constraining women's attempts to re-enter the employment sector during mid-life or later years.

Sources of Income

Women's disadvantaged economic status in old age is directly related to the sources of income available to them, primarily Social Security benefits, asset income, private pension benefits, and employment earnings. These income sources are themselves directly related to women's earlier family and work activities and their secondary status in both the employment and policy sectors.

Dependency on Social Security as the primary, and often only, source of income is a major factor in older women's precarious economic standing. One in three unmarried older women receiving Social Security depends on it for more than 90 percent of her income (34). In 1987, the average old age Social Security benefit was 6,924 dollars for men and 5,292 dollars for women (32). Not only are women's Social Security payments less than men's, but they are relied on to a much greater extent by women than men as their primary, often only, source of old age income.

The gender inequities, and disadvantages to women, of the Social Security program are well documented (25, 34). Broad-based income inequalities, based on gender and class status, are both reinforced and reproduced through the Social Security program. Because Social Security is modeled on an insurance scheme, wage earners who remain attached to the labor force throughout their adult years until retirement age—usually men and not women given the latter's family care responsibilities—secure relatively greater protection from this public pension system. Women's lower earning records and more frequently interrupted work histories result in lower Social Security benefits. Further, over 70 percent of women take early retirement at age 62, often because of the need to take on added caregiving responsibility for a parent or spouse, and so receive reduced monthly benefits. Even though most women who reach age 62 will live an additional two decades or more, their Social Security benefits remain at the reduced amount. The average Social Security monthly benefit paid to retired men in 1987 was 577 dollars compared to 441 dollars paid to retired women, 265 dollars paid to dependent wives, and 342 dollars paid to widows (35).

Several Social Security reforms of the 1980s adversely affect women, including those who will enter old age in the coming years: 1) the 1983 and other intermittent periods during which Social Security cost of living adjustments (COLAs) were frozen, even for limited periods of time. For example, it has been projected that a delay in the COLA for only one year brings 500,000 more elderly, mostly women, below poverty; 2) the gradual increase of the retirement age to 67 and the stepped-up penalties for early retirement (which nearly three-quarters of older women take); 3) the termination of the widow's benefit when the youngest child reaches age 16 rather than 18; 4) the phase-out of student benefits for children of retired, disabled or deceased workers, all of which impact on older women; and 5) the elimination of the minimum Social Security benefit (which earlier had been only 122 dollars per month) for persons retiring after January 1982; this change further disadvantaged the poorest women by removing them from the respectability of Social Security coverage and forcing them to seek public assistance in the form of Supplemental Security Income (SSI) (7).

The major policy changes of the 1980s that are likely to positively affect older women were in the pension reforms, particularly those of 1984 and 1986, that reduced the time for pension vesting (from ten to five years) and required the signature of the pensioner spouse who wishes to receive higher pension benefits during his lifetime by resigning the rights to a pension for the surviving spouse. Also likely to benefit older women is one of the few remaining provisions of the repealed Catastrophic Health Care Act; this reform is aimed at preventing spousal impoverishment by protecting a minimum income and assets for spouses of those who are institutionalized in nursing homes.

Women's low Social Security payments are not compensated for by income from private pensions. Only about 13 percent of older women receive income from private pensions and, even then, the amounts received are less than half the amounts received by men. According to Moon's 1984 estimate, women's pensions average 59 percent of men's in amount (36). Women's lower earnings and intermittent attachment to the wage labor force contribute to their lower pension coverage. Also, many women who become widowed or divorced are inadequately protected with regard to legal claim to their husband's accrued pension funds, even though the "pension accrued by the working spouse is often the single largest asset of an older married couple" (37).

Assets contribute relatively little to older women's overall income. Even though approximately one-half of the older population receives income from assets, most people receive very small amounts of asset income and the proportion of total income it represents is low. Evidence indicates that individuals whose lifetime incomes are high will accumulate more assets than those whose incomes are relatively low. This means that women, whose lifetime incomes are significantly lower than men's and whose economic status depends primarily on their marital status, are not likely to benefit from asset income during old age.

Only 7.2 percent of older women improved their economic status through employment in 1986 and the majority of these women had only part-time employment (7). Thus, the total amounts of income derived by older women from pensions, assets, and employment generally do not add significantly to Social Security benefits. Most older men, however, rely on a combination of income sources and are relatively secure economically.

Income Supports for the Very Poor

The Supplementary Security Income (SSI) program is a federal-state cash assistance program for the poor aged, blind, and disabled. Eligibility for SSI benefits requires extreme poverty and almost no assets (a maximum of 2,000 dollars). Nationally, there are four and a half million beneficiaries, about three-quarters of whom qualify on the basis of age. Not surprisingly, considering the much higher poverty rate of older women compared to men, three-quarters of the aged SSI recipients are women. The income assistance provided through the SSI program is so minimal that its recipients remain below poverty (38). The monthly federal benefit level for SSI for aged persons living alone in 1988 was 354 dollars. Twenty-six states supplemented this amount but only at a very limited level, averaging about one dollar per day (32). In nominal dollars, this supplementation has been cut directly by 16 percent since 1980 and has been eroded additionally by an estimated 40 percent due to inflation (32). Further, SSI benefit levels discriminate against single individuals by setting the maximum federal benefit level at 76 percent the poverty rate for individuals (mostly women) and at 90 percent the poverty rate for couples. Eligibility requirements for SSI are so rigid that few options exist for moving out of this program once a woman becomes a beneficiary (39). Moreover, it is estimated that only half of those eligible for this assistance receive it (37).

The economic status of older women in the future must remain serious cause for concern. The projections of the Commonwealth Fund that by 2020 the percent of older men living alone who are poor or near-poor will have declined from 38 to 6 percent while the proportion of poor and near-poor older women will have dropped little, from 45 to 38 percent (40), suggests that the issue of the economic status of the aged will remain a gendered story.

HEALTH CARE

A large body of data has shown consistently that social class and health are correlated, with the poor and near poor being most compromised. Older women's lower incomes are coupled with ill health and the likelihood of increased need for medical care. Medical and health care costs have increased for older women due both to higher patient cost sharing and the increased need for care due to advancing age. As aggregate medical care costs continue to rise, publicly financed health programs are faced with growing constraints. Yet, older women's available income remains relatively fixed or falls with the death of a spouse.

It has been well-documented that Medicare meets only 44 percent of the elderly's health care costs (41, 42). However, a recent study showed that while Medicare meets about 44 percent of the health care expenditures of elderly married couples, it meets only about 33 percent of these costs for an elderly single woman (42). This is easily understood in the context of Medicare's acute care policy that, on average, pays more for men than for women in both Part A (hospital) and Part B (physician) benefits. Women are shortchanged in terms of the chronic illness care they need (43).

Few private insurance dollars, less than 16 percent, go to health services for the aged (24). Since most private health insurance coverage is a benefit of full-time employment, those who are unemployed, retired, or low-wage casual employees are likely not to have private health insurance coverage. "The lack of health insurance is most common among those least able to afford the consequences of poor health or lack of preventive health care" (24). Further, since women's marital status is a more significant predictor of their health insurance coverage than is their own employment status, many older women lose access to health coverage when they lose their spouse through death or divorce (44). Since women make up the majority of the elderly poor and unmarried, it is women who are least able to cover out-of-pocket medical expenses or to afford supplementary private insurance coverage.

Due to escalating health care costs, aged persons actually expend a greater share of their income on health care costs now than they did prior to the enactment of Medicare (33, 38). A Congressional report in March 1984 states that the average out-of-pocket costs for doctors' bills was "virtually the same for older persons with incomes under 5,000 dollars as for those few older persons with incomes of 35,000 dollars and up" (23). Older women, who are at greater risk for chronic disability and disadvantaged economic status, bear a heavier out-of-pocket burden for health care costs in terms of absolute dollars and proportion of income expended. While an elderly married couple paid about 9 percent of its income on direct out-of-pocket payments and health insurance premiums in 1986, a single elderly woman paid over 16 percent of her income on these expenses (42). Further, as noted earlier, single women's spending increases proportionately with age, with monthly out-of-pocket expenses being greater for the oldest old.

Older women must purchase supplementary medical insurance, Part B premiums of Medicare for physicians' services and medigap coverage, to cushion the cost of hospital and physician deductibles and copayments not covered by Medicare. Alternatively, they must pay out-of-pocket for the costs that are not covered by Medicare directly. Out-of-pocket and cost-sharing expenses for hospital and physician services have increased substantially in the 1980s for all elderly, but low-income individuals clearly are most handicapped by these changes.

Aged recipients of SSI cash assistance may qualify for publicly financed health coverage through the Medicaid program, but the eligibility requirements of many states are more restrictive than those for SSI (45, 46). State Medicaid programs have tightened eligibility requirements in the last decade, contributing to a decline in the percent of the poor who are eligible for Medicaid to 40 percent in 1987 from 63 percent in 1975 (33, 42, 47). Over 15 billion dollars were cut from the Medicaid program between 1980 and 1987. Medicaid cuts, intended to constrain expenditures and access in this program for the poor, were implemented through reductions in the federal share of the costs and incentives provided to states. One result has been that the variability among the states in eligibility and utilization has increased, as the percent below poverty who are covered by Medicaid declined (48, 49). Thus, many aged who are poor and near poor are denied this health coverage.

No publicly financed health coverage exists for non-disabled American adults below age 65, the age of eligibility for Medicare, unless they qualify as economically destitute or as medically needy under Medicaid. Women below age 65 and past the years of raising minor children cannot qualify for Medicare coverage unless they are disabled. Given that displaced homemakers are likely to have no private health insurance, since most policies are a benefit of husbands' employment, divorced women are twice as likely as any other group to be without any kind of health insurance coverage (44). Recent legislation (COBRA) has been adopted to require employers to offer conversion plans to retain health insurance for women following widowhood or divorce for a limited time period (18 months); however, women needing coverage must be able to afford to purchase it, paying both their own and their employer's share of the insurance. Following this coverage, women attempting to obtain *new* coverage will be particularly disadvantaged if they have preexisting medical conditions because of the exclusions that insurers typically impose.

Lack of money and the presence of certain medical conditions simply preclude access to private health insurance for many unmarried mid-life and older women. In future years not only are more women likely to enter old age already poor, but—without major health care policy reform—more women will enter old age without having had adequate preventative medical care during important periods earlier in their lifetime as a result of inadequate financial access to such care.

Several limited advances of import to older women occurred in recent years in health care policy. These include the ability to extend health insurance coverage under COBRA, the inclusion under Medicare of coverage for pap-smears, and the requirement that, for the elderly poor, Medicaid programs cover copayments, deductibles and premiums. However, the continuing omission of long term care coverage under Medicare is particularly damaging since women are asked to provide approximately 80 percent of these services. The individual costs of women's providing such care have begun to be documented.

CAREGIVING, WOMEN AND IDEOLOGY: THE CONSEQUENCES

The 1980s were marked by an ideological revolution in which the New Right that was forged promoted simultaneously a revival of the free market, under neo-liberalism, and an open longing for the return of the (now-mythical) patriarchal autonomous family, under neo-conservatism. The former ideological strain, neo-liberalism, is distinctly oriented toward a "minimalist state" in being hostile to anything that may impede the (natural) order of the market (and its natural superiority). The latter, neo-conservatism, appeals to authority, allegiance, tradition, and to "nature." "A corollary . . . is that the [traditional nuclear] family is central to maintaining the state" (50). Because this New Right model "squares the circle between an intellectual adherence to the free market and the emotional attachment to authority and imposed tradition" (51), it melds the interests of capitalism and patriarchy. Further, the New Right has reminded us that the primary, if not the only, justification for government intervention is the national defense and law enforcement.

Natural rights individualism is the "ideological cement" binding together contemporary neo-conservative and neo-liberal ideas and U.S. politics (52), supporting principles of self-help based on economic initiative and productivity, individual autonomy, and voluntary association. Restoring "both the giant corporation and the autonomous family . . . to their 'rightful place' in American life [requires] . . . faith and patriotism" (52). Ronald Reagan's commitment to the retrograde project was one of the most significant hallmarks of his presidency.

Reagan's ideological project was operationalized through a policy agenda designed to promote both the privatization of the welfare state and the isolation of the "family" from "society" (53). Policies advocating privatization promoted the belief that the "proper" and best form of health and social services to the elderly is non-governmental. In U.S. health and social policy, privatization efforts have operated hand-in-glove with the increased informalization of care, bolstered by the rhetoric of family responsibility. The message once again was that women workers should return home to care for their elderly (54); this message was coupled, however, with the contradictory one that those who do not participate in the labor market on the male model will not be helped by the state. Phrases such as "the sandwich generation," "the daughter shortage," and "the baby dearth" were uttered, and in some quarters were bemoaned, but policymakers remained firm in their refusal to move toward a long-term care policy or beyond reaffirmations of the need for renewed and continued family support (55).

Informal care or family support means women's labor: the average American woman can expect to spend 18 years helping an aging parent and 17 years caring for children (56). It has been estimated that over 27 million days of unpaid caregiving are provided older Americans alone every week (57). Family labor—more precisely, women's unpaid labor—is viewed as free labor (if recognized as labor at all). It is noteworthy that "over 40 percent of adult offspring participating in one survey reported that the time spent on caregiving tasks was equivalent to the time required by a full time job" (16). It is in government's interest to secure as much of this free work as possible, since it relieves the public costs of providing adequate long-term care.

Women's caregiving directly affects both their economic status and their health in old age. These effects again point to the structural conditions that contribute to women's lower socio-economic status and to the direct and indirect economic costs of caregiving. The women who give care to their disabled spouses may have to drain their savings and assets acquired during the marriage, "spending them down" on their spouses' or parents' needs.

Additionally, costs of caregiving include "opportunity costs" and these costs may well be the greatest economic expense of caregiving. Studies suggest that changing work patterns and even quitting work are common coping strategies of caregivers (58). Data from the Informal Caregivers Survey, a component of the larger National Long Term Care Survey, indicate that a majority of caregiving women had either reduced their paid working hours, rearranged their work schedules, taken time off without pay, or quit their jobs to resolve conflicting demands of caregiving and employment (59). Women who take early retirement or otherwise modify their employment to provide care not only lose wages and wage-related benefits, but also jeopardize their own sources of income for their later years. Specifically, because a total of only five years can be dropped out from the averaging of accrued Social Security credits, women who quit their employment to caretake (either their children or elders) directly affect their future Social Security benefits, and perhaps risk even their eligibility. Private pension benefits are also tied directly to wages and employment patterns. These caregiving women find themselves in a no-win situation: they are expected to provide care to their husbands or elderly relatives, yet public policy economically penalizes them for doing so and contributes to reproducing women's economic dependency. Because the majority of older women's economic situations are precarious, at best, the added costs of caregiving are significant.

Caregiving carries high physical health risks (58, 60). Physical labor, sometimes excessive, is part of caregiving and disabled persons need various kinds of assistance. Since many caregivers themselves are old or approaching old age (59), they too are vulnerable to, and may be experiencing, chronic ailments. Older women have more health problems than do older men (11, 12), yet it is women who do most caregiving work. Additionally, there are somatic outcomes of high levels of stress: high blood pressure, fatigue and exhaustion, and greater susceptibility to physical illness are some of the physical health risks (12). Lack of respite and relief from responsibilities, lack of assistance in performing physical tasks, and emotional fatigue and overload thwart a caregiver's own recovery from illness (61). These women's physical health is also endangered by a lack of preventive health care resulting from a scarcity of financial resources, time, and personal attention to the onset of disabilities (58, 60).

UNSETTLED FUTURE

Social policies are shaped largely by the requirements of the economy and the politics surrounding it. Women's positions as workers, caregivers, and beneficiaries of public programs in a gender stratified society continue to be systematically unequal to those of men. By failing to address these structural inequities, social policies perpetuate, both directly and indirectly, the disadvantaged economic and health situations of women throughout old age.

Under the politics and fiscal retrenchment of the 1980s, the position of women has been further undermined, and there has been a distinct shift of resources away from women to men and from minorities to whites. The most important elements of the Reagan legacy for older women are (55): 1) intensified commodification and medicalization of care for the aging in ways that are consistent with capitalist expansion of the medical-industrial complex (62); 2) the continuing refusal of the state to provide meaningful long term care benefits to the elderly and disabled; 3) the accumulation of multiple pressures on a beleaguered network of traditionally nonprofit home and community-based health and social service providers, stretched thin by the demands of very sick and very old patients who are discharged from the hospital earlier than ever before (63), and a growing population of oldest old (85 and over); and 4) the use of policies to promote family responsibility and increase the informalization of care. These efforts to restore a traditional family life and to regulate families, especially women within families, are congruent with the deep concerns of both the state and capital to minimize public costs for the elderly. These efforts are consistent with the desires of those in the New Right to restore patriarchal family arrangements and to assure a continuing supply of women's free labor, viewed as essential to the reproduction and maintenance of the work force (64). The Reagan Administration's resistance to a federal policy solution to the problem of long-term care and its unstated policy of informalization must be understood as part of a larger austerity strategy and in the context of the state's need for women, regardless of their labor force participation, to continue to perform large (and increasing) amounts of unpaid servicing work (26).

The economic and health issues confronted by aging and aged women challenge the very structure of our social institutions; to end the social and economic inequities experienced by women requires broad-based social reforms. The economic and health situations of older women require deep structural and policy changes that will redress inequities and provide access to basic resources, including housing, health and long-term care, and Social Security benefits.

In conclusion, some points warrant reemphasis. The complex interrelationships between the private and public spheres have profound effects on the economic and health conditions of women. These effects vary across different, critical periods of women's lives. With advancing age, women's overall health status and available financial and social resources typically decline. The means for responding to increasing needs vary not only by gender but also by class and race.

The measures of austerity imposed on publicly funded social programs have entailed a shift away from the previous decade's efforts to increase access to, and make more comprehensive, social and health care services. Because of the deep structural origins of the problems identified here—older women's impoverishment and lack of access to health care—a public commitment to a strong state role remains essential. Today, the need for an adequate income policy is more important than ever given the political economic emphasis upon individual self-reliance. Women's income issues cannot be ignored in the health policy debate, and health must be defined in the broad sense to include well-being, not merely the absence of disease. The situations faced by older women call for development and implementation of programs and policies that abridge, and compensate for, the gendered division of labor and consequent situation of lifelong discrimination.

ACKNOWLEDGMENTS

Portions of this chapter were previously published under the title, "Unsettled Future: Older Women—Economics and Health" in *Feminist Issues*, Spring 1987 Volume 7 No. 1. Used with permission of Transaction, Inc.

REFERENCES

1. Estes, C. L., Gerard, L., and Clark, A. Women and the economics of aging. In *Readings in the Political Economy of Aging*, edited by M. Minkler and C. L. Estes, pp. 209–224. Baywood Publishing, Amityville, New York, 1984.

2. Marmot, M. G., Kogevinas, M., and Elston, M. A. Social/economic status and disease. In *Annual Review of Public Health*, Volume 8, edited by L. Breslow, J. E. Fielding, and L. B. Lave, pp. 111–135. Annual Reviews, Inc., Palo Alto, California, 1987.

3. Dutton, D. B. Social class, health, and illness. In *Applications of Social Science to Clinical Medicine and Health Policy*, edited by L. H. Aiken and D. Mechanic, pp. 31–62. Rutgers University Press, New Brunswick, New Jersey, 1986.

4. Butler, L. H., and Newacheck, P. W. Health and social factors affecting long term care policy. In *Policy Options in Long-Term Care*, edited by J. Meltzer, F. Farrow, and H. Richman, pp. 38–77. University of Chicago Press, 1981.

5. Kane, R. A., and Kane, R. L. *Long-Term Care: Principle, Programs, and Policies*. Springer Publishing Company, New York, 1987.

6. Luft, H. S. *Poverty and Health: Economic Causes and Consequences of Health Problems*. Ballinger, Cambridge, Massachusetts, 1978.

7. United States Bureau of the Census. Statistical abstract of the United States, 1988. *National Data Book and Guide to Sources*. Government Printing Office, Washington, D.C., 1989.

8. King, N., and Marvel, M. *Issues, Policies, and Programs for Midlife and Older Women*. Center for Women's Policy Studies, Washington, D.C., 1982.

9. Schultz, J. *The Economics of Aging*. Van Nostrand Reinhold Company, New York, 1985.

10. Stone, R. *Recent Developments in Respite Care Services for Caregivers of the Impaired Elderly*. Institute for Health & Aging, University of California, San Francisco, July 1985.

11. Rice, D., and Estes, C. L. Health of the elderly: Policy issues and challenges. *Health Aff.* 3(4): 25–49, Winter, 1984.

12. Verbrugge, L. Women and men: Mortality and health of older people. In *Aging in Society: Selected Reviews of Recent Research*, edited by M. Riley, B. Hess, and K. Bond. Lawrence Erlbauns Association, Publishers, London, 1983.

13. Rice, D. Sex differences in mortality and morbidity: Some aspects of the economic burden. In *Sex Differentials in Mortality: Trends, Determinants, and Consequences*, edited by A. Lopez, and L. Ruzicka. Department of Demography, Canberra, 1983.

14. Manton, K., and Soldo, B. Dynamics of health changes in the oldest old. *Milbank Mem. Fund Q. Health and Soc.* 63(2): 252, Spring, 1985.

15. Vladeck, B. *Unloving Care: The Nursing Home Tragedy*. Basic Books, New York, 1980.

16. Feldblum, C. Home health care for the elderly: Programs, problems, and potentials. *Harv. J. Leg.* 22(1): 194–254, 1985.

17. Grad, S. Incomes of the aged and nonaged, 1950–1982. *Soc. Sec. Bull.* 47(6): 3–17, Washington, D.C., 1984.

18. Minkler, M., and Stone, R. The feminization of poverty and older women. *Gerontologist* 25(4): 351–357, 1985.

19. Markides, K. S., and Mindel, C. H. *Aging and Ethnicity*, pp. 31–35. Sage Publishers, Beverly Hills, California, 1987.

20. Torry, B. Sharing increasing costs on declining income: The visible dilemma of the invisible aged. *Milbank Mem. Fund. Q. Health and Soc.* 63(2): 385 & 387, Spring, 1985.

21. Arendell, T. *Mothers and Divorce: Legal, Economic, and Social Dilemmas*. University of California Press, Berkeley, 1986.

22. Arendell, T. A review: Women and the economics of divorce in the contemporary United States. *Signs: Journal of Women in Culture and Society*, Winter, 1987.

21. Arendell, T. *Mothers and Divorce: Legal, Economic, and Social Dilemmas*. University of California Press, Berkeley, 1986.
22. Arendell, T. A review: Women and the economics of divorce in the contemporary United States. *Signs: Journal of Women in Culture and Society*, Winter, 1987.
23. Coalition on Women and the Budget. *Inequality of Sacrifice: The Impact of the Reagan Budget on Women*. National Women's Law Center, Washington, D.C., March, 1984.
24. Kasper, A., and Soldinger, E. Falling between the cracks: How health insurance discriminates against women. *Wom. and Health* 8(4): 77–93, The Haworth Press, Winter, 1983.
25. Rix, S. *Older Women: The Economics of Aging, Women's Research and Education*. Institute of the Congressional Caucus for Women's Issues, Washington, D.C., 1984.
26. Sassoon, A. S. Women's new social role: Contradictions of the welfare state. In *Women and the State*, edited by A. S. Sassoon. Hutchinson, London, 1987.
27. Quadagno, J. Race, class, and gender in the U.S. welfare state: Nixon's failed Family Assistance Plan. *Am. Soc. Rev.* 55(1): 11–28, 1990.
28. National Center for Health Statistics. *Monthly Vital Statistics Report* 33(11; Suppl.), February. U.S. Department of Health and Human Services, Washington, D.C., 1985.
29. Weitzman, L. *The Divorce Revolution*. The Free Press, New York, 1985.
30. U.S. Senate Special Committee on Aging. *Aging America: Trends and Projections, 1985–86*. U.S. Department of Health and Human Services, Washington, D.C., 1986.
31. Markson, E. *Older Women: Issues and Prospects*. Lexington Books, Lexington, Massachusetts, 1985.
32. *Families U.S.A. Foundation: Three Year Report (1986–1987–1988)*, p. 28. Families U.S.A. Foundation, Washington, D.C., 1989.
33. United States Congress. Problems of working women. Hearing before the Joint Economic Commissions, April 4, 1984. U.S. Government Printing Office, Washington, D.C., 1984.
34. Women's Equity Action League (WEAL). *WEAL Facts: Letter to the Editor, Equity for Women*. WEAL, Washington, D.C., 1985.
35. Social Security Bulletin. *Annual Statistical Supplement, 1988*. U.S. Department of Health and Human Services, Social Security Administration, Washington, D.C., 1988.
36. Moon, M. Economic issues facing a growing population of older women. Paper presented at the American Sociological Association, New York City, September 1986.
37. United States Senate. Special Committee on Aging. *The Future of Medicare*, p. 172. U.S. Government Printing Office, Washington, D.C., 1983.
38. United States Congress. *An Analysis of the President's Budgetary Proposals for Fiscal Year 1986*. Congressional Budget Office, U.S. Government Printing Office, Washington, D.C., February 1986.
39. Crystal, S. *America's Old Age Crisis: Public Policy and the Two Worlds of Aging*. Basic Books, New York, 1982.
40. Commonwealth Fund Commission on the Elderly People Living Alone. *Report on the Quality of Life for Older Women: Older Women Living Alone*. Testimony of Karen Davis, Director, to Select Committee on Aging, U.S. House of Representatives. U.S. Government Printing Office, Washington, D.C., 1988.
41. National Health Law Program (NHLP). *In Poor Health: The Administration's 1985 Health Budget*. Health Law Program, Los Angeles, 1985.

42. ICF, Inc. *Medicare's Role in Financing the Health Care of Older Women*. Submitted to American Association of Retired Persons, July 1985.
43. U.S. Department of Health and Human Services, Health Care Financing Administration, Division of Program Statistics. Unpublished data for 1984.
44. Berk, M., and Taylor, A. Women and divorce: Health insurance coverage, utilization, and health care expenditures: National health care expenditures study. Paper presented at Annual Meeting of the American Public Health Association, November 1983.
45. Estes, C. L., et al. *Correlates of Long Term Care Expenditures and Utilization in 50 States*. Final Report, National Center for Health Services Research, 1985.
46. Estes, C. L. Long term care and public policy in an era of austerity. *J. Pub. Health Pol.* 6(4): 464–475, 1985.
47. Davis, K., and Rowland, D. Uninsured and underserved: Inequities in health care in the United States. In *Securing Access to Health Care 3, Presidential Commission for the Study of Ethical Problems in Medicine and Biomedical and Behavior Research*. U.S. Government Printing Office, Washington, D.C., March 1983.
48. Holahan, J. F., and Cohen, J. W. *Medicaid: The Trade-Off Between Cost Containment and Access to Care*. Urban Institute, Washington, D.C., 1984.
49. Darling, H. The role of the federal government in assuring access to health care. *Inquiry* 23: 286–295, 1986.
50. Levitas, R. Competition and compliance: The utopias of the new right. In *The Ideology of the New Right*, edited by R. Levitas, p. 93. Polity Press, Cambridge, 1986.
51. Edgar, D. The free or the good. In *The Ideology of the New Right*, edited by R. Levitas, pp. 74–75. Polity Press, Cambridge, 1986.
52. O'Connor, J. *Accumulation Crisis*. Basil Blackwell, New York, 1984.
53. Myles, J. Personal communication, March 1989.
54. Binney, E. A., Estes, C. L., and Humphers, S. Informalization and community services for the elderly. Paper presented at the American Sociological Association, San Francisco, 1989.
55. Estes, C. L. The Reagan legacy: Privatization, the welfare state, and aging. In *States, Labor Markets, and the Future of Old Age Policy*, edited by J. Quadagno and J. Myles. Temple University Press, Philadelphia, (in press).
56. Quinlan, A., et al. *The Womanly World of Long Term Care: The Plight of the Long Term Care Worker*. Older Women's League, Washington, D.C., 1989.
57. Liu, K., and Manton, K. G. Disability and long term care. Paper presented at the Methodologies of Forecasting Life and Active Life Expectancy Workshop, Bethesda, Maryland, June 25–26, 1985.
58. Brody, E. Parent care as a normative family stress. *Gerontologist* 25(1): 19–29, 1985.
59. Stone, R., Cafferata, G., and Sangl, J. *Caregivers of the Frail Elderly: A National Profile*. NCHSR, Bethesda, Maryland, 1986.
60. Bader, J. Respite care: Temporary relief for caregivers. *Wom. and Health*, Special Issue 10(2/3): 39–52, 1985.
61. Corbin, J., and Strauss, A. Issues concerning regime management in the home. *Ageing and Soc.* 5(3): 249–265, 1985.
62. Estes, C. L., and Binney, E. A. The biomedicalization of aging. *Gerontologist* 29(5): 587–596, 1989.

63. Wood, J. B., and Estes, C. L. The impact of DRGs on community-based service providers: Implications for the elderly. *Am. J. Pub. Health* (in press).
64. Abramovitz, M. *Regulating the Lives of Women*, pp. 349–379. South End Press, Boston, 1988.

CHAPTER 14

COMMUNITY CARE POLICIES
AND GENDER JUSTICE

Suzanne E. England, Sharon M. Keigher,
Baila Miller, and Nathan L. Linsk

*When men and women are given the opportunity and the capacity to choose,
then justice is possible.*
D. Kirp, M. Yudof, and M. Franks, Gender Justice, 1986

What is the proper role of government in family care for the ill and disabled elderly? The question raises the thorny policy conflict between the public's concern with the needs of a dependent population and the presumed right of families to decide most matters privately, without interference by the State. Family-provided and other "informal" (i.e., unpaid) care of the dependent elderly is largely structured along gender lines, with women providing most of the personal and health-related care for elderly relatives. The feminized structure of family caregiving raises issues of equity because, in order to fulfill what can be viewed as both a private and a public responsibility, women must often forego other opportunities and the freedom to make choices that may be critical to their well-being.

In the United States, the debate about policies to support or encourage family and informal caregiving has largely ignored the issue of gender. The issues are most often framed in terms of the need to reduce or control public expenditures and to design policies that achieve a "proper balance" between incentives and disincentives to families to provide care [see, for example, Burwell (1)]. With a few notable exceptions (2–4), discussion of these policies, which fall under the general rubric of community care policy, tends to assume that the processes and outcomes of these policies are gender neutral.

The conceptualization of community care policy options must extend to include the gender structure of family caregiving and the effect of these policies on women who are the spouses, daughters, and other relatives of ill and disabled elderly persons. The social dynamics underlying present community care policies are rooted in traditional concepts about the family, women, and the responsibility of the State. These concepts have generally supported a laissez-faire approach to family caregiving, including an appropriate concern for preserving the liberty of the family to make its own decisions about allocating carer tasks. However, the privacy of these decisions is largely illusory. The capacity of women to freely choose caring is severely limited by the paucity of caregiving alternatives and the constriction of their choices elsewhere.

The assumptions underlying present policies arise from a social system in which, despite much-heralded change, women as a class remain at an economic disadvantage. Socialized to accept the caregiver role, and finding fewer opportunities in the work-place, their choices are further limited by services that are fragmented and difficult to obtain. Policies that accept this constriction of choice are supported by a political climate that regards the marketplace as an efficient and sufficient mechanism for distributing services to families. The result is that nothing is being done to protect carers from the undue risks to which they are exposed, and many women are left with no choice but to provide care.

The design and implementation of policies that affect family care of the elderly must take into account how policies foster inequities. Because family caregiving is feminized, government policies should be organized in such a way as to assure "gender justice" (5) by providing support that promotes the capacity of both sexes to make life choices unhampered by limitations rooted in sexual stereotypes.

Most analyses of community care policy options assume that the policies have been developed and implemented without gender bias. In this article, we challenge those assumptions by analyzing the relationship between community care policy and the gender structure of caregiving, and by explicating two major dynamics:

1. The interaction of community care policy provisions with the gender structure of family caregiving, which results in heavy dependence on the unpaid labor of female family members.
2. The inequities for women, which result from the current emphasis on controlling costs by restricting supportive services and benefits.

The intent of our analysis is threefold: to examine community care policies from a perspective of gender justice; to direct attention to the needs of carers and to the social costs of neglecting these needs; and to suggest a direction for future policy development.

DYNAMICS OF COMMUNITY CARE POLICY AND GENDER

Assumptions Underlying Present Policies

Our perspective is similar to that of the symbolic interactionists, who view social policy as "constructed" from social negotiations and based on cultural assumptions (6). Present community care policies are derived from a general acceptance of an interrelated set of assumptions, as outlined in the left-hand column of Table 1. The basic policy model is the welfare safety net in which government-supported care is the "last resort" for families.

The safety net approach has meant that elders (not their carers) qualify for benefits according to need as defined by lack of income or resources. By excluding as many persons as possible, and limiting benefits to the minimum needed for survival outside a nursing home, costs are "saved." Underlying the present community care model is the fear—so far unsubstantiated by research—that people will cease or reduce their own efforts and let the government take over. Apparently, this so called "substitution effect" is of central concern to those who develop the Medicaid regulations at the U.S. Department of Health and Human Services (HHS) and at the Office of Management and Budget. According to a report in the *Washington Post*, officials from both agencies based their restrictions on Medicaid coverage of home care on the belief that new or extended benefits would just substitute government money for the home care now being provided "free" by relatives and friends (7).

Also underlying present policies is the concern that even programs designed to help only those who would otherwise have to live in a nursing home would bring numbers of people "out of the woodwork" to apply for them (7). In fear of the "woodwork effect," Congress imposed two major restrictions on Medicaid. First, a state cannot provide Medicaid-funded home care benefits unless HHS agrees to waive normal Medicaid rules—hence the term Medicaid waivers; and second, to prevent the states from making home care an entitlement program, a ceiling was imposed so that per capita costs can be no higher than if the waiver were not granted.

By supporting home-based care only as a lower-cost substitute for institutional care, the Medicaid waiver-related policies shape programs to limit payment for home support solely to those who are so ill or disabled as to be eligible for nursing home care. A key concept of those community care policies is that the target for benefits should meet the "but for" criterion, as in "this person would be in a nursing home 'but for' the services provided by the community care program" (8). The "but for" approach discounts the unpaid caregiving of friends and relatives from the total amount of benefits to be paid. Thus, an elderly person without friends and family available to provide care will receive a higher benefit than an equally disabled person who is receiving care from family members. This family care is not calculated as a direct contribution to the program, nor are the family

Table 1

Comparison of assumptions of present care policies with policies to maximize gender justice

Policy dimensions	Assumptions	
	Present policies	Policies to maximize gender justice
Basic policy model	Community care is welfare e.g., a safety net. It must be rationed and means-tested Only the minimum benefits should be given Government-supported care should be the "last resort"	Community care must be a social utility, like public education. It should be available according to a broadened definition of need Equal access should be provided through income support, availability of goods and services, and, when appropriate, compensated family care Public provision should be the foundation for care
Locus of responsibility	Care of the elderly is a family responsibility Government's only responsibility is to fill the gap. Families should exhaust their own resources before turning to the government for help Government-assisted care should not substitute for unpaid family care	Care of dependent individuals is a responsibility shared by family and government Most families provide as much care as they can. Many families need government help to carry on Government help is an add-on rather than a substitute for family care
Values	Women are the primary caregivers in the family Women are responsible for the direct care of dependent members of the family, even if they have to give up other roles It is more important for men to realize their full economic potential than it is for women	Women are not obliged to be the primary caregivers in the family Men and women family members should be equally free to choose between caregiving and other roles Women are entitled to realize their full economic potential

	Family care is a "private good"	Family care is a "social good"
	The State's primary responsibility to the family is to assure freedom from State intrusion	In addition to free *from* intrusion, the State should assure the freedom *to* provide care, by making the necessary resources available
	Families, not society, benefit from family care	Families contribute to society by providing care
	Most family care is not compensable	Family care is compensable
Target of benefits	The impaired individual at highest risk is the sole target	Those too ill or disabled to be helped effectively by the health care system alone and those who care for them are the targets
	Those with available family carers need fewer services	Over-burdened caregivers need service and support
	Those without available family qualify for government help	Those with family qualify for government help
Objectives	Avoid or delay institutionalization as a way to curtail costs to the government	Provide support for family care and protection to family carers
	Encourage families to provide care	Integrate family care into a continuum of services and programs
	Maintain the "balance" between family and government care, that is, let families "pay the first dollar"	Provide family cash transfers to elders and/or their carers
Cost-benefit concerns	Benefits are measured by savings to taxpayers first and the welfare of caregivers last	Benefits are measured by family and community welfare
	Benefits or incentives to caregivers would bring caregivers "out of the woodwork" and drive up costs	There is no evidence of the "woodwork effect"; initial increase in cost may be due to pent-up demand but costs will probably level off
	Family-provided care saves government money because it does not cost anything	Family stress from unsupported caregiving burden can result in costs to the community
	The costs borne by families are not accounted for, even if they become public costs in the future	Women presently bear an inequitable share of the social and economic costs of caregiving

caregivers accorded any recognition or provided any compensation for their services.

The assumption underlying present policies is that the costs incurred by families in providing care are not a critical factor in the decision to place a relative in a nursing home and therefore are of no concern to government. One estimate of the total cost to individual carers was $18 billion dollars in 1979 (9). A pilot project in Maryland found that families were making a significant monetary contribution toward providing care and that subsidized families reported an increased capacity to cope and higher levels of life satisfaction (10).

Interaction of Policies with the Feminized Structure of Family Care

Policies designed to avoid the costs of institutionalization by providing for home-based services to those elderly who are at risk of placement in nursing homes affect mainly those areas of caregiving associated with health problems, difficulties with self-care, and relatively severe limitations in mobility and activities of daily living. These are the areas of family caregiving that are the most sex-segregated (3, 11). Because functionally impaired elderly men are much more likely than functionally impaired women to be married (12), the burden on wives is especially great. In addition to the greater likelihood that they will be less well off financially, they tend to provide care for the more disabled elderly (13), over longer periods of time (14), with fewer outside sources of assistance (15), and at a greater risk to their own health and well-being (16, 17).

It has been demonstrated that the relative involvement of adult sons and daughters in the care of an elderly parent is influenced by the nature of the caregiving tasks performed and certain characteristics of the parent's situation. In a study by Coward and Rathbone-McCuan, adult daughters were eight times more likely to be helping with indoor household chores and personal health care than were adult sons (11). Adult sons were more likely to be named as helpers with routine household maintenance and repairs. In addition, daughters were more likely to be identified as the caregiver when the parent perceived that his or her health represented a major obstacle to performing the daily tasks of living—the circumstances in which government-supported services come into play for elderly persons with no available family members. This means that many female relatives are providing care that might otherwise be assisted by the government. In policy terms, the presence of an unpaid female carer results in reduced eligibility for services and benefits. Not only are the contributions of these women minimized and unacknowledged by society, but when family caregiving is taken into account in determining eligibility, they and their families are also being indirectly penalized.

Present community care policies ignore the very cornerstone of their construction: the interaction between the economic structural conditions of women's lives and a set of social expectations that devalues and underestimates the care they provide. Indeed, some critics have suggested that "community care" is a euphemism for female members of families (18). Policies based on the assumption that women are and should be available as unpaid caregivers do not legitimize family carers as targets for services or benefits. The inequity of the situation aside, this arrangement is unlikely to survive in the future, when the costs of caregiving will become too great for women who must also work outside the home.

Impact of the Carer Role on Women

The shift to more egalitarian attitudes toward family roles notwithstanding, the care of dependent family members is still largely the responsibility of women (3, 19, 20). Preliminary data from the 1982 National Long Term Care Study indicate that 72 percent of the estimated 2.3 million persons providing unpaid care to the 1.2 million noninstitutionalized frail elderly were wives or adult daughters (21).

There is some evidence that economic position may influence the caregiving role, with lower income and less attachment to the paid labor force being associated with greater likelihood of being the provider of care. Archbold's phenomenological study of adult daughter carers found that the more affluent "career woman" daughters were more likely to be involved with a dependent parent as a "care manager," while less economically well-off daughters were more likely to be providing direct care (22). In a micro-analysis of caregiver selection, Ikels concluded that all other things being equal, if two candidates for carer are employed, the one with the least-paying job or the most marginal participation in the labor force is selected (23). This suggests that families may use a form of cost-benefit analysis, assigning caregiving roles to the member whose wages are lower and therefore more "disposable." Given the differential between the incomes of men and women, it is most likely the woman who will be expected to leave the paid work force to stay home with the relative or modify her paid work in ways that compromise her earning power. If the choice is between two women, the woman who is less attached to the labor force is more likely to find herself with the major caregiving responsibilities.

The "division of caring labor" within the family has both social and economic implications for women. The demands on one's time when responsible for the performance of indoor household chores, personal care, health care, and simply "being there" tend to be daily and ongoing, whereas household maintenance, helping with finances, etc., can be scheduled so as not to interfere with other role demands. Women, by their involvement in the time-intensive tasks of caring, more frequently report stress and burden in terms of "lack of discretionary or leisure time" and conflicts with other demands at work or from other family members (22). The tasks of caring that are most likely to be performed by women—personal care and body contact tasks—are most strongly associated with

234 / Critical Perspectives on Aging

perceived burden by caregivers (24). The responsibility that women take on when they carry out these indoor, personal, and health-related care tasks carries with it losses in other important areas of their lives.

Women, who continue to be economically disadvantaged as a class, lose more ground as individuals when they take on caring responsibilities. They lose wages by interrupting their employment or settling for lower paid work that fits into their caregiving schedule. Women who cannot work outside the home because of caregiving responsibilities, or who are simultaneously employed and attempting to care for an elderly relative, are at increased risk of economic dependency. Data from the survey of caregivers that was conducted as part of the 1982 National Long Term Care Study (4), document these risks: 14 percent of the wives and 12 percent of the daughters were forced to leave their jobs because of caregiving responsibilities; and of those who remained employed during their caregiver experience, 22 percent had taken time off from work (without pay) to provide care. Brody's study of families providing care to an elderly relative found that 28 percent of the women who were staying home to care for their mothers said they had quit work for that purpose (25). A similar percentage of the women who were employed said that they had reduced their working hours or were considering quitting. In her review of the research on family caregiving. Horowitz concluded that the impact of caregiving on the ability to work is substantial for significant numbers of carers (26).

A survey of workers in a large corporation found that of the employees who reported that they were caring for an elderly relative—some at levels exceeding thirty hours per week—women were much more likely than men to be the primary providers of care (27). The average amount of time per week that the women employees were providing direct care was reported as 16.1 hours, whereas the males reported an average of only 5.3 hours (27, p. 7). Most of these women reported that the combination of work and caregiving interfered with other family responsibilities and social and emotional needs. Despite the conventional wisdom that employment draws women from caregiving roles, it appears that it draws men much more than women. The employee survey found that in addition to the disparity between the overall caregiving responsibilities reported by men and women, men reported relying more heavily on outside help or their spouses to provide the primary care (27, p. 7).

Many women apparently struggle with the dual roles of employee and caregiver. Stoller, for example, found that employment significantly decreased the hours of assistance provided by sons, but not by daughters (20). Others have found that while women who are employed may produce fewer hours of direct care than those who are not, the level of total care received by the elderly person is not affected by the employment status of the primary carer (28, 29). There is even evidence that the parents of employed daughters may be at an advantage in that, in addition to receiving levels of care similar to those with nonworking daughters, they are also more likely to receive financial help (26).

Warshaw and associates report that many female employees are involved in providing care for elderly relatives (30). For these women, the strain of caregiving on role performance at work can result in excessive absences, lowered productivity, and less job security. What has not been reported, but is an obvious cost to these women, is the reduction in their opportunities to get additional training or education or to take on additional work responsibilities that could result in advancement and/or higher pay.

The interruption and compromising of their work lives by caregiving responsibilities contributes to women's overrepresentation in the "secondary" labor market in which workers receive low wages and few benefits. For many women, the "tricycle" of caregiving begins when they have children, is renewed when a parent becomes ill, and again when their aging spouse needs care. As a result of job segregation, discrimination, and role expectations, most women reach retirement age with significantly lower benefits, asset income, and pension protection than men (31).

The research to date strongly supports the proposition that much of family caregiving is structured along gender lines, with women providing more of the caring overall and doing more of the personal and health-related tasks that tend to be daily and ongoing and associated with greater perceived burden. Although research has yet to adequately document the nature and extent of the social and economic costs to families and individual carers, there is sufficient evidence that many family caregivers, most of whom are women, are incurring the costs of lost or reduced opportunities in the workplace and elsewhere. These costs are likely to have a lasting impact on them, their families, and society.

GENDER JUSTICE AND PRESENT COMMUNITY
CARE POLICIES

Medicare/Medicaid

Because the major purpose of present community care policies is to avoid the government expense of providing institutional care, present policies and programs for community care of the elderly, particularly those tied to state Medicaid waivers, depend heavily on the unpaid care provided in the home by relatives. The hidden sexist bias in Medicaid policies, perhaps the most pervasive and far-reaching of the policies that affect care of the elderly, has recently been recognized in the courts and by recent changes in state policies regarding "spend-down" requirement. The bias may be seen by examining both the impact of Medicaid policies and the efforts to provide financial incentives to families.

An example of the problem was described in an article in *The New York Times* about Bertha Hafner, seventy-five, who was left so impoverished by the spend down that Medicaid required before it would provide payment for nursing-home care for her husband that she was left with no alternative but to sue him for support (32). Because New York law did not allow the inclusion of the spouse's living expenses in the calculation of Medicaid spend-down requirements, suing was Mrs. Hafner's only means of securing some income to keep her from being forced to live in poverty. Mrs. Hafner, like most women of her generation who married, was dependent on her husband's pension and social security, yet was considered by law to be financially responsible for her spouse and required to pay for his nursing home costs out of their joint income. For her and others in her position who carried out the traditional responsibilities of homemaker and mother, the economic costs of resorting to institutional care for a husband are potentially devastating. Many have spent months and years taking care of their husbands at home, yet when it becomes necessary to use institutional care, their contribution to saving Medicaid costs is not acknowledged.

Until recently, the options that Medicaid's rules left for women whose spouses needed long-term care were: (a) spend down to poverty level in order to be eligible, (b) divorce or sue for support, (c) quit work to provide full time care, or (d) pay for care (2). Each option puts these women at risk of poverty and permanent economic dependency. The salvaging, from the Medicare Catastrophic Coverage Act, of a spousal protection benefit has partially, though by no means fully, ameliorated this situation (see Chapters 12 and 13).

Other dilemmas exist for the women who provide most of the informal care for the estimated 5.2 million elderly disabled Americans who remain in the community (19). Many of the same women who are caught in the spend-down problem have spent years taking care of their ill and disabled husbands at home, receiving little or nothing in the way of services or compensation for the care they provided during those years. The small minority [estimated at 15 percent by Macken (12)] who do receive publicly supported services to help care for their relatives are constrained by Medicare-related community care policies that limit the services to the minimum amount of additional care that is needed to prevent institutionalization.

Such cases highlight a major issue concerning the impact of policies for long-term care of the elderly on female carers. Policies to promote home-based informal care for ill and disabled elderly that are driven by concerns of controlling costs on an individual-by-individual basis actually constrict the choices of the elderly and their carers, and in so doing, have the potential to reduce the capacity of families to provide adequate care. Those provisions that attempt to control costs by limiting eligibility and rationing benefits raise the threshold of access to services and benefits to heights that require many elders and their carers to choose between no support and total support. The feminized structure of caregiving means that women may be reduced to choosing between providing all of the care or none of it.

Compensation for Family Caregiving

One approach to reducing some of the inequities of community care is to provide some form of compensation for family caregiving. At present, there are three types of community care policies that have potential for compensating family carers: the federal Child and Dependent Care Credit that provides a benefit to families through a tax credit; various state community care programs that allow in one way or another for direct payments to family members for some portion of the care they provide; and the Veterans' Administration's Aid and Attendance Allowance.

Child and Dependent Care Credit. The Child and Dependent Care Credit is the least adequate of these mechanisms for compensating family members who provide direct care. At present the credit is not refundable and therefore of no benefit to families who owe no taxes or do not itemize deductions. For example, it has been estimated that in 1981 only 6 percent of the credits—including credits for child care as well as care for elderly family members—went to families with incomes below $10,000 (33). The result is that many low-income families, which are predominantly headed by women, derive no benefit from the program.

In addition to these and other problems that limit the distribution of the benefit, the tax credit does not presently benefit families unless all taxpayers in the household are gainfully employed. Women who are not employed outside the home, or who prefer to leave or reduce their employment to provide some or all of the care themselves, are not eligible for the credit. The credit, which differs from a deduction in that it reduces the taxpayer's total tax liability, is only for expenditures for care, not for direct care provided by a relative. Although it may enable some women and men to continue to work outside the home, the subsidy, which ranges from 20 to 30 percent of the expenditures up to a maximum of $2,400 (1), may not be a sufficient incentive to families who are deciding between the benefits of the subsidy and having a member of the family (usually a woman) leave employment to stay home and provide the needed care. In an analysis of the benefits of current tax provisions for offsetting a family's costs for caregiving, Perlman concluded that, because the provisions take into account only a small part of the family's actual effort and exclude all unpaid work by family members, they are "woefully inadequate" (34).

State Policies. Similar problems exist with state-level policies that allow some family members to receive payment for the care that they provide. In a recent study of state policies on paid family caregiving, Linsk, Keigher, and Osterbusch found that some provisions for payment to family members were made by at least thirty-four states and the District of Columbia (35). Only thirteen states clearly prohibited reimbursement or payment to relatives for care (35).

While state policies vary widely in the amount of benefit and the eligibility of family members to receive payment, most tend to provide a benefit based on the gap between the informal care already provided and the care necessary to keep the elderly person from being institutionalized. Medicaid regulations restrict payment for personal care to those who are not members of the recipient's family, but some states have used other definitions of the family or service, and other sources of funding to circumvent this policy.

Some states take the restriction against paying relatives to mean those related to the recipient while others, such as Illinois, deny eligibility only to those family members who are "financially responsible" for the recipient. When the "financially responsible" definition is used, the regulations usually deny payment to spouses. The denial of eligibility to spouses tends to affect more wives than husbands since impaired elderly males are far more likely to be married than are elderly females (12).

Many states have programs other than Medicaid that place less stringent limits on the payment of relatives (1, 35). All but two states provide supplementation to Supplemental Security Insurance (SSI), which clients can spend at their own discretion. In most cases these payments are not sufficient to benefit caregivers. Of the 25 states that administer their own supplementation program, payment levels vary greatly from state to state, with lows of $10 in Utah and $20 in Wyoming to highs of $294 in Indiana and $248 in North Carolina (36). The study by Linsk and associates (35) reported provisions for payments to relatives ranging from virtually no restrictions on the eligibility of relatives to receive payment, to requirements that carers meet welfare income guidelines. Other restrictions tend to severely limit the eligibility of family carers, including payment only if no other home help is available; payment to family members only if they had to give up employment; licensing of carers; and requirements that the carer must be employed by a provider agency.

Aid and Attendance Allowance for Veterans. The Veterans' Administration's Aid and Attendance Allowance allocates an amount based on need to the elderly person who may use the funds to pay someone for care provided. This can be used to compensate family caregivers. By allowing veterans to employ relatives, the program gives eligible families decision-making power regarding distribution of the benefit. The benefit is set according to the disability level rather than unmet need and allows a measure of freedom to families. The Allowance is discounted by dollar amounts contributed by other sources but not by the in-kind contributions of friends and relatives. Moreover, surviving spouses are also eligible for the benefit. Although the benefit is not tied to the care-giving relationship, the allowance is a more equitable approach than those that indirectly penalize families who provide a carer. Of the existing approaches to compensating family carers, the Aid and Attendance Allowance is a relatively unobtrusive method of cash transfer and no doubt does more than other approaches to reduce the caregiving burden on wives and other family carers.

Trends

Profound demographic and social changes threaten the present social contract between families and society. Changes in family roles and expectations, the increasing attachment of women to the labor force, the increase in the ratio of dependent elderly to available family members (2), and the advent of prospective payment for medical care combine to put more strain on the entire long-term care system. Women and their families will experience increasing conflict as women make choices and compromises in their dual roles as caregivers and breadwinners. Many families will rely upon community services or nursing homes, or be forced to "make do," in effect neglecting the needs of their older relatives. Others may suffer from the consequences of women being unable to realize their full economic potential. Many are risking permanent financial dependency due to the demands of providing care in a context of competing family and employment demands. When these social and personal costs are taken into account, traditional models of community care become inadequate.

Among the options currently being considered are policies and programs that are thought to act as incentives for families to continue to provide care. These include (1):

- Expansion and formalization of state policies and programs to allow family members to be paid as Medicare providers.
- Changes in the dependent tax credit that would expand eligibility criteria for the credit, increase the level of the credit to compensate family care costs, and expand the types of care expenses that could be claimed.
- Caregiver leave and dependent-care benefits as employee benefits.
- Requirements that families contribute toward the care of their elderly members.

The latter so-called "family responsibility" policies have ominous implications for women. Policies that attempt to define and prescribe the role of the family in providing care would pressure families, especially low-income women, to take on caring tasks, irrespective of personal resources or needs of either the carer or care recipient. The social and individual costs of policies that coerce families into caregiving would fall most heavily on those least able to bear them.

Policies to provide benefits to caregivers are one way to address the question of how to maintain the family caregiving effort in a changing environment. Although some form of compensation to carers is certainly fairer than no compensation at all, the basic intent of these policies remains reducing government costs. The inequities are still not addressed, because the benefits do nothing to lower the threshold of access to alternative forms of care, or to compensate carers for the opportunities they forego by taking on caregiving responsibilities.

POLICIES TO MAXIMIZE GENDER JUSTICE

Changing the Assumptions

What is necessary is development of policies based on a different set of assumptions about family and community care. The right-hand column of Table 1 summarizes these assumptions. The central model for community care policies that would maximize gender justice is that of the social utility—a universally available array of supports to dependent adults to which families would have access as needed. Direct cash transfers to elders and/or their carers would be an integral part of such a system. Instead of attempting to ensure family responsibility by requiring families to participate in care, government would provide the resources necessary to enable families to respond adequately to the needs of their elderly members. The present approach, which pressures families with the entire caregiving burden until they break down to the point of "eligibility" for government support, is not only mean-spirited; it is inevitably a more costly alternative (37).

The values underlying community care policies are shifting somewhat as sex role expectations change. There is evidence that the needs of the elderly and their families are being increasingly recognized. Public opinion tends to support increased access to community care even if it means tax increases (38). Sheppard and Kosberg (39) report that a majority of their public opinion poll respondents still believed in 1981 that government should assume more responsibility for the elderly. However, family-provided care continues to be regarded as a "private good." Without an acknowledgment that family-provided care is a "social good"—a contribution to society made by women and men who often incur substantial personal, economic, and social costs—benefits to carers will continue to be minimal.

The cost-benefit concerns of community care policies that would maximize gender justice differ from the present concern with avoiding the costs of institutionalization. Policies to maximize gender justice would take into account the needs of the elderly who are disabled and ill but not necessarily at risk of placement in a nursing home. Research indicates that those who are placed in nursing homes are a much smaller and substantially different population than those who are cared for in their communities, suggesting that more effective targeting to meet the "but for" criteria could lead to higher costs for screening and less efficient programs (40). The evidence is that when community care is available, it is used more as an add-on than as a substitute for nursing home care, and it may be cheaper to extend home-care benefits and serve the very sickest and most dependent patients in nursing homes (37,40).

Although research on the substitution effect is somewhat contradictory because the question is posed differently in different studies, there is little evidence to support concern that community care would substitute for family efforts (26). The results from the Channeling Demonstration, which tested the feasibility and cost-effectiveness of alternative community-based long-term care service delivery, show that formal interventions did not significantly reduce the amount and type of informal care provided to clients (1). There is also evidence that when formal services are used, families continue to provide the major portion of the care (29). They seek support in the form of respite, help with very highly impaired elders, or with selected tasks (26) rather than total relief from caregiving. In her review of the research on the substitution effect, Horowitz concluded that "the provision of formal services does not significantly reduce the previous level of care provided by family caregivers" (26, p. 224).

Contrary to the fears of policymakers (7), there is no evidence to date that carers will come "out of the woodwork" just because a benefit is available. Based on the findings of Montgomery and Hatch (14) who reported a low level of participation by families in a respite care program, the more appropriate metaphor might be "beating the bushes" (35). There is, however, evidence of a relationship between level of carer stress and the use of community services, with higher levels of care need being associated with greater use of community services. Bass and Noelker found that elders whose primary caregivers were experiencing greater burden and stress effects from providing care were using more in-home community services (41). Even when elder need was controlled, caregiver need explained a significant portion of the variance in the elders use of services. These results directly contradict the assumptions of present policies which determine need based on the individual recipient, not the recipient's informal helpers.

Several researchers have concluded that, if the definition of need were extended beyond the highly impaired individual in need of nursing home care, an integrated continuum of services based on functional disability could be cost-effective (37, 40). The Canadian experience as documented by Rosalie and Robert Kane led them to conclude that a very desirable package of services can be offered at about 10 percent of the nursing home budget, and the presence of an alternative system of care makes it both politically and economically feasible to restrict the growth of the institutional sector (37). Kane and Kane found that "despite the fear . . . that expanded home care benefits might lead to runaway use, the Canadian experience shows a consistent pattern of demand leveling off after about three years" (37, p. 1362).

Other analysts have suggested that home- and community-based care has been oversold as a way of controlling long-term costs (8, 40). Weissert's review of a decade of research on the cost-effectiveness of community care led him to conclude that "few who use home- and community-based services would otherwise have been long-stayers in nursing homes" (40, p. 423). He proposes that an alternative to the cost-savings rationale for community care is one which would recognize that those not sick enough to be placed in a nursing home but too sick and otherwise too dependent to be helped by the existing episodic and medically oriented health care system and their caregivers, are deserving of help.

how?

CONCLUSIONS

?

Private family decisions about caregiving roles are not within the purview of public policy, nor should they be. Government's role is to assure that those who contribute to society by providing care to dependents have the full opportunity to choose that role free from coercion. Adequate and accessible supports to families, which include, when appropriate, compensation to family carers commensurate with that paid to others who provide comparable care, provides the capacity to choose.

The inequities and hidden personal costs associated with unpaid care cannot be fully rectified by changes in community care policies alone. Related issues of gender justice, including the distribution of social security benefits and the treatment of wives by the tax code [see Kirp and associates (5) for a discussion of these issues], directly affect the equity of remedies. Broader issues related to employment and economic opportunity also affect the ultimate outcome of community care policies designed to be gender-neutral, and even those policies that would maximize gender justice cannot replace necessary government programs for housing, income, health care, and transportation. However, by reexamining these policies from a perspective that acknowledges the fact and impact of the feminized structure of informal care, we can devise alternatives that preserve the freedom of individuals to choose to provide care by providing the support that is essential to that freedom. *how?*

REFERENCES

1. Burwell, B. O. *Shared Obligations: Public Policy Influences on Family Care for the Elderly*. Medicaid program evaluation working paper 2.1 U.S. Department of Health and Human Services, Health Care Financing Administration, Office of Research and Demonstration, Washington, D.C., May 1986.
2. Estes, C. L., Gerard, L. E., and Clark, A. Women and the economics of aging. In *Readings in the Political Economy of Aging*, edited by M. Minkler and C. L. Estes, pp. 75–93. Baywood Publishing, Amityville, New York, 1984.
3. Brody, E. M. "Women in the middle" and family help to older people. *Gerontologist* 21(5): 471–480, 1981.
4. Stone, R., Cafferata, G. L., and Sangl, J. *Caregivers of the Elderly: A National Profile*. Paper presented at the 32nd Annual Meeting of the American Society on Aging, San Francisco, March 1986.
5. Kirp, D. L., Yudof, M. G., and Franks, M. S. *Gender Justice*. University of Chicago Press, Chicago, 1986.
6. Estes, C. L., and Edmonds, B. C. Symbolic interaction and social policy analysis. *Symbolic Interaction* 4(1): 75–85, 1981.
7. Rich, S. The home-care debate. *The Washington Post National Weekly Edition*, June 10, 1985, p. 84.

8. Doty, P. *Family Care of the Elderly: The Role of Public Policy*. Office of Legislation and Policy, Health Care Financing Administration, Washington, D.C., 1985.

9. Paringer, L. Forgotten costs of informal long term care. *Generations* 9(4): 55–58, 1985.

10. Whitfield, S., and Krumpholz, B. *Report to the General Assembly on the Family Support System Demonstration Program*. State of Maryland Office on Aging, Baltimore, 1981.

11. Coward, R. T., and Rathbone-McCuan, E. *Illuminating the Relative Role of Adult Sons and Daughters in Long-term Care of their Parents*. Paper presented at the 1985 Professional Symposium of the National Association of Social Workers, Chicago, November 1985.

12. Macken, C. *A Profile of Functionally Impaired Persons in the Community* (draft report). Health Care Financing Administration, Office of Research and Demonstration, Washington, D.C., 1985.

13. Hess, B. B., and Waring, J. Family relationships of older women: a women's issue. In *Older Women: Issues and Prospects*, edited by E. W. Markson, Lexington Books, Lexington, Massachusetts, 1983.

14. Montgomery, R. J. V., and Hatch, L. R. The feasibility of volunteers and families forming a partnership for caregiving. In *Families and Long Term Care*, edited by T. H. Brubaker, Sage Publications, Beverly Hills, California, 1986.

15. Johnson, C., and Catalano, D. A longitudinal study of family supports to impaired elderly. *Gerontologist* 23(2): 612–618, 1983.

16. Cantor, M. H. Strain among caregivers: A study of experience in the United States. *Gerontologist* 23(6): 597–604, 1983.

17. Noelker, L. S., and Wallace, R. W. The organization of family care for impaired elderly. *J Mar. Fam. Issues* 6: 23–44, 1985.

18. Greater London Council Women's Committee. *Community Care and Women as Carers— Revised Report*. Report submitted to the Greater London Council, London, 1984.

19. Day, A. *Who Cares? Demographic Trends Challenge Family Care for the Elderly*. Population Trends and Public Policy No. 9. Population Reference Bureau, Washington, D.C., 1985.

20. Stoller, E. P. Parental caregiving by adult children. *J. Mar. Fam.* 45(4): 851–858, 1983.

21. Stone, R. *The Feminization of Poverty and Older Women: An Update*. Paper presented at the 113th Annual Meeting of the American Public Health Association, Washington, D.C., November, 1985.

22. Archbold, P. G. Impact of parent-caring on women. *Fam. Relations* 32(1): 39–45, 1983.

23. Ikels, C. The process of caretaker selection. *Res. Aging* 5: 491–510, 1983.

24. Hooyman, N., Gonyea, J., and Montgomery, R. The impact of in-home services termination on family caregivers. *Gerontologist* 25(2): 141–145, 1985.

25. Brody, E. M. Parent care as a normative family stress. *Gerontologist* 25: 19–29, 1985.

26. Horowitz, A. Family caregiving to the frail elderly. *Annu. Rev. Gerontol. Geriatrics* 5: 194–246, 1985.

27. Ball, G. T., and Greenberg, B. *The Travelers Employee Caregiver Survey*. The Travelers Companies, Personnel Research, Personnel Services Division, Personnel-Administration Department, Hartford, Connecticut, 1985.

28. Brody, E. M., and Schoonover, C. B. Patterns of parent-care when adult daughters work and when they do not. *Gerontologist* 26(4): 372–381, 1986.
29. Arling, G., and McCauley, W. J. The feasibility of public payments to family caregiving. *Gerontologist* 23: 300–306, 1983.
30. Warshaw, L. J. et al. *Employer Support for Employee Caregivers.* Paper presented at the 113th Annual Meeting of the American Public Health Association, Washington, D.C., November 1985.
31. Minkler, M., and Stone, R. The feminization of poverty and older women. *The Gerontologist* 25(4): 351–357, 1985.
32. Sullivan, R. Nursing costs force elderly to sue spouses. *The New York Times*, March 6, 1986, pp. 1, 17.
33. U.S. House of Representatives, Select Committee on Children, Youth and Families. *Demographic and Social Trends: Implications for Federal Support of Dependent-Care Services for Children and the Elderly.* U.S. Government Printing Office, Washington, D.C., December 1983.
34. Perlman, R. Use of the tax system in home care: a brief note. *Home Health Care Serv. Q.* 3(3–4): 280–283, 1982.
35. Linsk, N., Keigher, S., and Osterbusch, S. E. *Paid Family Caregiving: A Policy Option.* Final Report to the Illinois Association of Family Service Agencies. University of Illinois at Chicago, Department of Medical Social Work, Chicago, 1986.
36. Social Security Administration, U.S. Department of Health and Human Services. Current operating statistics. *Soc. Secur. Bull.* 48(8): 72, 1985.
37. Kane, R. L., and Kane, R. A. *A Will and a Way: What the United States can Learn from Canada about Caring for the Elderly.* Columbia University Press, New York, 1985.
38. Harris, L. *Aging in the Eighties.* National Council on Aging, Washington, D.C., 1981.
39. Sheppard, H., and Kosberg, J. I. *Public Opinion about the Issues of Public Responsibility for the Aged and Means Testing.* Paper presented at the Annual Scientific Meeting of the Gerontological Society of America, New Orleans, November 1985.
40. Weissert, W. G. Seven reasons why it is so difficult to make community care cost-effective. *Health Serv. Res.* 20(4): 421–433.
41. Bass, D. M., and Noelker, L. *The Influence of Family Caregivers on Elder's use of In-home Services: An Extended Conceptual Framework.* Paper presented at the Annual Scientific Meeting of the Gerontological Society of America, New Orleans, November 1985.

CHAPTER 15

GENDER, RACE, AND CLASS: BEYOND THE FEMINIZATION OF POVERTY IN LATER LIFE

Paula L. Dressel

Increasing popular and scholarly attention is devoted to the feminization of poverty argument, which is focused both on women in general (1, 2) and on older women in particular (3, 4). Such publications have made important contributions to the understanding of gender inequalities. For example, their discussions of the family wage system, the sexual division of paid and unpaid labor, and the existence of dual labor markets have highlighted structural and ideological bases of different economic opportunities and barriers for men and women. The writings have also provided a wealth of statistics that have documented gender inequalities and described the many social policies that undergird and reproduce different experiences by gender. Political activism by various age-based and feminist advocacy organizations has been fueled by the growing literature on the feminization of poverty across women's lives.

Although acknowledgment is due the contributions made in the literature, a concern is that the feminization of poverty argument in isolation also has the potential for distorting and simplifying the issue of old age poverty and for being politically divisive. In this chapter, it is maintained that gerontology scholars and activists need to move beyond the feminization of poverty argument to acknowledge how complexly the factors of race and gender are interlocked with the variable of social class in the United States. Emphasis on only one of these factors, gender, seriously misrepresents the phenomenon of poverty in later life, promotes policy and programming decisions with limited efficacy, and has the potential to undermine broad-based political coalitions seeking economic equality.

In part, in the arguments which follow, recent criticisms of social science in general and specific criticisms of the feminization of poverty argument in particular (5) are applied to the topic of the feminization of poverty in later life.

Recent general criticisms (6, 7) explicate ways in which social science research and theory reflect racism, either by omission (such as through the untested assumption that research findings or theoretical formulations apply similarly across groups) or commission (such as through the use of biased research instruments). Writings on the feminization of poverty in later life reveal both types of errors: authors tend to ignore the inextricable link between race and social class in the United States and they bolster their claims through selective utilization and interpretation of statistics.

The purpose herein is not to challenge the argument that patriarchy creates significant burdens for older (as well as younger) women. Nor is it to engage in debate over whether one form of stratification is more oppressive than another or that the experiences of one oppressed group are any more tolerable than those of another. Rather, the point is to argue that racial stratification is also a primary feature of the political economy of the United States. Once the racialized character of social class is made explicit, it is then possible to show how this feature of the political economy differentiates women with regard to later life experiences and vulnerabilities and renders racial-ethnic men disproportionately vulnerable to poverty in old age. The criticisms and reconceptualizations that follow are offered with the hope that a more complex understanding of poverty in later life will generate more effective efforts to eliminate economic inequalities.

ACKNOWLEDGING RACIAL OPPRESSION

The writings of selected black political economists have detailed the central way in which racial oppression informs the development of the U.S. political economy (8–10). Although the forms of oppression have changed historically with transformations of the economic base, shifting from slavery to sharecropping to low-wage labor, racism is nevertheless an ever-present, if increasingly subtle characteristic of U.S. capitalism.

The economic marginality of racial-ethnic groups is built on capital's need for low-wage labor. Ideologies that systematically devalue racial-ethnic groups rationalize their low pay and occupational clustering and legitimate their location at the bottom of the socioeconomic structure. Within a dual labor market, racial-ethnic workers are found disproportionately in the peripheral sector, where jobs are characterized by low wages, minimal, if any, fringe benefits, virtually no union protection, and high vulnerability to economic fluctuations (11). The limited individual mobility that has occurred for some black Americans since the 1960s is due largely to government employment and work in black-owned businesses, both of which are highly vulnerable to economic downturns and to government anti-discrimination initiatives whose level of enforcement varies with political administrations (12).

As a result, racial-ethnic group members, male and female alike, are more susceptible to the experiences of unemployment, underemployment, and unstable low-wage employment than are their white counterparts (13). As noted elsewhere (14), the limited upward mobility that has occurred within the past two decades for some members of racial -ethnic groups has not significantly altered inter-group inequalities (12, 13, 15). Furthermore, any advances may be short-lived, having most recently been negatively affected by economic decline (13, 16), judicial action upholding the primacy of seniority over affirmative action (17), and budgetary cutbacks for civil rights enforcement by the federal administration (18).

In sum, race is a primary stratifier of people's lives, as is gender. Recognition of this fact mandates reconceptualization of the bases of poverty in later life. Furthermore, it challenges implicit assumptions of the feminization of poverty argument.

Burnham cites several problems created by the feminization of poverty argument precisely because it fails to account for the complex interplay of gender, race, and class in the United States (5). Among the problems are that it obscures class differences among women, understates racial oppression, and ignores the poverty of black men. Furthermore, she takes issue with what gerontologists have frequently conceptualized as double or triple jeopardy by arguing that oppression is not an additive phenomenon. Rather, because black women experience the intersection of racism and sexism, their circumstances are qualitatively, not quantitatively, different from those of white women. Although Burnham speaks to the general feminization of poverty argument, her criticisms are applicable to its specialized emphasis on later life as well.

Racial-ethnic women have not been overlooked in most writing on the feminization of poverty in later life. The tendency has been, however, to take the "add-and-stir" approach (19), which leads to race-blind theoretical formulations. That is, what are meant to be general statements about gender and poverty are made, and then, as an afterthought or elaboration, specialized statements about black (or Hispanic or Native American) women are made. For example, "In 1982, over half of women aged 65 and over with incomes below the poverty level reported fair or poor health. . . . Among poor Black women the proportion approaches two-thirds" (4).

The point here is subtle but critical. In the illustration of the add-and-stir approach (of which there are many instances in a variety of gerontological publications), it is implied that similar outcomes in women's lives are produced by the one and only factor of patriarchy. Acknowledged, but not accounted for, are the worse (and sometimes different) conditions faced by racial-ethnic women. Indeed, the differences cannot be accounted for because the model of the feminization of poverty glosses over the variable of race for heuristic and political purposes. In other words, racial-ethnic women's experiences are forced into the model rather than being utilized to refine or critique the model itself.

The important fact that racial-ethnic men are systematically rendered economically marginal is also ignored in the literature on the feminization of poverty in later life. An insistence on dichotomizing elders by gender alone dismisses fundamental political economic dynamics with respect to race as unimportant for understanding poverty in old age. In other words, the claim that poverty is "feminized" makes patriarchy the primary factor in socioeconomic stratification. A parallel argument could be developed about the "racialization of poverty" in later life (as well as across the life span), thereby claiming white supremacy as the primary motive in socioeconomic stratification. The point, however, is that neither argument integrates the variables of gender, race, and class into a richer appreciation of poverty and economic vulnerability. What is required is movement away from debates in which implicity, if not explicitly, one form of oppression is posited as more serious, primary, or worthy of attention than another.

REEXAMINING STATISTICS

Once race is acknowledged as a central factor in how people fare economically, statistics can be reexamined with race and gender in mind. Upon re-examination, what is frequently found is that white women fare better than black and Hispanics, female or male, and that white family units fare better than other family units.

With gender as a filter for examining statistics, it can be argued that elderly women are worse off than their male counterparts. For example, Minkler and Stone (3) report that 49 percent of nonmarried elderly white women compared to 34 percent of nonmarried elderly white men fell below 125 percent of the poverty line; similarly, 80 percent of nonmarried elderly black women compared to 64 percent of nonmarried elderly black men fell below that line. They also found that nonmarried white women have a median Social Security income of $4490 compared to $5080 for their male counterparts; similarly, nonmarried black women receive a median $3050 from Social Security compared to $3710 for their male counterparts. If the analysis stopped here, then the conclusion that "elderly women represent . . . the single poorest segment of American society" (3) might be tenable. Now let race be used as a filter for examining the same sets of statistics. What is seen is that nonmarried black men are more likely (64%) to fall below 125 percent of the poverty line than are nonmarried white women (49%); the median income from Social Security for nonmarried black men is $3710 compared to $4490 for nonmarried white women; married white couples receive a median $7670 form Social Security benefits compared to $5920 for their black counterparts. From this perspective, an argument could be made for the racialization of poverty in later life.

But again, the point is not to debate which oppression is worse, gender or race. Rather, it is to argue that the history of U.S. political economy mandates that analysts take race into account, along with gender, age, and other relevant factors (20, 21), when trying to understand economic inequality and impoverishment. Patriarchy and racism are played out similarly in some respects (such as with occupational clustering) but differently in other respects (such as with opportunities for advancement). Consequently, both must be considered for a more complete understanding of economic marginality. Furthermore, because some sources indicate that race-sex patterns of economic marginality characterizing current elders are not substantially different for younger cohorts of workers (13), gerontologists cannot assume that each succeeding cohort of elders will benefit [or benefit equally (18)] from antidiscrimination legislation, whether directed toward race or gender.

In part, the feminization of poverty argument depends on selectively interpreted statistics. Caution must also be employed in terms of the particular statistics utilized to develop arguments about poverty in later life. For example, if Social Security benefits alone (including SSI) are analyzed, economic differences between blacks and whites appear considerably smaller than when private pensions and income from assets are also factored in. Schultz cites data indicating the differential sources of income for black and white elders, with the latter more likely to be covered by private pensions and to receive income from assets (22). Although it is true that women's work is also less likely than men's to offer pensions as a fringe benefit, it is also true that white women married to white men have greater access to private pension benefits than black women married to black men. Once again, the picture is incomplete unless both race and gender are taken into account.

RETHINKING POLITICAL ACTION

For several reasons, the feminization of poverty argument is politically appealing to various age-based and feminist advocacy groups. Most importantly, it directs much-needed attention to the widespread implications of patriarchy for women of all ages. No doubt it has also engendered sympathy for the poor by being focused on a relatively nonthreatening subsegment, women. Indeed, elderly women may be the least threatening and politically palatable of all possible categories of economically marginal adults. Finally, the feminization of poverty argument underlies attempts to develop links across age, racial-ethnic, and social class strata of women, whose political alliances historically have been problematic (23–26). To be sure, exposing sexism, generating concern over poverty, and attempting to unite women are all worthy goals. The pursuit of these goals through emphasis on the feminization of poverty, however, has important shortcomings as well.

As suggested above, a singular focus on gender and a consequent disregard for the factor of race as another primary stratifier of people has negative latent functions. First, it creates the tendency for fruitless and diversionary debates about which form of oppression is worse. Second, it disregards the fact that some men also are systematically marginalized in the economy, thereby diminishing opportunities for cross-gender coalitions. Third, by failing to paint the full picture of exploitation and discrimination, it impedes a more complex analysis of both welfare state and capitalist contradictions.

Furthermore, whatever concern the feminization of poverty argument generates about the poor will be limited because of the inherent limitations of the analysis. That is, all who are poor will not be embraced by whatever policy and programmatic actions arise from attention to the feminization of poverty. As already noted, racial-ethnic men's systematic marginality is ignored. In addition, there is legitimate concern that only selected groups of impoverished women will become the focus of political interventions, namely downwardly mobile white women who comprise the "nouveau poor" (27). For example, displaced homemaker legislation, in which critical needs of a specific segment of women are addressed, provides politicians with evidence of their concern over the feminization of poverty. It also enables them to sidestep long-entrenched working class and underclass poverty whose alleviation requires far more extensive social change. Even progressive social democratic groups have purposefully emphasized the female nouveau poor and underplayed race and class issues in efforts to broaden their base of political support (5). In other words, the feminization of poverty argument has been appropriated to serve limited ends at the expense of other historically dispossessed groups.

Consequently, the feminization of poverty analysis may prove to be a fatal remedy (28), despite the desire of its proponents to build coalitions among diverse groups of women. That is, they may accomplish just the opposite of their intentions. In the analysis, the failure to acknowledge race as a primary stratifier of peoples' life chances diminishes utility for black and other racial-ethnic women; insistence on the primacy of gender implies the unrealistic expectation that racial-ethnic women separate their political interests from those of racial-ethnic men. Finally, the failure to incorporate class and race into the analysis of women's conditions provides convenient opportunities for politicians to target for intervention those women who are the least fiscally and politically costly. As a result, women may become divided because only some will benefit from the selective targeting of putatively limited resources.

A more complex understanding of old-age poverty is needed by gerontology scholars and activists. Single-variable conceptualizations of political economic dynamics (whether based on gender, race, age or any other variable) may serve short-term consciousness-raising functions for select categories of people, but the detail necessary for the formulation of well-targeted social policies cannot be provided (19). And in the long run, the potential for broad-based political alliances among the heterogeneous people comprising the working poor, the underclass, and other economically vulnerable groups in the United States can be undermined. Gerontologists have realized the diversity contained within age groups; likewise they must recognize the diversity within gender groups and move beyond the feminization of poverty argument. To do so does not require abandoning concern over women's disproportionate impoverishment. But it requires abandoning political rhetoric built on an incomplete model of the U.S. political economy.

ACKNOWLEDGMENTS

Appreciation is expressed to Gerri Moreland and Frank Whittington for their contributions to the project.

REFERENCES

1. Ehrenreich, B., and Piven, F. F. The feminization of poverty. *Dissent* 31: 162–170, 1984.
2. Pearce, D. The feminization of poverty: Women, work, and welfare. *Urban and Soc. Change Rev.* 11: 28–36, 1978.
3. Minkler, M., and Stone, R. The feminization of poverty and older women. *The Gerontologist* 25: 351–357, 1985.
4. Older Women's League. Report on the status of midlife and older women. Older Women's League, Washington, D.C., 1986.
5. Burnham, L. Has poverty been feminized in Black America? *The Black Scholar* 16: 14–24, 1985.
6. Scott, P.B. Debunking sapphire: Toward a non-racist and non-sexist social science. In *But Some of Us Are Brave*, edited by G. T. Hull, P. B. Scott, and B. Smith, Feminist Press, Old Westbury, New York, 1982.
7. Zinn, M. B., Cannon, L. W., Higginbotham, E., and Dill, B. T. The costs of exclusionary practices in women's studies. *Signs* 17: 290–303, 1986.
8. Baron, H. M. Racism transformed: The implications of the 1960s. *Rev. Rad. Pol. Econ.* 17: 10–33, 1985.
9. Hogan, L. *Principles of Black Political Economy*. Routledge and Kegan Paul, Boston, 1984.
10. Marable, M. *How Capitalism Underdeveloped Black America*. South End Press, Boston, 1983.
11. O'Connor, J. *The Fiscal Crisis of the State*. St. Martin's Press, New York, 1973.
12. Collins, S. M. The making of the Black middle class. *Soc. Prob.* 30: 369–382, 1983.
13. U.S. Commission on Civil Rights. *Unemployment and Under-Employment Among Blacks, Hispanics, and Women*. Clearinghouse Publication 74, U.S. Commission on Civil Rights, Washington, D.C., 1982.
14. Dressel, P. Civil rights, affirmative action, and the aged of the future: Will life chances be different for Blacks, Hispanics, and women? An overview of the issues. *The Gerontologist* 26: 128–131, 1986.
15. Oliver, M. L., and Glick, M. A. An analysis of the new orthodoxy on Black mobility. *Soc. Prob.* 29: 511–523, 1982.
16. Gramlick, E. M., and Laren, D. S. How widespread are income losses in a recession? In *The Social Contract Revisited: Aims and Outcomes of President Reagan's Social Welfare Policy*, edited by D. L. Bawden. Urban Institute Press, Washington, D.C., 1984.
17. Jacobs, J., and Slawsky, N. Seniority vs. minority. *Atlanta Journal and Constitution* 35:1D, 7D, 1984.
18. U.S. Commission on Civil Rights. *Civil Rights: A National Not a Special Interest*. U.S. Commission on Civil Rights, Washington, D.C., 1981.

19. Anderson, M. L. *Thinking About Women—Sociological and Feminist Perspectives*. Macmillan, New York, 1983.
20. Palmore, E. B., and Manton, K. Ageism compared to racism and sexism. *J. Gerontology* 28: 363–369, 1973.
21. Whittington, F. Personal communication. 1986.
22. Schultz, J. H. *The Economics of Aging*. (3rd Edition). Wadsworth, Belmont, California, 1985.
23. Davis, A. *Women, Race & Class*. Vintage Books, New York, 1981.
24. Dill, B. T. Race, class, and gender: Prospects for an all-inclusive sisterhood. *Fem. Stud.* 9: 131–150, 1983.
25. Hooks, B. *Ain't I a Woman: Black Women and Feminism*. South End Press, Boston, 1981.
26. Hooks, B. *Feminist Theory from Margin to Center*. South End Press, Boston, 1984.
27. Ehrenreich, B., and Stallard, K. The nouveau poor. *Ms.* 11: 217–224, 1982.
28. Sieber, S. *Fatal Remedies: The Ironies of Social Intervention*. Plenum, New York, 1981.

CHAPTER 16

THE POLITICAL ECONOMY OF
HEALTH CARE FOR ELDERLY BLACKS

Steven P. Wallace

In the mid-1960s the black ghettos of many large cities in the United States erupted in flames and rioting. The Kerner Commission, established to investigate the causes of the civil unrest, wrote "Our nation is moving toward two societies, one black, one white—separate and unequal" (1). Over twenty years later, we remain a racially stratified nation, despite the efforts of a multitude of public policies designed to reduce racial disparities (2). Inequities in health status and medical services are among the most persistent (3). Health policy, however, is following a race neutral course by focusing on income or specific conditions.

This chapter analyzes health care for older blacks to assess the relative importance of class and race factors. Specifically, it asks whether race has an independent role in determining the health status of elderly blacks and whether race has an independent role in the relationship of older blacks to the medical care system. If race is an *independent* factor in the health and health care of the black elderly, then current and proposed health policies that are color blind are not enough. If being black is a *dependent* factor, important primarily because so many blacks are poor, then health policies that address the needs of all poor persons equally are sufficient.

PUBLIC POLICY AND THE HEALTH OF THE BLACK ELDERLY

The largest public programs established in the 1960s generally assumed that the problems of blacks could be remedied at the individual level. Most antipoverty programs focused on measures such as increasing the educational levels of individuals under the assumption that individual characteristics were the root cause of poverty. Problems of racism were addressed through civil rights laws that mandated equal opportunity for individuals in the area of public accommodations, education, and employment (4).

The major health care programs also followed this pattern. Medicare was established as an entitlement health care program for the elderly that purchased health care services (primarily hospital and doctor care) for the old from within the existing medical care system. Black elderly, who are disproportionately poor and unable to afford medical care, benefited *as individuals* from the increased ability to afford care provided by Medicare. The Medicare program was also instrumental in desegregating hospitals by prohibiting payment to formally segregated hospitals. This was an important step in opening up medical institutions to older blacks *collectively*, but was one of the few aspects of the program that attempted to change existing medical structures.

Medicaid is a means-tested program for families, the aged, blind, and disabled who live in poverty. The program was enacted at the same time as Medicare with the goal of "mainstreaming" the poor into the medical care system. It has unintentionally become the largest payer of long-term care for the aged in the United States. As a state administered program, Medicaid income and other eligibility standards vary widely. As a result, only about half of all poor persons in the United States are covered by Medicaid (5). The intent of both Medicare and Medicaid was to provide the aged and poor the same medical services enjoyed by middle-class Americans by changing the characteristics of the individuals (i.e., their ability to pay) rather than by changing the characteristics of the medical care system.[1] The groups targeted were defined by age, family status, and poverty, but not by race.

While the social programs of the 1960s have ameliorated a few of the problems they were directed to, none of the problems have been "solved" (2, 4,). About one-third of all black elderly remain in poverty, with an additional 40 percent being economically vulnerable (7). Our inner cities have become increasingly populated by poor blacks, with a disproportionate proportion of that population being aged. This segregation affects the availability of medical resources for the old just as it affects educational opportunities for the young. The failure of policies to eliminate racial differences in poverty, ill health, and other social injuries have contributed to the debate between contending analyses of racial inequality, each of which focuses on divergent forces to explain the persistent inequality.

Theories of Why Inequality Persists

Three basic types of theories are used to explain continued racial disparities: cultural, class, and race.

---

[1] An attempt *was* made to establish an alternative institutional structure by placing community health centers in underserved areas. These centers did not, however, receive the financial support necessary to grow to their potential (6).

The cultural analysis argues that the beliefs and attitudes of blacks are the primary cause of any disadvantages they experience (8). This approach informs the popular rationale for treating the victims as the problems. Research on pubic policies argues that government programs have actually exacerbated problems by stifling individual initiative and the ability of the free market to satisfy human needs (9, 10). This research notes that many ghetto problems have worsened rather than improved during an unprecedented era of federal antipoverty efforts. This body of theory contends that government programs have unintentionally reinforced values among poor blacks that perpetuate poverty and social inequality. This builds on the culture of poverty theory (11) and is similar to theories that black culture, through processes such as matriarchal families, is the cause of the problems of blacks (8, 12).

As applied to medical care, a cultural explanation would examine the beliefs and attitudes of blacks and whites about health and medical care. This research looks at feelings of alienation and skepticism about medical care in an effort to explain the lower use of preventive care and other services (13). Blacks tend to seek cancer treatment later in the course of the disease than whites, for example. A cultural explanation draws on the fact that blacks are less knowledgeable about cancer and more pessimistic about a cure (14). Higher black mortality from cancer is then explained as a result of those attitudes. There is also literature that emphasizes folk healing in the black community as a partial explanation of different treatment patterns (15). Those studies view the folk alternatives as diverting some blacks from more efficacious early treatment by medical doctors.

Among the elderly, a cultural preference for family care is a common explanation of why older blacks use nursing home care significantly less than older whites (16). Despite extensive concern about the "decline" of the black family as it impacts on children (8), the family is seen as a strong resource for elder care (17). Family values are seen to be the primary cause of black families caring for disabled elderly more often than white families. The cultural analysis of black health care focuses on the "demand" side of medical care, making the individual the central unit of analysis. Health policies would therefore try to educate individuals about proper health practices or work with local referral networks to encourage the proper use of medical care and health practices (18).

In contrast, a class analysis argues that the basic economic structure of the nation creates a situation in which minorities are exploited and prevented from enjoying the same life chances as whites (19–21). Some class analyses view past as well as present racial divisions as a result of a capitalist economic system within which race is created as an ideological force. The state is seen as a key force in reproducing race relations in a form that benefits the capitalist system (22, 23). Other versions of this theory allow that in the *past* racism placed and kept blacks at the bottom of the economy, but since World War II the structure of the economy has been the primary determinant of impeded mobility by poor blacks (4, 24).

Class analyses of health care have shown how the structure of the American medical care system reflects the capitalist system within which it is situated (25, 26). In many ways the medical care system is better suited to enhancing profits than it is to maximizing the health of the population. For the elderly, class position is determined in large part by preretirement class position. State policies help perpetuate the class position of retirees through social security, pension and tax laws, and senior services that reinforce the class disparities created by preretirement income (27). This theory highlights how economics creates structural barriers for many elderly in obtaining health care and provides a stronger focus on the supply side of health care than does the cultural explanation. It also draws attention to the unhealthy consequences of a capitalist organization of production that may accumulate and affect a person in old age (e.g., occupational cancers and other diseases and pollution-related disease).

The health problems of older blacks are viewed in a class analysis as primarily a function of the disproportionate presence of blacks in the lower class, subsuming racial differences under the broader determinant of class. When data are adjusted for income, in particular, many of the health status and medical utilization differences between older blacks and older whites disappear (28). To eliminate black–white differences, health policy changes would ultimately have to involve a basic restructuring of the profit motive in the American economy and a dramatic redistribution of wealth. In the short term, though, policies could ameliorate health disparities by eliminating all economic barriers to obtaining health care.

The third analysis argues that race remains an independent causal force in explaining the social and economic position of blacks (29–31). In the area of employment, this research shows that there is a continuing "cost" of being black as demonstrated in decreased wages earned by blacks compared to whites in the same part of the country with similar education, skills, and seniority (2). This theory, like the class perspective, is grounded in an analysis of the United States economic structure and the world system. Unlike the class perspective, however, racial dynamics are conceptualized as operating independently of class forces in society.

Miller argues that equalizing black and white incomes would not fully eliminate health status disparities because some studies show black–white differences that are independent of income (32). For example, blacks are more likely to use emergency rooms and public clinics than whites with similar incomes (33). Blendon and associates found that access and satisfaction measures for health care were lower for blacks nationally even after controlling for income and other variables (34). This suggests that the medical care system is institutionally structured in a way that treats blacks differently than whites, regardless of their class position. It should be noted that these studies tend to look at the continuous variable of income rather than at the interval variable of class. The point remains, however, that if blacks were in the same economic position as whites, there would still be health differences between blacks and whites.

One theory that asserts the independent effect of race specifically for the aged is the multiple jeopardy hypothesis (35). Discussions of multiple jeopardy are based on empirical observations that older blacks have a lower quality of life than either younger blacks or elderly whites. The hypothesis views race as one of several possible types of stratification that disadvantages older blacks. Particularly in the area of health status and health care, older blacks suffer from the combined status of age and race, and often poverty (36). While the multiple jeopardy hypothesis lacks a strong theoretical basis and the supporting evidence is mixed (37), this commonly used theory suggests that race is an independent force in the poor health of older blacks. If this is the case, health policies aimed only at the poor will fail to eliminate the jeopardy of racial stratification in the health of older blacks.

All three theories begin from the position that continuing differences between blacks and whites are undesirable. Because of their different analyses, however, each makes different proposals for the best way to eliminate those differences. Cultural explanations focus on the black elderly as the problem, class explanations focus on the political and economic structure of society as the problem, and racial explanations focus on institutionalized racism within medical care and other sectors of society. These theories inform the following discussion of the health status and health care of older blacks.

THE INDIVIDUAL LEVEL

Health and Social Characteristics of Older Blacks and Whites

The social and economic characteristics of older blacks and whites show that there are continuing disparities between the races across a wide variety of measures. These findings are similar to national trends on the continued disparities between blacks and whites at all ages.

Much has been written about the continuing disparities in the health status between older blacks and whites (38–40). While the black-white gap has decreased since the 1960s when Medicare and Medicaid began, many indicators show a continued disparity. The life expectancy for older blacks has improved, but remains lower than that of whites (Table 1). Older blacks report hypertension and diabetes twice as often as older whites. They also report diseases of the circulatory system and arthritis about one and one-half times more often (38). When asked about their overall health (Table 1), older blacks are less likely than whites to report their health as excellent or good (50%, 64%). Although older blacks are somewhat less likely to report that an illness or disability restricted their activities (32.9%, 37.8%), older blacks whose activities are restricted have substantially more days of restricted activity. Older blacks report that they are more dependent than whites over the entire range of home management, personal care, mobility, and continence measures [Table 1, (41)].

Table 1

Health status of persons aged sixty-five and over

	Black		White	
	Female	Male	Female	Male
Life Expectancy at age 65[a]				
1960	15.1	12.7	15.9	12.9
1970	15.7	12.5	17.1	13.1
1980	16.8	13.0	18.5	14.2
1987	17.2	13.6	18.7	14.9
Self-Reported Health Status[b]				
Excellent	20.9%		26.0%	
Good	28.2%		38.0%	
Fair	28.4%		25.1%	
Poor	22.5%		10.9%	
No. Bed Restricted Activity Days[b] (per person with any restriction)	81.5		48.0	
Proportion Dependent in:[c]				
Shopping	12.4%	8.5%	8.3%	5.1%
Bathing	8.4%	6.0%	6.8%	5.1%
Dressing	5.7%	7.3%	4.1%	4.2%
Mobility	13.0%	6.4%	9.8%	5.2%
Continence	19.5%	16.7%	13.4%	9.4%

Sources:
[a]U.S. Senate, Special Committee on Aging (42).
[b]Kasper, J. D. (28).
[c]U.S. National Center for Health Statistics (41).

Overall health patterns differ for blacks and whites during old age. The most commonly discussed difference is the "mortality crossover." This is the point (in the early eighties age range) when the remaining life expectancy of blacks *exceeds* that of whites (43). It has been suggested, but not proven, that this is the result of only the most rugged blacks surviving to that age while a larger number of ill whites do so (40). Research by Gibson and Jackson supports that interpretation (44). They found that black elderly aged sixty-five to seventy-four were *more* disabled than black elderly aged seventy-five to seventy-nine (45). This suggests that heavily disabled blacks are unlikely to survive to more advanced ages.

Older blacks are also at an economic disadvantage relative to older whites (Table 2). By the government's conservative estimate, about one-third of all black elderly were living in poverty in 1987, compared with 10.1 percent of white elderly. The multiple jeopardy hypothesis draws attention to the fact that median

Table 2

Economic characteristics of elders aged sixty-five and over

	Blacks		Whites
Persons aged 65 and over in poverty, 1987	33.9%		10.1%
Families with householder age 65 and over in poverty, 1987	23.7%		5.4%
Age 65-69: % of median income of white males ($14,504	57.4%	males	100.0%
in 1987)	32.0%	females	49.4%
Age 70 and up: % of median income of white males	58.7%	males	100.0%
($11,336 in 1987)	39.1%	females	62.0%
Source of income for families with householder age 65 and over			
Earnings[a]	54.1%		42.6%
Social Security	93.3%		95.2%
Pensions[b]	34.1%		54.6%
Investments	30.5%		81.2%
SSI	18.5%		3.6%
Distribution of aggregate income, families with householder age 65 and over			
Earnings[a]	42.8%		28.8%
Social Security	35.8%		31.7%
Pensions[b]	13.0%		16.8%
Investments	2.3%		21.1%
SSI	2.8%		0.4%
Other	3.3%		1.2%

[a]Includes wage and salary income, and self-employment income.
[b]Includes private pensions, government employee pensions, alimony, annuities, etc.
Source: U.S. Bureau of the Census (46) and U.S. Senate, Special Committee on Aging (42).

income of the elderly is lower for blacks than whites, that income declines with advancing age, and that women have the lowest income.

Contrary to the hypothesis, however, advancing age slightly *decreases* (or makes no significant change in) the income gap between those with the highest income (white males aged seventy and over) and other race-sex groups (see Table 2). This finding can be used to support the analysis that increasing age tends to "level" the differences attributed to race and gender (37). If race and class differences are eliminated simply by the process of aging, the *cultural* differences that exist throughout the life-course are suggested as the most significant aspect of aging for blacks.

Markides also points out, however, that a lack of growing disparities with age may be a consequence of the large racial differences created at earlier ages (37). The lack of continually widening disparities in total income should not be taken to mean that more general economic disparities do not widen. Table 2 presents data on the sources and distribution of income for families headed by a person aged sixty-five or over. The data show that older black families are more dependent on the earnings of family members, and substantially less dependent on investments. Earnings are much more volatile than investments, putting older blacks in a less secure economic position.

Gibson, on the other hand, notes that the *subjective* quality of retirement may be more desirable for blacks than whites (47). While white elderly may be negatively effected by the loss of earnings and work related status, black elderly who fully retire may be positively affected. Older blacks who struggled to find and keep low-waged work earlier in their lives are more likely to experience relief from the receipt of retirement income from Social Security and SSI because it is steady and predictable (even if low).

Health is particularly important in the ability of older blacks to maintain a job that contributes to family income (Table 3). Older blacks and whites have similar rates of labor force participation (about one-quarter of older men and 10 percent of older women are in the labor force), but the reasons for *not* being employed differ significantly. Older blacks are two to three times as likely as older whites to cite health problems as their reason for not being in the labor force.

Table 3

Employment status of individuals aged sixty-five and over, 1987

	Blacks	Whites
Male		
Did not work last year	76.7%	77.8%
Of those not working:		
Health primary reason	(20.4%)	(9.3%)
Retired primary reason	(76.6%)	(89.4%)
Worked only part of year	11.8%	10.0%
Of part-year workers:		
Health primary reason	(26.5%)	(11.2%)
Female		
Did not work last year	90.3%	89.1%
Of those not working:		
Health primary reason	(32.7%)	(11.2%)
Retired primary reason	(47.8%)	(56.9%)
Keeping house primary	(17.7%)	(30.7%)
Worked only part of year	4.3%	5.1%
Of part-year workers:		
Health primary reason	(21.0%)	(9.3%)

Source: U.S. Bureau of the Census (46).

Employment patterns differ *significantly* between black and white men in the period before normal retirement age (before age sixty-five). In 1987, 43.1 percent of black men aged fifty-five to sixty-four had not worked in the previous year compared with 25.4 percent of white men (46). While one-third of the nonworking white men reported that they were ill or disabled, over half (57%) of black men reported health reasons for not working. About half of both black and white women aged fifty-five to sixty-four had worked in the previous year, but black women were three times as likely to report health reasons for not working (44% versus 15%). Gibson calls the large number of blacks over age fifty-five who consider themselves disabled rather than retired as the "unretired-retired" (47). They typically have histories of discontinuous work, low education, and low-waged occupations. Poor health, therefore, further perpetuates the lifelong economic hardship endured by a significant number of older blacks.

The material situation of older blacks reflects the heritage of racial discrimination that was still overt when they were obtaining their education in the pre-World War II era, and when they were establishing careers during the mid-1900s. The occupational differences are a product of the historical segregation of blacks into a segmented labor force characterized by low wages, poor benefits, and difficult working conditions (2). Regardless of why these occupational differences existed in the past, public policies continue the lower economic status of this segment of the black working class. Social Security payments are based on past earnings, so low-income workers become low-income retirees even though benefits are weighted to help low-income retirees (7). Retirees with investments (mostly whites) benefit from Social Security not considering investment income as "earnings" reducing retirement benefits because of continued employment earnings.

The financial status of the elderly is a health consideration in part because Medicare covers only one-half of the medical expenses of the elderly (48). This Medicare gap is important because older blacks carry private insurance to supplement Medicare at half the rate of older whites (38.5% versus 79.0%), although they are substantially more likely to be covered by public assistance health care (23.9% older blacks versus 5.0% older whites) (49). This difference in health insurance helps maintain a two-class system of health care in which many black elderly are dependent on the subset of health care providers who accept Medicaid as well as Medicare.

With lower incomes, fewer sources of retirement income, and more limited sources of health insurance, older blacks would be expected to be in a more precarious situation than whites if they fall ill. Social support, however, appears to be more equal for older blacks and whites. While older blacks are less likely than older whites to live with a spouse, they are more likely to live with children and other relatives (17). In addition, Gibson and Jackson note that most black elders have a wide network of supportive relations that includes family, friends, and church members (44). These networks in turn can play an important role in mediating and buffering some of the complications of poor health among older blacks. Because each support network is likely drawn from the same social class as the affected elder, the buffering role should be most effective when caregiving and social support is needed, but least useful when economics is the critical factor.

At the individual level, older blacks appear in a particularly precarious economic position but a stable social position. Most cultural analyses do not go beyond the individual level to explain the black-white differences in the health of the elderly. Black culture and/or a culture of poverty is used in conjunction with risk factors among older blacks to explain the differences between blacks and whites. In particular, findings of higher rates of smoking, hypertension, obesity, drinking, and other unhealthy behaviors among blacks are shown to be associated with adverse health consequences (38, 39). Jackson notes, however, that these studies typically overlook the social determinants of individual behaviors, such as how class status influences obesity (39). Manton, Patrick, and Johnson also point out that blacks usually have higher death rates than whites even when controlling for the number of unhealthy behaviors (38).

A major flaw in the cultural analysis is that it fails to incorporate an analysis of the institutional patterns in the current health care system. Both the class and race analyses rest on a structural analysis that considers the economic and medical care systems and their effects on the health of older blacks.

CLASS AND RACE IN INSTITUTIONAL PRACTICES

Regardless of the individual preferences and behaviors of older blacks, the institutional context in which they live can be a powerful influence on their lives. The low income of older blacks clearly has an effect on their health status and medical care use. Moreover, the changing structure of the economy does not bode well for the income of future cohorts of black elderly. In moving towards a post-industrial capitalist economy, the labor market is increasingly bifurcated between the highly educated, well-paid workers and the low-skilled, poorly paid workers (49). While the black-white inequality in earnings declined after World War II, it began to increase again in the 1980s (2). Poor health and barriers to medical care are partly a function of life-long poverty, making the structure of our capitalist economy a significant barrier to the health status and medical care of older blacks.

Similarly, a class analysis provides a useful understanding of the structure of our medical care system. The problem of hospital flight to the suburbs is a nationwide phenomenon, with hospitals moving from areas with declining populations and/or increasing numbers of indigent patients to new areas that house workers who have private insurance. This is a matter of maximizing reimbursements, a process that both for-profit and nonprofit hospitals follow (50). The situation is similar for nursing homes with large sectors of the industry overtly trying to minimize the number of Medicaid-financed patients in their facilities. Some nursing homes require prospective patients to provide evidence that they can pay privately for up to three years. Other homes find ways to discharge patients who become eligible for Medicaid so that the bed can be filled by another private-pay patient (51). Older blacks, who were disproportionately exploited by the economic system as younger adults, continue to suffer in the health care arena because American medicine is structured around economic needs rather than human needs.

A class analysis is less useful in explaining the creation and maintenance of racial segregation. Residential segregation of blacks has declined modestly since 1960 in most large cities and metropolitan areas—but remained stubbornly high overall. In twenty-five large cities in 1980, 81 percent of blacks would have had to move to different neighborhoods to completely desegregate the average city (2). Even middle-class blacks who have left the inner cities in the past twenty years are likely to live in predominately black suburbs, despite a preference for integrated neighborhoods (2). This persistent residential segregation demonstrates the continued significance of race in the life chances of blacks.

The medical resources available to older blacks are determined, in part, by where they live. Inner cities and poverty areas typically have the least availability of hospitals, doctors, and other health providers. Table 4 shows that overall, the black population is more concentrated than the white population in the core of United States metropolitan areas. Black families are also more likely to live in areas that have a high proportion of poor persons, with almost one-third of all black families in the United States living in poverty areas of core cities. Black families headed by an older person are more likely than the average black family to live in nonmetropolitan areas rather than in the suburbs.

The most dramatic characteristic of all families headed by an older black person is that almost *two-thirds* live in poverty areas, compared to only 10.2 percent of all white families headed by older adults (Table 4). The poverty areas of core cities house about 40 percent of all black families headed by an older person, compared with only 3.7 percent of similar white families. Wilson discusses the consequences of this type of concentration for younger blacks who are trapped in inner cities (14). He notes that blacks living in high-poverty areas are less likely to have access to social networks that can assist with finding jobs and providing other mobility resources. While different economic resources are important for the elderly, the community infrastructure is critical for the health of the old.

Within poor neighborhoods of major cities, older blacks are heavily dependent on the hospitals and clinics located in those areas for both primary and acute care. Wan found that older blacks had private physicians as their usual source of care half as often as similar older whites (52). Older blacks were much more dependent than older whites on neighborhood health centers for care (24.2% versus 5.1%). While these centers were successful in improving the health of the poor and minorities, they were unsuccessful in obtaining the political support necessary to thrive (53). The number of federally assisted community health centers decreased by at least one-third during the 1980s as a result of federal budget cuts (5). This

Table 4

Family residence, 1987

	Blacks	Whites
All families		
In central (core) cities[a]	57.7%	25.5%
In suburban areas[b]	25.0%	50.1%
In nonmetropolitan areas	17.3%	24.4%
Total	100.0%	100.0%
Living in poverty areas[c]		
All poverty areas	47.7%	10.1%
Central city poverty areas	32.2%	4.0%
All families with head age 65 and over		
In central (core) cities[a]	56.5%	26.6%
In suburban areas[b]	17.3%	46.6%
In nonmetropolitan areas	26.2%	26.8%
Total	100.0%	100.0%
Living in poverty areas[c]		
All poverty areas	62.2%	10.2%
Central city poverty areas	39.2%	3.7%
Families living in poverty with head age 65 and over		
In central (core) cities[a]	47.4%	30.7%
In suburban areas[b]	16.2%	36.8%
In nonmetropolitan areas	36.3%	32.5%
Total	100.0%	100.0%
Living in poverty areas[c]		
All poverty areas	68.4%	27.6%
Central city poverty areas	36.7%	11.3%

[a]City designated by the census as the central or core city of a larger metropolitan area.
[b]Metropolitan area minus the central city.
[c]The census bureau defines a poverty area as a census tract where the poverty rate is 20 percent or higher.
Source: U.S. Bureau of the Census (46).

decline, along with increased financial and other barriers, may have contributed to the *declining* number of physician visits made by those in poor health with low incomes. This 1980s trend reversed the trend of the 1960s and 1970s, when access to primary care by the poor increased as a result of community health centers, Medicaid, and Medicare (54).

Older blacks also face decreasing resources with the closure and relocation of many inner-city hospitals. Wan found that black elderly living in poor inner-city areas were twice as likely as similar elderly whites to depend on hospital clinics for their usual source of care (36.6% versus 16.6%) (52). Rice notes that hospitals are more likely to close in, or relocate from, neighborhoods that become heavily black (55). While this is likely a result of the hospitals following wealthier and privately insured patients into the suburbs, the net result is that inner-city black residents are faced with declining health care resources. The closure or sale of many public hospitals during the 1980s and into the 1990s has further compounded access problems for older blacks. Residential concentration driven by *racial* factors creates conditions that the medical system avoids because of its economic structure. The dynamic between race and class factors makes the situation different from the simple additive model of the multiple jeopardy hypothesis. This interplay of race and class forces is initially shaped by independent race factors but ends up following the patterns established by a capitalist economic system.

There is also evidence that blacks may receive a different intensity of hospital care. Wenneker and Epstein report that blacks received less intensive cardiac care than whites in Massachusetts, even after controlling for age, sex, payment source, income, primary diagnosis, and secondary diagnosis (56). The hospital care received by blacks nationally leads them to be more dissatisfied with their care and more likely, compared to white respondents, to believe that the length of their hospitalization was too short (34). Any skepticism of medical care by blacks might be better explained as a result of poor experiences rather than poor culture. Such experiences would be particularly likely for older blacks who lived for a substantial proportion of their lives during an era of legal segregation and an overtly two-class system of medical care (see 57, 58 for examples of how medical care has been used *against* blacks). These differences are direct outcomes of racial dynamics.

Nursing home use is a topic that has received ongoing attention because of a persistent difference between the proportion of older blacks and whites who use nursing homes. Aged blacks use nursing homes 20 percent less than aged whites with the gap growing to 40 percent among those aged eighty-five and over (59). There are no conclusive national data to show whether this variation is caused by a cultural preference for family care, a class barrier to the use of institutions by the poor, or racial discrimination (60).

One study in New York City, however, found a clear pattern of racial discrimination by the more desirable nursing homes in the city (61). Nearly all of the residents were white in over one-third of the nursing homes, but one-half of the residents of public nursing homes were from minority groups. Medicaid paid for most of the nursing home care in all types of institutions. This pattern was attributed to a combination of discrimination by nursing homes and steering by hospital discharge planners.

Similarly, in St. Louis, striking racial patterns in nursing homes were found. In the primarily white third of the city, private and voluntary nursing homes averaged only 4 percent black residents, compared with 75 percent black residents in facilities located in the primarily black third of the city. As with the New York City study, primarily black nursing homes had more quality-of-care problems than primarily white nursing homes (62).

CONCLUSIONS AND POLICY IMPLICATIONS

Elderly blacks in the United States continue to fare poorly compared to elderly whites on most measures of health and economic status. The *quantity* of doctor and hospital care received by most older blacks has achieved rough parity with whites as a result of federal health care programs. There are still questions, however, about the relative *quality* of that care and about the permanence of the quantity parity.

An analysis of differences that draws solely on the cultural practices and values of black elderly fails to explore the influences of structural forces in society, such as the effect of class and race on the health and health care of older blacks. Disparities in sources and amount of income can be traced in part to historic employment patterns. Blacks were much more likely to work in low-skilled and low-wage occupations, resulting in a lower material status in old age. The low incomes of older blacks combines with their heavy concentration in urban centers to work to their disadvantage in a medical care system oriented towards maximizing profits.

The class position of older blacks is compounded by the institutional patterns of racism that perpetuate residential segregation, racially different medical care practices, and plain discrimination. There is no indication that these racially specific practices would cease if black and white incomes were equalized.

There is clearly a mismatch between resources and needs in the area of health care of older blacks. Policy solutions to this problem depend on the theory used to explain these facts. Cultural theories would suggest that if older blacks are living in a culturally prescribed manner, the mismatch may not be such a problem. At most, education would be called for to make sure that older blacks know about available resources. The continued existence of institutional segregation, however, contradicts reliance solely on a theory of cultural preferences.

A class explanation, on the other hand, would suggest that policy should work to eliminate the profit motive from health care and that disparities in income and insurance coverage should be attenuated. The reduction or elimination of health status differences based on race when income is controlled for suggests that improved economic justice might help the health status of the next generation of elderly. The patterns of institutional practices based on race in hospitals and nursing homes, however, suggests that a class-based approach alone will not eliminate differences in the health care provided to older blacks. Policies such as a national health insurance or national health system (designed to eliminate the barriers of income and profit, respectively) can therefore be seen as a necessary but not sufficient measure to address racial disparities.

The institutional patterns discussed in this article include an independent racial factor. Addressing the individual-level problems of older blacks will not open the doors to nursing homes or change the patterns of hospital practice. To the extent that medical care patterns reflect residential segregation, health care for older blacks will be influenced by the general level of segregation of the community. Race-conscious efforts in the planning and provision of medical care services will be required to assure that medical care is provided equitably to both blacks and whites.

REFERENCES

1. U.S. Riot Commission. *Report of the National Advisory Commission on Civil Disorders*. Bantam Books, New York, 1968.
2. Farley, R. A., *The Color Line and the Quality of Life in America*. Oxford University Press, New York, 1987.
3. Willis, D. P. *Currents of Health Policy: Impacts on Black Americans*. Supplements 1 and 2 of *Milbank Q.,* Cambridge University of Chicago Press, Chicago, 1987.
4. Wilson, W. J. *The Truly Disadvantaged*. University of Chicago Press, Chicago, 1987.
5. Butler, P. A. *Too Poor to be Sick: Access to Medical Care for the Uninsured*. American Public Health Association, Washington, D.C., 1988.
6. Starr, P. *The Social Transformation of American Medicine*. Basic Books, New York, 1982.
7. Villers Foundation. *One the Other Side of Easy Street*. Villers, Washington, D.C., 1987.
8. Baca Zinn, M. Family, race, and poverty in the eighties. *Signs* 14(4): 856–874, 1989.
9. Mead, L. *Beyond Entitlement: The Social Obligations of Citizenship*. Free Press, New York, 1986.
10. Murray, C. *Losing Ground*. Basic Books, New York, 1984.
11. Lewis, O. *Five Families: Mexican case Studies in the Culture of Poverty*. Basic Books, New York, 1959.
12. Moynihan, D. P. *The Negro Family: The Case for National Action*. U.S. Department of Labor, Washington, D.C., 1965.
13. Bullough, B. Poverty, ethnic identity and preventive health care. *J. Health Soc. Behav.* 13(4): 347–359, 1972.
14. National Cancer Institute. *SEER Programs: Cancer Incidence and Mortality in the United States, 1973–1981*. National Institutes of Health, Bethesda, Maryland, 1984.
15. Spector, R. E. *Cultural Diversity in Health and Illness*. Appleton-Century-Crofts, Norwalk, Connecticut, 1985.
16. Morrison, B. J. Sociocultural dimensions: Nursing homes and the minority aged. In *Gerontological Social Work Practice in Long-Term Care*, edited by G. S. Getzel and M. J. Mellor, pp. 127–145, Haworth Press, Binghamton, NewYork, 1983.
17. Taylor, R. J. Aging and supportive relationships among black Americans. In *The Black American Elderly*, edited by J. S. Jackson, pp. 259–281. Springer, New York, 1988.

18. Milligan, S., Maryland, P., Ziegler, H., and Ward, A. Natural helpers as street health workers among the black urban elderly. *The Gerontologist* 27(6): 712–715, 1987.

19. Barrera, M. *Race and Class in the Southwest*. University of Norte Dame Press, Norte Dame, Indiana, 1979.

20. Marable, M. *How Capitalism Underdeveloped Black America*. South End Press, Boston, 1983.

21. Bonacich, E. Advanced capitalism and black/white race relations in the United States: A split labor market interpretation. *Am. Soc. Rev.* 41(1): 34–51, 1976.

22. Miles, R. *Racism and Migrant Labor*. Routledge and Kegan Paul, London, 1982.

23. Wolpe, H. Class concepts , class struggle and racism. In *Theories of Race and Ethnic Relations*, edited by J. Rex and D. Mason, pp. 110–130. Cambridge University Press, New York, 1986.

24. Kasarda, J. Urban change and minority opportunities. In *The New Urban Reality*, edited by P. E. Peterson. Brookings Institution, Washington, D.C., 1985.

25. Navarro, V. *Crisis, Health, and Medicine*. Tavistock, New York, 1986.

26. Waitzkin, H. *The Second Sickness*. The Free Press, New York, 1983.

27. Estes, C. L. Public policy and aging in the 1980's. In *Empowering Ministry in the Ageist Society*, edited by D. Hessell, pp. 23–38. United Presbyterian Church, USA, Atlanta, 1981.

28. Kasper, J. D. *National Medical Care Utilization and Expenditure Survey. Series B. Descriptive Report # 14*. U. S. Government Printing Office, Washington, D. C., 1986.

29. Boston, T. D. *Race, Class & Conservatism*. Unwin Hyman, Boston, 1988.

30. Wellman, D. *Portraits of White Racism*. Cambridge University Press, New York, 1977.

31. Willie, C. *Caste and Class Controversy on Race and Poverty* (2nd Edition). General Hall, Dix Hills, New York, 1989.

32. Miller, S. M. Race in the health of America. *Milbank Q.* Suppl. 2, 65: 500–531, 1987.

33. Okada, L. M., and Wan, T. H. Impact of community health centers and medicaid on the use of health services. *Pub. Health Rep.* 95(6): 520–534, 1980.

34. Blendon, R. J., Aiken, H., Freeman, H., and Corey, C. Access to medical care for black and white Americans. *JAMA* 261(2): 278–281, 1989.

35. Dowd, J. J., and Bengtson, V. L. Aging in minority populations: An examination of the double jeopardy hypothesis. *J. Gerontol* 33(3): 427–436, 1978.

36. Jackson, M., Kolody, B., and Wood, J. L. To be old and black: The case for double jeopardy on income and health. In *Minority Aging*, edited by R. Manuel. Greenwood Press, Westport, Connecticut, 1982.

37. Markides, K. S. Minority aging. In *Aging in Society: Selected Reviews of Recent Research*, edited by M. W. Riley, B. B. Hess, and K. Bond, pp. 115–137. L. Erlbaum Associates, Hillsdale, New Jersey, 1983.

38. Manton, K. G., Patrick, C. H., and Johnson, K. W. Health differentials between blacks and whites: Recent trends in mortality and morbidity. *Milbank Q.* Suppl. 2, 65: 129–199, 1987.

39. Jackson, J. S. (ed.), *The Black American Elderly: Research on Physical and Psychological Health*. Springer, New York, 1988.

40. Markides, K. S., and Mindel, C. *Aging and Ethnicity*. Sage, Beverly Hills, California, 1987.

41. U.S. National Center for Health Statistics. *Physical Functioning of the Aged: United States, 1984*. Vital and Health Statistics, Series 10, #167. Public Health Service, Hyattsville, Maryland, 1989.

42. U.S. Senate, Special Committee on Aging. *Aging America: Trends and Projections*. U.S. Government Printing Office, Washington, D.C., 1989.

43. U.S. National Center for Health Statistics, *Vital Statistics of the United States*, 1986, Vol. II, Mortality, Part A. U.S. Government Printing Office, Washington, D.C., 1989.

44. Gibson, R. C., and Jackson, J. S. The health physical functioning, and informal supports of the black elderly. *Milbank Q.* Suppl. 2, 65: 421–454, 1987.

45. Manton, K. G., and Soldo, B. J. Dynamics of health changes in the oldest old: New perspectives and evidence. *Milbank Mem. Fund Q.* 63(2): 206–285, 1985.

46. U.S. Bureau of the Census. *Poverty in the Unites States 1987*. Series P-60, No. 163. U.S. Department of Commerce, Washington, D.C., 1989.

47. Gibson, R. C. Defining retirement for black Americans. In *Ethnic Dimensions of Aging*, edited by D. E. Gelfand and C. M. Barresi, pp. 224–238. Springer, New York, 1987.

48. Davis, K., and Rowland, D. *Medicare Policy*. Johns Hopkins University Press, Baltimore, 1986.

49. U.S. National Center for Health Statistics. Health care coverage by age, sex, race, and family income: United States, 1986. *Advance Data* Number 139. Public Health Service, Hyattsville, Maryland, 1987.

50. Gray, B. (ed.). *For-Profit Enterprise in Health Care*. National Academy Press, Washington, D.C., 1986.

51. Hawes, C., and Phillips, C. D. The changing structure of the nursing home industry and the impact of ownership on quality, cost, and access. In *For-Profit Enterprise in Health Care*, edited by B. H. Gray, pp. 492–541. National Academy Press, Washington, D.C., 1986.

52. Wan, T. H. Use of health service by the elderly in low income communities. *Milbank Mem. Fund Q.* 60: 82–107, 1982.

53. Geiger, H. J. Community health centers: Health care as an instrument of social change. In *Reforming Medicine*, edited by V. Sidel and R. Sidel, pp. 11–30. Pantheon, New York, 1984.

54. Freeman, H. E., Blendon, R. J., Aiken, L. H., Sudman, S., Mullinix, C. F., and Corey, C. R. Americans report on the access to care. *Health Aff.* 6(1): 6–18, 1987.

55. Rice, M. F. Inner-city hospital closures/relocations: Race, income status, and legal issues. *Soc. Sci. Med.* 24(11): 889–896, 1987.

56. Wenneker, M. B., and Epstein, A. M. Racial inequalities in the use of procedures for patients with ischemic heart disease in Massachusetts. *JAMA* 261(2): 253–257, 1989.

57. Jones, J. H. *Bad Blood: The Tuskegee Syphilis Experiment—A Tragedy of Race and Medicine*. Free Press, New York, 1981.

58. Petchesky, R. P. 'Reproductive Choice' in the contemporary United States: A social analysis of female sterilization. In *And the Poor Get Children*, edited by K. L. Michaelson. Monthly Review Press, New York, 1981.

59. Hing, E. Use of nursing homes by the elderly: Preliminary data from the 1985 national nursing home survey. *Advance Data from Vital and Health Statistics*. No. 135. U.S. Public Health Service, Hyattsville, Maryland, 1987.

60. Institute of Medicine. Racial differences in use of nursing homes. In *Health Care in a Context of Civil Rights*, pp. 72–104. National Academy Press, Washington, D.C., 1981.
61. Sullivan, R. Study reports bias in nursing homes. *New York Times*. January 28, 1984.
62. Wallace, S. P. Race versus class in the health care of African-American elderly. *Social Problems* 37(4): 101–119, 1990.

PART VI. RETIREMENT, SOCIAL SECURITY, AND ECONOMIC DEPENDENCY

The utility of an analytical approach combining political and moral economy perspectives is perhaps best illustrated in the evolution of retirement and social security systems. In this section, retirement and old age dependency are examined by Kohli from a moral economy perspective, and by Myles, within a political economy framework that implicitly also considers some of the moral economy notions underlying the evolution of modern pension systems. Complementing the focus of these analysts on the experiences of two advanced industrialized nations (Germany and the United States, respectively), Neysmith then addresses the situation of elders in Third World nations, where pension systems remain underdeveloped and underfunded, and where serious economic constraints on both the national and the family and community levels place the majority of elders in a dependent and vulnerable economic position.

The section begins with Kohli's analysis of the development and evolution of the world's first pension system. The moral impact of retirement is seen as involving its creation of lifetime continuity and reciprocity by linking welfare with the evolution of an institutional mechanism to regulate the individual's movement through a succession of positions in life, by which his or her experiences and plans were organized. Within this theoretical framework, Germany's welfare system is seen as having developed as an attempt to construct a reliable life course by covering illness, disability, and old age—the risks associated with the organization of work—and thus providing workers with a stake in the existing social order.

While moral economy helps explain such phenomena as the significant role of labor in fighting for expanded pension coverage, such considerations represent only a partial explanation of the evolution of retirement and social security systems. Moral economy perspectives therefore must be complemented by a careful look at ways in which the needs of capital have shaped the modern welfare state including, importantly, its pension schemes.

In Chapter 18, Myles looks specifically at the U.S. experience with retirement, examining the evolution of social security into a true "retirement wage" on which superannuated workers could live without a major downward turn in their economic circumstances. He argues that changes in Social Security under the

Nixon Administration (when major benefit increases were legislated) were what really transformed the public pensions into a retirement wage. It was these reforms in turn which greatly decreased poverty rates among the old during the 1970s and early 1980s. Although the Social Security system in the United States has successfully withstood large-scale cutbacks, Myles argues that piecemeal dismantling must still be guarded against in a nation in which rugged incrementalism has been both the way welfare advances and welfare retreats have tended to take place.

Although public pensions constitute the major source of income for the elderly in developed countries, such schemes remain a luxury in the Third World. The already vulnerable economic position of the old in many of these countries, moreover, worsened still further during the 1980s as a consequence of deteriorating economic conditions. In Chapter 19, Neysmith examines the situation of the elderly in the Third World stressing that the causes and consequences of underdevelopment, and hence of the vulnerable position of disadvantaged groups including the elderly, are heavily influenced by the economic relationships which bind Third World nations to advanced capitalist countries.

While Chapter 19 focuses most heavily on the political and economic realities which determine the experience of old age in Third World nations, moral economy concerns are also highlighted. Neysmith thus notes that in both Third World and developed countries, societal assumptions concerning moral obligations to the old include strong implicit notions linking responsibility for the day-to-day care of the elderly with the "informal sector" of unpaid female labor. She argues that policy considerations must begin to address the contradictions inherent in micro-macro relations (e.g., family-state tensions and public [paid] and private [unpaid] labor) if the injustices in this critical aspect of the moral and political economies of both developed and Third World nations are to be redressed.

CHAPTER 17

RETIREMENT AND THE MORAL ECONOMY: AN HISTORICAL INTERPRETATION OF THE GERMAN CASE

Martin Kohli

The evolution of the German welfare system presents in a nutshell most of the basic questions and controversies of modern welfare policy. This is due to its temporal primacy as well as to its specific salience for German society. The history of welfare—and of retirement as a major part of it—is not only pertinent for identifying some key features of the German modernization process; the German case is also especially useful for uncovering the social logic of retirement more generally.

The conservative critique of the welfare state today takes essentially two forms. On the material level, the welfare state is held responsible for stifling the economy by its heavy financial drain and its bureaucratic regulations. On the moral level, it is criticized for destroying the motivational basis of the economy by decoupling income from productive work, and of society by eroding one's responsibility for self and kin. Within the welfare system, retirement takes a prominent place, and is thus especially well-suited for assessing the merits of these critiques.

The public pension scheme is in the Western nations today the largest machinery of redistribution; the welfare state is mostly a state of welfare for the old (1). But interestingly enough, the current conservative attacks on the welfare programs do not directly reflect this order of relevance. Retirement is usually the last domain to be touched. While there are proposals for raising the retirement age limit or for reducing the size of public pensions, nobody has as yet seriously proposed to abolish them. Such leniency may be due to the fact that retirement, while it certainly represents a financial burden for the economy, does not threaten the motivation for productive work: its aim is not to compensate for a temporary lack of work and income but to remove people permanently from the workforce. But this alone would not be a sufficient explanation for maintaining such a costly institution. We are therefore led to examine more closely the moral dimensions of retirement, in other words, what it contributes to the social order.

During the last decade, the research literature on retirement as a social institution (2) has expanded rapidly. It is especially the historical studies that have added to our understanding of its structural features. Methodologically, any such study is confronted with the problem of how to do justice to the specific context of each national system and still achieve comparability and theoretical generalizability. Historians have preferred the bottom-up approach, starting with a detailed account of a national system and then cautiously trying to extend the scope of the analysis to incorporate other cases for comparison. Thus, Ritter (3) and some of the contributors to the volume by Mommsen and Mock (4) explore the possibilities of a comparative history of the German and English system. Sociologists, on the contrary, have preferred the top-down approach by starting with a comparative grid, usually within the framework of theories of the welfare state and of modernization (1, 5, 6).

Unlike this deductive approach, this chapter centers on a single case. Unlike the historical approach, however, it reconstructs the case in more general theoretical terms: it examines the social logic of retirement as part of the development of the Western "work societies." The wealth of empirical material made available by the historical studies is selectively used in view of what it contributes to this theoretical aim. Thus, the historical account given here is constructed so as to throw light not only on the place of the institution of retirement in the particular path to modernity that German society has taken, but also on the structural impact of retirement in modernization as such, however differently it may be contextualized in other national systems.

A THEORETICAL MODEL: THE INSTITUTIONALIZATION OF THE LIFE COURSE AND THE MORAL ECONOMY

The theoretical model proposed here goes beyond what has usually been covered in the discussion of the welfare state to incorporate issues of the institutionalization of the life course and its relevance for the moral integration of modern societies. Speaking of a "moral economy" shifts the emphasis from individual motivations—as in the conservative critique—to the system of reciprocal relations. On the other hand, it allows us to extend the argument beyond the political and economic sphere in a narrow sense, thus avoiding the reductionist assumptions that have guided much of welfare state theorizing in the marxist vein, and also to go beyond a schematic representation of the relations between "welfare" and the "economy" or the "polity" as separate subsystems, stating that welfare has the function of securing legitimacy for the latter two, by putting the question of legitimacy squarely into an analysis of the moral structure of the economy and polity themselves.

The concept of "moral economy" has been introduced by E. P. Thompson in his analysis of eighteenth-century "food riots" (7). Thompson refers to the "social anthropology" of Durkheim, Weber, and Malinowski as the theoretical source of his concept and defines it as the "popular consensus as to what were legitimate and what were illegitimate practices. This in turn was grounded upon a consistent traditional view of social norms and obligations" (7, p. 79), in other words, upon the collectively shared basic moral assumptions constituting a system of reciprocal relations. He argues against the usual view of the price riots as "spasmodic" happenings, and shows them instead to be collective sanctions for a violation of the social logic of reciprocity.

Another part of his argument is less convincing: that the moral economy is valid only in the preindustrial economy, and after a prolonged agony is giving way to the newly emerging market economy. It is more plausible instead to consider the latter as a new form of economic organization giving rise to its own moral economy on which it depends for its functioning. In other words, the market economy is not "dis-embedded," in Polanyi's terms (8), but needs to be embedded just as well. This can be argued theoretically, following Durkheim's analysis of the division of labor and its preconditions (9), or perhaps more convincingly, with historically contextualized studies such as the one by Moore (10) on the relevance of collectively validated beliefs of justice and injustice in the forming of the modern workers' movement. What occurs is not a collapse of the moral economy but a shift of the main arena of moral conflict from the consumption market to the labor market: it concerns no longer the price of goods but the "just reward" for work. While consumptive goods become largely commodified, the use of labor— even in its new form of wage labor exchanged on markets—remains morally restrained. As we have shown in our study of aging in work settings (11, 12), norms of reciprocity—in the sense of taken-for-granted beliefs of fairness in the relation of efforts and rewards—are important features of the internal labor markets of industrial firms; they define a system of mutual obligations beyond what is and can be regulated by formal contracts. Although informal and somewhat vague, they are nevertheless a powerful reality, whose violation by the firm leads to costs such as diminishing work efforts and open conflict. It is not only the day-to-day transactions that are thus normatively regulated, but even more importantly the long-term engagements of workers and management, in other words, those in the lifetime dimension.

Ironically, the Durkheimian tradition provides some authors with arguments for a critique of the welfare state (5, p. 363; 13, 14): it is said to undermine all elements of reciprocity by putting the premium on utilitarian-individualistic behavior and thus eroding the more genuinely social forms of integration by morally grounded solidarity. This assumption, however, is based on too narrow a concept of the moral economy. Mauss (15), in his classic work expanding Durkheim's notions of moral solidarity into an analysis of the systems of reciprocity to be found in primitive societies, finds analogous patterns in the modern organization of work (15, p. 75):

> There is no better way of making men work than by reassuring them of being paid loyally all their lives for labor which they give loyally not only for their own sakes but for that of others. The producer-exchanger feels now as [she/] he has always felt—but this time [she/] he feels it more acutely—that [she/] he is giving something of himself, his [/her] time and his [/her] life. Thus [she/] he wants recompense, however modest, for this gift.

Mauss refers to modern social insurance as a possibly equivalent form of reciprocity: the worker "gives his [/her] life and labour," and "those who benefit from his [/her] services are not square with [her/] him simply by paying [her/] him a wage. The state, representing the community, owes [her/] him . . . a certain security in his [/her] life against unemployment, sickness, old age and death" (15, p. 65). And Titmuss (16), whose influential book takes up Mauss' idea, analyzes the contemporary institutions of the welfare state—in this case, the British Health Service and more specifically its blood donorship service—in terms of moral solidarity.

Retirement pensions, in the form that they assume in most western states today, could to a certain extent be viewed in a utilitarian perspective: they are not pure reciprocity in the sense of a system of moral obligations without any element of individually calculable returns, and the latter may be quite relevant, e.g., in individual decisions about when to retire. The correspondence between individual contribution and return may even function as a powerful instrumental motivation for gainful work. But the correspondence is far from complete, not even on the aggregate level of a population (such as that provided, e.g., by private life insurance contracts); public pensions thus contain a clear element of reciprocity based on morally bounded claims and expectations, or—as it is usually termed in the German welfare discussion—of solidarity between the generations (17). They mix instrumental elements in the sense of calculable returns for investments with reciprocal elements in the sense of a normative system of mutual obligations. The decisive point, however, is that the former elements are "embedded" in the latter; therefore, it is feasible to interpret retirement in terms of the moral economy.

The issue can be stated more precisely by clarifying the organization of work in society. In German sociology, the term "work society" has come to be preferred over the rival ones such as "industrial" or "capitalist society" (18, 19). While the latter terms refer to a form of organization of economic production, the former conceives of work as a reality not only of the economy but also of culture and life-world; it emphasizes how people are engaged into society, in other words, how social life in the broadest sense is regulated. The impact of work goes far beyond simply assuring material survival or organizing economic and political interests; by providing the legitimate basis for the allocation of life chances in a very broad sense, it defines the cultural unity of modern society as well as the identity of its members (20).

But to fully appreciate the moral impact of the welfare system, we have to take the argument one step further. It consists of linking the development of welfare with the historical institutionalization of the life course (as discussed more broadly by Kohli (21)). It is by the creation of lifetime continuity and reciprocity that the welfare system contributes to the moral economy of the work society. This becomes especially clear when we look at retirement. The emergence of retirement has meant the emergence of old age as a distinct life phase, structurally set apart from active life and with a clear chronological boundary. But the other parts of the welfare system can be viewed in this perspective as well: as elements in the construction of a stable lifecourse, covering the gaps ("risks") that are created or left open by the new organization of work.

The notion of "institutionalization of the life course" refers to the evolution, during the last two centuries, of an institutional program regulating one's movement through life in terms of a sequence of positions and a set of biographical orientations by which to organize one's experiences and plans. What it has consisted of can be summarized in four propositions:

1. The relevance of the life course as a social institution has greatly increased. There has been a change from a regime in which age was relevant as a categorical status only to a regime in which lifetime is one of the core structural features (*temporalization*).
2. The temporalization of life has been largely keyed to chronological age as the basic criterion; this has resulted in a chronologically standardized "normative life course" (*chronologization*).
3. This evolution has been part of the more general process in which individuals are set free from the bonds of status, locality, and family, i.e., part of the new social programs that are focused on individuals as the basic units of social life (*individualization*).
4. The life course has been structured around the new *organization of work* based on wage labor, resulting (among other things) in its tripartition into periods of preparation, "activity," and retirement.

It is in the construction of this regulated life course that retirement is important for the fabric of modern society. The life course has become one of the key institutions for achieving social order by processing people through the social structure and articulating their actions. It can be shown to "answer" some of the structural problems that arise with the transition from a household economy to an economy based on free labor:

• the problem of *rationalization*, both of economic production and of individual lives;

- the problem of *succession* (in terms of regulating the flow of cohorts through the economy);
- the problem of *integration* of the newly differentiated life domains (especially work and family) and their corresponding "careers";
- and the problem of *social control* under the conditions of an individualized life form with a high degree of geographical and social mobility.

By continuing this line of reasoning, I will argue that retirement—even in its present form of a highly bureaucratized machinery of redistribution—is still a major factor of social integration, and thus a key element of the moral economy. And even more poignantly: it is a form of integration geared to the individualized life course regime of the modern work society, and thus more appropriate as an element of our moral economy than other forms based on family solidarity. The moral universe is no longer the kinship network or—as in Thompson's analysis— the local community but the new nation state, or more exactly, its formal sector of work. Such an expansion of the morally relevant boundaries is, as Elwert (22), convincingly argues, a prerequisite for the functioning of a national market economy. In this sense, the welfare system has also a political impact: it helps to construct the nation as a collective framework for identity. This is especially important in a case such as nineteenth-century Germany where national utility was still a fragile project.

RETIREMENT IN PREINDUSTRIAL GERMANY

The history of retirement in Germany is usually addressed in terms of the emergence of the public old-age pension insurance as part of the Bismarckian social security laws, put into effect just about one hundred years ago. By necessity, it will be the focus of my own discussion as well. But it did not spring to life from scratch; it is contingent on its earlier precursors in a double sense: positively, as a continuation of some earlier realities and projects, and negatively, as a response to problems that had been left unsolved or even created by them. Among these precursors are 1) the forms of retirement in preindustrial agriculture and crafts; 2) the regulations created for the emerging public bureaucratic structures (civil service and army); and 3) the pension funds created by some of the early industrial firms and branches. In addition, the evolution of public welfare prior to the social security system of the 1880s has to be taken into account.

Retirement in the preindustrial peasant society took the form of a transfer of a farm holding to an heir in exchange for the lifelong provision of shelter, food, and other services to the retiree (23). The transfer is usually connected with the marriage of the heir. This pattern can be found in large parts of middle and northern Europe, which is an indication for its relevance as part of the "European marriage pattern"; not surprisingly, it has been analyzed in terms of the structure of the preindustrial family (24). At first glance, this retirement arrangement could appear to be a functional equivalent to the pension-based retirement of industrial workers. However, such an impression not only disregards the different every-day reality of these two forms (in terms of support and work), and the different extension of the moral community that it refers to (family vs. nation state); more importantly, it overestimates the relevance of the transfer pattern as a normal part of the life course. The transfer of property was not clearly tied to chronological age, and its prevalence was quite low. Held (23), in his careful study of thirty-two Austrian communities between 1632 and 1909, found that less than 8 percent of those aged fifty-one to seventy were living as "Altenteiler" (i.e., had turned over their former property). As to the age of those who did retire in this manner, Held reports from a community study that the age at retirement ranged from thirty-seven to eighty-one, and that the "majority" retired between fifty and sixty-five. It should also be noted that retirement had no place in traditional European folk culture; its life cycle system consisted only of birth/marriage/death, and thus old age was not a distinctive period set off by specific transition rites or other customs (25).

For the state sector, it can again be shown that the first forms of material assistance in old age had nothing to do with retirement in the modern sense; they were considered in terms of disability. The state assumed a kind of patronage for its faithful servants, but the patronage came into effect in case of need only. According to Conrad, three phases in the provisions of the state for its officials can be distinguished (27, p. 11):

> Starting in the 18th century and going far into the 19th, pensions were awarded on a case-by-case basis (following application by the official himself or his department). No rules on age limits or guaranteed minimum benefit existed. After 1825, Prussia established a pension fund and made it mandatory for the civil servants to become paying members. There had already been a special fund for survivors' benefits (since 1775). After 1868 in Prussia and 1871 in the German Empire as a whole, contributions from the civil servants to these funds were no longer made; a retirement income became then a part of their general life-long remuneration. Not before the late 19th century, however, did the idea of normal retirement (irrespective of health reasons) become institutionalized, when the reaching of age 65 was finally considered the equivalent of disability.

Thus, the institutionalization of retirement for civil servants paralleled that created by public social insurance for workers.

In the industrial sector, the first branch in which early forms of insurance funds were created was mining, with its especially high risks. With growing industrialization, several firms created assistance funds, usually financed by contributions from both firms and workers (see the overview by Wessel (28)). While some entrepreneurs wanted to keep these institutions in the responsibility of the private firms, others joined forces with members of the political and cultural elites in an attempt to develop broader solutions for the growing problems of industrialization. The main forum of these bourgeois social reformers was the "Centralverein für das Wohl der Arbeitenden Klassen" (Central Association for the Welfare of the Working Classes, founded in 1844). In its project for an old-age insurance, initiated in 1848 (!), concepts of welfare were linked with those of social control; it was intended to replace the poor relief in old age and to motivate workers to long-range provision for and planning of their life course (29). While the project was not successful, many of its features and motifs played a role in the later development of the public pension system.

It should be noted that at this time, public poor relief was already well-established (30). It consisted of an obligation of the local authorities to provide the indispensable means of subsistence to those in need. It was thus means-tested, and deprived its recipients of their public rights. This was one of the problems that fueled the projects for a public insurance system. Even more important was the massive overload of the locally-based poor relief due to the effects of industrialization. The local authorities were obliged to provide relief for all those legally settled in their commune. This originally meant their place of birth. Although it was later modified to account for the growing geographical mobility of the poor—a law which provided that one was entitled to poor relief in a commune after two years of residence was passed right after the founding of the Reich (1871)—this proved to be no feasible solution. It was not only the growing size of the poor population, but also the massive migration that caused the overload.

THE EMERGENCE OF THE PUBLIC
SOCIAL SECURITY SYSTEM

Since Germany was the first nation to adopt a large-scale public social security system, including old-age insurance, the solutions found in this process served as a model—positive or negative—for political discussions in the other Western states (3, p. 11). The actors themselves were quite conscious of their pioneering role. For the economist Schmoller, the new laws represented "not merely a German, but a world-historical transformation of social policy." The first president of the Imperial Insurance Office compared the importance of the insurance system in the "moral domain" to that of steam power and electricity in the "material domain." The government used it as a means for international propaganda, e.g., in the large universal exhibitions.

Before going into the questions of retirement proper, we have to be concerned with the system as a whole. There can be no doubt that it was basically a response to the new pressures and consequences of industrialization. The concern about pauperism shifted to that about the "social question," in other words, the question of the integration of the new industrial workers into the existing patterns of political and social life. It is also clear, however, that these structural arguments are not sufficient to explain the emergence of public social insurance. The latter is not simply the consequence of a certain stage of economic and social development. If this were so, England would have had to be the first country to adopt such a system, while Germany—the proverbial late-comer on the industrial scene and on that of modernity in general—would have come later in this respect, too (3).

Thus, we need to take a closer look at the specific set of conditions given in Germany, and at how they were dealt with in the political process. Among the complex interplay of forces, a few points should be singled out. One is the peculiar brand of political culture, with its tradition of an interventionist authoritarian state responsible for the welfare as well as for the control of its subjects. (In the conceptual scheme of mercantilism, the term "police" meant the regulation both of public welfare and of internal security.) Another is the success of the political-administrative elite in enlisting the support of parts of the entrepreneurial and cultural elites for a state-based solution. And finally, such a solution became an important element of the struggle towards political unification, especially in Bismarck's design for a strong unified state dominated by Prussia. Bismarck had originally hoped to gain at least part of the emerging labor movement as an ally in this process. When this failed, he started to contain it as best he could, a strategy which culminated in the well-known "socialist laws" (1878) which declared the Social Democratic Party and the unions illegal. However, he remained convinced that this had to be complemented by an expansion of public welfare ("candy and whip").

The immediate situation of the late 1870s was characterized by two threats to the existing order. One was the experience of the Paris Commune of 1871, which epitomized the possibility of a socialist revolution. The second was the massive economic crisis, which started in 1873 and reached its culmination point in 1879. It aggravated further the misery of the proletarian masses and was a deep blow to the belief in the self-regulation of the economy and the stabilization of social order by way of unrestricted markets. Economic and political liberalism, still comparatively weak due to the late onset of capitalist expansion, lost its legitimacy. In this context, interventionist economic policies by the state were coupled with projects for social reform—projects which took up many of the features discussed earlier but gained a new urgency due to the manifest inability of the market economy to provide even a minimum level of social welfare by itself.

In a surprisingly short period, the plans for three public insurances were drafted: for health, accidents, and disability and old age. The first two were put into effect in 1883 and 1884, respectively, while the last proved to be the most difficult, partly because of the lack of the necessary statistical information, but more importantly because of the conflict over its form. Bismarck had originally planned a unitary pension paid by state subsidies, thereby hoping to link the creation of the welfare system to a reform of the state finances. This plan failed, however; the law that was finally (and rather narrowly) passed in 1889 provided for an insurance paid mainly by the firms and workers, with only a small contribution by the state, and with a differentiation of the pension according to previous income. The age threshold was set at seventy. The insurance was declared mandatory for all blue-collar workers and for white-collar workers (Angestellte) with a yearly income of not more than 2,000 Marks.

For our argument, stressing the link between the moral economy of retirement and the institutionalization of the life course, the creation of an age threshold for pension eligibility—and thus for the full participation in the labor force—is the main feature. It has been the key component in the constitution of old age as a distinct life stage. There is some debate on how important the age threshold was in the beginning of the insurance system. Generally, most of the interest in the literature is focused on the health insurance, while the disability and old age insurance is not given nearly as much attention. Within the latter, it is argued that old age was perceived secondary to disability, and that the emergence of old age as a problem and topic by itself occurred only later (27). In support of such arguments, one can point out that during the early years of the insurance, most of the pensions were paid for disability, and only a minority for people having reached the age limit. One could also cite statements such as that by the chamberlain von Helldorff in the first reading of the bill in 1888: "in the old age pension there is present a case of disability; after reaching a certain year of life this pension is given because disability naturally is assumed to be established by old age" (31, p. 35).

But what this means is not that age and retirement were irrelevant. In Bismarck's early design, the concept of retirement—modeled after the French concept of a retirement fund under Napoleon III—figured prominently (3). Old age was thus an important structural element of the emerging welfare state right from the start. The period of old age which was chronologically defined by the introduction of an age threshold was indeed seen in terms of (partial) disability; but disability was operationally assumed to be the defining characteristic of a whole life stage. The contemporary medical discourse on decrepitude (or "old-age weakness," as it was called in German) functioned as a background for this view. Only later did old age acquire other meanings of its own.

THE DEVELOPMENT OF RETIREMENT TO THE PRESENT

The first two decades of the pension insurance brought an increasing discussion of the adequacy of the system both in terms of the political struggle between Social Democracy and government and *entrepreneurs*, and in terms of the empirical reality of life for the older workers and their dependents or survivors. The latter was spurred by a series of surveys of the "Verein für Socialpolitik," which are among the pioneering studies of empirical social research in Germany (32). The main change during this time, besides the eventual extension of the insurance to the surviving widows and orphans, was the creation of a separate insurance for white-collar workers (Angestellte) in 1911. It was motivated by a clear political strategy to promote a separate identity of this stratum in opposition to the workers' movement, and thus to prevent its organization as part of the Social Democrats and the socialist unions. To the extent that this strategy was successful, it contributed to the constitution of a "petite bourgeoisie" which later became an important factor in the Weimar Republic and in its overthrow by the Nazis. The "Angestelltenversicherung" set the age threshold at sixty-five and provided for much better conditions, albeit at the price of higher contributions. While the age threshold in the "Arbeiterversicherung" was also changed to sixty-five a few years later (1916), the full equalization of the two systems had to wait until 1957.

Following these two decades of relative stability, the massive crises of German history became crises of the pension insurance as well (33). The war, and especially the inflation of 1922/23 brought about a complete financial collapse. It impoverished those parts of the middle class which had relied on personal savings, which resulted in the formation of vociferous social movements with strong authoritarian and anti-Semitic overtones. What was left of the insurance system was little more than an institutional facade, and there were thoughts of replacing it by a system of public welfare in the traditional sense (34). After only a few years of reconstruction, the Great Depression starting in 1929 again led to an imbalance marked by rising demands and falling contributions. The issues of welfare policy again took center stage in the struggles for political control. The authoritarian governments of the last years of the Weimar Republic coped with the imbalance by lowering the pension amounts. It is interesting to note, however, that the pensioners, due to the even stronger fall of the costs of living, were the only social stratum that was better off in the Depression (34).

The financial problems were resolved again by the (relative) economic success of the Nazi regime in its early years. Surprisingly, the regime, except for directly subordinating the insurance institutions to the state, left the structure largely intact. In other respects, however, the Nazi period was a dark chapter in the history of old age. It got under pressure not only due to the shortage of labor during the war, with a tendency to delay the retirement from the labor force, but also for ideological reasons. In important aspects, the Nazi movement was a youth movement; its dominant code of strength and militancy made the position of old age rather precarious, and those who fell into mental disability were even threatened by the programs of extermination of "unworthy life." In the moral economy of the Nazi regime, old age did not have a prominent place.

After the Second World War, the pension system was again in shambles. The chances for repair came with the surprisingly fast renaissance of the German economy during the economic and political reconstruction beginning in 1948. Following a series of pension rises, a basic reform of the system came into effect in 1957 and created the structure which in its main features is still valid today.

With this reform, old age was restored to the center of the welfare state. The reform consisted essentially of three parts: 1) the pensions were "dynamized," i.e., linked to the evolution of the real (gross) wages; 2) the pension level was raised to an amount which made possible an adequate, if somewhat restricted, level of living at least for those with a continuous full-time work career; and 3) the provisions of the different insurance branches were largely equalized. Although the institutional framework remains highly conservative—the origins of the different forms of insurance are still visible in the existence of separate institutions for blue-collar and white-collar workers, miners and a few others—the contributions and levels of payment are the same (with the one exception of the civil servants; even today, they have a privileged position, reflecting a specific form of structural patronage by the state).

The solution for the financing of the pensions that was adopted in 1957 represents a clear break with the principles of accumulation of capital; it consists instead of a transfer of income from the active population to the pension beneficiaries. The German experience of financial instability and even collapse through the rapid succession of wars, depressions, and inflations was a powerful motive for such a solution. It was also strongly suggested by the advances in economic theory: in a circulation model of the economy, it is clear that all welfare payments of a given period have to be covered by the national income of the same period.

This economic logic has become the basis of the social logic of the "contract of solidarity between the generations," which is the formula used in the political discourse to characterize the income transfer of the pension system (17). In the analytical terms of an age-cohort-model, the income redistribution is mainly one between the different age strata; there is, however, also a cohort element in the true sense, in that the transfer organized by the law of 1957 was seen as a just compensation for those cohorts that had lost much of the value of their pension entitlements as a consequence of the historical catastrophes, and at the same time borne much of the burden of them.

In 1972, there was another series of changes which, although smaller in scope, have had substantial financial consequences. This is particularly true for the incorporation of the self-employed (on a voluntary basis), who got extremely favorable conditions of entry; this also meant the inclusion into the public security system of the one group which had still been socially defined as independent and self-providing, in other words, as not being part of the clientele of the welfare state. Other changes consisted in the creation of some flexibility of the age threshold, and the adoption of separate provisions for unemployment and disability. Although they have left the basic elements of the 1957 system untouched, these changes—and even smaller ones, such as the administrative change of criteria for assessing disability—have produced immediate effects, mainly in terms of drastically lowering the retirement age. They can be seen as a series of institutional responses by the state to the crisis of the labor market. The latter has not only provoked these responses, it also determines their impact by making it more or less attractive for the firms and their workers to use these various forms of early withdrawal from the labor force. This is one point where the role of retirement as a feature of the work society has become dramatically clear.

THE IMPACT ON RETIREMENT AS A LIFE STAGE

Our discussion so far has been focused on the organizational regime. For assessing the social reality of retirement, we need to look systematically at the extent to which the insurance organizations have shaped the life course. This is a task which goes beyond what has been covered by the research literature so far, and certainly much beyond the scope of the present chapter. But we should at least examine briefly two dimensions of the generalization of retirement: the growing proportion of the population that has reached the retirement limit, and the growing proportion of those covered by the insurance.

The first dimension refers to the data on survival. In 1881-90 (i.e., immediately prior to the establishment of the old-age insurance), 19.7 percent of German men survived to the pension limit of seventy (35, p. 109); today (1981-83), 73.1 percent survive to age sixty-five (the upper pension limit), and 81.4 percent to age sixty (the mean factual retirement age being fifty-nine) (36, p. 78). Thus, the proportion of those that can possibly benefit from retirement has increased from one-fifth to over four-fifths. Even if we want to eliminate the effects of the changes in child and adolescent mortality, and restrict our analysis to those having reached age twenty, the differences in survival to the pension threshold are striking. More striking still are the differences in life expectancy for those having reached the retirement threshold, in other words, the differences in the mean duration of retirement. In 1881-90, the mean life expectancy at age seventy was 7.51 years for men and 7.84 years for women (at age sixty, 12.43 and 13.14 years) (35, p . 110); while today, the corresponding figures for age sixty are 16.61 and 20.93 (36, p. 78). A woman's life in retirement is thus already half as long as her active work life (if she has been in gainful work continuously).

As to the second dimension, it should be remembered that the evolution of retirement has proceeded unevenly, by a series of different models for specific groups and branches (27). By now, however, these differences have been largely evened out, and the proportion of those insured has risen from 54 percent (in 1985) to 84 percent (in 1975) of the economically active population (6, p. 238); if we add to the latter figure those covered by the civil service pension, the total rises to 94 percent. An even better indicator of the impact of the pension system is provided by the data on labor force participation, which is a function not only of the proportion covered but also of the level of pensions relative to previous income and of the state of the labor market. Although there are as yet no studies of historical changes in the transition to retirement comparable to those of the transition to adulthood, we have at least this simple set of data indicating to what extent there *has* been a transition. The data show that the change in labor force participation of older men in Germany has been dramatic. Between 1895 and 1980, it has decreased from 79.0 to 25.1 percent for the men aged sixty to seventy, and from 47.4 to 5.2 percent for those above seventy (21, p. 282). In other words, the retirement limit set by the public pension scheme has now become the factual limit of labor force participation as well. Only now do we have a structurally distinct phase of life with a relatively uniform beginning and a sizeable length for the major part of the population. It is by providing the material basis for such a phase of life beyond gainful work that the pension scheme has contributed to the institutionalization of the life course.

A COMPREHENSIVE INTERPRETATION

In what ways is this process related to the moral economy of the work society? As stated above, the new life course regime was, among other things, a transition to a new form of social control, adapted to the more individualized life form that evolved during the process of industrialization. It may be recalled that social control was prominent in the designs of the creators of the social insurance system. In the project of the "Centralverein für das Wohl Arbeitender Klassen," the key thought was that—as one of its promoters put it—the promise of a "modest but secure income during the age of weakness" would turn even the younger worker into a "conservative citizen" (29, p. 418). Bismarck was similarly motivated. As is well-known, he repeatedly asserted that nothing would reconcile the workers better with the state and society, and thus lower the risk of a proletarian revolution, than the prospect of a stable life course with a public guarantee of material security; to his critics, he pointed out that money spent on this purpose was well-spent (3, 38).

The provisions for old age were a key element in this design, but the whole social security scheme can be interpreted along these lines. The benefits of the system consisted essentially of wage replacements during the periods of inability to work. This was originally true even for the health insurance; it was intended and used at first not so much as a means for getting medical services than as a replacement of income in times of illness. Thus, in contrast to the traditional welfare system which was means-tested and deprived its recipients of their public rights, the new system created a "social citizen" with legitimate claims to continuity through the life course. Social control is here projected to operate not simply through monetary transfers but through its long-term expectability, i.e., through biographical perspectives.

On the other hand, such claims are also resources for individual autonomy based on the continuity of material support, and thus confer more political and social weight to those entitled to them. These ambivalent consequences—social control as well as more resources to resist social control—have been a crucial dimension of the controversy surrounding the further evolution of the welfare state, and may still be an important latent issue of the present debates, behind the more manifest concerns for economic motivation and productivity.

A second line of interpretation refers to the relation of retirement to work. It is evident that retirement is linguistically and socially defined by its structural opposition to work. But the relation goes deeper. We have seen that the institutionalization of the life course has been shaped around the social organization of work. More specifically, the new forms of social security were addressed to the constituency of the newly emerging work society. The "social question" has been reframed as the "workers' question." By restricting its benefits to those in the (formal) labor force, the social security system in effect made the worker into a citizen of the new work society (and excluded from such citizenship those not continually engaged in salaried work). Up to the present day, this structural logic has shaped the pension system; it has created the problems that are still unsolved—an adequate provision for those without a continuous career in the formal sector, such as housewives—and those that arise today as a consequence of the growing importance of discontinuous and informal work.

The salience of the social organization of work for the development of the old age pension insurance can again be assessed by examining the motives of its designers and the economic interests involved. There is ample evidence that at least some parts of the entrepreneurial class looked upon the state to assume the burden of providing for those not fit to work (or not needed by the firms), and thus to enable them to rid themselves of those workers without excessive social costs. In other words, they opted for a new social pact allowing them to externalize parts of their moral obligation, with the state now assuming the support of the old and freeing the enterprises from having to (paternalistically) care for them.

Structurally, this can be viewed in the context of the emergence of internal labor markets (21). The welfare measures adopted by the firms were an element of their personnel policy, aimed at creating a stable core workforce; this had to be complemented by public provisions for those outside this core, and especially by a system of retirement making possible an orderly exit from the internal (firm-specific) labor market, and an orderly succession through its positions. This interest has persisted, and has provided for some measure of continued support for the welfare state from the entrepreneurs, in spite of the controversies about its costs.

All this is valid for most Western nations (for the United States, see Graebner (37)), and accounts for the considerable degree of unity of their welfare systems—surprising to a student of their highly differentiated political starting points. But in Germany, the work society has gained an especially high salience, and its evolution has proceeded in a specific form. The creation of the modern welfare regime was part of an authoritarian state activity—which has sometimes been called a "revolution from above"—trying to take control of the economic process of industrialization as well as of its social consequences, with the aim of modernizing within the existing social order. The construction of the "citizen of the work society" was a crucial element of this project.

In a model which has become influential not only in the welfare literature (1) but also in that on social inequality and class (38), Marshall has interpreted the evolution of the welfare state in terms of acquiring citizenship rights: it is the last step in the sequence of legal, political, and social rights (39). In Germany, this sequence is different: social citizenship has been attained (or conferred) before—according to some interpretations even instead of—full political citizenship, and it has been attained not qua being a member of the political community but qua being a worker. This is one aspect of the often-noted "delay" of German modernization—an aspect that is usually overlooked. Social rights have been formally realized long before the other nations; and with regard to old age, there are some indications that there has also been a material impact from early on. Taking the data on labor force participation in old age, we find some reduction already in the decades before World War I, thus partly falsifying Myles' thesis that the implementation of retirement essentially occurred only after World War II (1).

There are arguments that the social fabric of the Wilhelminian Reich would have disintegrated even without the war, because the balance between economic and political expansion and social pacification could not have been kept much longer (40). In an influential statement, Wehler has even argued that the unsolved inner tensions of the Reich, in other words, its inability to cope with the problems of industrial development within an authoritarian political structure, were at the root of the German "special path" ("Sonderweg") which ultimately led to Nazism (41). But there are also indications to the contrary. The revisionist tendency of the Social Democratic Party in the decades before the war, and its surprising tameness during the war, may be read as showing that the balance was still functioning. In this sense, the movement towards integration of the working class begun by the Bismarckian social security system, based on its construction of a citizen of the work society, had been successful. It constituted an "historical compromise" of unique proportion, and to the extent that it was socially validated, the work society became a common focus of social as well as individual identity.

There was a high amount of polarization during the Weimar Republic, due mainly to basic economic difficulties. During the Nazi period, it is debatable how much support for the political dimension of the social program was mobilized by the regime, but it seems safe to assume that most of the population converged at least on the work side of it. The collapse of the Nazi state had as its consequence that all political convergence of identity was outruled, which channeled all social energies even more into the work society (20). This became the main societal project, and it was historically vindicated to an extraordinary degree by the "economic miracle" of the 1950s. The metaphor is telling. In terms of the Calvinist ethic, it may have appeared that if the German people had been rejected politically, it had been elected in and by its economic success.

The basic reform of the pension system of 1957 can be seen in this context; it was a move to make old age participate in this economic success (which had surpassed all anticipations), and thus to reconfirm the validity of the model on which the integration of society had increasingly come to depend. While there had been attempts at a fundamental reform of social security in general, they were abandoned for a focus on old age as the most salient part of it; and it is instructive to see that the 1957 reform law was overwhelmingly popular (34). Again we find that retirement is the core element of the publicly ratified moral economy. The new form of the "intergenerational contract" adapted retirement to the new conditions of the "economic miracle." It was in this new moral context that the SPD, two years later, adopted the "Godesberg Program" in which it dismissed most of its remaining marxist commitments and moved to a clearly centrist position.

The high salience of the work society may also explain why there is so much concern, in German society and sociology, with its present crisis. At stake is the crucial basis of social integration—more so than in other western states where nationalism is still a viable focus of identity—and it thus raises the possibility of renewed class polarization. In the present situation, this would probably cut across traditional class lines, and be aligned rather along the emerging divide between those who (as the ironic terminology has it) "own" work and those who do not. Here, the construction of the pension system as part of the work society would not be a feasible solution, as the main problems would increasingly occur for those without a continuous full-time work life in the formal sector, who are therefore not adequately covered under the present system. Thus, it is logical that the Green party, which not only opposes much of the program of the work society but also recruits its supporters largely among those who do not fully take part in it, favors the replacement of the present work-based welfare system by one based on a general citizen's wage.

On the other hand, those with a high stake in the work society—the unions, the management, and most of the political right—are in favor of retaining the present system with its mixture of collective redistribution and individual "insurance" elements. From the union side, it is argued that the work-based system could be saved by a policy of assuring employment for all, including women, in other words, by finally completing the project of the work society.

To come back to our original question, it would appear that the welfare state in general, and retirement in particular, have been a success: they have embedded the emerging capitalist market economy within the new moral economy of the work society, and thus made it socially viable. For those who like it pure, the success may not be all that desirable; the critique from the left sees no merit in the contribution of welfare to the survival of capitalism. But to put matters into these terms of death or survival is too simple; with Heimann (42), we could rather say that the welfare system has realized the social idea within capitalism against capitalism. It has to a certain extent transformed the structure of society by providing the material basis for individualization—and the legitimate aspirations for personal development and autonomy that go with it—thus creating a dynamic which is still effective.

It is of course possible that the welfare system would now have outlived its historical usefulness, in other words, that its costs would have reached a level that far surpasses its returns. One might even say that the historical success of the welfare state has produced the threats to its survival—especially at a time of economic crisis, when a work-based system is confronted by rising demands and falling contributions. In this situation, it may be tempting to cut down the welfare system in order to "solve" its financial problems and by the same token to weaken the claims for individualization that it allows to develop. But given the importance of welfare for the moral economy, such attempts meet with resistance and generate high social costs, so that even well-established conservative governments shrink back from transforming their anti-welfare rhetoric into reality.

It seems more likely that the success of the welfare system contributes to changing the basis on which it is constructed; and it is on these unplanned consequences that we should focus our research attention. As to retirement, the pressure of the labor market has resulted in a striking drop of the factual age limit—a process to be observed in all western countries, irrespective of the institutional retirement arrangements and of any age discrimination laws. Together with the projected demographic evolution, this not only makes the financial burden heavier, it also deepens the cultural dilemma posed by the fact that people are first expected to be active and work-oriented and then passive and leisure-oriented. It is somewhat paradoxical that retirement should be an integral part of the work society, with its deep valuation of inner-worldly activity. The paradox becomes more marked with the lengthening of retirement. The emergence of a growing population of "young old" (with their resources for activity still intact) is likely to create a pressure towards new forms of activity in retirement—whether as "second careers," shadow work, unpaid volunteer activity, or even "consumption work" (12, 43); it will thus tend to erode the boundaries of the formal sector of work, and to alter the tripartition of the life course that is connected with it.

REFERENCES

1. Myles, J. *Old Age in the Welfare State: The Political Economy of Public Pensions.* Little Brown, Boston, 1984.
2. Atchley, R. C. Retirement as a social institution. *Ann. Rev. Soc.* 8: 263–287, 1982.
3. Ritter, G. A. *Sozialversicherung in Deutschland und GroBbritannien.* Beck, München, 1983.
4. Mommsen, W. J., and Mock, W. (eds.). *The Emergence of the Welfare State in Britain and Germany.* Croom Helm, London, 1981.
5. Flora, P. Solution or source of crises? The welfare state in historical perspective. In *The Emergence of the Welfare State in Britain and Germany*, edited by W. J. Mommsen and W. Mock, pp. 343–389. Croom Helm, London, 1981.
6. Alber, J. *Vom Armenhaus zum Wohlfahrtsstaat.* Campus, Frankfurt/M., 1982.
7. Thompson, E. P. The moral economy of the English crowd in the 18th century. *Past and Present* 50: 76–136, 1971.
8. Polanyi, K. *The Great Transformation.* Beacon Press, Boston, 1967.

9. Durkheim, E. *The Division of Labor in Society*. Macmillan, New York, 1933 (originally published in 1893).

10. Moore, B. *Injustice*. Sharpe, White Plain, New York, 1978.

11. Kohli, M., and Kondratowitz, H.-J. von. Retirement in Germany: Towards the construction of the "citizen of the work society." In *Retirement in Industrialized Societies*, edited by K. S. Markides and C. L. Cooper. Wiley, New York, 1987.

12. Kohli, M., and Wolf, J. Altersgrenzen im Schnittpunkt von betrieblichen Interessen und individueller Lebensplanung. *Soziale Welt* 37, 1986.

13. Bell, D. *The Cultural Contradictions of Capitalism*. Basic Books, New York, 1976.

14. Janowitz, M. *The Social Control of the Welfare State*. Elsevier, New York, 1976.

15. Mauss, M. *The Gift*. Cohen and West, London, 1966 (originally published 1925).

16. Titmuss, R. M. *The Gift Relationship*. Penguin, London, 1973.

17. Kaufmann, F.-X., and Leisering, L. *Studien zum Drei-Generationen-Vertrag*. Universität Bielefeld, Institut für Bevölkerungsforschung und Sozialpolitik, 1984.

18. Matthes, J. (ed.). *Krise der Arbeitsgesellschaft?* (Verhandlungen des 21. Deutschen Soziologentages in Bamberg 1982). Campus, Frankfurt/M., 1983.

19. Offe, C. *Arbeitsgesellschaft—Strukturprobleme und Zukunfts-Perspektiven*. Campus, Frankfurt/M., 1984.

20. Härtel, U., Matthiesen, K., and Neuendorff, H. Kontinuität und Wandel arbeitsbezogener Deutungsmuster und Lebensentwürfe. In *Berufs-Biographien im Wandel*, edited by H. G. Brose. Westdeutscher Verlag, Opladen, 1986.

21. Kohli, M., Rosenow, J., and Wolf, J. The social construction of aging through work: Economic structure and life-world. *Ageing and Soc.* 3: 23–42, 1983.

22. Elwert, G. Märkte, Käuflichkeit und Moralökonomie. In *Soziologie und Gesellschaftliche Entwicklung* (Verhandlungen des 22. Deutschen Soziologentages in Dortmund 1984), edited by B. Lutz, pp. 509–519. Campus, Frankfurt/M., 1985.

23. Held, T. Rural retirement arrangements in seventeenth to nineteenth-century Austria: A cross-community analysis. *J. Fam. His.* 7: 227–254, 1982.

24. Mitterauer, M., and Sider, R. *The European Family*. Blackwell, Oxford, 1980.

25. Schenda, R. Bewertungen und Bewältigungen des Alters aufgrund volkskundlicher Materialien. In *Gerontologie und Sozialgeschichte*, edited by C. Conrad and H.-J. von Kondratowitz, pp. 59–71. Deutsches Zentrum für Altersfragen, Berlin, 1983.

26. Gennep, A. van *Les Rites de Passage*. Nourry, Paris, 1909.

27. Conrad, C. Work and the life-course: Historical perspectives on retirement. Paper presented to the XIIIth International Congress of Gerontology, New York, July 12–17, 1985.

28. Wessel, H. A. Probleme der Altersversorgung im 19. Jahrhundert und Ansätze zu ihrer Bewältigung: Das Beispiel betrieblicher Sozialpolitik. In *Gerontologie und Sozialgeschichte*, edited by C. Conrad and H.-J. von Kondratowitz, pp. 425–479. Deutsches Zentrum für Altersfragen, Berlin, 1983.

29. Reulecke, J. Zur Entdeckung des Alters als eines sozialen Problems in der ersten Hälfte des 19. Jahrhunderts. In Gerontologie und Sozialgeschichte, edited by C. Conrad and H.-J. von Kondratowitz, pp. 425–479. Deutsches Zentrum für Altersfragen, Berlin, 1983.

30. Sachße, C., and Tennstedt, F. *Geschichte der Armenfürsorge in Deutschland*. Kohlhammer, Stuttgart, 1980.

31. Kondratowitz, H.-J. von Societal and Administrative Definitions of Old Age. Paper presented to the Conference on the Elderly in a Bureaucratic World, Cleveland, 1983.

32. Weber, A. Das Berufsschicksal der Industriearbeiter. *Archiv für Sozialwissenschaft und Sozialpolitik* 34: 377–405, 1912.

33. Döring, D. *Das System der Gesetzlichen Rentenversicherung*. Campus, Frankfurt/M., 1980.

34. Hentschel, V. *Geschichte der Deutschen Sozialpolitik 1880–1890*. Suhrkamp, Frankfurt/M., 1983.

35. Statistisches Bundesamt (ed.) *Bevölkerung und Wirtschaft 1872–1972*. Kohlhammer, Stuttgart, 1972.

36. Statistisches Bundesamt (ed.) *Datenreport 1985*. Bundeszentrale für politische Bildung, Bonn, 1985.

37. Graebner, W. *A History of Retirement*. Yale University Press, New Haven, 1980.

38. Giddens, A. Klassenspaltung, Klassenkonflikt und Bürgerrechte. Gesellschaft im Europa der achtziger Jahre. In *Soziale Ungleichheiten* (Soziale Welt, Sonderband 2), edited by R. Kreckel, pp. 15–33. Schwartz, Göttingen, 1983.

39. Marshall, T. H. *Class, Citizenship and Social Development*. University of Chicago Press, Chicago, 1964 (originally published 1949).

40. Tampke, J. (1981). Bismarck's social legislation: A genuine breakthrough? In *The Emergence of the Welfare State in Britain and Germany*, edited by W. J. Mommsen and W. Mock, pp. 71–83. Croom Helm, London, 1981.

41. Wehler, H.-J. *Das Deutsche Kaiserreich 1871–1914*. Vandenhoeck and Ruprecht, Göttingen, 1973.

42. Heimann, E. *Soziale Theorie des Kapitalismus*. Suhrkamp, Frankfurt/M., 1980 (originally published 1929).

43. Joerges B. Konsumarbeit: Zur Soziologie und Ökologie des "informellen Sektors". In *Krise der Arbeitsgesellschaft?* (Verhandlungen des 21. Deutschen Soziologentages in Bamberg 1982), edited by J. Matthes, pp. 249–264. Campus, Frankfurt/M., 1983.

44. Kohli, M. The world we forgot: An historical review of the life course. In *Later Life: The Social Psychology of Aging*, edited by V. W. Marshall, pp. 271–303. Sage, Beverly Hills, 1986.

CHAPTER 18

POSTWAR CAPITALISM AND THE EXTENSION OF SOCIAL SECURITY INTO A RETIREMENT WAGE

John Myles

In American social politics old age is unique. Unlike family or health care policy, in this area the United States has developed a truly "modern" welfare state. Because of this, Social Security does its job reasonably well, has acquired a solid basis of political support, and is relatively immune to political efforts to dismantle or erode its basic structure. My purpose in the first part of this chapter is to document these claims and to describe the development of this "modern" side of the American welfare state. The major step in the development of America's modern welfare state for the elderly, I argue, occurred under the administration of Richard Nixon, not Franklin Roosevelt. The reforms of the late sixties and early seventies are responsible for the fact that Social Security now does its job reasonably well and has developed a political constituency that makes it immune to political attack. When the reforms were complete, as Robert Ball, head of the Social Security Administration, remarked, America had a "new social security program."

Not everyone was happy with the new program, however. During the seventies and early eighties, it underwent an astounding assault. American society, it was claimed, was about to collapse under the weight of an aging society and rising Social Security entitlements (1). Ronald Reagan came to power announcing that it would be necessary to slash Social Security in order to save it. In the end, the assault was a failure for two reasons. First, few of the more radical claims advanced by the critics were able to withstand critical scrutiny (2). Second, whatever the merits of the criticisms, politicians quickly leaned that to tinker with Social Security was to court electoral defeat.

Though it failed, the attack and its aftermath mark a watershed in the history of American social policy. The bipartisan agreement of 1982 that officially brought

293

"the crisis" of Social Security to a close was not the beginning of a new round of reforms to address the serious problems that continue to face America's elderly. Neither did it begin an effort to extend the principles of Social Security to other areas of social life. The agreement was not a victory but a truce, symbolizing the current impasse of the welfare state. In the second part of the chapter, I elaborate on the reasons for both the attack and the impasse.

AMERICA'S MODERN WELFARE STATE

The phrase "modern welfare state" has become an integral part of the contemporary sociological lexicon. But just what is it that defines the modernity of the welfare state? In an important essay written to commemorate the fiftieth anniversary of the International Labour Organization, Guy Perrin suggested that the development of social security could be divided into two major periods: first, the social insurance era prior to World War II, and second, the period of social security proper, following the war (3). Though the beginnings of the social insurance era can be dated to the German sickness insurance scheme of 1883, social insurance developed largely in the period between the two great wars, when compulsory insurance schemes (and less frequently, noncontributory benefits financed from public funds) flourished in Europe and several non-European countries. As Perrin points out, however, the function of these schemes differed little from that of traditional public assistance programs—to ease the extreme poverty of the least privileged members of society (3). Benefits were low and targeted at those of limited means. The average monthly benefit of an old-age pensioner in Munich in 1905, for example, was 13.5 marks, significantly below the prevailing public assistance rate of twenty marks (4). A British investigatory committee reported in 1919 that even doubling the existing five-shilling pension would be insufficient to provide a subsistence-level income (5). Nowhere were public pensions intended to provide elderly workers with a level of income sufficient to permit withdrawal from economic activity—that is, to retire—in advance of physiological decline. This traditional welfare state was a welfare state *for the poor*.

The transition to the era of social security involved the gradual implementation of two quite novel principles of distribution. The first was the principle of universality. Coverage and benefits were extended to all citizens or, alternatively, to all members of the labor force. The second was the principle of substitutive benefits; in effect, benefits related to the worker's former earnings but at a level sufficient to allow continuity in living standards in the event of unemployment, illness or retirement (3). This is what distinguishes the modern welfare state. No longer are old age pensions merely to provide subsistence for those who through age and disability fall out of the labor market. Instead, old age pensions became a "retirement wage" sufficient to permit (or induce) the older worker to withdraw from the labor market in advance of physiological decline (6).

The main result of the implementation of these two principles was to break the historic link between public provision and the "poor." "Modern" social society programs were designed to provide income security for the expanding middle strata of the postwar period—workers with average incomes and regular employment as well as the professionals and managers of the "new middle class." The poor were excluded under this new arrangement; rather the boundaries of public provision were expanded. This gradual process of middle class incorporation into the welfare state was subsequently to prove of enormous political as well as economic importance. By virtue, and to the extent of, their incorporation, the growing middle strata became allies rather than enemies of the welfare state.

How well does the transition described by Perrin characterize the American experience? In broad terms, the answer is: not very well. For the most part, the American welfare state continues to be a welfare state for the poor. Instead of a universal system of family allowances, Americans got Aid to Families with Dependent Children (AFDC) and instead of a universal system of national health insurance, Americans got Medicaid. By the mid-1970s, the percentage of families headed by a person aged twenty-five to fifty-four receiving some form of transfer income was only 16 percent in the United States compared to 80 percent in Sweden and 59 percent in Britain. In the United States, 61 percent of transfer income went to the lowest income sextile and only 2.4 percent to the highest income sextile; in Sweden, the corresponding figures were 28 percent and 13.7 percent, respectively (7). In one sense, the American welfare state is quite efficient: it has the highest proportion of transfers going to the poor. But by the same token it is the least effective: among the advanced capitalist democracies it has among the highest levels of relative poverty (8). The reasons for this apparent contradiction were noted by Titmuss and his colleagues (5). Benefit structures created in the poor law tradition that fail to incorporate the middle strata do not generate the broadly based political support necessary to ensure the growth and survival of the welfare state. For middle-aged, middle-income America, the welfare state is virtually all cost and no benefit. Consequently, it remains "programmatically underdeveloped, symbolically demeaned and politically vulnerable" (9).

But this is not the case with old age security. From the base established during the New Deal, Social Security has evolved into a system that provides the major source of income for the vast majority of elderly Americans and is not unlike the most advanced old age security systems of Western Europe (10). Evidence for this conclusion is presented in Table 1. Panel 1 provides earnings replacement rates of old age security systems in five countries for workers with a history of average earnings in manufacturing. The earnings replacement rates are computed by dividing social security just after retirement by earnings just prior to retirement. These are hypothetical rates and should not be confused with actual replacement rates that are affected by labor force interruptions and variations in career-cycle earnings. Their main purpose is to demonstrate what would happen to similar

Table 1

Selected indicators for old-age security and the economic status of the
elderly in five countries

	Canada	Germany	Sweden	U.K.	USA
1. Earnings replacement rates of sicuak security old-age pensions for workers with average wages in manufac-turing, 1980					
Single worker	.34	.66	.68	.31	.44
One-earner couple	.49	.49	.83	.47	.66
2. Adjusted disposable income of the elderly in relation to national mean[a]					
Age 65–74	.94	.84	.96	.76	.99
Age 75+	.81	.77	.78	.67	.84
3. Gini index for adjusted disposable income					
Age 65–74	.309	.298	.143	.266	.342
Age 75+	.291	.340	.126	.240	.355
4. Poverty rates[b]					
Age 65–74	11.2%	12.7%	0.0%	16.2%	17.8%
Age 75+	12.1%	15.2%	0.0%	22.0%	25.5%

Sources: Panel 1 data from Jonathan Aldrich, "Earnings Replacement Rates of Old-Age Benefits in 12 countries, 1969–80," Social Security Bulletin 45, no. 11 (November 1982): 3–11. Panels 2, 3, and 4 data from Peter Hedstrom and Stein Ringen, Age and Income in Contemporary Society: A Comparative Study (Stockholm: The Swedish Institute for Social Research, 1985).

[a]After tax income adjusted for family size.

[b]Percentage of persons belonging to families with an adjusted disposable income below half of the median for all families.

workers under different pension regimes. For single workers (or two-earner couples), American replacement rates are modest in comparison with Sweden and Germany but generous in comparison with Canada and the United Kingdom. In contrast, American replacement rates for a traditional one-earner couple are high by international standards.

Panels 2, 3 and 4 give us some indication of the actual economic status of the elderly in the United States relative to other countries. These data are drawn from the important analysis of Hedstrom and Ringen based on the Luxembourg Income Study and are constructed from microdata files for the year 1979 except for the data from Canada and Sweden which are for 1981 (8). Panel 2 indicates that the American elderly have the highest level of income security among the five countries: their average standard of living differs little from that of the population as a whole. But as panel 3 shows, security does not imply equality. As indicated by the Gini index, income inequality within the elderly population is highest in the

United States. The explanation for this apparent contradiction is straightforward. The American system of income distribution does provide the elderly with a high level of income security, but for the poor this means little since it merely secures them in their poverty. The United States has the highest incidence of relative poverty across all age groups and this pattern is reproduced among the elderly as well (8). In sum, the United States does the most effective job of providing income security—continuity of living standards after retirement—but because it has one of the least egalitarian income distributions prior to retirement, it produces a very high level of relative poverty among the elderly after retirement.

But if Social Security fails to substantially alter the distribution of income in old age it does maintain it relatively intact, precisely what a modern welfare state based on universal substitutive benefits is intended to do. This explains why, unlike other sectors of the American welfare state, Social Security has proven so resistant to the attacks of the New Right. As Skocpol and Ikenberry conclude, its natural political base is not the "poor" but rather the "better off, stably employed industrial workers and the broad 'middle class'" (11). As elsewhere, public provision for the elderly in the United States has acquired the form of a retirement wage.

THE ORIGINS OF THE RETIREMENT WAGE

In conventional accounts, the philosophical foundations of the postwar welfare state are typically associated with the publication in the United Kingdom of the Beveridge Report in 1942. Prepared during wartime when the costs and risks of war were being borne by rich and poor alike, the Beveridge report became an important symbol of postwar social reconstruction, promising a new era of collective self-help and social responsibility. The state, acting on behalf of all citizens, would provide a safety net below which no member of the community would be allowed to fall. In the spirit of equality, benefits would be equal for all. Reproducing the inequalities of the market was not to be the task of the state. The basic flat-benefit formula proposed by Beveridge guided postwar reforms in many countries, including Britain (1946), Sweden (1946), Holland (1947), and Canada (1951). What is frequently ignored in such accounts is the fundamentally liberal character of the Beveridge proposals. Beveridge did not advocate, and indeed was opposed to, a system of substitutive benefits that would replace the market wage. This was made clear in the third of the three principles he prescribed as the basis for social provision: "The State in organizing security should not stifle incentive, opportunity, responsibility; in establishing a national minimum, it should leave room and encouragement for voluntary action by each individual to provide more than the minimum for himself and for his family" (12). In discussing the problem of employment and old age he explicitly rejected the necessity of anything resembling a retirement wage since the elderly were more able than ever, in his view, to support themselves by their own labor (13).

In those countries where the Beveridge principle was implemented, the eventual creation of a retirement wage to replace the market wage lost on retirement required a more radical transformation than where existing benefit structures were already linked to contributions. And, remarkably, Britain, the so-called cradle of the modern welfare state did not implement such a system until 1978, the result of legislation passed in 1975.

In contrast to Britain's status as a "welfare laggard" in the area of pension reform, America, at first glance, appears to have been remarkably precocious. In William Graebner's account, the retirement wage in the United States can be dated to the Social Security Act of 1935. For Graebner, the Social Security Act of 1935 was first and foremost a piece of "retirement legislation" designed to solve the massive unemployment of the Great Depression by removing older people from the work force and freeing up their jobs for younger workers (14). Graebner points to the awareness among many policy advisors of the labor force implications of a system of old age benefits linked to contributions and, most critically, to a retirement test as a condition for eligibility (an exception among modern welfare states).

It is not my intention here to adjudicate among the many debates over the "real origins" of Roosevelt's New Deal in general or of the Social Security Act in particular. Undoubtedly, this is an exercise that will preoccupy academics well into the next century. In large measure, these debates are over the proximate forces (the agents and their intentions) that brought the Social Security Act into being. Graebner's important, and lasting, contribution, however, is to draw our attention to what are unquestionably the remote causes of Roosevelt's old age security legislation, the series of changes within the American political economy that made such legislation an objective possibility. From at least the turn of the century, the search for a means to remove older workers from the industrial labor force had become a key item on the agenda of the "efficiency movement." Modern methods for organizing the labor process, it was concluded, required modern methods for the selection of those workers most "fit" for production. And, as Graebner amply documents, this selection did not include the older, slower members of the work force. The growing awareness of the economic implications of the retirement principle as a means for "rationalizing" labor inputs provided the context within which it became objectively possible to seriously consider a program for the superannuation of elderly workers. And with the passive unemployment of the thirties, possibility was transformed into probability.

But if it was the intent of the reformers of the 1930s to establish a retirement wage, then their victory was only a partial one. The provisions of Old Age Insurance (OAI) were set up so that benefits would not exceed minimum wage levels (15). And by 1949, the average Old Age Assistance (OAA) benefit, a program designed in the poor law tradition, was 70 percent higher than the average primary insurance benefit (16). Though perhaps designed as a piece of "retirement legislation," the Act itself did not provide for a "retirement wage," a benefit that would allow withdrawal from economic activity in advance of physiological decline. But what the Act did provide was a policy framework of earnings-related benefits that allowed subsequent generations of reformers to construct a system of retirement wages through what would appear to be a series of incremental reforms rather than a radical transformation of the policy structure itself. In short, in the United States the road to the retirement wage was made smoother by virtue of the fact that reforms could be presented as a series of improvements to an already existing benefit structure. This "ratchet" approach to social reform appears to have been a deliberate strategy of the program's chief executives almost from inception (16). Elsewhere (Sweden, Canada, Great Britain), comparable results could be achieved only through radically new policy initiatives to construct an earnings- related system on top of the existing flat-benefit structure.

During the first two and one-half decades of the U.S. system's operation, the major changes in it were directed at achieving the first of the two objectives identified by Perrin as characteristic of a modern welfare state, namely universal coverage. This objective was accomplished through a series of social security amendments in 1950, 1954, 1956, and 1965 (17). Coverage was extended to regularly employed farm and domestic workers, state and local government workers, farm operators, most self-employed professionals and members of the armed forces. In contrast, the benefit increases that were legislated during this period were aimed at merely maintaining the real value of benefits against price increases (17). The enormous benefit increases of 1950 (77%) simply restored the purchasing power that had been lost since the plan's inception. The result was that during the period between the end of the war and the mid-1960s, there was a continual erosion of the economic status of the American elderly (18). Benefits did not keep pace with a general rise in the standard of living or replace the labor market income being lost through a rising retirement rate. The combination of low benefits and rising retirement was progressively pauperizing the American elderly.

If we adopt Perrin's conception of universal substitutive benefits as indicating the transition to a "modern" welfare state, as stated at the beginning of this chapter, it is the administration of Richard Nixon, not of Franklin Roosevelt, that marks this development in American social history. Because the transformation that occurred in the period 1969-1972 did not require the addition of a major new program to America's old age security network, the drastic character of the changes introduced during this period was less noticeable than the legislative innovations that marked comparable developments in Sweden (1958), Canada (1965), or the U.K. (1975). But when the transformation was complete, as Robert Ball remarked, America had a "new social security program" (16).

The process of transformation had begun modestly under the Johnson administration with a 13 percent increase in benefits in 1967 and an increase in the level of covered earnings from $4800 to $7800. But under the Nixon administration major increases were legislated in 1969 (15%), 1971 (10%), and 1972 (20%). The result was a real increase in benefits (i.e., net of inflation) of 23 percent in just three years. Of equal importance was the fact that the 1972 legislation added indexing against inflation. The results were soon apparent. In 1965, the income replacement rate for a retired worker with a dependent spouse who had average earnings before retirement was .44. By 1975 it was .57 and by 1980 it had risen to .66 (19, 20). And, not surprisingly, after 1965 the relative economic status of the elderly began to rise until, in the mid-1970s, it was approximately at the level it had been after the war (18).

LAUNCHING THE COUNTERATTACK: AMERICAN BUSINESS AND THE CRISIS OF SOCIAL SECURITY

Until 1972, the relationship between American business and the Social Security program had always been an ambivalent one. A number of important business leaders had supported the initial Roosevelt reforms and, according to Derthick, took the lead in pushing through the amendments of 1939 that extended benefits to aged dependents and survivors as well as in urging universal coverage for the aged in 1953 (16). In those sectors of the economy in which strong labor unions were able to demand high corporate pension benefits, many corporate leaders became enthusiastic supporters of the system, seeing in it a means of offsetting corporate labor costs. But throughout most of its history, the dominant strategy of business and conservative critics was not to dismantle Social Security but merely to "hold the line, wherever the line might be at the moment" (16). Until 1965, this was a successful strategy; after 1965, it failed and failed massively. By 1972 the modernization of America's welfare state for the elderly was a *fait accompli*. And throughout the rest of the decade, corporate America set out, in concerted fashion, in an effort to undo the damage. As a result, the "crisis" of Social Security was discovered.

At first glance, it might appear that corporate America had fallen asleep at the wheel during the 1969-72 period, only to reawaken, like Rip Van Winkle, to discover the world had changed in the interlude. In reality, both the transformation of the U.S. Social Security system and the subsequent attack on it correspond to one of the most dramatic turnarounds in class politics in American history. As Derthick points out, the traditional conservative strategy of merely "holding the line" reflects the fact that to "oppose, rather than merely to resist change, would have required internal consensus and considerable organizational effort," a consensus and organizational capacity that was generally absent in postwar corporate America (16). But after 1965, even this capacity to resist popular demands disintegrated. As Edsall demonstrates, during the period after 1965 corporate America was in retreat. The civil rights and anti-war movements made corporate America a special target of their efforts and the consequences of reports of corporate corruption and, finally, Watergate was that "public confidence in the chief executives of major corporations fell like a stone from the mid-1960s to the mid-1970s. The percentage of the public describing themselves as having a great deal of confidence in corporate leaders dropped from 51 percent in the 1966–67 period to an average of 20 percent in the 1974–76 period" (21).

The real weakness of corporate America during this period can be gauged within its own domain as well as in the public sphere. Until 1965, both American labor and American capital had generally adhered to the postwar "social contract" to link wage gains to productivity increases. Indeed, between 1961 and 1965 productivity gains had actually exceeded wage gains for labor. After 1965, however, this relationship was reversed. Between 1966 and 1972 real wages rose 18 percent while productivity rose only 13 percent (22). The result of this changing balance of power was a rise in labor's share of the national income and a profit squeeze (23). The seriousness of this turnaround in the balance of class power in America is indicated by the program of wage controls the Nixon administration introduced in August 1971 to halt the erosion of corporate profits. But what the administration offered with one hand, it withdrew with the other. In the following year, Americans won the largest real increase in their "retirement wages" in the history of the Social Security program.

The seeming contradiction between imposing limits on market wages while simultaneously expanding social wages can be reconciled when we recognize another special feature of the "retirement wage." Whereas any increase in market wages must be paid for immediately, the retirement wage is a deferred wage, an income entitlement to be claimed at some point in the future. The real "Social Security wealth" of the vast majority of Americans was dramatically increased by the reforms of 1972, but only those already retired began to consume that wealth immediately (24). In the short term at least, a deferred wage—a promise to deliver a benefit at some point in the future—provided a non-zero-sum solution to the problem of mounting wage pressure. Workers won real wage gains—because deferred retirement benefits eventually have to be paid—while employers avoided the cost of significant increases in current real wage bills. In the case of the 1972 reforms, these savings were enhanced by the fact that the benefit increases were not accompanied by increases in contribution rates.

The American experience shows a marked resemblance to the pattern of policy reform that emerged during this period in Europe where labor entered into formal agreements with governments to forego increases in market wages in exchange for increases in social wages. A case in point was the British pension reform of 1975, the direct result of an agreement between organized labor and the British government in 1974. Similarly, the Italian reforms of 1969 were the product of a formal truce with labor following three general strikes in 1968–69. While the Nixon reforms of 1972 were passed with an eye to an impending election rather than as part of an effort to bring a powerful labor movement to heel, the logic of reform was similar. In the short term at least, workers/voters could be appeased with expanded social benefits at the same moment that market wages were being subject to restraint.

After 1972, the balance of class power in America began to shift again. As Edsall writes (21):

> During the 1970s, the political wing of the nation's corporate sector staged one of the most remarkable campaigns in the pursuit of political power in recent history. By the late 1970s and the early 1980s, business, and Washington's corporate lobbying community in particular, had gained a level of influence and leverage approaching that of the boom days of the 1920s.

Edsall dates the origins of this mobilization of corporate America to November 1972, when two business organizations whose main purpose was to restrict the influence and bargaining power of organized labor joined to form the Business Roundtable, a policy forum and lobbying agency for America's largest corporations. In the latter half of the 1970s, this mobilization was manifested by the revitalization of the Chamber of Commerce, in which "many of the principals in the formation of the Roundtable participated" (21). What made this revitalization remarkable was not the amount of corporate activity in the political arena but, rather, the content of this activity. Unlike the situation Derthick describes as being typical of an earlier period, business now "refined its ability to act as a class, submerging competitive instincts in favor of joint, cooperative action in the legislative arena" (21). Rather than using up their political capital by competing with one another for a larger share of the government pie, corporations now joined together in the struggle to advance interests they shared in common—defeating consumer protection and labor law reforms, enacting favorable tax legislation, and rolling back America's recently modernized welfare state for the elderly.

Among the most important elements of the attack on social security was the extremely successful effort by corporate America to provide an institutional environment for the development of a conservative, pro-business intelligentsia. With a few notable exceptions (William Buckley, Milton Friedman), a major weakness of American conservatism until the 1970s was the absence of a critical mass of intellectuals, literati, and academics capable of presenting the conservative case in a coherent and persuasive fashion. In fact, the "new class" of America's educated elite was targeted as one of the main enemies of traditional business interests (25). To turn this situation around, business began to put large sums into the creation of think tanks and policy institutes to nurture scholarship and research that could be drawn upon to support its case at all levels of society. These organizations included not only such well-known agencies as the American Enterprise Institute and the National Bureau of Economic Research but also more specialized agencies such as the Employee Benefit Research Institute, which, after its foundation in 1978, poured out hundreds of carefully done analyses demonstrating the problems associated with a publicly financed old age security system and the advantages of shifting responsibility for this activity to the private sector.

Great care was taken to ensure that social security's critics backed up their claims with research that met rigorous academic standards, and that results of this research were disseminated in an appropriate form to a wide range of audiences. The work of Martin Feldstein, director of the National Bureau of Economic Research from 1977 until his appointment in 1982 as chair of President Reagan's Council of Economic Advisors, can usefully serve as an example. In 1974, Feldstein launched a spirited debate in U.S. economic circles with an article based on sophisticated econometric methods demonstrating that social security had reduced the capital stock of America by a dramatic 38 percent since its inception, as a result of its effects on personal savings (26). In the context of the discussions that followed in the late 1970s about the "deindustrialization" of America, a process blamed on America's historically low rate of saving, this was powerful stuff indeed.

To ensure that the message was communicated, various versions of this and similar articles prepared by Feldstein and his associates appeared in the Public Interest, a major disseminator of conservative economic and political views, and in the op-ed pages of America's major newspapers, and they were widely cited in the major articles on social security appearing in the business press (*Forbes, Fortune, Business Week*). In the end, Feldstein's main numbers were shown to be the result of a programming error which, when corrected, suggested (somewhat implausibly) that social security had actually increased the savings rate (27). But what is significant here is the pattern of intellectual production: from learned journal (replete with sophisticated econometric analyses), to political essay (without numbers) for the American literati, to the business press, and, finally, to the mass media. It was a pattern repeated many times in the late 1970s and early 1980s. The claims varied—social security was going broke, social security was a bad buy, social security was too generous—but the pattern of intellectual production and dissemination of ideas did not. By 1981, when the Reagan administration came to power, the "crisis of social security" had successfully penetrated American culture, both high and low. According to Henry Aaron, 80 percent of all Americans were reported to have less than full confidence in Social Security and disillusionment was particularly pronounced among the young (28).

When placed against the backdrop of the actual cycle of policy innovation, on the one hand, and the shifting balance of class forces in the American political economy, on the other, the timing of the attack on Social Security is understandable. But by themselves these factors do not account for the special significance of Social Security in the efforts of corporate America to reassert its dominance after 1972. In the end, most of the claims of the critics were discredited (29). Even Martin Feldstein admitted that so long as the voters were prepared to support it, Social Security could not go broke, and all available evidence suggested that the voters were prepared to do just that (30). In the following section I shall argue that the claims the critics advanced about the long term implications of the social security "debt," while misleading in their emphasis, do point us in the right direction.

CAPITAL, LABOR AND THE RETIREMENT WAGE

The fact that modern welfare states continue to reproduce market-based inequalities is often construed as evidence for the fundamentally "capitalist" character of such provisions. Ironically, however, it was labor, not capital, that provided the political support for the principle of substitutive benefits in the postwar capitalist democracies. As Perrin observes, the first systematic articulation of the substitutive principle is to be found not in the pronouncements of liberal policy reformers but rather in Recommendation 67 passed by the International Labour Organization at its twenty-sixth meeting in Philadelphia in 1944. "Real security" for the worker, Perrin notes, required benefits related to former earnings at a level that would allow the worker and his family to maintain their normal standard of living (3). Demands for a government-sponsored pension program based on the principle of earnings replacement was advocated by the Swedish Labour Organization as early as 1944, by the Canadian Congress of Labour in 1953, and by the British Trade Union Congress in 1957—all in countries where the more egalitarian flat-benefit formula was in place. Perhaps even more instructive is the fact that in these nations the major opponents of any departure from the flat-benefit principle came from the business community (31–33). The great virtues of a flat-benefit system were that it kept benefits low and left untouched the lucrative and growing private pension market among middle and upper income earners.

For labor, the institutionalization of the retirement wage was a victory that went far beyond income security in old age. Embedded in the retirement wage was an achievement that has tended to be devalued by liberal and leftist critics alike—the right to cease working before wearing out. The remarkable fact about old age in the late twentieth century is that while the elderly generally are not allowed to work, neither are they required to do so. And as the opinion polls amply demonstrate, the right not to work in old age is just as important to most workers as the corresponding denial of the right to continue working.

Now in principle, a retirement wage could have been established simply by having the employer or some other market actor retain control over the deferred wage for distribution during the retirement years. And in part, this was precisely what occurred, as witnessed by the dramatic growth of the private pension industry during the postwar period. But for a variety of reasons, governments in all countries quickly nationalized the bulk of this "new industry"; everywhere, responsibility for administering the retirement wage bill was assumed by the state (6). And despite national differences in political ideology and social structure, public pensions are now the major source of income for the retired in all capitalist democracies. This development was an event of enormous significance in the evolution of the distributive practices of these nations. For despite frequent protestations to the contrary, a state-administered pension scheme is not just another big insurance company. Instead, an ever-growing and increasingly important portion of the national wage bill is removed from the market and made subject to a democratic political process, one in which workers, in their capacity as citizens, are able to claim a share of the social product that is independent of any claims they possess in their capacity as wage earners. While a democratic polity may choose to respect the norms of the market—that is to link benefits to contributions—it is by no means constrained to do so and, in general, has not done so. All national pension systems, as they have evolved during the past decades, have incorporated democratic principles of equality, need, and adequacy into their distributive practices; all redistribute income—to a greater or lesser degree—from high wage earners to low wage earners; the majority make allowance for need in the form of supplements for dependent spouses and survivors; and, historically, the majority of countries have legislated increases for the elderly to provide them with a larger share of a growing economic pie. In effect, the retirement wage was transformed into a citizen's wage, an income entitlement partially independent of the commodity value of the worker's labor power. The extent of this transformation varies from country to country, a result of differential levels of working class power inside the state, but the tendency has been universal.

The retirement wage has aided labor in other ways. As Bowles and Gintis observe, the social wage increasingly insulates the working class from the reserve army of the unemployed (34). By absorbing the unemployed the welfare state also absorbs much of the downward pressure on wages that a rise in unemployment would otherwise produce. And among the first to be absorbed in periods of rising unemployment are the elderly: more workers retire and more choose to take advantage of early retirement provisions. Between 1970 and 1979 the labor force participation rate of males aged fifty-five to sixty-four declined from 83 to 73 percent (35).

But the main problem for capital lies in the deferred character of the retirement wage, for unless it can find political or other means to renege on its promises, the deferred wage bill must eventually be paid. Irrespective of how it is financed or whether it is public or private, the cost of today's benefits must ultimately be paid for out of current production, and tomorrow's benefits out of tomorrow's production. The real issue lying behind the trillion dollar Social Security deficit once projected for the next century was not that it could not be paid but, more simply, that it would have to be paid. And irrespective of how it is financed, future benefits promised to today's workers represent real wage costs to employers, a fact that is obvious to any elementary economic or business student exposed to "present value theory."

In short, expanding the retirement wage does not actually reduce the wage bill: it simply pushes an increasing portion of the wage bill into the future. And as it expands, so too does the portion of future real wage costs that are fixed in advance.

In the language of marxian economics, a portion of variable capital is in fact no longer variable, and the capacity of capital as a whole to manipulate the total wage bill (market wages + social wages) in response to changing economic conditions is increasingly constrained. This represents a fundamental change in the social character of the capitalist allocation process.

Under capitalism, as Przeworski observes, the trade-off between current wages and current profits is a societal trade-off that affects everyone (36). Future wage gains are as dependent as future profits on the retention and reinvestment of today's profits. But, Przeworski argues, the actual allocation of increases in the social product created by reinvesting today's profits is, in principle, indeterminate. It may be returned to labor in the form of wage gains, consumed by capital, or exported elsewhere: there is "nothing structural" in the capitalist system that determines this allocation in advance. The advent of the retirement wage bill, however, changes all this. The institutionalization and expansion of the retirement wage in the capitalist democracies mean that the allocation of wealth to be produced in the future is increasingly fixed in advance. And, indeed, actuaries and economists have been busy generating estimates of this fixed portion of tomorrow's wage bill well into the next century. As a *New York Times* article observed, defined benefit plans are "a blank check against corporate assets" (37). In short, the rules of the allocation process under capitalism are changed. In terms of traditional market principles, a growing share of the national economy is "out of control."

Now it is important to recognize that securing the future incomes of the elderly in this way poses no inherent problem so long as other sectors of the economy are similarly secured. And, indeed, it was just such long-term stabilization of markets, for both labor and capital, that the Keynesian system of macro-regulation had provided the American economy during the preceding decades. The emergence of this system of market stabilization and its demise during the 1970s have been thoroughly documented elsewhere (38). Suffice it to say that by the early 1970s, a whole series of shocks and transformations in the national and international economies were signalling that these conventional mechanisms for long-term market stabilization were breaking down. With inflation and unemployment rising together, Keynesianism was losing its force.

A key element of this macro-regulatory structure was the welfare state itself. It had been intended not merely to stabilize the "wages" of the elderly and the poor, but also to provide a counter-cyclical stimulus that would stabilize the economy as a whole by sustaining demand during economic downturns. In sum, stabilizing wages, whether for active or retired workers, was acceptable so long as this served to stabilize corporate profits as well. When it appeared that wage stabilization was no longer serving to stabilize long-term corporate profits, the *raison d'etre* of these mechanisms disappeared, and indeed they became counter-productive. In the language that began to emerge during this period, welfare and efficiency could no longer be construed as compatible principles of economic organization (39).

Thus, the modernization of America's welfare state for the elderly occurred at almost the same moment when the system of macro-regulation for the economy that could legitimate such a program was beginning to break down. And Social Security was all the more visible a target due to its uniqueness within the American welfare state structure. Within this context the special significance that Social Security acquired in the conservative offensive becomes understandable. The future incomes of today's workers had been secured—that is what income security means—while future profits had not. The projected increase of America's elderly population simply exacerbated this problem. From the point of view of corporate America, a growing share of the national income was "out of control," and the problem would become even more severe in the future. Accordingly, the wages of the elderly, like the wages of the young, would have to be subjected to the rigors of market disciplines once again and be returned to the private sector.

CONCLUSION

If the attack on Social Security was successful in generating widespread alarm about the long-term viability of the system, it was less successful in achieving its objectives. American public opinion proved remarkably resistant to demands that the system be dismantled or significantly cut back. In 1981, Louis Harris polls showed the majority of Americans thought government should be doing more for America's elderly and were prepared to pay higher taxes to ensure the viability of the program (30). As a result, the Reagan administration was forced to back away from the more radical proposals that had been advanced to "save" the system. In the United States, as elsewhere, the modern welfare state that constructs broad political coalitions between lower and middle income earners has proven to be highly resistant to such direct assault. But resistance also points to the fact that the long-term viability of Social Security depends less on demographic developments than on the viability of the political coalitions that sustain it.

The attack on Social Security demonstrated that the "modern welfare state," one that incorporates a broad section of the middle classes as well as the poor, cannot easily be dismantled. It is less certain, however, that it is immune to a long-term process of slow erosion. Cuts were made during the first term of the Reagan administration, and, though modest, the cumulation of many such small "adjustments" can seriously erode the program over the longer term. This, after all, was how America's modern system of retirement wages was constructed—through a series of incremental changes to the base established in 1935. This, as Derthick (16) has pointed out, was a deliberate strategy of American policy reformers. There is nothing to prevent those who would dismantle the welfare state from adopting a similar strategy.

REFERENCES

1. *Forbes*, May 26, 1980.
2. Myles, J. The trillion dollar misunderstanding. *Working Papers for a New Society* 8: 22–31, 1981.
3. Perrin, G. Reflections on fifty years of social security. *Int. Labour Rev.* 99: 249–290, 1969.
4. Conrad, C. Aging with a minimum of property: The lower middle class and working classes of Cologne, 1830–1930. Paper presented at the annual meetings of the American Historical Association, Washington, D. C., p. 16, December 1982.
5. Heclo, H. *Modern Social Politics in Britain and Sweden: From Relief to Income Maintenance.* Yale University Press, New Haven, Connecticut, 1974.
6. Myles, J. *Old Age in the Welfare State*, Chapter 1. Little Brown, Boston, 1984.
7. Rainwater, L., Rein, M., and Schwartz, J. *Income Packaging and the Welfare State: A Comparative Study of Family Income.* Oxford University Press, 1985.
8. Hedstrom, P., and Ringen, S. *Age and Income in Contemporary Society: A Comparative Study.* Swedish Institute for Social Research, Stockholm, 1985.
9. Ikenberry, J., and Skocpol, T. From patronage democracy to social security: The shaping of public social provision in the United States. In *Stagnation and Renewal*, edited by Esping-Anderson, G., Rainwater, L., Rein, M., and M. E. Sharpe. Armonk, New York (forthcoming).
10. Tomasson, R. Government old age pensions under affluence and austerity: West Germany, Sweden, The Netherlands, and the United States. Paper presented at the meetings of the Xth World Congress of the International Sociological Association, Mexico City, 1982.
11. Ikenberry, J., and Skocpol, T. The political formation of the American welfare state in historical and comparative perspective. In *Comparative Social Research*, edited by R. Tomasson, pp. 87–148. JAI Press, Greenwich, Connecticut, 1983.
12. Beveridge, W. H. *Social Insurance and Allied Services*, pp. 6–7. MacMillan, New York, 1942.
13. Beveridge, W. H. *Full Employment in a Free Society*, p. 69. W. W. Norton, New York, 1945.
14. Graebner, W. *A History of Retirement*, p. 184. Yale University Press, New Haven, Connecticut, 1980.
15. Quadagno, J. Welfare capitalism and the Social Security Act of 1935. Paper prepared for the annual meetings of the American Sociological Association, San Antonio, Texas, p. 9, 1984.
16. Derthick, M. *Public Policy for Social Security*, p. 26. The Brookings Institution, Washington, D.C., 1978.
17. Schulz, J., et al. *Providing Adequate Retirement Income: Pension Reform in the United States and Abroad*, p. 8. University Press of England, Hanover, New Hampshire, 1974.
18. Pampel, F. Changes in the labor force participation and income of the aged in the United States, 1947–1976. *Soc. Prob.* 27: 135, 1979.
19. Haanes-Olsen, L. Earnings-replacement rate of old age benefits, 1965–75, selected countries. *Soc. Sec. Bull.* pp. 3–14, January 1978.

20. Aldrich, J. Earnings replacement rates of old-age benefits in 12 countries, 1969–80. *Soc. Sec. Bull.* 45: 3–11, 1982.

21. Edsall, T. *The New Politics of Inequality*, p. 113. W. W. Norton, New York, 1984.

22. Scheible, P. Changes in employee compensation, 1966 to 1972. *Monthly Labor Rev.* 98: 10–16, 1975.

23. Bowles, S., Gordon, D., and Weisskopf, T. *Beyond the Wasteland: A Democratic Alternative to Economic Decline*, p. 103. Doubleday, Garden City, New York, 1983.

24. Feldstein, M., and Pellechio, A. Social Security wealth: The impact of alternative inflation adjustments. In *Financing Social Security*, edited by C. Campbell, pp. 91–118. American Enterprise Institute, Washington, 1979.

25. Bruce-Briggs, B. *The New Class?* Transaction Books, New Brunswick, New Jersey, 1979.

26. Feldstein, M. Social security, induced retirement and aggregate capital formation. *J. Pol. Econ.* 82: 905–926, 1974.

27. Leimer, D., and Lesnoy, S. Social security and private saving: New time-series evidence. *J. Pol. Econ.* 90: 606–642, 1982.

28. Aaron, H. Advisory report on Social Security. *Challenge*, pp. 12–16, March/April 1980.

29. Aaron, H. *Economic Effects of Social Security*. The Brookings Institution, Washington, D.C., 1982.

30. *Louis Harris Survey of the Aged*. Employee Benefit Research Institute, Washington, D.C., 1981.

31. Esping-Andersen, G. *Politics Against Markets*. Princeton University Press, Princeton, New Jersey, 1985.

32. Menzies, A. The Netherlands. In *Pensions, Inflation and Growth*, edited by T. Wilson, pp. 110–154. Heinemann, London, 1974.

33. Murphy, B. Corporate capital and the welfare state: Canadian business and public pension policy in Canada since World War II. Unpublished master's thesis, Carleton University, Ottawa, 1982.

34. Bowles, S., and Gintis, H. The crisis of liberal democratic capitalism: The case of the United States. *Pol. and Soc.* 11: 51–93, 1982.

35. Clark, R., and Barker, D. *Reversing the Trend Toward Early Retirement*, p. 13. American Enterprise Institute, Washington, 1982.

36. Przeworski, A. Material bases of consent: Economics and politics in a hegemonic system. *Pol. Power and Soc. Theory* 1: 21–66, 1980.

37. Rankin, D. The fading of the fixed pension plan. *New York Times*, p. F-15, March 20, 1983.

38. Piore, M., and Sabel, C. *The Second Industrial Divide*. Basic Books, New York, 1984.

39. Geiger, T., and Geiger, F. *Welfare and Efficiency*. MacMillan, London, 1978.

CHAPTER 19

DEPENDENCY AMONG THIRD WORLD ELDERLY: A NEED FOR NEW DIRECTION IN THE NINETIES

Sheila M. Neysmith

The last decade has witnessed increasing efforts among researchers in aging to examine systematically the social conditions of old people as a reflection of their relationship to the economy, the state, and the family. The emerging political economy of aging, however, has focused largely on the conditions of old people in western industrialized societies and thus has neglected the situation of more than half of the world's elderly—those residing in Third World nations (1).

A political economy approach to aging in the Third World would consider such issues as the nature of the economic relationships that bind advanced industrialized countries to Third World nations. These relationships help determine who grows old, the social existence of the old, the nature of state policy for the old, and the forms of assistance that developed nations offer Third World countries to meet the needs of an aging population (2).

In largely ignoring the phenomenon of aging in Third World countries, researchers have also missed important opportunities for comparative studies concerning, for example, the phenomenon in both Third World and advanced industrial countries of the large unpaid labor and personal costs borne by women as the caregivers of the old.

This chapter examines aging trends in the Third World and considers three recent approaches to addressing the deteriorating economic and social conditions that shape the lives of the elderly in these countries. In the last section, questions are raised about a position emerging in some of the development literature that advocates encouraging families, through such measures as tax deductions, housing benefits, and even legislation, to continue their traditional function of providing for their dependent members (1). The argument is made herein that families are unable to assume such responsibilities, not only due to a lack of resources, but because such policies are based on images of shared familial obligation and responsibility that do not correspond to reality.

AGING IN THIRD WORLD COUNTRIES

As noted above, the effects of an aging population continue to be seen as an issue primarily for industrialized nations, since less than 6 percent of the population is over sixty in most Third World countries. However, as Table 1 illustrates, 52 percent of the world's population aged sixty and above is living already in Third World countries, and this proportion will rise to over seventy percent by the year 2025. The proportion will grow more slowly in some regions, like Africa (only 6.1%) and Latin America (12.4%), and rapidly in others, like Oceania (18%) and East Asia (19.3%), reflecting the fact that the latter regions are "developing" more rapidly than the former (1).

Such numbers suggest that to think of the elderly as residents of developed countries is to ignore the demographic location of the majority of the world's older population. Because most gerontological research and writing continues to occur in and be focused on industrialized countries, the problems posed, the questions asked, the causes and explanations considered, and the social policies and programs designed are marginal to the needs of the majority of the world's aging peoples.

Since the World Assembly on Aging in 1982, there has been increased data gathering—albeit mainly at the descriptive level—and international discussions

Table 1

Population aged 60 and over, 1950-2025, the more developed regions
and the less developed regions (thousands)

Age	1950	1975	1985	2000	2025
More Developed Regions					
60+	94,559	166,423	185,948	234,563	329,534
	(47)	(48)	(44)	(39)	(28)
60–69	55,909	93,675	93,426	120,057	166,860
	(43)	(44)	(38)	(35)	(25)
70+	38,650	72,748	92,522	114,506	162,674
	(52)	(53)	(51)	(44)	(32)
Less Developed Regions					
60+	107,752	181,299	241,344	374,130	841,842
	(53)	(52)	(56)	(61)	(72)
60–69	72,709	117,690	151,643	226,666	503,686
	(57)	(56)	(62)	(65)	(75)
70+	35,043	63,609	89,701	147,464	338,156
	(48)	(47)	(49)	(56)	(68)

Note: Figures in parentheses are percentages of the world total.

focusing on the experience of the Third World elderly (e.g., 3–6; also, the U.N. Trust Fund for Aging has sponsored regional meetings on aging in developing countries). However, existing policies and programs often continue to rely on models imported from North America and Europe. Not surprisingly, Third World planners who are studying the needs of their aging populations are finding that the available research and policy models designed for advanced industrialized nations are ill equipped to address the needs of Third World countries.

As in industrialized nations, some elderly persons in Third World countries are doing very well. Others, due to gender, class, and race discrimination, are in an extremely vulnerable position. Deteriorating social and economic conditions in many countries during the 1980s have aggravated this vulnerability. The external environment has been constrained; for example, world commodity prices have reached some of their lowest levels since World War II. The per capita income in many countries either grew less or fell more rapidly than their per capita Gross Domestic Product (7, 8). The refinancing of debt has meant major cuts in domestic spending, with the Latin American and African regions being the hardest hit.

Such trends have affected disproportionately such vulnerable groups as the elderly (9, 10). Poor countries and poor groups within them have the least options for repositioning themselves when external and internal pressures mount. Warnings began to be raised in the late seventies that the focus of international money markets on short-term economic adjustments distracted from the fact that the development of *human* resources should be the primary concern of development policy. A preoccupation with increases in per capita income or cost cutting tends to confuse economic indicators, *a means*, with *an end*, improvement in the quality of people's lives.

Such a preoccupation has implications for development strategies. For example, although health care has been protected in some countries as growth has declined, how such scarce resources are used needs to be scrutinized. There is now considerable evidence showing that monies put into primary health care reap returns that similar amounts put into hospitals do not—yet there continues to be a bias toward an institutionally based model of health care delivery. This pattern is repeated in many international aid efforts. A recent U.N. document noted (9, pp. 34–35):

> It is widely believed that expenditure on human development programmes is either distributionally neutral or discriminatory in favour of the poor. This view, however, is not generally correct. *The major beneficiaries of human development programmes tend to be males, households in large urban areas, and people with middle or higher incomes.* Females, residents in rural areas and those with relatively low incomes benefit proportionately less. This is due in part to "urban bias" in the provision of services, in part to a failure, for cultural and sociological reasons, on the part of some of the intended beneficiaries to use the public services and facilities that are provided, but above all to a pattern of unequal subsidies among programmes that effectively favours upper income groups (emphasis added).

The above assessment suggests that gender, class, and race disparities exist in all countries and are probably more important than age per se as determiners of the quality of life, whether one lives in the development or developed world. Thus, our understanding of the political and economic underpinnings of these structures is pivotal in assessing which subgroups of the elderly are in jeopardy.

THE IMPACT OF ASSUMPTIONS IN DEVELOPMENT THEORY

The documentation of virtual economic stagnation, debt load, military dictatorships, and wars fueled by nationalism and/or fundamentalism has resulted in a continuing critique of development theories. The modernization paradigm paramount in the fifties and sixties envisioned Third World countries following a path similar to that of advanced capitalist countries. Economic and cultural penetration was seen as furthering modernization: as knowledge, skills, organization, values, technology, and capital diffused into poor nations, these inputs would become, over time, variants of those that made the Western community economically successful. This traditional-modern dichotomy was later transformed by Rostow into a theory of stages of economic growth (2, 11).

Such theories came under attack in the 1970s, particularly by Latin American theorists who argued that the capitalist development of the now developed countries engendered the underdeveloped structures in today's Third World and continues to reproduce them. Such writers, known variously as *dependistas*, structuralists, marxists, and/or world systems theorists, have been subjected to a fairly severe grilling during the 1980s. (For a short review of the strengths and weaknesses of these perspectives see 12; for a more sympathetic assessment see 11, especially Chaps. 6 and 7.) The critical weaknesses are summarized by Kay (11, pp. 195–196):

> By overstressing the dependency relationship, dependency analysis provided a convenient scapegoat for the development problems of Third World countries. Imperialism and the dominant countries are held to have generated them in the first instance and to be responsible for their continuance. This creates a distorted historical picture of conditions in the pre-independence period, which is explicitly or implicitly idealized and seen as unproblematic. Second, by underemphasizing the internal causes of underdevelopment, dependency analysis pays insufficient attention to the class contradictions and obstacles to development within the country. Third, dependency analysis fosters the "autonomist" illusion that if only the ties of dependence could be cut, all would be well. . . . As dependency is seen as the source of the problem it is small wonder that *dependistas* are bereft of concrete policy proposals for development. Thus, dependency analysis has few specific proposals for raising the rate of economic growth, improving the distribution of income, diversifying exports, generating employment, reducing social inequalities, removing racial and sexual discrimination, and so on. By thinking in terms of a new international order, they underestimate the room for maneuvering within countries. It is an all or nothing scheme.

SHIFTING TO AN INTERNAL FOCUS

Although the responses to these criticisms put much more emphasis on the human aspects of development than is found in classic development theory, there are important differences among them. One response, well-exemplified in the UNICEF document *Adjustment with a Human Face* (10), argues for the need to protect vulnerable groups, including the elderly, while promoting economic growth. Although humanitarian reasons for such an approach are self-evident, the report emphasizes that there are also strong economic reasons for such a focus. The evidence presented shows that development actually ceased during the 1980s as Third World countries grappled with economic adjustment. The goal, therefore, according to proponents of this "human face" perspective, is to get development going again, but with the caveat that restructuring that does not protect groups like children, mothers, and the elderly, is not enough. These analysts consciously take a macro focus because they are directing their recommendations to policymakers. However, the former argue further that adjustment with a human face also must include: more expansionary macro-economic policies; the use of meso-level policies; sectoral policies aimed at restructuring within the productive sector; improving the equity and efficiency of the social sector; and compensatory programs (10, pp. 290–291).

A second type of response to the macro bias of dependency theory has been a rediscovering of microsystems. Urban populations in shantytowns have become centers for local-level organizations designed to meet the needs of the elderly and other vulnerable groups, e.g., children, women, and the disabled. Nongovernmental organizations (NGOs), using the principles of popular education and liberation theology, have built on the existing networks of support found wherever daily living is precarious (13). Probably the best known examples of such projects are in the areas of primary health care, food production in rural areas and marketing within the informal economy, most of which focus on and are organized by local groups of women. As will be suggested below, the obvious advantages of this perspective can hide assumptions about the unpaid labor women are expected to provide in caring for others.

Theorists of the human scale development school see micro-level networks as critical seeds for development. They focus on internal production rather than goods and services that are geared to export, since the latter depend on the vagaries of external demand and are usually heavily capitalized, with much of the profit going to foreign owners. Resultant growth has not touched the masses of poor or led to policies of redistribution. Most assessments agree that such growth has contributed to greater inequalities *within* countries, as well as failed to develop the internal markets for local products that are essential to long-term development (14–16).

The existence of dependencies is not questioned by human scale development theorists, but is seen as coming in a variety of forms—economic, financial, technological, cultural, and political—and as operating on local, regional, national, and international levels. Thus, the new problem is to understand the differing patterns of and spaces within which dependency occurs from country to country.

Much of the above literature refers to invisible sectors which make up the subhistory of everyday life. Traditional survival and productive strategies are seen as having emerged within a cultural context which must be respected and considered in subsequent development efforts. As a prelude to arguing for a strengthening of micro organizations, proponents of human scale development note that such enterprises currently fill in where capitalism has left gaps. Since rewards are meager, the work is done by marginal groups—women, children, the old, and the disabled.

This changing script, however, has allowed women to enter the social development drama. One is tempted to conclude that an analytical shift to the micro level made ignoring the labor of women more difficult. Women care for the children, the ill and disabled, and the elderly. In addition, women are the main actors in small local economies of selling and trading in goods and services, or of food production in the rural areas. At a minimum, a focus on women in development delegitimized an earlier perspective that saw the main "problem" of women as being their lack of involvement in the otherwise beneficial process of growth and development (15).

After the role of women as primary providers came into view, a male-centered paradigm left too much unexplained. Thus, in the 1980s, development theory on the left and right had to grapple with accusations that its macro perspective did not fit micro experiences and, further, that its male assumptions ignored the labor of half the world's population. The question remains, however, whether these new perspectives will be able to address their own criticisms and marry praxis to theory.

Most Third World countries, unfortunately, have patterns of patriarchal attitudes and privilege structures as deeply engrained as those found in industrialized nations (17). These patterns are the basis for assumptions behind current economic and social policy, and their effects are only beginning to be documented in the development literature. The slowness of the process is not surprising when one considers the conceptual and methodological barriers that faced feminist analyses in Europe and America. A large part of the job is rendering discrimination processes visible, giving them a name so that they can be described. Only after this visibility is conferred is it possible to undertake analysis and to debate alternative possibilities. The centrality of women in micro rather than macro organizations partially explains their historical invisibility in development theory.

The necessity of micro-macro articulation for long-term change has not gone unnoticed. There is a danger, however, that local-level efforts can get isolated from larger development plans. On the one hand, isolation may lead to cooptation. On the other, it can result in an approach that favors people in the micro social realm while perpetuating in the larger realm an order that excludes the mass of people and, eventually, reduces this alternative to a mere idea that cannot be widely implemented (16).

This possibility does not seem to be such a dilemma for those focusing on women in development. Part of the explanation is that the contradictions inherent in micro-macro relations—the public world of paid labor and the private world of unpaid labor, and family-state tensions—are dualisms with which feminists are constantly grappling and which they bring together conceptually in expressions like "the personal *is* political." Feminist theory and practice suggests that gender, confounded by class, race, and age inequities, will result in development continuing to be uneven both within and between countries and regions. Perhaps the most we can expect is a commitment both nationally and internationally to putting in place a process that will facilitate rather than block, that will include rather than exclude what UNICEF has referred to as vulnerable groups, among them the elderly. Within this process, some cooptation, inequities, and failures are to be expected. Fortunately, however, experience suggests that even so, some pathways are opened that did not exist before. At a minimum, priorities get rearranged, issues get redefined, and the agenda is modified as different players bring in new themes. Over time, a new discourse takes shape; new standards emerge for deciding what is fair and just.

REDEFINING WHAT IS JUST

Minkler and Cole note in Chapter 3 that whether we are examining the experience of the elderly in advanced capitalist or socialist nations or in Third World countries, shared moral assumptions about reciprocity and fairness, and collective visions of what is due the old, should form an integral part of the database. Concepts of reciprocity, altruism, and community appear with regularity in the social welfare and gerontology literatures. Studying peasant societies, writers like Scott (18) and Kohli (19) point out that, although past relationships should not be romanticized, they ensured that people had the minimum. The moral economy of the subsistence ethic dictated that all members of a community had a right to a living, as local resources permitted, including sufficient provisions to carry out such culturally dictated roles as caring for elderly parents (18). Such economies were embedded in a web of social relationships expressed as reciprocal and moral obligations. However, even in this literature on the peasant's moral economy, obligation and claims to resources are discussed at the household level. Issues of distribution within the household are absent, a point to be discussed below.

Although capitalist economies are embedded in their own moral economies, the concept has yet to be widely applied to the study of these countries (see Chapters 3 and 17). Moreover, as Hendricks and Leedham note (Chapter 4) societal assumptions concerning what is due the old sometimes conflict with the ethos of individualism prevalent in market economies. The latter ethos gives rise to new forms of moral economy grounded in exchange value which devalue both the old and caregiving for the old. Assumptions about supportive families contained in modern rhetoric about responsibility of the family versus that of the state are instructive, and differ importantly from the social norms and obligations worked out in peasant societies. Elder advocates argue today that a "responsive community services system" must recognize changing family structures if the goal of maintaining elders in the community is to be achieved in a fair and equitable manner.

As suggested in Chapter 15, current formulations of state/family obligation that consider the family as a unit with sole or primary responsibility for its aged members may be unjust. North American and European literature documents the depth and breadth of familial obligation borne by women. Even in advanced welfare states, the work load is heavy and carried almost exclusively by women as unpaid kin carers, low-paid service personnel, and volunteers. As the costs to women have become more visible, a different set of equity questions is being asked (20–23).

Feminist scholarship can inform planners in both developed and developing countries about the domestic scene, the worlds of paid and unpaid labor, and how the state and family act out their respective parts. In policies and programs focused on the needs of the old, as in other areas, reforms will be isolated unless micro-macro connections become central rather than peripheral to our analyses. A micro-macro view would result in revolutionary structural changes in relationships among the private and public spheres. Since both modernization and dependency theories center on economic relations, neither is able to comprehend the ways in which this micro-macro perspective is fundamental (23, p. 175).

> However important are questions of resources, distribution of wealth and ownership, it is the logic implanted in the organization and assumptions of wage work itself which is in growing contradiction with social needs, a contradiction which has always existed but has to a larger extent been absorbed by women. . . . The presence of women in production reveals that *neither equality nor liberation is possible whether under capitalism or socialism, unless the world of work, the domestic sphere, and the relation between state and social needs are transformed* (emphasis added).

CONCLUSION

In a recent paper, Clark and Filinson (24) examined social security expenditures in seventy-five core, peripheral, and semiperipheral countries over a twenty-year period, using variables that both modernization and dependency theory would suggest are important. A growing gross national product (GNP) seems to be basic. Regions with a history of social welfare programs, (e.g., Latin America) and with foreign investment that uses educated urban workers rather than the extraction of natural resources seemed most associated with expanding social security. Figures presented above indicate that these conditions deteriorated in many Third World countries during the 1980s. Such trends do not bode well for the growing number of persons over sixty in these regions in the next decade.

The position developed in this chapter sees a renegotiated social contract between the development and developing worlds as setting a different stage. Such a realignment will open up possibilities for Third World countries to build infrastructures that can meet human need. However, even a renegotiated social contract cannot touch well-entrenched class and gender barriers. Therefore, vulnerable groups including the poor, women, children and the elderly will continue to suffer. Micro-level development approaches seem to have a greater potential in this regard. They focus on the actors using the material conditions of their daily lives as the starting point for social analysis.

The emergence of dependency theory in the seventies, whatever its shortcomings, forced policymakers to recognize that relations between developed and developing countries are pivotal. The causes and consequences of underdevelopment are as much a responsibility of developed as of developing countries.

Less explicit in this dependency perspective, however, was the realization that development takes place within the context of a constantly changing set of national and international events. Thus, the changing face of Eastern Europe will influence development possibilities in the 1990s as surely as world commodity prices did in the 1980s.

In the next decade, we can expect important questions to be raised about the ability of socialism, as well as capitalism, to meet the needs of people. However these are all macro-level dynamics. At any moment in history they set the stage, even dictate the scenes within which players must construct their parts. But no matter how restrictive the set, more than one script is possible.

A potential pitfall for development in the 1990s lies in getting caught at this level—failing to connect personal experience to the social structures that maintain the disadvantaged positions of vulnerable groups, including the low-income elderly and women as unpaid caregivers for the old. I argued that the history of the women's movement and experience with international projects focusing on women offer some optimism. Actors do not remain unchanged when problems are viewed as socially, not personally, constructed.

This chapter has focused on vulnerable groups within Third World nations, including the elderly. The concerns raised in the pages above will affect primarily the elderly who are poor and/or female. By viewing the population profiles of developing countries as another version of the "aging crisis" "discovered" earlier in Europe and North America, the truly vulnerable groups will remain invisible.

Even less defensible would be a continued deployment of scarce resources to favor national elites as social security and health care programs frequently do. Likewise, policies that place the locus of responsibility for care of the elderly within the family will be as unfair in Third World countries as they have proven to be in Europe and North America. A political economy perspective on aging, and related attention to the moral economy assumptions underlying current policies and practices affecting the old, can help to highlight some of the inequities and contradictions raised in this chapter. By rendering more visible the needs of Third World elders, their unpaid caregivers, and other vulnerable groups, such a perspective can further illuminate fruitful policy directions for helping to overcome some of these problems.

REFERENCES

1. United Nations. Department of International Economic and Social Affairs. *Economic and Social Implications of Population Aging.* United Nations, New York, 1988.
2. Neysmith, S., and Edwardh J. Economic dependency in the 1980's: Its impact on Third World elderly. *Ageing and Soc.* 4(1): 21–44, 1984.
3. Hampson, J. Elderly people and social welfare in Zimbabwe. *Ageing and Soc.* 5(1): 39–67, 1985.
4. Brathwaite, F. The elderly in the commonwealth Caribbean: A review of research findings. *Ageing and Soc.* 9(3): 297–304, 1989.
5. Andrews, G., Esterman, A., Brounack-Mayer, A., and Rungie, C. *Aging in the Western Pacific: A Four Country Study.* World Health Organization, Manila, Philippines, 1986.
6. Brown, C. Aging in Swaziland: Accentuating the positive. *Social Development Issues.* 12(1): 56–70, 1988.
7. United Nations. Department of International Economic and Social Affairs. *Development Under Siege: Constraints and Opportunities in a Changing Global Economy.* United Nations, New York, 1987.
8. The World Bank. *World Development Report 1989.* Oxford University Press, New York, 1989.
9. United Nations. Department of International Economic and Social Affairs. *Human Resources Development: A Neglected Dimension of Development Strategy.* United Nations, New York, 1988.
10. Cornia, G., Jolly, R., and Stewart, F. *Adjustment With a Human Face: Protecting the Vulnerable and Promoting Growth.* Vol. 1. A Study by UNICEF. Clarendon Press, Oxford, 1987.
11. Kay, C. *Latin American Theories of Development and Underdevelopment.* Routledge, London and New York, 1989.
12. Browett, J. Out of the dependency perspective. In *Neo-Marxist Theories of Development,* edited by P. Limqueco and B. McFarlane. Croom Helm, London and Canberra, 1983.
13. Campfens, H. Forces shaping the new social work in Latin America. *Can. Soc. Work Rev.* 5(Winter): 9–27, 1988.
14. United Nations. Department of International and Social Affairs. *The World Aging Situation: Strategies and Policies.* United Nations, New York, 1985.
15. Sen, G., and Grown, C. *Development, Crises, and Alternative Visions: Third World Women's Perspectives.* Monthly Review Press, New York, 1987.
16. Max-Neef, M., Elizalde, A., and Hopenhayn, M. Human scale development: An option for the future. *Development Dialogue* 1: 1–80, 1989.
17. Rogers, B. *The Domestication of Women: Discrimination in Developing Societies.* Tavistock Publications, London, 1980.

18. Scott, J. *The Moral Economy of the Peasant: Rebellion and Subsistence in Southeast Asia.* Yale University Press, New Haven and London, 1976.
19. Kohli, M. Retirement and the moral economy: An historical interpretation of the German case. *Journal of Aging Studies* 1(2): 125–144, 1987.
20. Dalley, C. *Ideologies of Caring: Rethinking Community and Collectivism.* Macmillan, London, 1988.
21. Finch, J. *Family Obligation and Social Change.* Polity Press, London, 1989.
22. Ungerson, C. *Policy is Personal: Sex, Gender, and Informal Care.* Tavistock Publications, London and New York, 1987.
23. Showstack Sassoon, A. (ed.). *Women and the State: The Shifting Boundaries of Public and Private.* Hutchison, London, 1987.
24. Clark, R., and Filinson, R. Multinational Corporate Penetration, Industrialism, Region and Social Security Expenditures: A Cross-National Analysis. Paper presented at the annual meetings of the Canadian Association on Gerontology. Ottawa, Canada, October 1989.

PART VII. CONCLUSION

Woven throughout this volume are concepts of the needs of the economy and the primacy of politics as they shape policies and programs for the old. There is a growing need for policies that address broad structural inequities and human needs across generations. In Chapter 20, Shindul-Rothschild and Williamson forecast prospects for U.S. policy reform in the areas of aging and health. The authors base their analysis on a political economy perspective with attention to moral economy notions of fairness in resource allocation, as these are reflected in policy history, and changing perceptions about the aged and the diversity of the population. An optimistic review of possible alternatives to balance particularistic and universalistic reform measures is provided. The authors argue that although expensive new social programs are unlikely to be initiated, the sustained collective action of the elderly in concert with other disadvantaged groups may be able to prompt just and cost-effective solutions to health and social problems across the life course.

The Epilogue proposes an intellectual project to address the questions raised in this volume. Acknowledging the contradictions and tensions between capital and democracy and between polities and people, this section calls for a critical examination of the social and cultural production of aging on which theory and praxis may be reasonably based. Such critical theory and theory-based action in turn should be aimed at meeting human needs across the life course including, importantly, the need for a higher quality and more meaningful old age.

CHAPTER 20

Future Prospects for Aging Policy Reform

Judith Shindul-Rothschild and John B. Williamson

In this chapter, we analyze the prospects for future public policy gains for the elderly. The policy shift to the right in recent years leads many scholars to believe it more appropriate to discuss where the least harmful cuts in spending on programs for the aged could be made. However, we do not anticipate major additional cutbacks, even though there will certainly be continued efforts to slow the rate of increase in spending on many programs. If the assumption that the most severe cuts have already been made is correct, it is reasonable to ask whether there may even be policy gains for the elderly in the foreseeable future.

The political realities of the current era, however, are reflected in our attention to such issues as cost containment, discussing how it can be managed to minimize the negative impact of the elderly. Before analyzing public policy reforms currently being debated, it is useful to review some of the factors that contributed to the public policy gains made by the elderly during the 1960s and 1970s and to the lack of such gains during the 1980s.

THE ECONOMY AND THE ELDERLY ELECTORATE

When Medicare and Medicaid were enacted in the 1960s, and mandatory cost-of-living adjustments (COLA) were added to the 1972 Social Security Amendments, policymakers and politicians alike were narrowly addressing issues of equity and access. The policy preference was for universalistic programs with the goal providing benefits to as many of the aged as possible, but particularistic in focus on programs for the elderly to the exclusion of other age groups. This approach was influenced by political as well as philosophical considerations. At that time, because the plight of the elderly was beyond question and the perceived strength of the elderly electorate was considerable, opponents dared not risk engaging in open conflict with America's senior citizens (1, 2). Means tests were also avoided because stereotyping and stigmatization were assumed to occur if eligibility criteria singled out a particular group for assistance (2). Finally, with America's economy at its height of productivity, relatively little attention was given to the long-run costs of these programs.

During the 1970s, the economy deteriorated and one consequence by the end of the decade was a shift to a less generous assessment of the worthiness of the elderly. By the mid-1970s, reports began to refute the perception that large numbers of the elderly were impoverished (3, 4). Although the median income of the elderly relative to other age groups had increased only modestly, when in-kind benefits were considered, the standard of living for the aged had improved substantially over the decade of the 1970s (5, 6). Fairly typical was a study by Brotman (7) which reported in the mid-1970s that 14 percent of persons over age sixty-five were in poverty. A Congressional Budget Office study reduced this estimate to 6 percent after considering in-kind government transfers (8).

In the past decade, a growing controversy has surrounded the formerly unquestioned "deserving status" of the elderly. The controversy has arisen largely due to reports that the number of aged in poverty has steadily declined over the past twenty-five years while the number of children or young families in poverty has risen. This trend suggests that the entitlement programs implemented in the 1960s and 1970s that have been so successful in creating a middle-class of elderly Americans in the 1980s, may receive less broad public support in the 1990s.

Increasingly, the ability of the elderly to maintain visibility for their economic concerns has been separated from their ability to actually wield political power. Groups like the National Council of Senior Citizens (NCSC) continue to be quite successful at persuading legislators to support income-maintenance programs, mobilizing their membership, and targeting key legislators for direct contact (9). But, in general, elderly organizations including the National Council of Senior Citizens, the American Association of Retired Persons (AARP), and the National Association of Retired Federal Employees (NARFE) tend to focus their efforts solely on Social Security and Medicare, rather than Medicaid or other programs of benefits to the indigent aged (10).

A close look at voter polls and studies of the attitudes of the elderly towards public policies suggests that on issues other than those involving direct economic benefit, the elderly could hardly be described as a cohesive constituency. Particularly on issues such as abortion and racial integration, voting behavior of the elderly follows traditional party and demographic voting patterns. The inability of aging organizations to redress the problems of the disadvantaged or frail elderly and the clear absence of bloc voting behavior by aged Americans have led some authors to conclude that there is little possibility the elderly will ever fully develop into a strong, viable political constituency (11, 12).

The increasing skepticism over the intensity of the needs of the elderly, the growing absolute and real costs of aged programs, and mounting competition over dwindling social welfare dollars will present a tremendous challenge to public policy advocates for the elderly in the years ahead (2). Demographic projections consistently conclude that in future years, the percentage of elderly Americans to the general population will markedly rise as will the demand of the aged for supportive services—especially for the very old (13). Nonetheless, it is also important to note that this significant growth in the number of elderly citizens only explains a small portion of the anticipated increase in future program costs (14, 15).

POLICY REFORM PROPOSALS

Medicare, Medicaid, and Social Security have all been plagued by high rates of inflation. Low productivity and high unemployment also added to Social Security trust fund problems in the late 1970s and early 1980s (16). In the case of Medicare and Medicaid, both the volume of services per beneficiary and the rise in the cost of services have intensified (17). Since these broader social problems are the primary reasons that programs benefiting the elderly have dramatically risen in cost, it seems illogical that the proposed reforms focus on the beneficiaries rather than on the broader structural flaws.

Health care costs could be brought into line by paying hospitals and physicians less or by expecting the elderly and other taxpayers to pay more (17). At the 1984 Conference on the Future of Medicare, the three options proposed for maintaining solvency in the Medicare/Medicaid programs included: paying for fewer services, paying less for each service, or shifting a greater financial burden to the beneficiaries or taxpayers (17). Only one of these possible solutions—paying less for each service—targets those who bear the primary responsibility for cost increases, the providers.

One physician has characterized this struggle as "a classic pocketbook issue pitting the economic standing of physicians against the out-of-pocket liability of the elderly beneficiary" (17). If political pressure from the American Medical Association or the American Hospital Association (AHA) causes increased cost sharing for the elderly beneficiaries, the elderly will be forced to shoulder the burden of medical costs. A different perspective is that the administrative costs associated with the existing health care delivery system are prohibitive and rapidly draining shrinking resources from direct health care services. In that scenario, the health care delivery system would be scrapped altogether and efforts redirected toward formulating a universal health care program that would streamline administrative costs and provide health care services to all Americans.

At the present time, radical restructuring of health care delivery still appears to be too politically volatile and efforts remain focused on freezing reimbursements to providers or minimizing services to beneficiaries. One proposal gaining support is the use of "managed care programs" in which a health care organization would receive a prospectively negotiated fixed budget for providing care to a specialized Medicare/Medicaid population (18). There are, of course, problems in converting such seductive theoretical concepts into practice (19). Under the managed care program, elderly clients would lose their freedom of choice and be assigned to a specific provider group such as a Health Maintenance Organization (HMO) or a preferred provider organization (PPO) for treatment. In the absence of options the elderly would inescapably fall victim to a delivery system where savings may be realized without any concern about alienating the elderly consumer. Not surprisingly, a report recently released by the U.S. Senate Special Committee on Aging revealed that the elderly enrolled in HMOs sometimes experience life-threatening delays in treatment and various tactics, including intimidation, to discourage the use of services (20).

A key question in the debate over controlling health care costs is whether the elderly should be held more personally responsible for their medical and hospital bills. Some medical economists argue that increased cost sharing will hold down excess utilization and enhance competition (21). Others note that 28 percent of all Medicare expenditures are made in the last year of a person's life, hardly implying an abuse of services (22). Furthermore, if cost sharing were increased, those who could most afford supplemental health insurance would purchase additional protection, placing added financial pressure only on those who can least afford any increased out-of-pocket expense (17).

Solutions to maintain the solvency of Social Security call for either bureaucratic maneuvering or for the elderly to assume more direct cost. Reliance on income maintenance programs could be severely curtailed by limiting accessibility and promoting the private pension system through more favorable tax laws (23). More moderate reforms, recommended in 1982 by the National Commission on Social Security Reform, include: delaying the cost-of-living adjustment (COLA), accelerating payroll tax increases, taxing the benefits of high-income persons, and requiring Social Security coverage of new federal employees and all nonprofit organizations (24).

Attempts to improve the economic security of the elderly that rely on individual responsibility, not government intervention, stress the importance of individual retirement accounts (IRAs) Keogh plans, and employee stock ownership plans (ESOPs) (25). Inherent in this emphasis on individual responsibility is the supposition that economic hardship is a product of one's unwillingness, rather than inability, to save. Therefore, there is a risk that greater divisiveness will be created among the elderly by pitting those who are perceived to be "frugal" against those who are unwilling or unable to save.

Even in the private sector, the retirement security of American workers has been seriously threatened over the last few years by the termination of 114 private pension plans and the subsequent reversion to employers of over $1 million (26). In some cases, the pension plan has been transformed into an employee/stock ownership plan (ESOP)—a concept heralded by both labor and management. However, by not diversifying the investment, there is the potential danger that the employee could completely lose his or her retirement income (27).

Other legislative initiatives, such as lowering the minimum age for pension participation, granting pension credit during maternity or paternity leave, and safeguarding survivor benefits are all sincere efforts to make the private pension system more equitable (27, 28). Despite the virtues of such reforms, making the private pension system more equitable through the Employee Retirement Income Security Act (ERISA) or any other legislated means is not going to be of any great value to a little less than half (45%) of all Americans who do not participate in a private pension program (29).

UNIVERSALISTIC VERSUS PARTICULARISTIC REFORMS

Perhaps the basic problem with current public policies benefiting the aged is that they fail to account for the prominent differences that presently exist in the aged population. For example, in the age group over eighty-five, 57 percent are limited in their ability to carry on major activities compared to 34 percent in the sixty-five to seventy-four age group (30). Only a very small percentage (5%) of all the elderly account for over half (53%) of all Medicare expenditures (31). By the year 2000, the over-eighty-five age group will increase by 84 percent compared to a 56 percent increase in the sixty-five and older age group (30). In the future, we can anticipate it will be the over-eighty-five age group who, due to their projected numbers and sheer intensity of debilitation, will require far more services than those aged sixty-five to seventy-five.

There are also significant differences between older men and older women. Seventy-two percent of all persons over sixty-five who live in poverty are women (28). In 1981, only 10.5 percent of women over sixty-five received pensions averaging $2,427 a year compared to 27.7 percent of men who received pensions averaging $4,152 a year (28). Living arrangements between men and women also differ greatly, with far more men over sixty-five than women (83% to 57%) living with a spouse or relative (32).

Economic differences among the aged have been widely recognized for some time. Overall, older women have substantially lower incomes than older men, and more older blacks and Hispanics live in poverty than older whites (33). Less widely known is the extent to which out-of-pocket expenses, particularly for health care, impact to a far greater degree on the poor, whom Medicare and Medicaid are supposed to protect, than on the fairly well-to-do. For instance, the proportion of out-of-pocket health expenses for people with incomes less than $6,500 is 5.4 percent, and it is 8.7 percent for those with incomes less than $4,000. However, for those with incomes greater than $15,000, the proportion of out-of-pocket health expense is only 1.4 percent (34). Under these conditions, it is not surprising that the fairly well-to-do elderly seldom identify with aging issues (35).

In the face of such disparities and the scarcity of economic as well as human resources, would targeting benefits to the elderly in the greatest need be a feasible policy alternative? In other words, despite historical American dislike of means or eligibility tests, has their time now come? Since only 15 to 20 percent of persons over sixty-five require some special form of health or social service, are we over-serving the vast majority of aged Americans and under-serving the ones who are truly in need (36)? Should, as Governor Bruce Babbitt of Arizona advocated, those who have "fortunate economic circumstance" forgo government subsidies in order to target a tight federal budget where the need is greatest (37)?

There are certain political advantages for the elderly in pursuing particularistic policy reforms. Narrow particularistic programs offer a recognizable rallying point for advocates and proponents (2). A clearly defined program serving a very circumspect group can also facilitate monitoring to ensure program goals are met. Traditionally, age has been used as a criterion to define public program eligibility if positive entitlements are being granted. But there is strong opposition to the notion of using age as a criterion for limiting or rationing expensive treatments (38).

Differentiating need according to an economic yardstick certainly has presented a plethora of problems for other social-welfare programs such as Aid to Families with Dependent Children (AFCDC), Medicaid, and Women, Infants, and Children Program (WIC). Fragmenting programs to serve particular populations can make it easier for policymakers to gradually erode funding support. By definition, particularistic programs serve narrow populations that often are not large enough to sustain significant opposition should continuance of a program be threatened.

One group whose "deserving" status has rarely been questioned is the disabled; yet, between March 1981 and September 1983, nearly one-half million beneficiaries of the Social Security disability program were terminated (39). More disturbing is that upon review by administrative law judges, approximately 70 percent of those removed from the liability rolls were found eligible for reinstatement (40). The hardship this callous and precipitous action imposed by the Social Security Administration had on scores of disabled persons is amply documented in testimony before the U.S. Senate Committee on the Budget (39).

Another potential danger of particularistic reforms is that they heighten competition between groups who must vie for scarce resources. Such divisive competition among age groups could unintentionally serve the interests of those wishing to decrease the government role in providing social welfare programs across the life span (41). There is also the possibility that as the elderly make gains in political influence, others in society, in particular the taxpayers who will be called upon to fund additional aging programs, will rise up in opposition. The potential for such a backlash is not unprecedented. One only has to witness the conflict between pro- and antiabortion activists to see how mounting strength in one constituency mobilizes an adversarial response in another. It is also possible that if younger taxpayers perceive the aged population to be less debilitated and dependent than in the past, they are likely to characterize the aged as "undeserving" and be less willing to subsidize aging programs (42).

If one assumes, as does Etzioni (43), that particularistic programs heighten tension between the aged and the rest of society, perhaps the elderly will ultimately lose more than they could gain by pursuing particularistic reforms (44). These political considerations suggest that it may be far more fruitful to avoid singling out the aged as special, different, and dependent and instead focus the energies of the elderly on policies that will be of benefit to all Americans. For example, cost-effective national health insurance is advantageous not only to the elderly, but to all age groups. For some social problems, such as abuse, alcoholism, and housing, the required service may differ according to the age of the individual, but the need for services is not specifically age-related (42). However, not all programs now targeted for the elderly may be easily expanded to include other age groups.

Currently, the work cycle is fairly fixed with leisure and retirement set arbitrarily at age seventy and uninterrupted participation in the workforce occurring through the middle years of life. In such a system, the displacement of older workers to make room for younger aspirants is encouraged and facilitated by Social Security and private pension programs. Yet, one study found that four of five workers would prefer to reduce their years of retirement and redistribute more leisure time to the middle portion of their working years (45).

Redefining and redesigning the work cycle to accommodate both the needs of working adults and the elderly could ease the strain on Social Security trust funds. But, pragmatically, the immediate demands of the marketplace are not likely to yield to the long-term interests of labor. It is far more likely that inflexible work schedules will be maintained, and, in addition to sustained participation in the work force throughout adulthood, the elderly will be enticed or expected to extend the length of their work life. On a more ideological level, Kingson, Hirshon, and Cornman (40) argue that intergenerational transfers, which meet the needs of vulnerable citizens at varying stages of the life cycle, are critical to social stability.

Policy analysts who support universalistic reforms claim that comprehensiveness will facilitate administration, minimize fragmentation and duplication, and ultimately be more cost effective. Other advantages include spreading the risk among a larger pool of beneficiaries and expanding the funding base. But, again realistically, the impact of economic scarcity and American values of individualism and limited government suggest that any effort to expand existing programs is unlikely to gain widespread support.

Moreover, for programs covering a wide range of ages to be implemented, the elderly and their advocates would have to form political alliances with other disadvantaged Americans and their advocates or with the population at large. On a variety of public policy initiatives, competition among special interest groups has made coalition building extremely difficult. Whether those who are similarly repressed identify with one another and join forces to mandate universal reforms, or view each other as adversaries in a struggle to capture limited resources, remains to be seen. In either of these scenarios, the definition of "beneficiary" is the critical component of reform. In neither instance is attention given to economic restraints or sanctions on those who provide or indirectly benefit from programs for the elderly.

SOURCES OF RESISTANCE TO REFORM EFFORTS

Although by the end of the 1960s, the National Council of Senior Citizens (NCSC), American Association of Retired Persons (AARP), and National Council on Aging (NCOA) received $10 million for aging programs, their activities did little to address the economic and social problems confronting the disadvantaged aged (10). The public posture of the major aging organizations has been to insist that "all programs benefiting the aged, and those who make their living off them, are sacred . . . without much attention to those who are not saved by Social Security or any other programs" (12, p. 142). Unfortunately, it would appear that this pattern of pursuing self-interest to the detriment of the disadvantaged elderly became graphically apparent during the enactment and subsequent repeal of the Medicare Catastrophic Coverage Act.

Over the past three decades, the rapid rise in the cost of entitlement programs benefiting the aged and changes in economic and social conditions have triggered a rethinking of how one can balance the protection to the aged who would otherwise suffer financial hardship against the distortions that result when protection levels are set too high or benefits are badly structured (46). Thus, when the Medicare Catastrophic Coverage Act was passed in 1988, there was a radical change in the financing mechanism from a traditional social insurance funding concept to the "user fee" principle. In addition, the surtax to be levied against the elderly to pay for the program was to be progressive—that is, the wealthiest elderly would share the burden of providing services to their poorer counterparts. The American Association of Retired Persons (AARP) initially supported the progressive surcharge, but another organization—the National Committee to Preserve Social Security and Medicare (NCPSSM)—led a counterattack. By using a direct mail campaign, Jim Roosevelt, Chairman of the NCPSSM, persuaded vast numbers of elderly that the catastrophic health bill offered seniors little and cost them a lot (47). When the seniors began to attack the AARP and several thousand of its own members resigned, AARP was forced to back down from its original support of the catastrophic bill (48).

Not only did the AARP back down, but Congress, flooded with preprinted messages and tear-away cards, for the first time in the nation's history, repealed a social insurance program. Pundits were quick to characterize the actions by the aged as reflective of a "core of greedy and not at all needy geezers who pretended to speak for a much larger pool of poor" (48, p. 11). Others viewed the maelstrom as heightening intergenerational conflict and cast the aged as just another special interest pursuing and preserving its economic self-interest (49, 50). Unfortunately, all the divisive debate pitting the poor aged against their more well-to-do counterparts obscures a larger issue. Although the aged may have maligned Congress for many years to come, the debacle over catastrophic health insurance merely reinforces the importance of restructuring the entire delivery system so that all Americans may be equitably served (51).

The American Medical Association (AMA), the American Hospital Association (AHA), and two groups representing the insurance industry, the Life Insurance Association of America, and the National Association of Blue Shield plans, have all consistently opposed any government-sponsored national health program. This insistence by the insurance and medical industry on maintaining regressive financing mechanisms has assured that no serious debate on national health insurance has ever taken place and that efforts to hold down costs have placed excessive burdens on the consumers of health care services (52). Even though liberal reimbursement policies (on a fee-for-service basis for physicians and a cost basis for hospitals and nursing homes) amply rewarded providers, by 1970 gross gaps in coverage were apparent in Medicare and Medicaid, as well as in private insurance.

Today, not only are the elderly paying more out-of-pocket expenses, but medical costs in general are consuming larger and larger portions of total family budgets (53). Clearly, neither employer-based health insurance nor Medicaid and Medicare are any guarantee that Americans will be adequately protected under existing health insurance programs. Remarkably, on an issue that impacts all ages, no coalition has yet to be formed among the elderly, business, and labor to limit health care providers' "overwhelming sense of self-interest and self-preservation" (54).

In the area of medical technology, where every type of technology is applied more often to the aged than to the general population, the question of cost has far-reaching social and ethical implications (55). The cost of medical technology can be controlled either by decreasing demand by raising charges to the consumer, limiting distribution by assessing the cost/benefit of individual technologies, or changing the reimbursement procedures by reversing the monetary incentive for physicians and hospitals (55).

How one weighs psychological aspects and measures the potential for improvement in the quality of an individual life have polarized the medical community (56). The use of cost-benefit analysis, which completely avoids addressing larger questions of social justice, has dire connotations for the elderly who are presumed to have a higher cost-benefit ratio (57). Undaunted by issues of distribution, fairness, and equity, some have argued that with demand exceeding supply, the only option is to evaluate explicitly, systematically, and openly using an approach like cost-benefit analysis or continuing to evaluate implicitly, haphazardly and secretly, as has been the pattern in the past (58).

Any regulatory approach that relies on subjective guidelines for the distribution of capital-intensive technology is obviously subject to bias (55). A number of analysts agree that even with such regulation, unnecessary utilization will continue as long as doctors and hospitals can reap enormous profits and extensive reimbursement policies (59, 60). Ultimately, a choice will have to be made as to whether the rights of the individual, the state, or providers will be infringed upon in an effort to reasonably control the application of medical innovation (61, 62). Binstock fears that the widespread perception that the aged are exacerbating hospital costs will cause disturbing moral decisions to be made regarding the allocation of health care resources (63).

The conflict between the interests of capital and those of labor is also evident in the Social Security system. In 1972, when amendments to the Social Security Act were enacted, aging organizations had gained a strong political foothold. The economic need of the elderly was beyond reproach, and the solvency of the program appeared certain. Barely a decade later, the Social Security trust fund seemed doomed to bankruptcy, assertions were made that Social Security was a bad investment for younger generations, and critics characterized the program as an instrument of social control with a minimal redistributive effect (64, 65). Although only a few business lobbyists and administration officials dared question the effect Social Security might have on the federal budget and inflation in the early 1970s, the funding crisis of the late 1970s irrevocably changed the image of Social Security as a "sacred" entitlement program.

The compromise negotiated in 1983 to maintain the solvency of Social Security is an example of how in a crisis the beneficiaries and the taxpayers are called upon to make sacrifices. We should anticipate that heightened antitax sentiments on the part of business and the American public will significantly limit options that call for added revenues through substantial tax increases in the future. State governments, in particular, are very vulnerable to threats by businesses to relocate their industries if local taxes become too costly (66). In light of these considerations, when the President's Commission on Pension Policy (67) recommended a sweeping reform, called the Mandatory Universal Pension System (MUPS), concern was expressed that even with a generous tax credit, the increase in cost to business could potentially result in higher unemployment and lower wages, lower benefits, or both, to employees.

CONCLUSION

In America, our pluralist public policies attempt to maintain individualism and liberty while simultaneously sanctioning limited government intervention should the free market be incapable of providing certain necessary social goods. Not surprisingly, contradictions erupt between the state—charged with redressing social and economic inequities—and the capitalist economy—driven by profit. Some economists refer to this struggle as the balance between equity and efficiency. We have attempted to document throughout this chapter that, due to a variety of constraints, the redistribution effect of American old age policies has been limited.

We have raised questions regarding the "worthiness" or "deservedness" of the elderly. Throughout the 1960s and early 1970s it appeared that the sanctity of the aged as a political constituency had steadily grown—empowering the aged as a group to benefit from government entitlement programs targeted to serve all the aged regardless of need. However, the strident opposition by seniors to the enactment of the Catastrophic Coverage Act has left many analysts wondering, to what degree elected officials will, in the future, spearhead reforms targeting the aged. In fact, because there is a widespread perception that seniors will exercise considerable political muscle to preserve their economic self-interest—even to the detriment of their poorer counterparts—there may be a backlash. Already there are indications that the attentions of Congress are beginning to shift away from the aged and toward programs benefiting children and families (50). If this trend continues, new public policies benefiting the aged are less likely to be forthcoming. Further, even if the elderly could be mobilized around a particular policy initiative, the growing perception that the elderly are not as dependent and incapacitated as once perceived has put them in a vulnerable position when their interests are pitted against the interests of other groups. As Callahan notes, expanding medical care for the elderly while some 35 million Americans have no health insurance at all would represent an enormous neglect of other age groups (68).

As for the type of program reform the elderly might most effectively promote, we have analyzed the advantages and disadvantages of particularistic versus universalistic reforms. Pragmatically speaking, particularistic reforms are probably easier to enact, but by targeting one narrow group for assistance, the implication is made that the remainder of the population is more directly accountable for their own well-being. Universalistic reforms, which recognize the heterogeneity of the aged, would expand government's role (a prospect most Americans oppose) and diminish or curtail the activities of various special interests in the private sector (i.e., the AMA, the AHA, and American business). Even with these limitations, certain old age programs may well benefit from each of these approaches.

The long-term care needs of the elderly seem well suited to a reform measure that would comprehensively administer and fund a program addressing both the social and health care needs of the frail elderly regardless of economic status. Currently, five pilot projects are underway in the United States to create Social/Health Maintenance Organizations (S/HMO's). S/HMO's coordinate health and chronic care needs for the frail elderly through a prospective prepaid plan using a variety of alternative, less expensive providers. The S/HMOs represent a reform that is particularistic in its focus on the needs of the frail elderly but universalistic in availability to the frail elderly in all income groups.

A particularistic reform measure of significance to elderly women is the Private Pension Reform bill enacted in August of 1984. The Private Pension Reform Act provides additional protection of women's pension rights by improving both joint and survivor benefits, reducing the minimum age for pension plan participation, and granting credit for maternity or paternity leave. Former Representative Ferraro described this reform as "a practical cost-effective approach to many of the problems women face in the private pension system," which will hopefully go far in "making a difference between poverty and comfort for retired women" (27, p. 145). This measure is universalistic to the extent that it is available to women in all income groups, but it is particularistic in its focus on women to the exclusion of men.

Whether a particularistic or universalistic reform measure is appropriate and implementable will largely be determined by the degree to which the elderly are perceived to be in need and the extent to which all interested parties can agree on a cost-effective solution. The difficulty with the first step is that the elderly are not a homogeneous population. Nor does it appear likely that even if pockets of "deserving" elderly could be identified, they would be capable of strengthening their position by forming coalitions with other similarly disenfranchised groups.

As for the second step, virtually all recent reforms have held down costs by placing added financial burdens on the elderly beneficiary. Those who tend to promote this approach are administration officials, representatives of industry, professional organizations, and taxpayers. Although the crux of the seniors' opposition to the Catastrophic Coverage Act was the progressive surcharge, it appears that in light of budgetary constraints, the user-fee concept of financing will remain a viable option. If such user-fees or surcharges are regressive, we anticipate that the inadequacies of public policies will become more apparent, discord from those in need who are adversely affected will intensify, and ultimately pressure will once again be brought to bear on the government to more evenly balance the interests of government, the private sector, and the public at large.

With the exception of the Catastrophic Coverage Act debacle, advocates for the elderly have been successful in emphasizing programs and policies that are particularistic in providing benefits targeted for the elderly to the exclusion of other age groups, but universalistic in the sense of providing benefits to as many of the aged as possible. In the years ahead, it would seem that two alternative strategies might be viewed as being more just and at the same time prove to be more cost effective. One would be to emphasize programs for the aged that are particularistic in the sense that they are aimed at the aged who are clearly disadvantaged. The second strategy would be to emphasize programs and policies that are universalistic in the sense of providing benefits to the nonaged as well as the aged and to middle- as well as low-income groups.

The first or particularistic strategy is designed to deal with the criticism that many of the aged have adequate means to provide for themselves. By restricting program benefits to persons who can demonstrate need, the resources that we know will be limited, would go to those who are most in need. In addition, this emphasis will undercut the opposition of those who tend to view the elderly as a homogeneous and relatively affluent segment of the population.

The second or universalistic strategy is designed to deal with the criticism that the elderly are already getting more than their fair share of government resources. To the extent that the elderly are viewed as a homogeneous and relatively well-off group, there will be continued opposition to new programs and policy changes that tend to benefit the elderly to the exclusion of other age groups. But if a way can be found to design more universalistic programs that benefit the nonelderly as well, it might be possible to obtain the political support needed.

Today, neither the particularistic nor the universalistic strategies we have described would be likely to result in support for bold new social program initiatives that will directly or indirectly benefit the elderly. However, these strategies will become increasingly appropriate if and when the nation returns to a period of sustained economic growth without substantial federal budget deficits— that is, a period similar to that of the 1960s. Until then, it would seem that there is no plausible strategy for increasing the share of our national product that goes to the elderly. The one major exception to this generalization will be the increases due to purely demographic changes. As the proportion of the population eligible for Social Security and Medicare increases, we can expect at least some increase in the share of the national product spent on programs for the aged.

In any case, meaningful political change will only be effected as a response to the sustained collective action of the elderly and other groups acting on their behalf. Success also will require attention to cost-effective solutions and not merely reliance on social justice rhetoric, which, of late, has lost much of its persuasive appeal. And finally, trade-offs will have to be made between particularistic and universalistic reforms—choices that should be governed by the needs of the aged rather than political expediency or private gain.

REFERENCES

1. Marmor, T. R. Enacting Medicare. In *The Aging in Politics: Process and Policy,* edited by R. Hudson, pp. 105–134. Charles C Thomas, Springfield, Illinois, 1981.
2. Hudson, R. The graying of the federal budget and it's consequences for old-age policy. In *The Aging in Politics: Process and Policy,* edited by R. Hudson, pp. 261–281. Charles C Thomas, Springfield, Illinois, 1981.
3. U.S. Bureau of the Census. Characteristics of the population below the poverty level. Current Population Reports, Series P-60. U.S. Government Printing Office, Washington, D.C., 1977.
4. U.S. Bureau of the Census. Money income and poverty status of families and persons in the United States: 1978. Current Population Reports, Series P-60, No. 120. U.S. Government Printing Office, Washington, D.C., 1979.
5. Schulz, J. H. *The Economics of Aging,* 2nd Edition, p. 18. Wadsworth, Belmont, California, 1985.

6. Johnson, E. S., and Williamson, J. B. *Growing Old.* Holt, Rinehart and Winston, New York, 1980.

7. Brotman, H. B. The aging of America: A demographic profile. *National Journal* 10: 1625, 1978.

8. Congressional Budget Office. *Poverty Study of Families Under Alternative Definition of Income.* U.S. Government Printing Office, Washington, D.C., 1977.

9. Pratt, H. J. The politics of Social Security. In *The Aging in Politics: Process and Policy,* edited by R. Hudson, pp. 135–150. Charles C Thomas, Springfield, Illinois, 1981.

10. Binstock, R. H. The politics of aging interest groups. In *The Aging in Politics: Process and Policy,* edited by R. Hudson, pp. 47–73. Charles C Thomas, Springfield, Illinois, 1981.

11. Weaver, J. L. Issue salience. In *The Aging in Politics: Process and Policy,* edited by R. Hudson, pp. 30–46. Charles C Thomas, Springfield, Illinois, 1981.

12. Binstock, R. H. The aged as a scapegoat. *Gerontologist* 23: 136–143, 1983.

13. Aaron, H. J. When is a burden not a burden? The elderly in America. *The Brookings Review* Summer: 17–24, 1986.

14. Clark, R. L., and Menefee, J. A. Federal expenditure for the elderly: Past and future. *Gerontologist* 21: 132–137, 1981.

15. Judge, K. Federal expenditure for the elderly: A different interpretation of the past. *Gerontologist* 22: 129–131, 1982.

16. Congressional Budget Office. *Paying for Social Security: Funding Options for the Near Term.* U.S. Government Printing Office, Washington, D.C., 1981.

17. U.S. House of Representatives. Proceedings of the Conference on the Future of Medicare, before the Committee on Ways and Means. U.S. Government Printing Office, Washington, D.C., November 29, 1984.

18. Magnusson, P. Health Maintenance Organizations in Massachusetts: Issues for Public Sector Initiatives. A Working Paper for the Massachusetts Department of Public Health, 1985.

19. Sapolsky, H. M. Prospective payment in perspective. *Journal of Health Politics, Policy and Law* 11(4): 633-645, 1986.

20. U.S. Senate Special Committee on Aging. The Crisis in Medicare: Exploring the Choices. U.S. Government Printing Office, Washington, D.C., August 20, 1984.

21. U.S. House of Representatives. Oversight Hearing on Title III, Older Americans Act and the Effects of Medicare's DRG Implementation, before the Subcommittee on Human Resources of the Committee on Education and Labor. U.S. Government Printing Office, Washington, D.C., July 30, 1985.

22. Lave, J. R., and Silverman, H. A. Financing the health care of the aged. *Annals of the American Academy of Political and Social Science* 468: 149–164, 1984.

23. Myles, J. F. *Old Age and the Welfare State,* pp. 116–117. Little, Brown and Company, Boston, 1984.

24. U.S. House of Representatives Select Committee on Aging. *Proposals to Address the Financing Problem of Social Security,* p. 4. U.S. Government Printing Office, Washington, D.C., 1983.

25. Olson, L. K. *The Political Economy of Aging: The State, Private Power and Social Welfare,* p. 221. Columbia University Press, New York, 1982.

26. U.S. House of Representatives Select Committee on Aging. *Pension Asset Raids.* U.S. Government Printing Office, Washington, D.C., 1984.
27. U.S. House of Representatives. Hearing on Pension Legislation, before the Subcommittee on Labor-Management Relations. U.S. Government Printing Office, Washington, D.C., 1983.
28. U.S. Senate. Hearing on the Retirement Equity Act of 1983, before the Subcommittee on Labor. U.S. Government Printing Office, Washington, D.C., 1983.
29. Schieber, S., and George P. Retirement opportunities in an aging America: Coverage and benefit entitlement. Employment Benefit Research Institute, Washington, D.C., 1981.
30. Callahan, J. J. The impact of federal programs on long-term. In *Federal Health Programs,* edited by S. H. Altman and H. M. Sapolsky, pp. 177–192. Lexington Books, Lexington, Massachusetts, 1981.
31. Hirsch, B., Silverman, H. A., and Dobson, A. *Medicare Summary: Use and Reimbursement by Person 1976–1978.* Health Care Financing Administration, Baltimore, 1982.
32. U.S. House of Representatives Select Committee on Aging. *Every Ninth American.* U.S. Government Printing Office, Washington, D.C., 1982.
33. Allen, C., and Brotman, H. *Chartbook on Aging in America,* p. 57. U.S. Government Printing Office, Washington, D.C., 1981.
34. Rosenblum, R. Out-of-pocket health expenses and the elderly. *Health Care Management Review* 8: 77–87, 1983.
35. Riley, M. W., and Foner, A. *Aging and Society,* Volume 1. Russell Sage, New York, 1968.
36. Neugarten, B. L. Policy for the 1980s: Age or need entitlement. In *Age or Need?: Public Policies for Older People,* edited by B. L. Neugarten, pp. 19–32. Sage Publication, Beverly Hills, 1982.
37. Babbit, B. It's time for a universal means test. *Boston Globe,* August 12, 1984.
38. Moody, H. R. Ethics and Aging: Old answers, new questions. *Generations* (Winter): 5–9, 1985.
39. U.S. Senate. Hearings on Social Security Disability Program Reform, before the Committee on the Budget. U.S. Government Printing Office, Washington, D.C., March 16, 1984.
40. Kingson, E. R., Hirshon, B. A., and Cornman, J. M. *Ties That Bind: The Interdependence of Generations,* p. 155. Seven Locks Press, Washington, D.C., 1986.
41. Samuelson, R. J. The withering freedom to govern. *Washington Post,* March 5, 1978.
42. Austin, C. D., and Loeb, M. B. Why is age relevant? In *Age or Need?: Public Policies for Older People,* edited by B. L. Neugarten, pp. 263–288. Sage Publications, Beverly Hills, 1982.
43. Etzioni, A. Old people and public policy. *Social Policy* 6: 21–29, 1976.
44. Schram, S. Title XX implementation and the aging. In *The Aging in Politics: Process and Policy,* edited by R. Hudson, pp. 220–235. Charles C Thomas, Springfield, Illinois, 1981.
45. Best, F., and Stern, B. Education, work, leisure: Must they come in that order? *Monthly Labor Review* 100: 3–10, 1977.

46. Feldstein, M. S. The Social Security explosion. *The Public Interest* 81(Fall): 94–106, 1985.
47. Roosevelt, J. Congress misleads seniors: Catastrophic care bill offers little. *Journal of Public Health Policy* 9(4): 453–455, 1988.
48. Weisberg, J. Cat scam. *The New Republic* 30: 11–12, October 1989.
49. Robinson, M. L. Backlash forces rewrite of catastrophic law. *Hospitals* 20: 28–29, September 1989.
50. Borger, G. Why the catastrophic-care fight will change generational politics. *U.S. News and World Report* 9: 18, October 1989.
51. Corn, D. De-taxification. *The Nation* 30: 480–481, October 1989.
52. Harrington, M. *Decade of Decision: The Crisis of the American System,* p. 74. Simon and Schuster, New York, 1980.
53. Health Insurance Association of America. *Sourcebook of Health Insurance Data, 1981–1982,* p. 64. Health Insurance Association of America, Washington, D.C., 1982.
54. Tomayko, J. The role of labor in containing health costs. In Proceedings of a Conference Sponsored by Blue Cross and Blue Shield Association. Health Care in the American Economy: Issues and Forecasts. Health Services Foundation, Chicago, 1978.
55. Banta, H. D., Burns, A. K., and Behney, C. J. Policy implications of the diffusion and control of medical technology. *Annals of the American Academy of Political and Social Science* 468: 165–181, 1983.
56. Najam, L. M., and Levine, S. Evaluating the impact of medical care and technologies on the quality of life: A review and critique. *Society, Science and Medicine* 151: 107–115, 1981.
57. Fox, D. *Economists and Health Care.* Prodist, New York, 1979.
58. Fuchs, N. E. What is CBA/CEA and why are they doing this to us? *New Engl. J. Med.* 303: 937–938, 1980.
59. Wolfe, S., and Berle, B. *The Technological Imperative in Medicine,* p. 95. Plenum Press, New York, 1981.
60. Relman, A. S. The new medical-industrial complex. *New Engl. J. Med.* 303: 963–970, 1980.
61. Bloom, B. S. Stretching ideology to the utmost: Marxism and medical technology. *Am. J. Pub. Health* 69: 1269–1271, 1979.
62. Callahan, D. *The Tyranny of Survival.* Macmillan, New York, 1973.
63. Binstock, R. H. Oldest old: A fresh perspective or compassionate ageism revisited. *Milbank Mem. Fund Q.* 63(2): 420–451, 1985.
64. Feldstein, M. S. Facing the crisis of Social Security. *The Pub. Int.* 47: 88–100, 1977.
65. Davis, K., and Van der Oever, P. Age relations and public policy in advanced industrial societies. *Population and Development Review* 7(1): 1–18, 1981.
66. Estes, C. L., and Newcomer, R. J. The future for aging and public policy. In *Fiscal Austerity and Aging: Shifting Government Responsibility for the Elderly,* edited by C. L. Estes and R. J. Newcomer, pp. 249–270. Sage Publications, Beverly Hills, 1983.
67. President's Commission on Pension Policy. *Towards a National Retirement Income Policy.* U.S. Government Printing Office, Washington, D.C., 1980.
68. Callahan, D. *Setting Limits: Medical Goals in an Aging Society.* Simon and Schuster, New York, 1988.

EPILOGUE

Carroll L. Estes

Social policy and gerontological knowledge need to be examined closely in terms of how they promote and reproduce the dominant institutions of society. State policies that treat the issues of aging as individual problems are ideologically and practically suited to the state's role in the process of capital accumulation and to the legitimacy needs of the state that are managed through processes of social control and social integration.

Social policy for the aging is an important battleground on which the social struggles presently engulfing the state are being fought as it attempts to address the growing tensions between capitalism and democracy. Elders are caught in the ideological manipulation of their ideals of democracy in which society is portrayed as a zero-sum game in which resources for the elderly are seen as taking away from resources for other imperative societal needs. Such notions succeed in separating the aged from an awareness or consciousness of the class basis of their own needs. Further, the zero-sum mentality and related constructions ignore moral economy notions of fairness and reciprocity across generations which remain strong among young and old alike, despite media rhetoric to the contrary. In this and other ways, the aged and the policies designed to assist them are an intrinsic part of the broader phenomenon of crisis construction and management.

The intellectual project before us is to specify the conditions under which the aged and aging policy responses are implicated in crisis formation and trajectory, and the role of ideology therein, providing an alternative framework for examining and analyzing contested domains within aging policy and related areas. Consonant with the underlying theme of Critical Theory of the Frankfurt School in the 1920s (1), our view of the larger project includes critical empirical analysis as well as a concerted project of praxis or action related to social change, in this case, to the betterment of elders in society.

Dominant crisis constructions in the past decade have promoted a "reluctant welfare state" (2) in which the state finds itself acting contradictorily in attempting

341

to promote the economic needs of capitalism while maintaining the social harmony of the populace, that is displaced by the state's responsiveness to the needs of capital (3). Social harmony or peace is achieved by increasing welfare costs to those who are dumped out of the market reward system (4).

The legacy of the 1980s includes a reconstruction of a number of "rights" and a challenge to a number of others. The successful cultural revival of the ideologies of individualism, the market, and the traditional autonomous (but increasingly rare) traditional "family" (complete with authoritarian pater) has pervaded social policy considerations. In the 1980s, health care has been firmly established as a market good rather than a right in terms of social policy, deepening divisions in the *de facto* rationing of U.S. health care based on ability to pay. Notions of self-help, economic entrepreneurialism, and individual autonomy (read responsibility) have been used to reinstate inherently pro-market and antifeminist solutions and perspectives. The primary legacy is social struggle on a number of crucial levels: 1) intergenerational, 2) gender, 3) racial/ethnic, and 4) class. Ideological attacks from the right have been successful on multiple fronts and are likely to continue to play a key role in these struggles.

The real and constructed crises of capital (profitability and accumulation) and the state (rationality and legitimation) have been transported into aging policy on both the subjective and objective levels. The subjective level is in the ideological labeling of crisis and the accompanying attacks on the elderly, who find themselves accused of being well-off "greedy geezers" portrayed as living well at the direct expense of society and of younger generations. The objective level is reflected in a complex struggle between 1) forces seeking a major retrenchment of the welfare state and the resurgence of patriarchy and 2) forces seeking both to restructure the welfare state by redirecting publicly financed resources from public and nonprofit providers to for-profit providers and to reinstate market forces as the medium for delivering state benefits and services.

Multiple contradictions are produced and responses to them represent vehicles, either for social change or for reinforcement of the status quo. An example, and an obvious source of potential struggle that could coalesce common interest, is medical care. Policies that have increased state underwriting of a booming private commercial for-profit sector for the delivery of medical care and technology will almost certainly lead to the state's bearing increased costs for medical services and technologies. This will be done, moreover, under the rationale of attempting to achieve cost savings to the state by contracting to the theoretically "more efficient" proprietary sector. The contradiction is that pursuing "competitive" policies to advance commercial interests in health and "reduce costs" is having the diametrically opposite effect of *increasing* costs.

State costs will assuredly continue to grow exponentially as long as there is pluralistic financing and the key actors in the medical-industrial complex successfully press for public subsidy of the most profitable components of the industry. In addition, state costs will grow as the state is increasingly forced to subsidize the "unprofitable" clients who cannot afford private coverage in the private medical care system. For example, the new estimates of 63 million Americans without regular health insurance (5) demonstrate the existence of the significant and growing segment of the U.S. population (particularly children, minorities, women, and the employed poor) that is severely disadvantaged by current policy. Recent data show that average elders annually spend 4.5 months of their Social Security payments for out-of-pocket health care (6). The common interest of the uninsured under age sixty-five and the underinsured over age sixty-five is clear. The issue is whether viable coalitional efforts can sustain the ideological and political shifts requisite to achieving a universal and equitable system of health care. Although collectively shared assumptions defining norms of fairness and reciprocity provide a critical base for such coalition building, they are contradicted and severely tested by other norms stressing individualism and competition. Particularly during the 1980s, policies which created and reinforced divisiveness among the working class and constructed images of generational and age/race "wars" over the allocation of scarce resources, further threatened moral economy notions of universal entitlement at the base of Social Security and other key welfare state programs.

Another example of the contradictions between policies and people that potentially could alter current directions is the area of gender relations. In the past decade, women's place in society has been reassessed. Women are needed in the labor force both for the public reason of fulfilling service roles, including temporary low-paid work without benefits, and for the private reason of maintaining individual standards of living. Yet, women are essential to fill the nation's growing need for long term care in ways that not only do not cost the state but enable it to reduce the costs of formal service provision in areas where greater voluntary labor can be extracted. (Shortened hospital stays based on DRG policy, for example, increased women's unpaid work in providing post-hospital care). The 1980s were a period in which the double binds in women's lives became starkly apparent as their roles in the labor market and the home were simultaneously but differentially reinforced and expanded—but not necessarily supported. Women are sandwiched not only between paid work and uncompensated caregiving and between multiple generations, but also between the structural interests of the state, the medical-industrial complex, and the rest of business. These interests are synonymously driving up the present high-cost, high-technology medical care system while constraining and distorting the health care system toward acute care and away from needed chronic and long term care policies.

With the current difficulties of advanced capitalism in the United States, the growing needs of an aging society and the deepening crisis of inadequate health and social programs set the nation on a collision course. At least two alternative scenarios exist. The first scenario is one in which the state continues and further extends the conservative economic and ideological policies and commitments of the 1980s; the move is toward an increasingly divided class state characterized by widening gaps between the rich and others, whites and nonwhites, and old men and old women. The second scenario is one in which the tensions and contradictions between capital and democracy crystallize and the resulting class, gender, generational, and racial/ethnic struggles erupt with the force to profoundly alter the present direction and agenda; the move is toward a universal state. This is a state in which the rights of citizens take precedence over the rights of property holders; a state in which productive capacity and resource distribution are geared toward meeting basic human needs. (Chapter 4) The question is whether social and ideological forces and the inherent dialectic of conflict and its resolution will promote a more deeply divided *class and patriarchical* state or whether the United States will move toward a more *universal* state. A universalistic state determines rights based on citizenship rather than position in the labor market or possession of property.

The outcome will, in part, be determined by the question of "agency," and the role of the historical subject, in determining "what is to be done." In the field of aging, as in many others, the role and commitment of the intellectual may have profound effects on the outcome of such struggles. The import of the intellectual in transformative change has been argued by a number of theorists (7, 8). Equally important is Antonio Gramsci's theory of praxis, in which he contributes the concept of "hegemony" to argue that class domination is imposed more through consent than through force. Those who possess the means of cultural production (i.e., the production of ideas and ideology) are crucial both in the maintenance of the status quo and in the creation of meaningful change. The ability to realize common interest and catalyze common power across age, class, gender, and race lines and the cultural production of a new ideological hegemony will be telling factors in the future course of aging.

It has been suggested (9) that there are important parallels between Gramscian theorizing on the role of the intellectual in the workers' movement and Daniel Callahan's treatment of aging advocates and intellectuals. Arguing for "setting limits" for the aged, Callahan implicitly acknowledges the crucial role of the intellectual and lashes out against gerontologists for encouraging the old in "unreasonable," "unfair," and "selfish" expectations for life expectancy and societal resources (10). In contrast is the argument that gerontologists have contributed directly to the construction of a better old age through early problem definition and data substantiation, particularly in the area of income (11, 12).

The broad intellectual "project" to which this book is addressed concerns the need to understand the construction of the fate of the aging. Consistent with the goal of Critical Theory, the project must inevitably engage in action. It requires moving beyond positivistic assumptions that objective demographic, epidemiological, and economic facts "speak for themselves." It is to critically examine the social and cultural production of aging and gerontological knowledge at their base, and to attend to the class, generational, gender, and racial/ethnic divisions and ideological forces embedded in their production and reproduction. Finally, the intellectual project is to help us move beyond the trivialization and alienation of old age. A crucial dimension of this project is the battle for the intellectual high ground in constructing resource and equity issues for the elderly, to the ultimate benefit of the whole of society.

REFERENCES

1. Held, D. *Introduction to Critical Theory: Horkheimer to Habermas.* Hutchinson, London, 1980.
2. Estes, C. L. The Reagan legacy: Privatization, the welfare state and aging. In *Old Age and the Welfare State,* edited by J. Quadagno and J. Myles. Temple University Press, Philadelphia, 1990.
3. O'Connor, J. *Fiscal Crisis of the State.* St. Martin's, New York, 1973.
4. Piven, F. F., and Cloward, R. *Regulating the Poor.* Vintage, New York, 1981.
5. U.S. Bureau of the Census. *Health Insurance Coverage, 1986–1988.* U.S. Government Printing Office, Washington, D.C., 1990.
6. U.S. House of Representatives, Select Committee on Aging. *Emptying the Elderly's Pocketbook: Growing Impact of Rising Health Care Costs.* U.S. Government Printing Office, Washington, D.C., 1990.
7. Gouldner, A. *The Coming Crisis of Western Sociology.* Basic, New York, 1970.
8. Gramsci, A. *Prison Letters.* Pluto Press/Unwin Hyman, United Kingdom, 1988.
9. Binney, E. A. Personal communication, 1990.
10. Callahan, S. *Setting Limits.* Simon and Schuster, New York, 1987.
11. Clark, R. L., Maddox, G. L., Schrimper, R. A., and Sumner, D. A. *Inflation and the Economic Well-Being of the Elderly.* Johns Hopkins University Press, Baltimore, 1984.
12. Maddox, G. L. Intervention strategies to enhance well-being in later life: The status and prospect of guided change. *Health Services Research* 19(6, Suppl., Pt. 2): 1007–1032, 1985.

CONTRIBUTORS

TERRY ARENDELL is Assistant Professor in the Department of Sociology at Hunter College of City University of New York. She received her doctorate in Sociology from the University of California, Berkeley, 1984, and subsequently completed a two-year National Institute of Aging postdoctoral fellowship at the Institute for Health and Aging at the University of California, San Francisco. She is author of *Mothers and Divorce: Legal, Economic, and Social Dilemmas* (1986), and is presently writing a book on men's postdivorce fathering activities and experiences.

ELIZABETH BINNEY is a research associate in the Institute for Health and Aging and doctoral candidate in the Department of Social and Behavioral Sciences, University of California, San Francisco. Ms. Binney is co-author of several articles and book chapters on the political economy of aging and health policy, older women's issues, and the state and the non-profit sector, and is presently conducting dissertation research on the social construction and political economy of osteoporosis.

THOMAS COLE is an Associate Professor of History and Medicine and Graduate Program Director at the Institute for Medical Humanities, University of Texas Medical Branch, Galveston, Texas. He is senior editor of *What Does It Mean To Grow Old?: Reflections from the Humanities* (1986) and of *The Handbook of Aging and the Humanities* (forthcoming, Springer Press). He is completing *The Journal of Life: A Cultural History of Aging,* a book that will appear in 1991.

PAULA DRESSEL is an Associate Professor of Sociology at Georgia State University in Atlanta where she teaches courses in poverty and welfare, social problems, and gender stratification. Her research focuses on the intersection of gender, race/ethnicity, and class implications in poverty and social policy. Among her publications are *The Service Trap: From Altruism to Dirty Work* (Charles C. Thomas, 1984) and recent articles in *Social Problems* and the *Journal of Sociology and Social Welfare* on welfare policies and social stratification.

SUZANNE E. ENGLAND (formerly Osterbusch) is Head of the Department of Medical Social Work and Associate Professor in the College of Associated Health Professions and Jane Addams College of Social Work, University of Illinois at Chicago. She also serves as Director of the Project for the Study of Families,

Health and Social Policy. Dr. England recently completed a study on the politics of family and medical leave policies in the U.S. and is currently investigating how family caregivers experience and assess the relevance of organized helping.

CARROLL L. ESTES, Professor of Sociology, is Chairperson of the Department of Social and Behavioral Sciences, School of Nursing, University of California, San Francisco, and is Director of the Institute for Health and Aging, University of California, San Francisco. Dr. Estes, whose Ph.D. is from the University of California, San Diego, conducts research on aging policy, long-term care, fiscal crisis, and new federalism. She is the author of *The Decision-Makers: The Power Structure of Dallas* (1963) and *The Aging Enterprise* (Jossey Bass, 1979), and co-author of *Fiscal Austerity and Aging* (Sage, 1983) and *Political Economy, Health and Aging* (Little Brown, 1984).

CHARLENE HARRINGTON is Professor in the Department of Family Health Care Nursing and Associate Director of the Institute for Health and Aging, University of California, San Francisco. She received her Ph.D. in Social and Higher Education from the University of California, Berkeley in 1975 and subsequently served as Deputy Director of the Department of Health Services and the State Licensing Certification Program for the State of California. Dr. Harrington's major publications include her co-authored books, *Fiscal Austerity and Aging* (Sage, 1983) and *Public Policies and Long Term Care* (Sage, in press).

JON HENDRICKS is Chair, Department of Sociology, Oregon State University and immediate past chair of the Behavioral and Social Sciences section of the Gerontological Society of America. Dr. Hendricks is the author of *Aging and Mass Society* (4th edition in press) and co-editor of the Foundations in Gerontology Series for Little Brown. He also serves as co-editor of the *International Journal of Aging and Human Development.*

MARTHA HOLSTEIN currently heads the West Coast office of the Hastings Center. She recently completed a thirteen-year term as Associate Director of the American Society on Aging, and teaches courses on ethics and aging at San Francisco State University and at the School of Public Health, University of California at Berkeley. She is contributing editor of *The Aging Connection* and is co-editor of *A Good Old Age? The Paradox of Setting Limits* (Simon and Schuster, August 1990), an exploration of categorical age-based rationing of health care.

SHARON M. KEIGHER is Assistant Professor of Social Work at the University of Michigan and adjunct Assistant Professor in the Department of Medical Social Work, College of Associated Health Professions, University of Illinois at Chicago. Her research interests include the risks of homelessness for the elderly, and cross-national and state-level comparisons of welfare policies as they affect family caregivers. She recently completed a study of consumers' satisfaction with Michigan's Adult Home Help program and is a co-author of *Wages for Caring: Compensating Family Care of the Elderly.*

MARTIN KOHLI is Professor at the Institute for Sociology of the Free University of Berlin. He received his doctoral degree from the University of Bern (Switzerland), and his habilitation from the University of Konstanz. His research centers on the sociology of the life course, especially with regard to work and social policy. His recent studies include an analysis of pre-retirement in Germany and a comparative assessment of the trend toward early exit from the labor force in Western societies (Cambridge University Press, forthcoming).

CYNTHIA A. LEEDHAM is a doctoral student at the University of Kentucky in Lexington. She received her M.A. in modern languages from Oxford University and her M.A. in sociology from the University of Kentucky. Her research interests include social and health policy for the aging and models of health. She has presented a number of papers and co-authored book chapters on these themes.

NATHAN LINSK is Associate Professor in the Department of Medical Social Work, Director of the Midwest AIDS Training Center and Co-Director of the Illinois Geriatric Education Center, College of Associated Health Professions, University of Illinois at Chicago. His research centers on linkages of families and formal programs to serve the elderly, and case management and long term care for persons with AIDS-related illnesses. He is senior author of *Wages for Caring: Compensating Family Care of the Elderly* and co-author of *Care of the Aged: A Family Approach and Effective Social Work Practice.*

RITA GASTON LUNG has an M.S. in nursing from Washington University (St. Louis) and an M.S. in Gerontology from the University of Missouri-St. Louis. Her interests are in health care issues of the elderly. She is an adjunct faculty member in the Gerontology Program at the University of Missouri-St. Louis.

BAILA MILLER is Assistant Professor in the Department of Medical Social Work, College of Associated Health Professions, University of Illinois at Chicago. Her current research interests include gender relationships in older couples, caregiver burden, and functioning of older persons. She has recently completed an investigation of the effect of caregiver burden on institutionalization, hospital use and stability of care networks of frail older persons. Prior research and publications are in the areas of family involvement in nursing home care, gender differences in caregivers of the frail elderly, and family caregiver strains and satisfactions.

MEREDITH MINKLER is Professor and Chair of the Community Health Education Program in the Department of Social and Administrative Health Sciences, School of Public Health at the University of California, Berkeley. She received her doctorate in Public Health Education from the University of California, Berkeley in 1975 and was a Kellogg National Fellow from 1980-1983. Dr. Minkler is co-editor of *Reading in the Political Economy of Aging* (Baywood, 1984) and has authored numerous publications in the areas of aging policy, social support and health, and alternative approaches to community health education.

JOHN F. MYLES is a Professor in the Department of Sociology and Anthropology at Carleton University in Ottawa, Canada. Dr. Myles' research centers on comparative class politics and comparative class structure in North America and Western Europe. His recent publications include the book, *Old Age in the Welfare State: The Political Economy of Public Pensions* (University Press of Kansas, 1989).

VICENTE NAVARRO is Professor of Health Policy at Johns Hopkins University and founder and editor-in-chief of the *International Journal of Health Services*. He has written extensively on sociology, political sociology, and the political economy of medical and social services. Dr. Navarro is the author of *Medicine under Capitalism, Social Security and Medicine in the USSR: A Marxist Critique*, and *Class Struggle, the State, and Medicine: An Historical and Contemporary Analysis of the Medical Sector in Great Britain*, and editor of collections *Health and Medical Care in the U.S.: A Critical Analysis* and *Imperialism, Health and Medicine*.

SHEILA NEYSMITH is a Professor in the Faculty of Social Work at the University of Toronto, Canada. She received a doctorate in social welfare from Columbia University, New York. Most of her research and writing has focused on how social policy affects women and the elderly. She is currently co-editing a book, *Women's Caring: Feminist Perspectives on Social Welfare*, to be published by McClelland and Steward in March 1991.

LAWRENCE ALFRED POWELL, received his Ph.D. from MIT and is currently Assistant Professor of Social and Policy Sciences at the University of Texas-San Antonio. His research interests include political gerontology, political psychology and communication, the dynamics of social movements, and comparative social policy in modern welfare states. Among his aging-related publications are two co-authored books, *The Politics of Aging: Power and Policy* and *Framing the Equity Debate: The Senior Movement and Aging Policy Reform in America*, as well as articles in *The International Journal of Aging and Human Development, Social Policy*, and *The Journal of Sociology and Social Welfare*.

ANN ROBERTSON is a doctoral candidate in health policy at the School of Public Health, University of California, Berkeley and a Research Associate at the Institute for Health and Aging, University of California, San Francisco. After obtaining an M.Sc. in Health Services Planning at the University of British Columbia in 1984, she worked as a Seniors' Wellness Coordinator with the Vancouver Health Department, and was also involved in the Strengthening Community Health movement in British Columbia. Ms. Robertson's academic interests are in aging policy, and particularly the effects of aging research on aging policy.

JUDITH SHINDUL-ROTHSCHILD, Ph.D., R.N., M.S.N., received her Ph.D. in Sociology from the Department of Sociology at Boston College. She is the past President of the Massachusetts Nurses Association and co-author of the book, *Aging and Public Policy: Social Control or Social Justice?*, and is presently serving on the Committee for the Uninsured which oversees the implementation of Universal Health Care in Massachusetts.

JAMES SWAN is an Associate Professor of Health Care Administration in the Department of Applied Anthropology and Sociology at California State University, Long Beach. He is co-author of *Fiscal Austerity and Aging* (1983), *Political Economy, Health and Aging* (1984), *Long Term Care of the Elderly: Public Policy Issues* (1985), and *Serving the Mentally Ill Elderly* (1987).

STEVEN P. WALLACE is an Assistant Professor in the School of Public Health at the University of California, Los Angeles and was previously on the faculty at the University of Missouri-St. Louis. His research interests include minority aging, long term care, and social policy, and he has published this research in journals such as *The Gerontologist, The Journal of Aging Studies, Society,* and *Policy Studies Review.* Dr. Wallace is currently investigating the causes of the racial difference in nursing home utilization.

JOHN B. WILLIAMSON, Ph.D. is Professor of Sociology in the Department of Sociology at Boston College. He earned his Ph.D. from Harvard University and his undergraduate degree from M.I.T. He has served as Chairperson of the Youth, Aging and Life Course Division of the Society for the Study of Social Problems. He has authored or co-authored ten books and over forty articles. Among his books are: *Age, Class Politics and the Welfare State* (1989), *Aging and Public Policy* (1985), *The Politics of Aging* (1982), *Aging and Society* (1980), and *Growing Old* (1980).

INDEX